BUDDHIST ICONOGRAPHY OF NORTHERN BACTRIA

Buddhist Iconography of Northern Bactria

KAZIM ABDULLAEV

Edited by

ALISON BETTS
FIONA KIDD

UNIVERSITY OF SYDNEY
CENTRAL ASIAN PROGRAMME

MANOHAR
2015

First published, 2015

ISBN 978-93-5098-097-2

Published by
Ajay Kumar Jain *for*
Manohar Publishers & Distributors
4753/23 Ansari Road, Daryaganj
New Delhi 110 002

Printed at
Salasar Imaging Systems
Delhi 110 035

Contents

Figures

(All illustrations are the work of the author unless otherwise indicated)

Foreword

After the Buddha passed into *nirvana*, his companions, it is said, followed his example and met in forests, to remember among themselves his words and deeds. Even lay adepts sometimes offered gardens for this purpose. This is believed to have taken place around the sixth century BC in India, near Kapilavastu in the Ganges Valley. From place to place and century after century, more *stupa*s were built to consecrate the relics of the Master, and monasteries to house the religious community in a quiet environment. The earliest of these establishments in northern India are considered to date from the second century BC onwards. Westwards from the Ganges Valley to the Indus, Buddhists followed the already well-worn tracks of travellers and merchants from east and west. The main town was then Taxila in Gandhara with its famed university. The rough crags of the Hindu Kush were not easy to cross, but they made it, nevertheless, and reached the Oxus River (modern Amudarya) and Bactria. They began to meet unknown people from eastern and northern countries, some of them from far away China. In resting places along the trail, the Buddhists left evidence of their existence and religious practices. Many different ethnic tribes and greedy conquerors had been along the same trail, leaving behind the remnants of destroyed buildings and the shattered fragments of images.

In northern Bactria, the concern of this book, the earliest traces of the presence of the Buddhist communities can be seen by the end of the first century AD. Kazim Abdullaev has worked for the last twenty-five years on the subject of Buddhism in Bactria and has collected from many sites a great volume of documentation which is presented here. This includes the large and well-studied monasteries at Old Termez, which are now the centre of modern research. Fayaztepa and Adjinatepa illustrate a fascinating group of local Buddhist buildings and wonderful pieces of Buddhist images, though often sadly ruined. But smaller places more lately discovered, too long misunderstood or found by chance, offer unexpected proof of a much more important presence of Buddhist communities than first expected, and also propose a longer time span for the religious presence of the Buddhist believers in Bactria.

Both general readers and researchers will find in this new book what is not so easily found in the great number of scientific reports by the very efficient specialists of these subjects. Those are, for the greater part, in the Uzbek and Russian languages and remain, of course, valuable sources of information. The facility of a book in the English language, however, will be a great help for Western readers. Thus, this book will be a guide to new approaches and discussions on new elements concerning the difficult subject of the spread of Buddhism in Western Central Asia.

FRANCINE TISSOT

Editors' Preface

This book has come about as the result of a promise made to the author, Kazim Abdullaev, well over a decade ago to produce an English language publication of his major work on Buddhist Iconography. One of the aims of the University of Sydney Central Asian Programme is to assist in making the work of Central Asian scholars available to a broader English-speaking readership. This volume is one of several that have been published under the auspices of the Programme. The role of the editors has been assistance with English language usage, copy editing, and the enhancement of illustrations. We hope that the volume will encourage interest in the archaeology and ancient history of Central Asia and inspire new generations of students to explore these fascinating lands.

ALISON BETTS
Professor of Silk Road Studies
University of Sydney
Sydney

FIONA KIDD
Assistant Professor of History & Art and Art History
New York University Abu Dhabi

Editors' Preface

Acknowledgements

The author would like to thank all who helped and encouraged him during the writing of his book: Particular gratitude for valuable advice goes to Professors P. Bernard, G.A. Koshelenko, F. Grenet and O. Bopearachchi; to the specialist of the Institute of Material Culture - V.A. Zavyalov; to the painter A. Naumov; to the archaeologist T. Annaev and others. He would like to express his deep gratitude to Gerda Panofsky, and Fiona Kidd and Alison Betts for their assistance with the correction of the English text. His warmest thanks are owed to his wife Eugenia Badanova, the inspirer of his deeds, for her untiring assistance and care.

KAZIM ABDULLAEV

Glossary

Abacus : in architecture, flat slab forming the top member of a capital.

Abhaya-mudra : gesture signifying protection made with the right hand.

Acrolith : (Greek) statue made of two materials, with some parts (e.g. head, hands, feet) made in stone while other parts (e.g. drapery) are made in another material.

Al secco : technique of painting over dry plaster, usually for murals.

Anda : the bell-shaped or dome-shaped upper part of a *stupa*.

Anjali-mudra : gesture of respect and greeting. The two hands rest on the chest and are held together with slightly cupped palms.

Ardokhsho : goddess with cornucopia, can be represented alone (on Kushan coins) or in couple with Pharro.

Aryk : an Uzbek/Tajik term for a small, artificially cut canal.

Avalokiteshvara : the most popular and beloved Buddhist *bodhisattva*, the spiritual son of the Adi (primordial) Buddha Amitabha and his female companion, Jnana (gnosis) Pandara.

Baysun : a district in the northern part of the Surkhandarya region.

Baysuntau : the southern range of the Hissar mountains.

Bhumisparsha-mudra : the gesture of 'touching the earth', calling the Earth to witness the enlightenment of Gautama (Siddhartha, the historical Buddha).

Bodhi : awakening or enlightenment, also alluding to the sacred tree under which Buddha attained enlightenment.

Bodhisattva : saintly individual who is on the path to enlightenment and has vowed to guide others to the True Path of the Buddha, also indicating the prince Siddhartha prior to achieving enlightenment (and therefore becoming a Buddha).

Brahma : the god of creation and one of the Hindu Triad with Vishnu and Shiva.

Brahmi : ancient Indian written language (the rock cut Ashokan edicts are written in Brahmi).

Buddha : 'awakened one' or 'the enlightened one'; it could also refer to an anthropomorphic image representing the ideal of spiritual development.

Boule : council, advisory citizen body of the Athenian democracy.
Bouleterion : meeting place of the Boule.
Calathos : a flared fruit basket borne on the head as a symbol in Greek and Egyptian art of fruitfulness; in architecture, a basket surrounded by acanthus leaves forming the upper part of a Corinthian capital.
Cauliculus : In the Corinthian capital, one of the eight stalks rising out of the lower leafage and terminating in leaves which seem to support the volutes.
Cannelure : also referred to as fluting, a rounded shallow concave groove on the shaft of a column, pilaster, etc.
Chakra : Sanskrit word for wheel, symbolizing the sun, and representing the Wheel of the Dharma.
Chakravartin : the King of the Wheel, universal monarch.
Capital : the crowning, decorative part of a column, which in the Corinthian order may be decorated with ornamental foliage.
Central Asia : here the term is considered mainly as the territory comprising the former Soviet Republics: Kyrgyzstan, Tajikistan, Turkmenistan, and Uzbekistan.
Chaganian : an historical and cultural region located in the central reaches of the Surkhandarya River Valley.
Cannelure : A decorative motif consisting of a series of uniform, usually vertical, flutes, incised on the surface of a column.
Chantaka : personal attendant of Prince Siddhartha. In the scene of the Great Departure, he is the bearer of the parasol.
Chaprak : textile, usually richly decorated, covering the back of an elephant.
Chattravai : multiple parasols over the *stupa*.
Chul : An Uzbek/Tajik term for steppe.
Citadel : a term used in Central Asian archaeological literature meaning a fortified area, normally the highest part of the site, set within the main fortifications.
Corona muralis : (Latin: 'mural crown') is a crown shaped in imitation of battlements or towers.
Cretula : white clay used for sealing (*signum in cretula*).
Devata : deity, can also indicate a guardian deity represented in human form in Hindu and Buddhist traditions.
Dharmacakra-mudra : the gesture of preaching the Law. It symbolizes the turning of the Wheel of Law.
Dhoti : cloth tied to cover the lower part of the body.
Dhyana-mudra : gesture of meditation.

Dipankara	:	one of the Buddhas of the Past, predecessor of Shakyamuni (Siddhartha) Buddha of the Present.
Ganch	:	plaster mixed with clay, usually covered with incised ornamentation.
Garuda	:	a large mythical bird or bird-like creature that appears in both Hindu and Buddhist mythology, the vehicle of Vishnu, with solar connotations, enemies to the *naga*s.
Gautama	:	the historical Buddha, Siddhartha Shakyamuni (the Sage of the Shakya), widely represented in Buddhist art.
Khalat	:	loose long-sleeved coat mostly worn by nomads, made in heavy textile or fur.
Harmika	:	a small platform with a railing located at the top of a *stupa*, over the *anda*.
Jainism	:	an ancient religious system considered heterodox by the Vedic tradition. The first Tirthankara under the name Rishabhanatha is mentioned in the *Vishnu* and *Bhagavata Purana* as belonging to the remote past.
Jataka	:	a collection of Buddhist literature concerning previous incarnations of Buddha Shakyamuni.
Iwan	:	a hall or space with a roof supported by columns, walled on three sides, with one end entirely open.
Kala	:	Turkic and Persian term for a fortress or a citadel (for example, the Citadel of Old Termez).
Kan	:	system for heating dwellings of the Early Medieval period using ceramic pipes set into the *sufa* and the walls of the rooms.
Kantaka	:	the horse ridden by Prince Siddhartha (the future Buddha) when he departed from Kapilavastu.
Kharoshthi	:	an ancient Indian script, in common use in the Indo-Greek and Kushan period.
Kurgan	:	tumulus or artificial mound, usually over a burial, used as a suffix on place names (e.g. Erkurgan).
Kushan	:	one of the five tribes of *Ta Yue-zhi* which subjugated the other four tribes and created a single political unit, and eventually an empire.
Kutan	:	a place for the location of a sheep-pen, used as a suffix on place names (e.g. Jarkutan).
Krishna	:	an incarnation of Vishnu, an important Hindu deity.
Maitreya	:	the Future Buddha. (Bodhisattva)
Makara	:	a fantastic animal in Indian mythology.
Mandorla	:	halo of light surrounding the entire figure of a holy person.

Merlon : architectural element on the rim of battlements to provide shelter for archers, often with a stepped outline. The merlon motif appears in ornamentation.
Mudra : a ritual hand-gesture.
Mukuta : an elaborate form of hair styling or a crown in the form of a turban. It can be associated with Hindu deities as well as with *bodhisattva*s.
Naga, nagi : a snake, semi-deity and genius of the Water.
Namaskara-mudra : gesture of salutation, adoration or prayer.
Nirvana : state of spiritual peace achieved by Buddha and the Arhant (Ascetics).
Ovuli : from Latin ovum, ornamental motive in relief in the shape of an egg, used *i*n Ionian and Corinthian orders.
Oxus : the Latin name of the Amudarya, Greek Oxos, derived from the Iranian name Waksh.
Padmasana : the lotus posture (cross-legged) used in meditation.
Pakhsa : compacted clay used in construction.
Panchika : king of the *yaksha*, deity of wealth and the hidden treasures of the earth.
Paridhana : length of cloth wrapped around the lower body as a garment, similar to the *dhoti* still worn in India.
Parinirvana : final extinction, the 'final' or 'highest' *nirvaana*, the state of *nirvana* entered by the Buddha at death.
Parvati : in Sanskrit 'She of the mountains', Devi, consort of Shiva, the Divine Mother.
Petasos : wide-brimmed hat with a conical crown worn in ancient Greece, used for travelling and made of felt or straw with a chin strap, so that when not in use it could be hung down the back.
Pharro : Iranian divinity of the royal splendour and glory, can be associated with Ardoksho.
Pipal : fig tree (*Ficus religiosa*) native to India and associated with events in the life of the Buddha (Bodhi tree).
Prakshna : sacred area around cultic constructions.
Propylon : a Greek structure forming an entrance or gateway, normally to to a sacred enclosure.
Rabad : suburb of ancient Central Asian city, usually the location for craft workshops. Normally there would be several *rabad*s surrounding the *shahristan*.
Shahristan : term used in Central Asian archaeological literature for the part of an ancient city surrounded by fortifications.

Saka : Iranian-speaking nomad tribes of ancient Central Asia.

Sakaraukes : nomad tribe of Saka origin documented by classical authors.

Sakaravles : nomad tribe linked to the Sakaraukes.

Sala : tree (*Shorea robusta*), in Hindu tradition said to be favoured by Vishnu.

Salabanjika : *yakshini*, a dryad, genius of the *sala* tree.

Sanghati : long, loose draped outer robe.

Say : an Uzbek/Tajik term for a small river of natural origin, used as a suffix on river names.

Scotia : a concave moulding between two fillets. A scotia is one of the elements used in the Attic base of columns.

Shakyamuni : the Sage of the Shakya clan, one of the titles of the historical Buddha.

Sheresh : an organic glue of vegetable origin. It is still used by modern masters of *ganch* decoration.

Shiva : a major Hindu deity, one of the Hindu triad, representing destruction and death.

Siddhartha : the name of the historic Buddha when he was a prince in his father's house.

Spandrel : the triangular area above and on either side of an arch, normally decorated.

Stupa : a Buddhist monument constructed as a solid structure without internal space, it can be built over sacred relics or can be a simple votive artefact.

Su : Turkic word for water, used as a suffix on the names of rivers and streams (Kyzilsu, Karasu, Aksu). The Tajik equivalent is 'ob' (Surkhob, Siyob).

Sufa : a bench, usually of clay or mud bricks, built along the wall of the room.

Sukhavati : the Buddhist paradise of the primordial Buddha Amitabha.

Tepa (tepe) : a mound or hill, normally of artificial origin located on flat ground.

Tympanon : in Classical architecture, the decorative recessed area enclosed by a pediment.

Torana : cultic construction in the shape of a gate found in Buddhist architecture.

Urna : one of the *mahalakshana* (major marks) of the Buddha, a dot placed on the forehead of Buddhist images as an auspicious mark. Sometimes it is represented by a jewel.

Ushnisha	: one of the *mahalakshana* (major marks) of the Buddha, an oval protuberance at the top of the head of the Buddha. It was originally depicted as a topknot, but later became simplified into a plain knob.
Uttariya	: item of clothing in the form of a long shawl used to drape over the arms and upper body, usually worn by *bodhisattva*.
Vajra	: the thunderbolt, the typical attribute of the Hindu god Indra and the Bodhisattva Vajrapani.
Vajrapani	: *bodhisattva*, protector of Buddha Shakyamuni.
Vasudeva	: the Great Deity, the other name of Krishna.
Varada-mudra (Vara)	: gesture symbolizing grace or boon. The palm of the hand with fingers extended downward is held as far below the waist as possible.
Vihara	: a Buddhist monastery.
Vishnu	: the second aspect of the Hindu Triad, power of preservation and conservation.
Vedika	: railing found in cultic constructions such as the *stupa*.
Yaksha-Yakshi (Yakshinis)	: semi-divinity, genius of nature and trees.
Yogi-yogini	: an ascetic.
Yue-zhi	: The Da Yue-zhi (Greater Yue-zhi) was a nomadic tribe forced westwards out of eastern Xinjiang and Gansu by the Xiong-nu around the second century BC. The Xiao Yue-Zhi (Lesser Yue-Zhi) moved south into the mountains while the Da Yue-zhi migrated into Transoxiana and Bactria where the tribes coalesced to found the empire of the Kushans.
Zhang Qian	: Chinese diplomat sent by Chinese Emperor Wu-ti (140-87 BC) to seek a military alliance with the Yue-zhi against the Xiong-nu.
Zoroaster	: prophet and reformer of the Mazdean religion.

Abbreviations

AI	:	*Arheologicheskie issledovaniya v Uzbekistane*. Samarkand.
Annali IUO	:	*Annali dell'Istituto Universitario Orientale di Napoli*. Naples.
ART	:	*Arheologicheskie raboty v Tadjikistane*. Dushanbe.
CRAI		*Comptes rendus de l'Académie des Inscriptions et Belles-Lettres*. Paris.
EW	:	*East and West*. Rome.
IAHCCA	:	*International Association of the History and Culture of Central Asia*. Moscow.
IAN Taj.:	:	*Izvestiya Akademii nauk Tadjikskoy SSR*. Dushanbe.
IMKU	:	*Istoria material'noy kul'tury Uzbekistana*. Tashkent, Samarkand.
JA	:	*Journal Asiatique*. Paris.
JNSI	:	*Journal of the Numismatic Society of India*. Varanasi.
JRAS	:	*Journal of the Royal Asiatic Society of Great Britain and Ireland*. London.
JS	:	*Journal des Savants*. Paris.
KSIA	:	Kratkie soobscheniya Instituta arheologii Akademii nauk SSSR. Moscow, Leningrad.
KSIIMK	:	Kratkie soobscheniya Instituta istorii material'noy kul'tury. Leningrad.
MDAFA	:	Mémoires de la Délégation Archéologique Française en Afghanistan. Paris.
MIA	:	Materialy i issledovania po arheologii SSSR. Moscow, Leningrad.
MKT	:	Material'naya kul'tura Tadjikistana. Dushanbe.
ONU	:	Obschestvennye nauki v Uzbekistane. Tashkent.
RA	:	*Rossijskaya arheologiya*. Moscow.
SA	:	*Sovetskaya arheologia*. Moscow.
SAA	:	*South Asian Archaeology*. London.
SGE	:	*Soobscheniya Gosudarstvennogo Ermitaja*. Leningrad.
SRAA	:	*Silk Road Art and Archaeology*. Kamakura.
StIr	:	*Studia Iranica*. Paris.
TAKE	:	Termazskaya arheologicheskaya kompleksnaya ekspeditsia. Tashkent.
TGE	:	Trudy Gosudarstvennogo Ermitaja. Leningrad.

VDI	:	*Vestnik drevney istorii*. Moscow.
YuTAKE	:	Yuzhno turkmenskaya arheologicheskaya kompleksnaya ekspeditsia. Ashkhabad.

1

Introduction

GEOGRAPHICAL BACKGROUND

Surkhandarya province – the south-eastern region of the Republic of Uzbekistan – has long attracted the attention of scholars and travellers. It has an abundance of ancient monuments located in the mountains, on the plains, and by rivers, canals, and small streams. The province occupies about 18,900 sq. km. It is bordered in the north by the majestic heights of the Hissar range, and divided into two southern regions – Surkhandarya and Kashkadarya. In the west the province is surrounded by the Baisuntau spurs and the Kugitangtau range, beyond which lies the territory of Turkmenistan. The eastern boundary of Surkhandarya is formed by the Babatag range, which also marks the border with Tajikistan. To the south, the region is bound by the Amudarya, the river that serves as the frontier with Afghanistan (Fig. 1). Between the mountain ranges, which occupy a large part of the Surkhandarya province, are two major plains, where flow the Sherabaddarya and Surkhandarya rivers, the main waterways of the province. Seasonal mountain streams caused by the melting snows feed both of these rivers. From the north, the powerful Hissar mountain range protects the Surkhandarya Valley from the cold winds, ensuring a microclimate of mild winters and hot dry summers that is similar to the subtropics. Ancient sources provide evidence of the wealth and fertility of the region.[1] Rich and abundant crops lured different peoples and tribes to Surkhandarya province. Nomads frequently settled here, attracted by the plentiful fruits and animals.

The Surkhandarya Valley is a narrow zone about 5 km wide, extending from north-east to south-west. The irrigated lands are located on the lowest agricultural terrace and follow the course of the Surkhandarya through the valley. In the south the valley is blocked by the Kattakum desert, created as the result of wind erosion in the semi-desert of the Khautag. The latter, together with the Utchkizil hills, separates the Surkhandarya from the Sherabaddarya Valley.

HISTORICAL BACKGROUND

To the north of the great ancient Oxus River, the modern Amudarya, lay an important historical and cultural area of the Orient in antiquity. Ancient

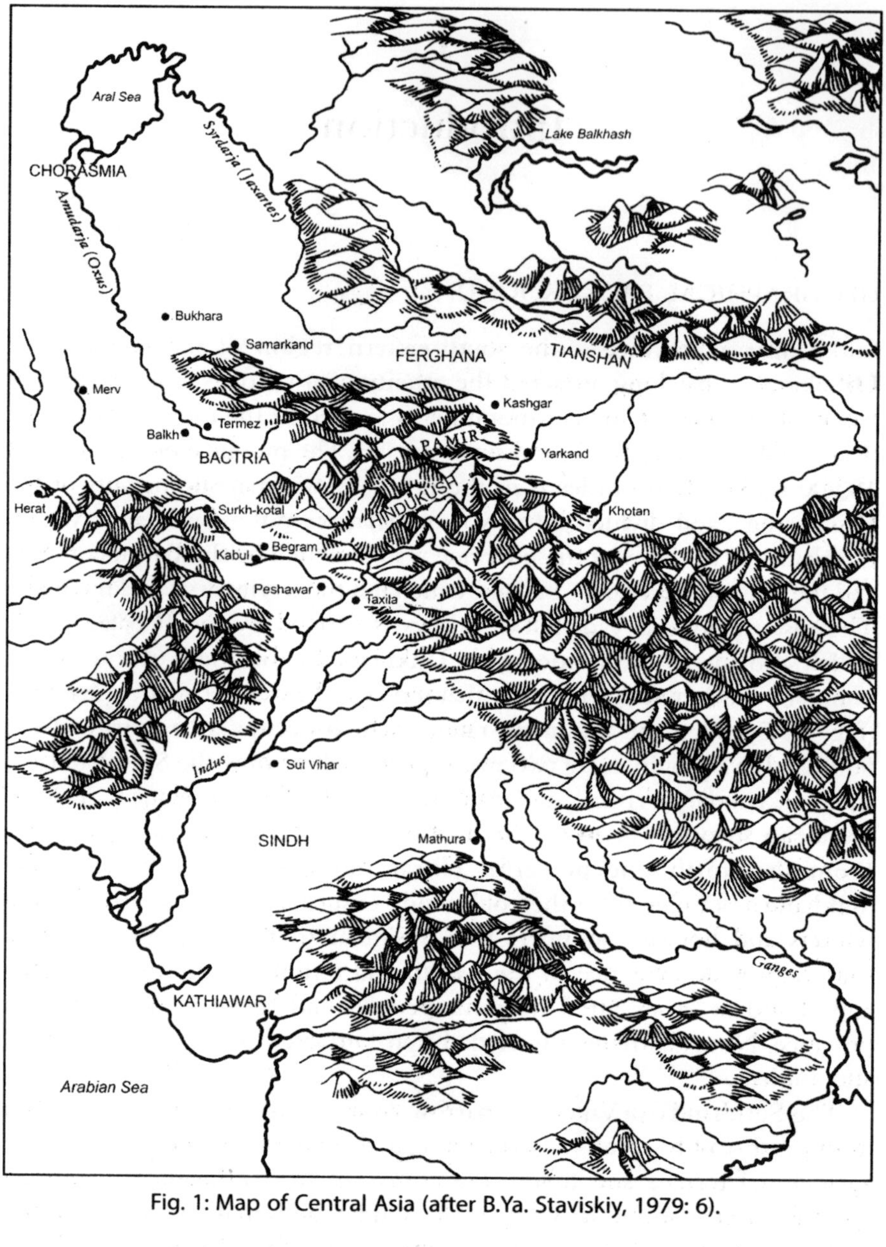

Fig. 1: Map of Central Asia (after B.Ya. Staviskiy, 1979: 6).

historians and geographers named it Sogdiana,[2] yet archaeological investigations of the region have demonstrated that the same culture extended on both sides of the river. Culturally, one can identify this area as Bactria (Bactriana). As a geographic border we can cite the Iron Gates near the modern village of Derbent. Much scholarly literature has been devoted to the problems of the Greco-Bactrian (Ta-Hsia of the Chinese chronicles of the first centuries BC) borders, especially their northern limits, and the state formation that followed.[3] After the collapse of the Greco-Bactrian kingdom this territory assumed another name based on the ethnonym of one of the large tribes, the Tokhars, who settled there.[4] It should therefore be specified that the term North Bactria or North Tokharistan refers to the territory to the north of the Amudarya, which is bordered by the spurs of the Hissar and Baysuntau systems in the north and east respectively. Thus, the territory spread over the regions of modern Tajikistan (Kulyab and Kurgantube) and the Surkhandarya province of Uzbekistan.

During the sixth to fourth centuries BC the countries of western Asia, together with the Greek cities of Asia Minor, comprised the Achaemenid Empire. The Achaemenid Empire included also most of Central Asia, which was divided into satrapies. Bactria, Sogdia, Parthia and others are mentioned in the enumeration of conquered lands on the rock inscriptions erected by order of the Persian kings.[5]

In 334 BC, the Greek-Macedonian army under Alexander the Great crossed the Dardanelles and from then on a new empire began to form, one no less in size than that of the Achaemenids. This event ushered in an epoch of Hellenism in the East. Within a relatively short period of time the vast expanses of Asia Minor, Mesopotamia, Iran, Egypt, and Central Asia had been conquered. Nevertheless, despite the swiftness with which this huge empire was created thanks to the strategic genius of Alexander, its collapse was just as rapid after his death in 323 BC. The satrapies of Central Asia were incorporated into the Seleucid kingdom. These satrapies maintained their power until the middle of the third century BC. Almost simultaneously, Parthia (modern Turkmenistan) became independent under the local Arsacid tribe, while Bactria (comprising modern northern Afghanistan and southern Tajikistan and Uzbekistan) likewise declared her independence under the governor Diodotes.[6] The emergence of the Greco-Bactrian kingdom that initially included both Bactria and Sogdiana reflected the flourishing of Hellenistic culture. The power of the Greco-Bactrian kings extended to include India.[7] However, after an existence of more than 100 years Greco-Bactria (Ta Hsia of the Chinese sources) succumbed to the pressure of the nomads north of the Oxus (Amudarya) River, known in the Chinese chronicles as the Ta Yueh Chih (Da Yuezhi).[8] The Kushans, the most powerful among this group of nomads, subordinated the other four tribes, giving their name to the future state.[9] Chinese sources of the fourth century AD mention Tokharistan (Tu-ho-lo), located on the territory of the modern Surkhandarya region, southern Tajikistan and northern and eastern parts of Afghanistan. Strabo and Justin also mention a great tribe, Tokhares, but without giving them a precise localization.[10]

The first capital of the consolidated tribes was the city to the north of the Gui (Kuei = Oxus) River, called, in the Chinese sources, Chin-shih[11] (located hypothetically at Dal'verzintepa[12]). Absorbing the traditions of the preceding periods, the Kushan Empire created a unique culture based on the colourful diversity of its people. The extent of this synthesis can be judged by the coins of Kanishka, one of the most eminent personalities of the Kushan period. Kanishka's coins display a whole gallery of different deities, Greek, Hindu, Buddhist and Zoroastrian, which aptly demonstrate his tolerant religious policy. It is also in the reign of this king that Buddhist art and culture flourished. Most scholars now accept the year AD 127 as the beginning of Kanishka's era.[13] The heyday of Kushan culture is dated to the second century and first half of the third century AD. The Kushan Empire was one of the most powerful empires in the ancient world aside from Parthia, Rome and Han China.

In the second half of the third century AD, the power of the Kushans began to decline. One of the last kings, Vasudeva II, was a contemporary of his terrible adversary Ardashir I, the founder of the Sassanian dynasty. The first of the Sassanian campaigns against the Kushans began with the march of Bahram II in AD 280 and Hormizd II (AD 303-9), and then specifically the march of Shapur II (AD 309-79), who was even married to a Kushan princess (the Sassanian rulers referred to themselves as 'Kushan shah').[14]

Around the turn of the fifth century (AD 390-430), the territory of Northern Tokharistan passed to the power of Kidara and his successors, the Kidarites. Some coins bear the legend in Brahmi, 'Kidara Kushana sha'.[15] Between AD 412 and 437, the Kidarites united Tokharistan with Gandhara.[16] The subsequent stages in the history of Tokharistan were closely linked with the events and peoples of the surrounding regions. The sources mention these peoples as Kidarites and Chionites – Hephthalites.[17] In the second half of the fifth century, the Hephthalites entered the historical arena as a mighty force. Historians recounted brilliant episodes of fighting between the Sassanian King Peroz (AD 459-84)[18] and the Hephthalites. For Peroz, the war was not successful.[19] His successor, the Sassanian King Khosrov I (AD 531-78), was luckier. He made a very strong alliance with the Turkic Kaghanate. In the middle of the sixth century , the consolidation of Turkic tribes, who initially inhabited the area around the Altai, presented a new and menacing force moving towards the borders of Central Asia. Thus, the Hephthalites found themselves caught between the Turks and Sassanians.

After a stubborn struggle, the Turks pushed the Hephthalites from the territory of Central Asia, but soon entered into conflict with their former ally Khosrov I. The territory of northern Tokharistan before the Arab invasion was one of several small, isolated kingdoms. The independence of these kingdoms is reflected by the fact that they could, for example, send their embassies to neighbouring or distant countries. The name of Turantash, the ruler of Chaganian, a kingdom located in the region north east of the Surkhandarya valley, is inscribed on the wall paintings of Afrasiab (the ancient site of Marakanda – Samarkand) dated to the seventh century.[20]

HISTORY OF RESEARCH

The historical and geographical study of this region began at the end of the nineteenth century (Fig. 2), although remains of ancient irrigation systems and mounds had been incidentally mentioned earlier in the notes of topographers, geographers, and military engineers.[21] Initial explorations were connected with the activities of 'The Circle of Archaeology Amateurs of the Imperial Society'. V.V. Bartold's works on the geography of the region were written at the turn of the twentieth century.[22]

The Termez Archaeological Complex Expedition under the leadership of M.E. Masson marked the beginning of systematic archaeological investigations.[23] The archaeological work of M.E. Masson focused primarily on the Termez region.[24] By analysing the architectural details of sites in this region, Masson was able to show that ancient craftsmen used limestone mined from the bank of Amudarya River near Orlinaya Sopka (Eagle Mound).[25] The first half of the twentieth century was associated with archaeological investigations at the site of Karatepa, undertaken by E.G. Pchelina.[26] In Tajikistan, the Kobadian region was studied by M.M. Diyakonov,[27] while the Angor region of the Surkhandarya province of Uzbekistan was thoroughly examined by L.I. Al'baum.[28]

From the beginning, archaeological excavations in Surkhandarya province resulted in the discoveries of magnificent art and architectural monuments. One of the most remarkable discoveries is that of the Airtam reliefs, illustrating the art of sculpture by Tokharistan masters.[29] The half-length

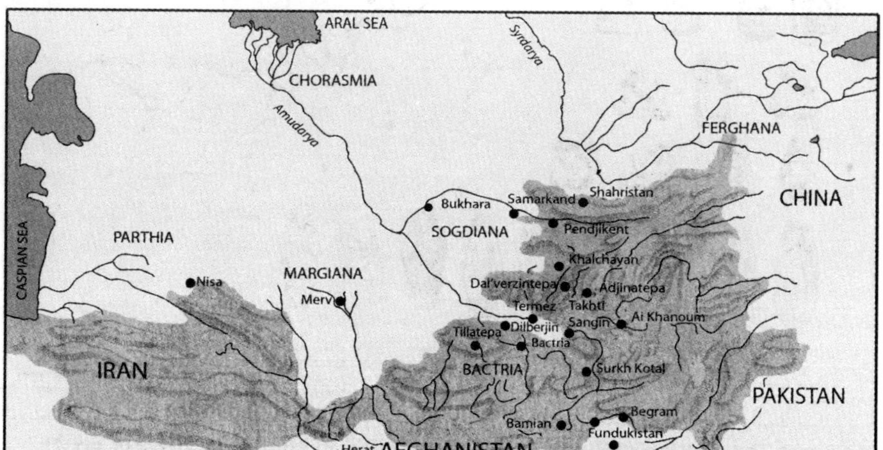

Fig. 2: Key archaeological sites in Central Asia.

portrait-like images, executed in a combination of high relief rendering of the head and low relief rendering of the body, represent musicians in calm grandeur and harmony. The compositions of the Airtam reliefs are a significant source not only for the study of the musical culture of the region, but also for the study of costume. These reliefs confirm the importance of the site in the development of plastic art in Bactria during the ancient period. The clay sculptures at Khalchayan in the upper Surkhandarya valley, uncovered by the expedition led by G.A. Pugachenkova in the 1960s, were another sensational find.[30]

The discovery of stone and clay sculptures, along with column bases, capitals, and other architectural decorative features, terracotta figurines, coins and other artefacts have become common during intermittent, but methodical, archaeological excavations in this region (Fig. 3). The Termez Archaeological Museum is one of the richest repositories of architectural decoration of the region for the ancient period, and objects of art from Bactria-Tokharistan have significantly enriched the collections of other republican museums.[31]

Another important site in the archaeological study of Surkhandarya is the Karatepa complex, first discovered by Denike's expedition.[32] From 1962 onwards, large-scale investigations were carried out by a team led by B.Ya. Staviski. From 1998 up to the present time, Karatepa has been

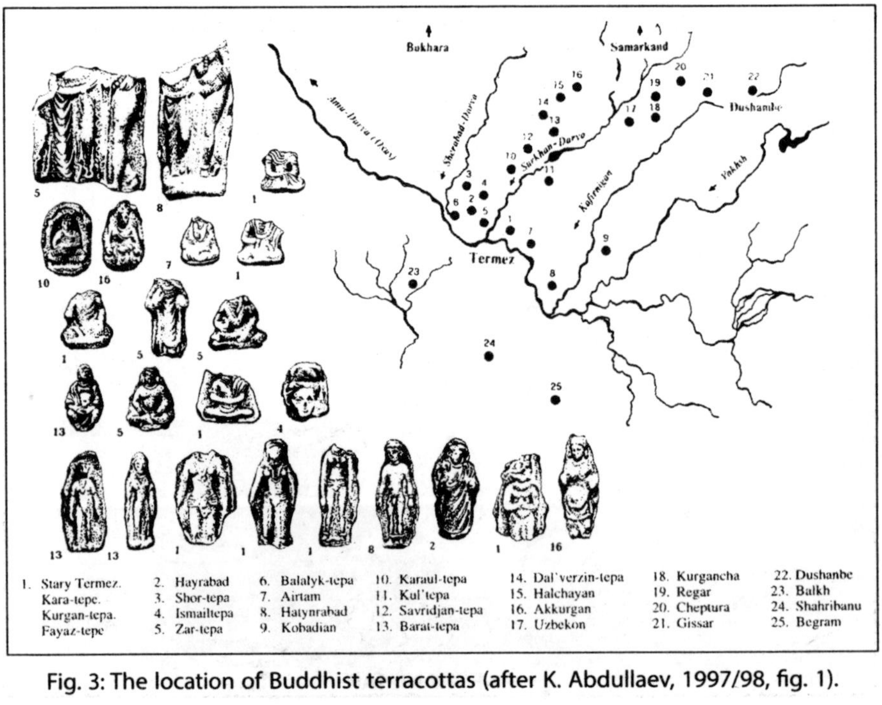

Fig. 3: The location of Buddhist terracottas (after K. Abdullaev, 1997/98, fig. 1).

investigated by the Uzbek-Japan Archaeological Expedition, directed by K. Kato and Sh. Pidaev.[33] In 1967, the expedition of the Institute of Art-Knowledge (Fine Arts), led by G.A. Pugachenkova, started regular excavations at the large ancient site of Dal'verzintepa.[34] This site has yielded brilliant finds of the artistic culture of the Kushans.

The splendid Buddhist complex of Fayaztepa was unearthed over several seasons of excavations led by L.I. Al'baum. By the end of the 1950s, a number of archaeological monuments had been found, many of which are included in Al'baum's comprehensive monograph *Balalyktepe.* The discovery of Balalyktepe yielded extremely fine wall paintings of the sixth century AD.[35] In the 1970s, the Bactrian Complex Expedition began its work. This expedition included archaeologists and other specialists from the Leningrad Department of the Institute of Archaeology (directed by V.M. Masson), the Institute of Archaeology of the Academy of Sciences of the USSR (directed by G.A. Koshelenko), and also from the Institute of Archaeology of the Academy of Sciences of Uzbekistan. The expedition was engaged in the recurrent and systematic excavations of Zartepa as well as survey work. In 1977, this team excavated Kuevkurgan, which yielded brilliant examples of plastic art. The participants in that expedition were G.A. Koshelenko, Sh. Pidaev, T. Annaev and others.

The results of the Kuevkurgan excavations have been published in an article by T. Annaev,[36] while the sculptural pieces have also been repeatedly published elsewhere.[37] However, an in-depth interpretation of the Kuevkurgan sculptures has not been undertaken yet. Thus, I will be attempting here, for the first time, a full analysis of the sculpture finds in its archaeological context. The goal is to describe in detail the archaeological complex of Kuevkurgan and to compare it with the archaeological complex of the final stage of settlement at Zartepa. These objectives will comprise the artistic evaluation of Kuevkurgan plastic art, defining its place in Bactrian Tokharistan art, as well as drawing parallels to other artistic centres. I will address questions concerning the way in which the Kuevkurgan tradition blended into the common evolution of sculpture and Bactrian art in general. Tracing the traditions of Bactrian sculpture of the pre-Kuevkurgan period, I will thereby reconstruct the artistic environment from which the plastic art of Kuevkurgan evolved. I will also explore the influence of Buddhist art on the images of the Kuevkurgan cycle, and examine the Buddhist monuments of North Bactria-Tokharistan.

NOTES

1. Strabo XI, XI, 1-2.
2. Strabo II, I, 15; Curtius VII, 4-5.

3. Staviskiy 1961, pp.108-14; Masson 1968, 8; *idem*. 1975; Abdullaev 1997b, pp. 54-60. Regarding the name Tokharistan (T'ou-ho-lo, Tou-ho-lo, T'ou-hou-lo) in the Chinese sources – Wei-shu (see Chavannes 1907, p. 155) appears in a literary source of AD 383.
4. Muller 1918, p. 575; Gafurov 1989, p. 284.
5. Dandamaev 1985, pp. 27-32.
6. Tarn 1951; Narain 1962; E.V. Zeymal' 1978, pp. 192-214.
7. Will 1979, pp. 281-90.
8. It should be pointed out that prior to the appearance of the Yue-zhi, the territory to the south of the Hissar range was occupied by another nomad tribe, probably the Sakaraukes or Sakaraules. See Abdullaev 1995c, pp. 151-61.
9. Koshelenko et al. 1994, pp. 171-89.
10. Strabo XI, VIII, 2; Justin XLII, 2; Ptolemaios VI, 11; Marcellinus XXIII, 57.
11. This is proposed hypothetically in Abdullaev 2001b, pp. 197-215.
12. Pugachenkova et al. 1978, p. 220.
13. Falk 2001, pp. 121-36.
14. Christensen 1944; Lukonin 1969, pp. 20-40; idem. 1967, pp. 16-33; idem. 1969a.
15. Bivar 1956.
16. Enoki 1955, n. 5; idem. 1958, n. 3.
17. Ghirshmann 1948, pp. XII-XIII, 66, 115; Altheim 1959, pp. 41-56; Enoki 1959.
18. The date of Peroz's ruling is given according to Ghirshman 1962, pp. 457-83.
19. Tabari 1977, pp. 118-19, 121.
20. Livshits 1965; Al'baum 1975, pp. 54-6.
21. Maev 1879, pp. 159-165; Massal'skij 1913.
22. Bartol'd 1963b, pp. 23-43; Bartol'd 1963c, pp. 4-75; Bartol'd 1964, pp. 263-471; Bartol'd 1965.
23. Masson 1940b.
24. Masson 1940a, pp. 5-122.
25. Masson 1940b, p. 114.
26. Pchelina 1946.
27. Diyakonov 1953, n. 37.
28. Al'baum 1960.
29. Masson 1933, idem. 1935, pp. 35-8; Turgunov 1973, pp. 52-77.
30. Pugachenkova 1966, idem. 1971.
31. There is no special publication devoted to the architectural decoration. Archaeological finds of this category are discussed in various articles. See for example, Pugachenkova 1945; Nil'sen 1966; Pugachenkova 1973, pp. 78-128.
32. Pchelina 1946; Strelkov 1927, pp. 27-30, 1928, pp. 41-7.
33. Pidaev and Kato 2000a, pp. 87-90.
34. Pugachenkova and Turgunov 1978; Pugachenkova et al. 1978.
35. Al'baum 1960.
36. Annaev 1984, pp. 188-200.
37. Masson 1985; Pidaev 1999b.

2

The Tradition of Plastic Art in Northern Bactria-Tokharistan

ORIGINS

The origins of plastic art in Bactria go back to the prehistoric period. Objects of artistic significance played a considerable role in the culture of the Bronze Age, although the majority of them were still of a raw, primitive quality (Fig. 4). Their creators could scarcely be called artists, but were more likely craftsmen, or priests, who in executing certain rituals tried to give the objects a certain form. Often these figures were found in burials (Fig. 5). Among the anthropomorphic representations there was a clay figure from the cenotaph of Jarkutan (2nd millennium BC), imitating the pose of the deceased (Fig. 6).[1] Another similar clay figure was found in the Tandyryul burial (Tajikistan), which also dates to the Bronze Age

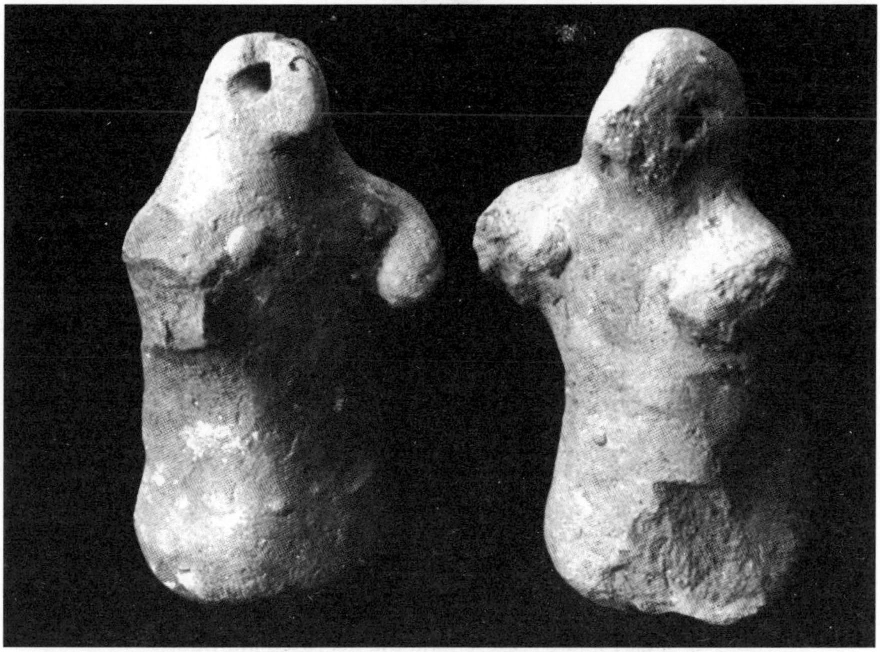

Fig. 4: Clay anthropomorphic figurines. Jarkutan. Bronze Age, 2nd millennium BC. H = 12 cm. (Institute of Archaeology, Samarkand).

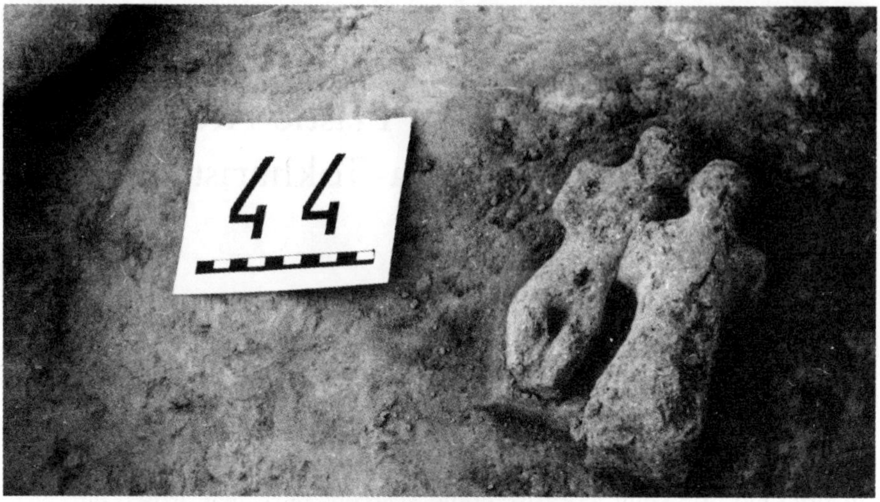

Fig. 5: Two clay figures found *in situ* in a burial. Bronze Age, 12th-11th century BC. Jarkutan IV, necropolis. (Institute of Archaeology, Samarkand).

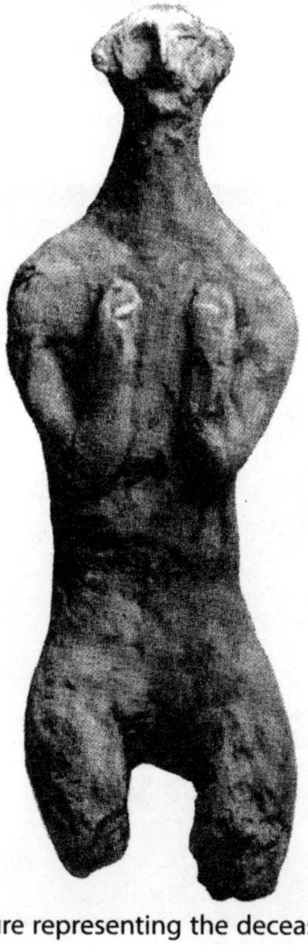

Fig. 6: Clay figure representing the deceased individual. Cenotaph. Bronze Age, 2nd millennium BC. H = 45 cm. (Archaeological Museum, Sherabad District, Surkhandarya Region).

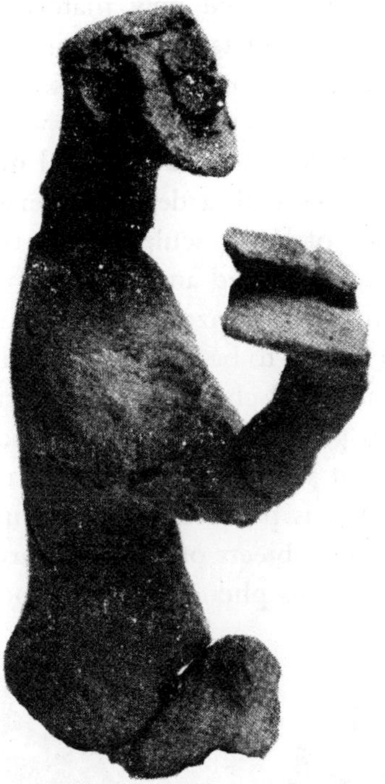

Fig. 7: Male clay figure. Burial, Tandyrjul Necropolis. Tajikistan. Last quarter of the 2nd millennium BC. H = 39.5 cm. (Institute of History, Dushanbe. Inv. No. 190).

(Fig. 7).[2] Two coarsely executed clay figurines from Jarkutan should also be mentioned.[3] They have only a remote likeness to a human image, but evidently fulfilled some function in the funeral rite and had a symbolic relation to the deceased.

Regarding objects, one can cite a stone head from Mirshade (Surkhandarya region), which has been dated to the tenth to ninth centuries BC (Fig. 8).[4] Archaeological excavation of the two main Bronze Age sites of the region,

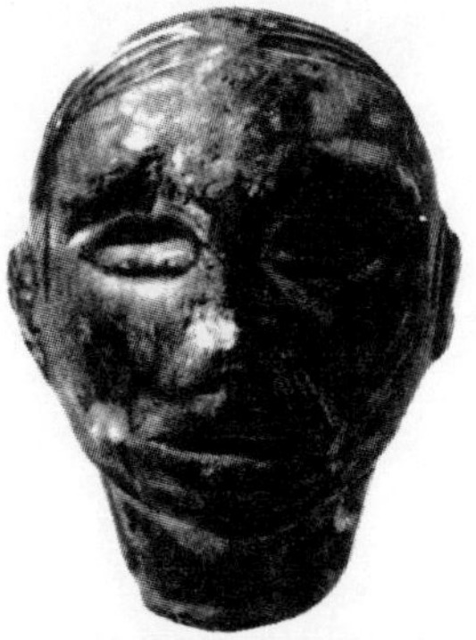

Fig. 8: Stone head. Mirshade, Surkhandarya Region. Late Bronze Age, 10th-9th century BC. H = 10 cm. (Institute of Art Research, Tashkent).

Sapallitepa and Jarkutan, provided new material for the figurative cult complex, including seals, amulets and figurines. These, as a rule, were zoomorphic, in relief or incised on ceramic vessels (Figs. 9, 10, 11). Recently at Jarkutan some clay figures were found that were modelled in the same primitive way. Apparently they too had a ritual meaning, as the similarity of a figure with closed eyes with a deceased person suggests. One of the remarkable peculiarities of these sculptures is their painted decoration (Fig. 12), using ochre to make red and soot to make black.[5]

Although the repertoire of Bronze Age plastic art is comparatively small, it allows for some conclusions to be drawn regarding the Bactrian figurative tradition. In spite of the ritual character of the primitive clay figures, one can assume that in this period there are some examples which testify to the first timid attempts at sculpture in the region.

The Bactrian Iron Age is particularly interesting as, in contrast to the Bronze Age, practically no objects of figurative art have come to light till now. At the present time this phenomenon cannot be explained. Does it

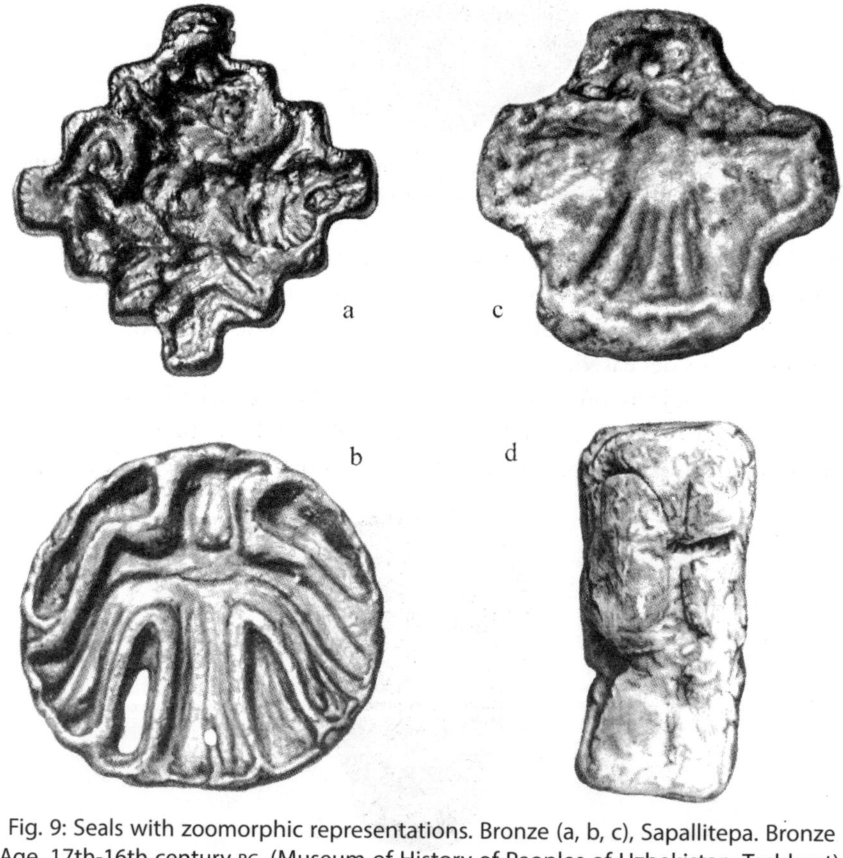

Fig. 9: Seals with zoomorphic representations. Bronze (a, b, c), Sapallitepa. Bronze Age, 17th-16th century BC. (Museum of History of Peoples of Uzbekistan, Tashkent). Stone (d), cylindrical seal with representation of two goats near Tree of Life. Jarkutan. 11th-10th century BC. H = 3 cm. (Institute of Archaeology, Samarkand).

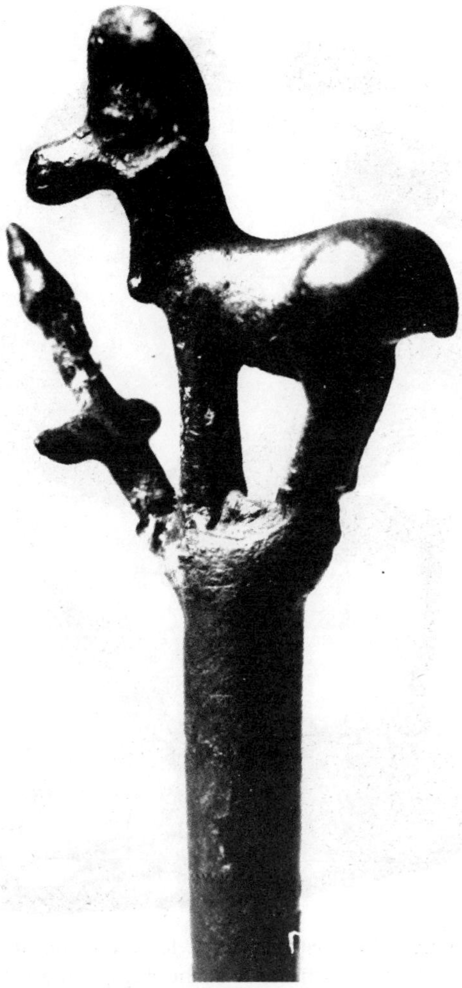

Fig. 10: Bronze hairpin (detail). Goat near Tree of Life. Sapallitepa. 2nd millennium BC. H = 19 cm. (Museum of History of Peoples of Uzbekistan, Tashkent).

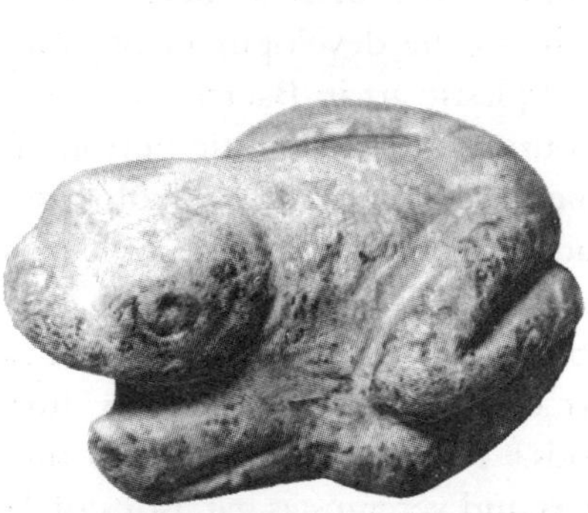

Fig. 11: Stone statuette of a frog. Sapallitepa. 17th-16th century BC. 4 × 3 cm. (Museum of History of Peoples of Uzbekistan, Tashkent).

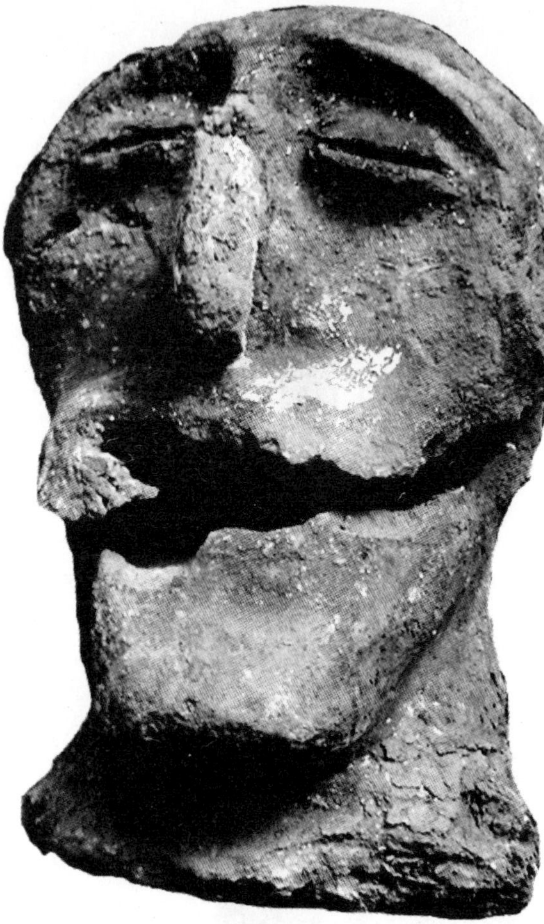

Fig. 12: Male bust. Clay with pigment. Jarkutan. 2nd millennium BC.
H = 17.5 cm. (Institute of Archeology, Samarkand).

relate to a crisis of economy and culture, or was there some great change in religion and ideology in the ancient society? Undoubtedly, Hellenism provided a new impulse in the development of figurative traditions. With regard to the origins of plastic art in Bactria, the genre of sculpture, which arose and developed during the Hellenistic period, it is necessary to draw a general picture of the development of the sculptural art of the Hellenistic world before it spread to Central Asia. The processes of Hellenization in Central Asia are closely related to the periods of Alexander the Great and the Seleucids. These processes began with the colonization of territory and the migration of part of the Greek population during the Seleucid and Greco-Bactrian periods.[6] This was in contrast to the policy of Alexander, who left invalid soldiers and veterans as garrisons of Asiatic cities. However, it is obvious that the Greek material and artistic cultural complex penetrated Central Asia above all in the Seleucid and Greco-Bactrian periods.

The Greek city of Ai Khanum, founded on the confluence of the Oxus and Kokcha rivers at the end of the fourth or very early third century BC, possessed a complete architectural ensemble, which was up to the expectations of the Greeks (whereby it comprised a communication system, city plan, theatre, gymnasium, etc.).[7] In the Seleucid period, town planning was truly developed. Many towns such as Seleucia, Antioches and Laodiceas sprung up within the newly created Empire.[8] Often they had dynastic temples with established cults of the kings. The fortification systems with great ramparts protecting not only the city, but also the surrounding agricultural area, belonged to the same period (a good example of this type of monumental defensive construction is the Wall of Antiochus in Margiana). During the time of the co-ruling of Seleucus I and his son Antiochus I, an expedition beyond the Jaxartes River in inner Asia was organised.[9] The aim of the expedition was not only to secure the conquered territory and to survey the potential external menace, but also to have a more complete understanding of the geographic and ethnographic situation. From this period, we have some finely executed examples of local Greco-Bactrian sculpture. Capitals of the Corinthian order, stone and clay sculpture including miniature images demonstrate the high level of skill of these local artists.[10]

The next stage in the development of the Hellenistic tradition in the Central Asian context was the period of the Greco-Bactrian kingdom, when the Asian satrapies of Bactria and Parthia became independent from the central Seleucid power. The crisis of the Seleucid state did not mean the total decline of the culture; on the contrary it reached its climax during this period. Justin called Diodotus – one of the first independent kings of Bactria – the ruler of a thousand Bactrian cities (Just. X, 1, 4 and 5). Strabo also named a thousand towns under the control of Eucratides (Strabo XV, 1, 3). Numerous imitations of Seleucid and Greco-Bactrian coins testify to the influence of Hellenistic culture,[11] while continuing archaeological discoveries add evidence that the penetration of Greco-Macedonian culture into Central Asia can be seen as an entire cultural complex, incorporating all aspects of life.

When we speak of Hellenism we mean the culture in all its diversity. Almost all spheres of creative activities were influenced by Hellenistic culture. The term that was introduced by Droysen implies not only the spread of Greek supremacy, but also the introduction of the Greek way of life.[12] We should try to clarify certain elements of this sophisticated process, especially those concerning the plastic arts. Above all, one question arises – what were the characteristics of the cultural complex that the soldiers of Alexander the Great brought with them? What did the Greeks and Macedonians carry into Central Asia?

Hellenistic culture in itself was the continuation of traditions that derived from the Late Classical period. These traditions had a direct relation to the artistic values that were created by the masters of previous periods.

There is an opinion that 'Hellenistic sculpture is not a creative art', and that the masters of the Hellenistic period only drew from the great reserve of forms and methods created in the fifth to fourth centuries BC.[13] There is, nevertheless, another opinion, which suggests that the sculptural works of eminent artists of this period manifest a new vitality in the 'expressive sculptural portrait'.[14] New elements of the figurative complex – a new conception of the artistic world outlook – were formed on the basis of the traditions of the cities of Asia Minor, external to Athens. But the deep humanistic ideas of the artistic genius of Greek culture, established in the Classical period, continued to feed the schools remote from the metropolis.[15]

For the Classical period it is a characteristic that 'the centre of gravity was replaced from the cities of Greece itself to the provinces of the Greek world, namely to those parts that had a closer connection with the Orient'.[16] Among the leading sculptural schools, the Syrian school deserves special attention.[17] It represented a region that was at the crossroads of Greek culture in the Hellenistic period, and was a zone of permanent cultural contacts promoting the development of new forms of artistic creation. The spirit of the epoch is observed also in the changing of the architectural structures of the cities, supplementing the traditional Classical ensemble with new elements. The palace of Ai Khanum, as with cities in Seleucid Mesopotamia, was not isolated, but contained within the heart of the city. This testified to radical changes in the ideology of society and state policy that began in the time of Alexander and were reinforced during the Seleucid period. Characteristic signs of the new style were also expressed by the majestic pomposity and greatness in form. Sculpture became a permanent fixture of architectural decoration. If monumentality was characteristic of Oriental art, the forms themselves were adopted from the Hellenistic world,[18] the main meaning of which was related to official art, propagandizing the king's power. Monumental constructions erected in honour and glory of the king, which we observe in both Early Hellenistic states and in the Roman empire, are analogous in content to the tradition of the Ancient East, glorifying the activities of the king, sanctified by the omnipotent will of the deity. Numerous examples are also known from the Seleucid state.[19]

Special priests were organizers of the cult of the king. In Dura Europos there was a priest of King Seleucus I Nicator and a priest of his ancestors (180 BC).[20] Seleucia on the Tigris also had a priest. Often the divine kings were represented in the guise of Olympic deities (for example, 'Seleucus Zeus Nicator') .[21] The temple of Athena in Ilion was an object of veneration, decorated with a statue of the King Antiochus I on a horse. Statues of Seleucus were erected in Athens (Paus. I, 16, I), in Antioch (Liban. I, 301R), in Miletus (Milet I, c.383; III, c.262), in Olympia (Paus. VI, II.I) and in Priene. There were also representations of the king in Delos and in Magnesia on Sipilos.[22]

The secular aspect of the cult of the king was reinforced in Seleucid art and in this context the religious architecture and plastic works are preserved as the main objects of the ritual requirements of the population. The realistic manner of the representation of secular images is also found in works of religious character. A well-known and representative work in this respect is the sculptural portrait of Seleucus from Herculaneum (from Naples, dated to the third to the second centuries BC).[23]

The Seleucid period in the history of Central Asia has been poorly studied and it is therefore difficult to trace the origins of Hellenization. One might speculate that in the early phase of its development the Hellenistic art of Bactria and Parthia rose from the mutual source of the Seleucid figurative complex.[24] However, this has not been well studied and it is hard to confirm this hypothesis. Nevertheless, it can be supposed that the art of the Seleucid period embraced both official and cult aspects and provided strong new impulse to the dynastic art of subsequent periods. In the plastic art of the Hellenistic period particularly, one can observe the tendency to personify ideas related to concepts such as abundance, richness, and fertility. This trait is often achieved by the embodiment of aspects both in images of certain historic personages and in cult statues of the respective deities.

In the Hellenistic period, previously minor deities including Asclepius, Cybele, Serapis, Tyche, and the Dioscuri become popular, displacing the older generation of gods.[25] The manner of sculpting is distinguished by a sensitive perception of the image and by a new understanding of modelling. This manner is clearest in the works of Skopas, one of the most outstanding sculptors of antiquity.[26]

The artistic methods developed during the Late Classic period were enriched by new creative methods. The soft painted plastic modelling of Praxiteles, which gives his works an expression of contemplation, was replaced by the dramatic tension of the works by Skopas.[27] This development achieved its climax in the sculptural images of Lysippos (for example, in a portrait of Alexander from Istanbul Museum).[28] The modelling of the eyes with the eyeball in relief and enlarged eyelids turned down at the external edge conveys the deep psychological insight of the works of Lysippos.[29] This modelling of the eyes reinforces the tragic tension of the up-turned stare. Works in this style were widespread in the Hellenistic world.[30]

The works of plastic art attributed to Bactrian masters are characterized by traits of a similar style and therefore are often associated with the sculptural school of Lysippos.[31] However, the Hellenistic traditions in the territory of Bactria and Sogdiana did not develop according to a universal scheme. These traditions represent a sophisticated process relating to a specific historical situation and the peculiarities of the local culture. In the art of Bactria, Ai Khanum, with its sculptures executed in the traditions of Hellenistic plastic art, has yielded the most representative figurative complex.[32] The stylistic peculiarities of the Ai Khanum works associate them with works of the Lysippos circle (for example, the funerary relief from the necropolis), although by their pathos and drama these images are reminiscent of the reliefs of the Pergamon circle.[33]

THE HELLENISTIC PERIOD

Ai Khanum

The significance of Ai Khanum in the history of Central Asia is paramount. The site is characterized by a number of different features. Firstly, Ai Khanum was a town founded by the Greeks and built for the needs of its citizens. Secondly, its peculiarities can be traced to the historical situation that came into being after Alexander the Great and the creation of the new Seleucid Empire. Thirdly, the Greco-Bactrian period in the history of Ai Khanum is long and brilliant. The majority of its plastic art works belongs, probably, to this period.

According to the excavators, approximately 2,500 small fragments of clay statues were found in room no. 9 (in the temple of indented niches).[34] Judging by these fragments they probably came from fifteen different statues.[35] They also demonstrate the preference of the Ai Khanum masters for clay, despite the fact that they had access to quarries. That stone was intensively used in Ai Khanum is manifested in the numerous bases and fragments of columns, and capitals, sometimes of considerable dimensions. But why was clay chosen? Is it because it was the cheapest and most accessible material or was it easier to handle for plastic modelling? It is very possible that both of these aspects made clay one of the most popular materials in plastic art. In Ai Khanum, we see one of the earliest examples (for Central Asia) of the modelling technique combining clay and stone, the so-called *acrolith* technique. This technique is demonstrated on the huge foot wearing a Greek sandal (Fig. 13) from the Temple with Indented Niches.[36] Nevertheless, many kinds of architectural decoration with sculptural works demonstrate that stone was widely used here. The high quality of the works of the Ai Khanum sculptors shows the superior level of their stone carving skills.

Turning to the most remarkable plastic works of Ai Khanum, it should be stated first that the traditions of the Ai Khanum masters reflect general tendencies which can be traced in Hellenistic art to Greece herself as well as her colonies. The Pergamon Altar, with its remarkable reliefs of Greek mythological subjects, is most representative of the sculptural art of the Hellenistic period.[37] Tension, drama, vivacious expression and dynamism

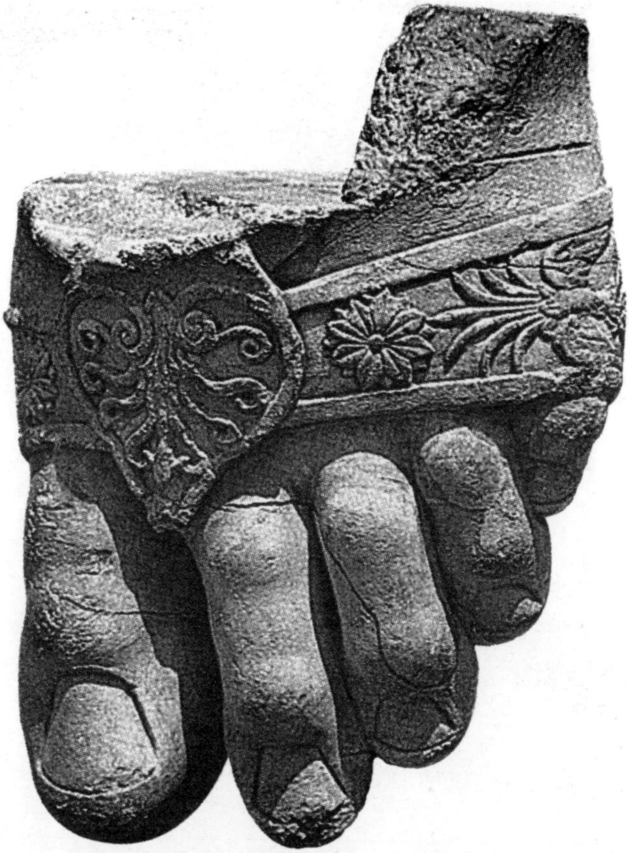

Fig. 13: Stone detail of an acrolith (combination of stone and clay) statue representing a Greek sandal with ornamentation in the form of a rosette and winged thunderbolts (symbol of Zeus). Ai Khanum. H = 27 cm. (National Museum of Afghanistan. Courtesy of P. Bernard).

are the traits of this style, which spread to the remotest corners of the Hellenistic world. The relief of a youth (Fig. 14) on a funerary stele found in the area of the necropolis at Ai Khanum reflects this trend.[38] Although the sculpture has not been completely preserved, it displays numerous characteristics of this style. The figure was executed in limestone. It has an athletic body with the left leg advanced. The figure is nude, except for the left shoulder and hand, which are draped with a *chlamys* (mantle) that is fastened by an *agraph* (fibulae) on the right shoulder. On the small head fragment can be seen long hair falling onto the shoulders and part of the forehead above the upward glancing eyes. The pose of the figure resembles, as noted by Paul Bernard, the figure of 'Apollo' with bow and arrow on Greco-Bactrian coins (for example, the coins of Eucratides and Apollodotus).[39] At the same time, as alluded to above, the figure is very close to the

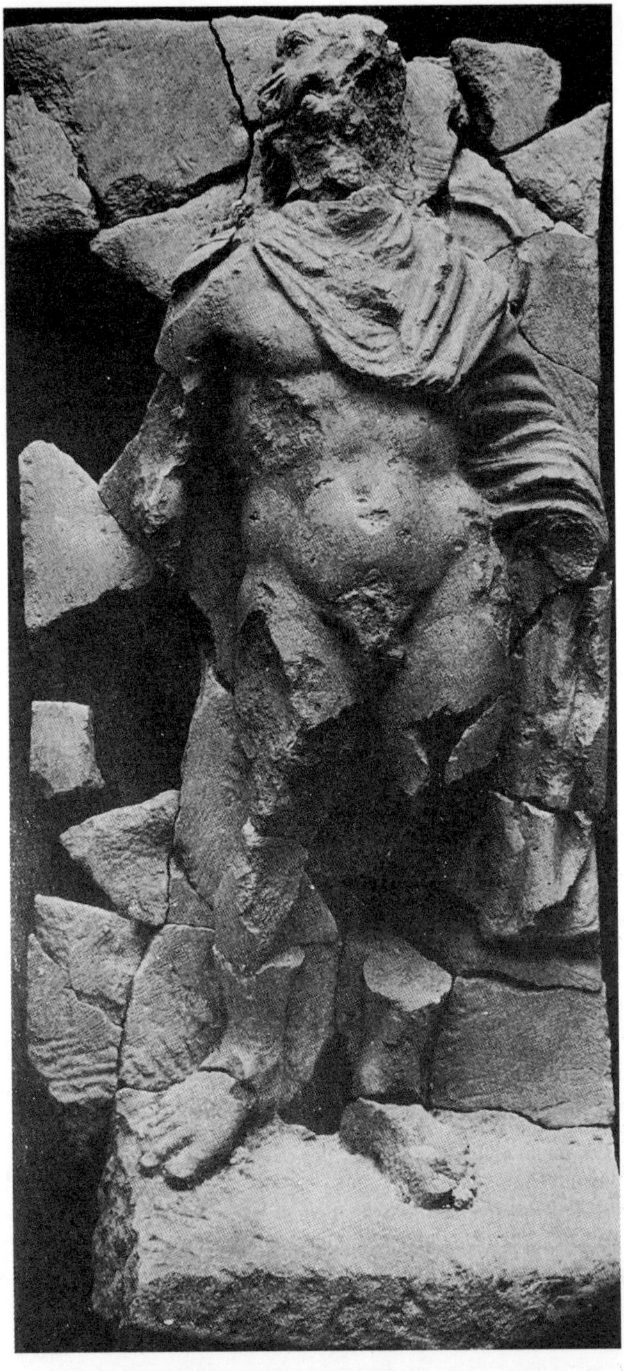

Fig. 14: Stone statue. Figure of a nude youth with a mantle draped over his shoulders and back, and a *petasos* hung behind his left shoulder. Necropolis of Ai Khanum. 50 × 26 × 11.5 cm. (National Museum of Afghanistan. Courtesy of P. Bernard).

sculptures of the Pergamon circle. While among the well-executed plastic pieces from Ai Khanum, there are several sculptures which show a certain decadence and artistic degradation, in this athletic figure just described – full of dynamism and expression – we can observe a high level of creative artistry. More images can be grouped around the latter: another nude figure of a youth wearing a diadem, a portrait of an elderly man, and a female portrait.[40] However, a female figure in a long dress, standing beside a small column (Fig. 15) is of lower quality, having certain flatness.[41] The pleats

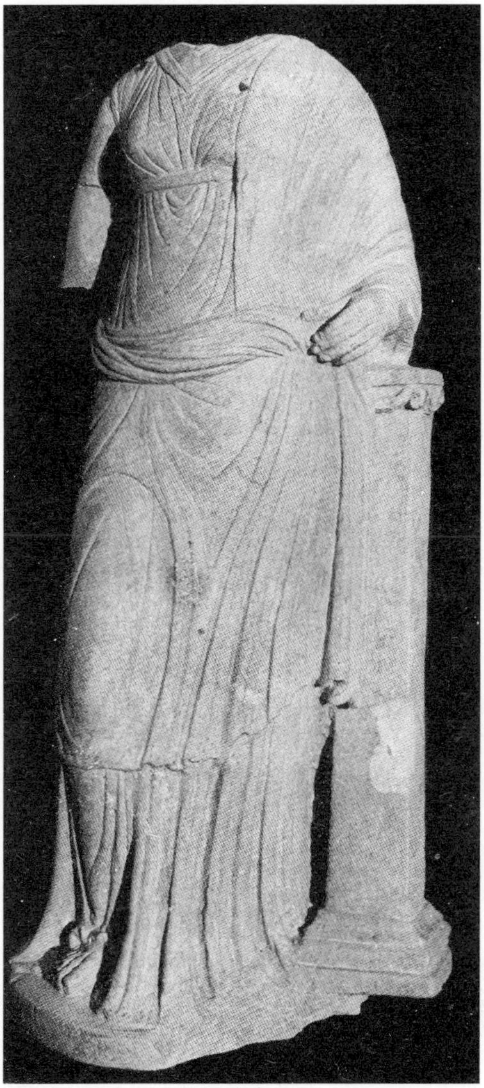

Fig. 15: Standing female figure leaning on small column. Ai Khanum. H = 13.7 cm. (National Museum of Afghanistan. Courtesy of P. Bernard).

of the dress are rather graphic and superficial. The contrast of soft, deep shadows is lost, replaced by linearity. The pose of the young woman is unnatural, with a hand held stiffly in the air over the column on which she is leaning. In the same category is the figure of Heracles.[42] His stocky body lacks modelling of the muscular system and is heavy and clumsy. The image of Heracles, the strong, dynamic hero of early Hellenism, has been substituted for a more simplified and static image (Fig. 16) typical of the

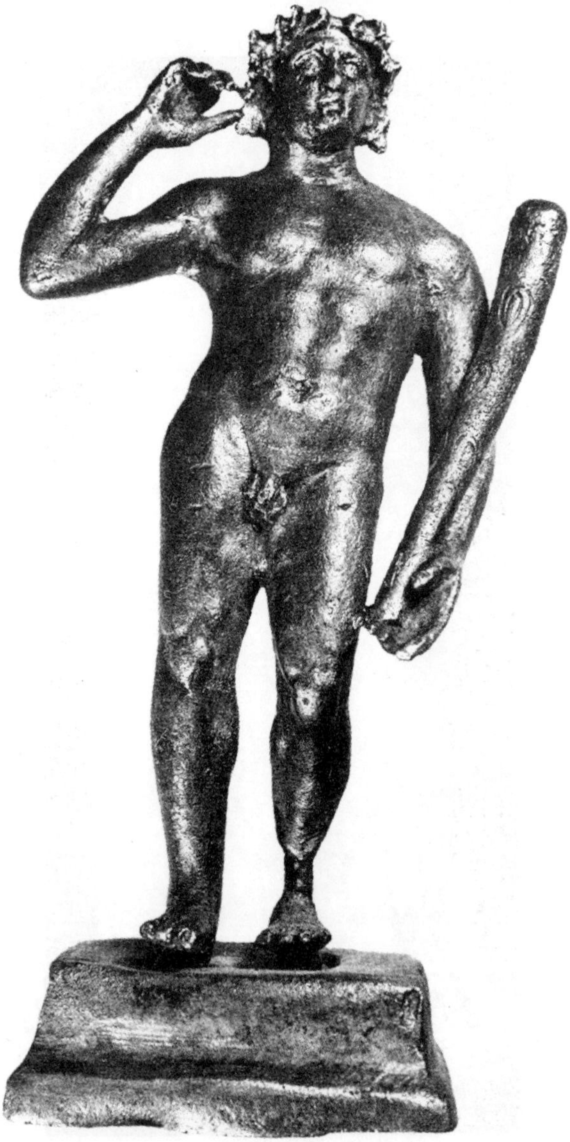

Fig. 16: Heracles with club. Bronze. Ai Khanum. H = 18.2 cm. (National Museum of Afghanistan. Courtesy of P. Bernard).

later period. This loss in plastic imagination occurred between the late third and the first half of the second century BC. The majority of plastic images of this period, not only in Bactria, but also in other regions of the Hellenistic world, tended towards linearity and flatness.[43]

The small group of terracotta figurines (emblemata and heads applied to vessels) from Ai Khanum is linked to the plastic school of Lysippos (Fig. 17).[44] In these figurines the manner of modelling the eyes and head-dress is the same. Locks of hair frame the face symmetrically, curling back over the diadem. The latter is characteristic of impressed heads decorating the handles of ceramic vessels.[45]

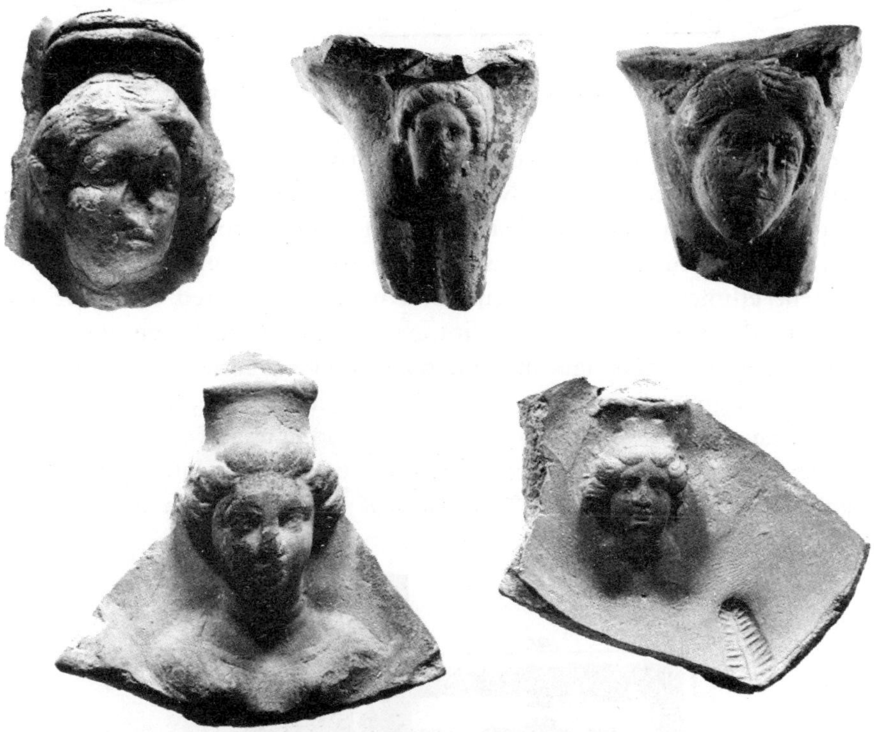

Fig. 17: Terracotta heads appliquéd on vessels from Ai Khanum. (National Museum of Afghanistan. Courtesy of B. Lyonnet).

TAKHT-I SANGIN

Excavations at another site, Takht-i Sangin, have yielded considerable material for the plastic art of Bactria. In addition to an Ionian capital (Fig. 18) that decorated the portal of the temple, a rich collection of small artefacts was found here: engraved bones (ivory), small sculptures in stone and bronze, terracottas and clay sculptures. The objects found in the sacred area of the temple were probably votive offerings.[46] As one votive inscription

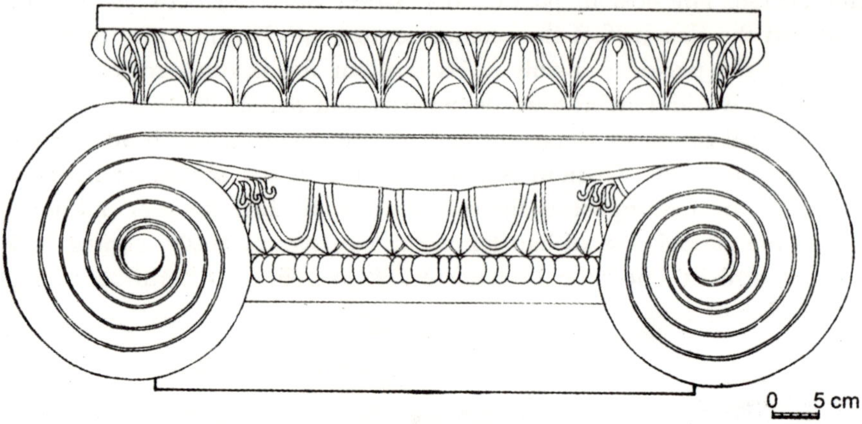

Fig. 18: Ionian Capital. Takht-i Sangin. Tajikistan. (After I.R. Pichikian, 1991, fig. 3).

reveals, the temple was consecrated to the river god Oxus (Fig. 19). The deity was venerated most likely by both the Greek and Iranian-speaking population. In any case, the character of the objects from the temple, and their ethno-cultural attributions, indicate that the donors belonged to different ethnic groups. The sculptural material gathered from the site confirms this supposition. Plastic images of clearly Greek appearance are found together with images showing traits of a local ethnos. As an example of this local group one can refer to a bearded head with a coiffure typical of Bactrian costume.[47] This testifies to a common cult devoted to the deity of the Oxus among the Bactrian population. The sculpture of Takht-i Sangin was executed in clay. The clay was then covered with a layer of

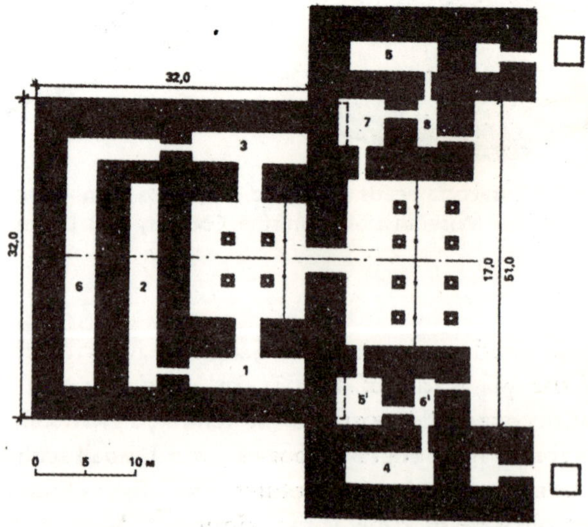

Fig. 19: Plan of the Oxus Temple. Takht-i Sangin. (After I.R. Pichikian, 1991, fig. 2).

alabaster, which in turn was decorated with polychrome paint and gilding.[48] Figures wearing royal wreaths with typical Greek modelling of the hair clearly show individual traits and perhaps represented local rulers. An identification of these sculptural portraits as Seleucid kings has been proposed by I. Pichikian according to whom there existed two different age groups.[49] The first proposed group is represented by the head of a man in his fifties (Fig. 20), which has been interpreted as an image of Seleucus.[50] The second proposed group is represented by the head of a younger man (Fig. 21),

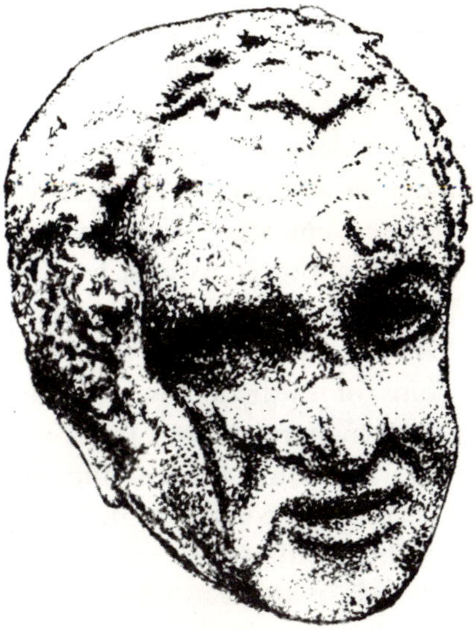

Fig. 20: Sculptural portrait of an old man. Painted clay. Takht-i Sangin. H = 13.1 cm. (Institute of History, Dushanbe).

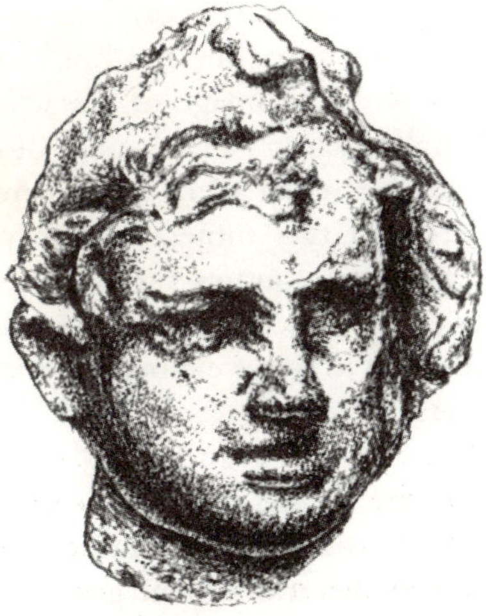

Fig. 21: Sculptural portrait of a young king. Painted clay. Takht-i Sangin. H = 16 × 12 cm. (Institute of History, Dushanbe).

which has been identified as Antiochus I (son of Seleucus). These two portrait sculptures were discussed by B.A. Litvinskiy, who, however, associated the 'second head' of Pichikian's classification with Seleucus and ascribed the image of the 'older man' to King Antiochus.[51]

We cannot deal here with the questions of attribution of the Takht-i Sangin clay portraits. The selected material belongs only to a certain phase and gives a general idea of its plastic art. It is evident, though, that the sculpture of Takht-i Sangin reflects the long evolution of sculptural art in Bactria. At the same time the finds of royal portraits as votive objects in a temple give them official weight. In this aspect the remarkable find of a Greek inscription from the Kulyab region in Tajikistan provides an extremely illuminating insight. This inscription, which was recently published by French scholars, concerns a dedication by one Heliodotus.[52]

Two great kings, Euthydemus and his son Demetrius, are mentioned in the inscription with the highest epithets.[53] The inscription could be read as a kind of proclamation of royal power. At least from this inscription one can deduce the popularity of these kings and the existence of a certain cult of them. Not by chance is the territory to the north of the Oxus River rich in finds of coins of Euthydemus and Demetrius, including copper ones.[54] Moreover, the clay portrait from Takht-i Sangin representing a head with curled hair and wearing a diadem and the coin portraits of Euthydemus have certain features in common, including the hairstyle and headdress with diadem and the profile with straight nose.[55] The repertoire of Bactrian artists included both images of deities and portraits of historic personalities. This repertoire demonstrates the diversity of genres and the excellence of the sculptors. However, whereas the identification and comparison of clay sculptures with historically recognizable Bactrian personalities must remain open to conjecture, the mythical images present less of a problem for interpretation. The head of Heracles carved in ivory that Pichikian associated with the image of Heracles-Alexander (Fig. 22) is an artistic work of high quality.[56] The handle of a sword decorated in the shape of the fighting figures of Heracles and Achelous (?) (Fig. 23)[57] speaks for the popularity of this subject in the plastic art of Bactria. In subsequent periods, this topic continues to be treated in terracotta plastic art.[58] Images of Marsyas (Fig. 24), Achelous and Hippocampus were, probably, part of a single cycle devoted to water elements, paying tribute to the main deity of the Oxus River.

The complex of Takht-i Sangin is an invaluable source for the study of plastic art in Bactria for the simple reason that the objects came from a single place – the temple – and were accumulated over a period of time. All aspects of research into this monument give an impressive picture of the evolution of figurative art traditions from the Achaemenid and early Hellenistic periods to the time of the destruction of the temple. While the

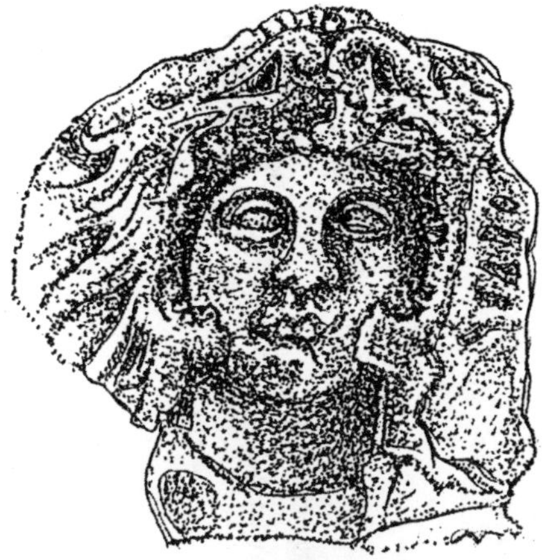

Fig. 22: Representation of Heracles (Alexander-Heracles). Ivory. Takht-i Sangin. H = 3.6 cm. (Institute of History, Dushanbe).

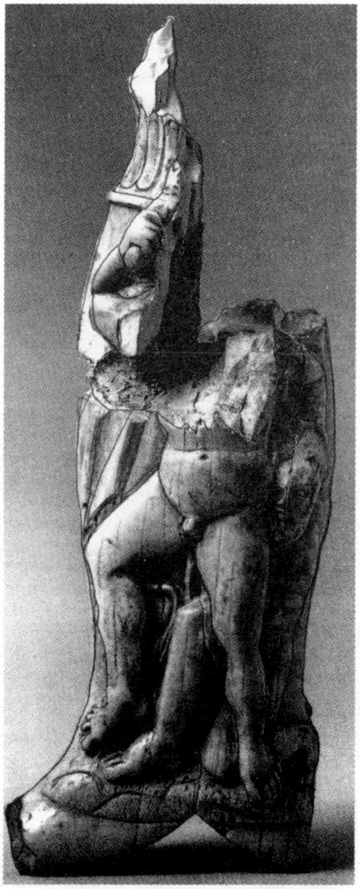

Fig. 23: Hilt of sword decorated with a struggle between Heracles and Achelous (?). Ivory. H = 10.8 cm. (Institute of History, Dushanbe).

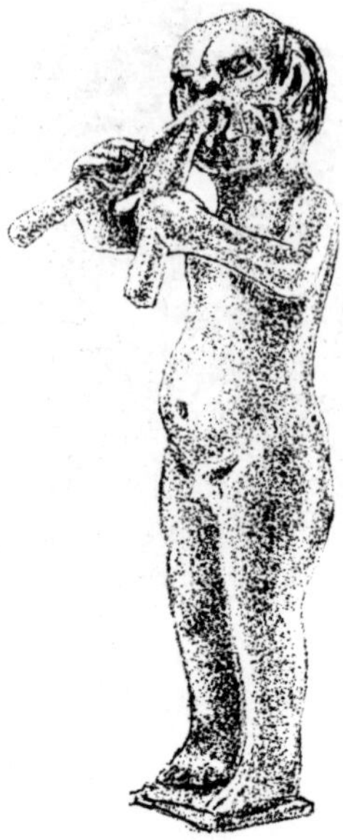

Fig. 24: Bronze figurine of Marsyas. Takht-i Sangin.
H = 7.2 cm. (Institute of History, Duṣhanbe).

figurative complex from Takht-i Sangin stands for the early Hellenistic period based on Achaemenid and Greek traditions, the plastic works of the Khalchayan sculptors represent the subsequent Post-Greek period.

THE LATE HELLENISTIC AND YUE-ZHI PERIODS

KHALCHAYAN

Khalchayan was located in the middle stretch of the valley of the Surkhandarya.[59] This amazing site with its reliefs is one of the most famous monuments of pre-Kushan art in Central Asia. In one of the rooms of a building richly decorated with antefixes and merlons, numerous clay sculptures were unearthed (Fig. 25). These fragments of life-size human

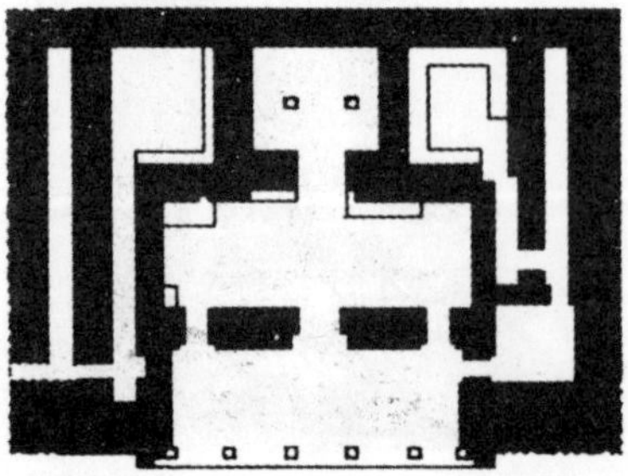

Fig. 25: Khalchayan. Plan of the palace.
(After B.Ya. Staviskiy, 1979: 92, 1966, fig. 23, I).

figures had belonged to wall reliefs of a large hall. The first investigator of this complex, G.A. Pugachenkova, interpreted the main scene of the Khalchayan reliefs as a triumphal procession of the victorious tribes of the Yue-zhi.[60] Indeed, the entire figurative complex of Khalchayan glorified the Kushan victory and the establishment of Kushan power (Fig. 26). Evidently some scenes do depict actual events, but it is difficult to identify particular individuals from the reliefs. On the basis of a male head with a moustache and diadem (Fig. 27), G.A. Pugachenkova identified the figures with the Heraius clan.[61] However, the numismatic data do not include any coins of this ruler.[62] Some figures and fragments of the Khalchayan complex (for example, the horseman shooting an arrow, the individual with the trophy armour and the horse's leg treading on the armour) seem to depict a battle between the Ta Yue-zhi and other nomadic tribes.[63] Other figures in the reliefs are distinguished by their expressive features and were believed by G. Pugachenkova to be satyrs and demonic creatures. These expressive figures with side-whiskers (Fig. 28) differ greatly from the tranquil, majestic

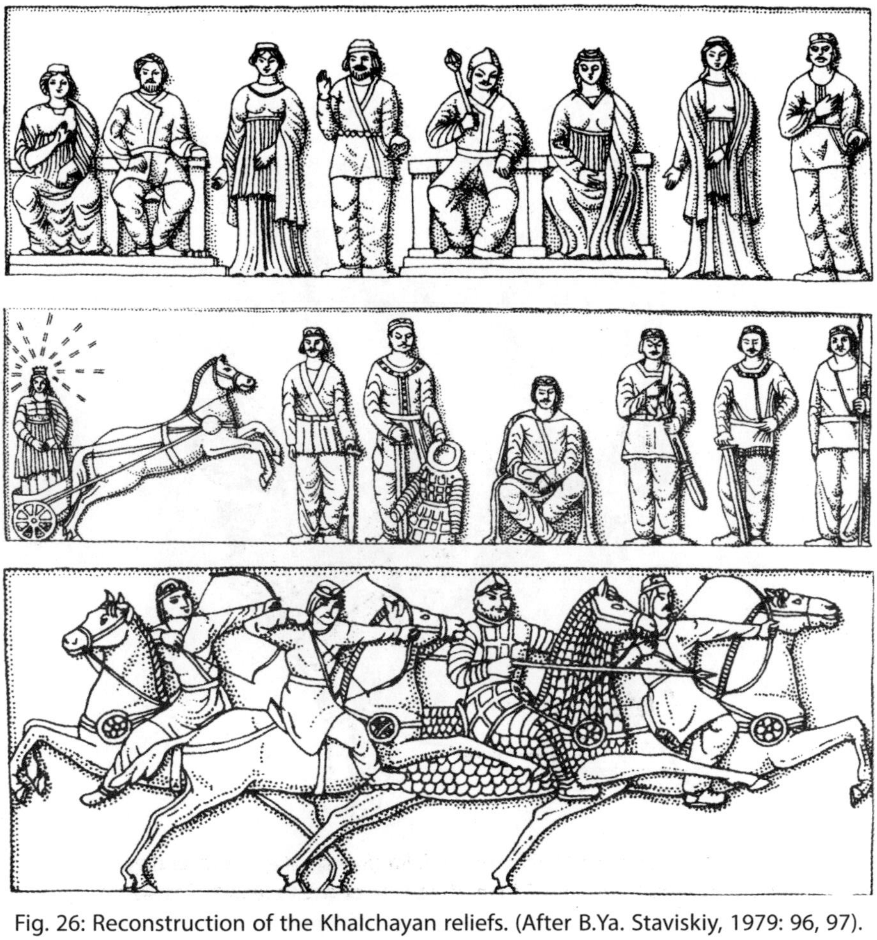

Fig. 26: Reconstruction of the Khalchayan reliefs. (After B.Ya. Staviskiy, 1979: 96, 97).

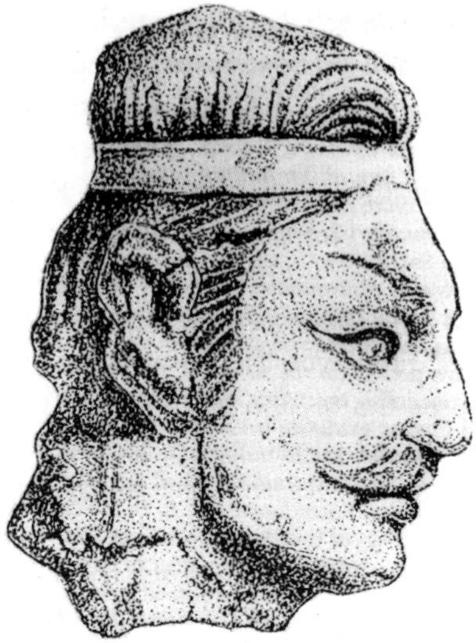

Fig. 27: Male portrait of a member of the Yue-zhi tribe. Painted clay. Late 2nd century BC. 19.5 × 16 × 12 cm. (Museum of History of Peoples of Uzbekistan, Tashkent).

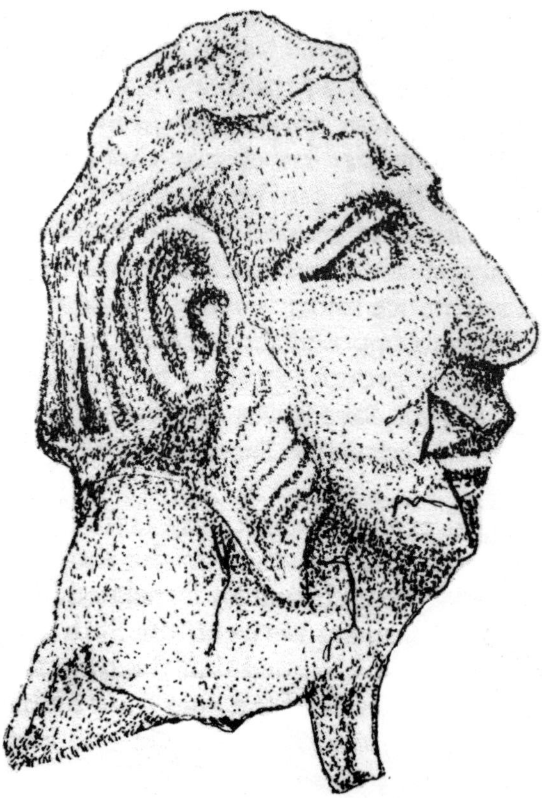

Fig. 28: Male portrait showing a Saka (Sakarauke). Painted clay. Late 2nd century BC. H = 27 cm. (Institute of Art Research, Tashkent).

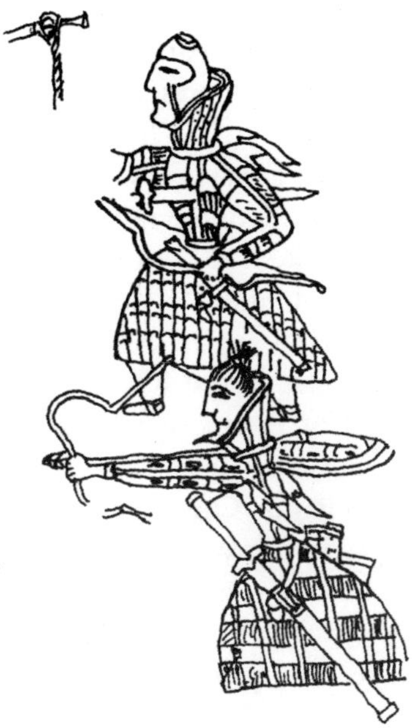

Fig. 29: Warriors in chain-mail armour from the Orlat necropolis. Bone plates. Samarkand region. Late 2nd century BC. (Institute of Art Research, Tashkent).

faces and poses of the Yue-zhi personages. It is not impossible that the Bactrian artists caricatured their foe[64] and that these figures with long whiskers were the enemies of the Yue-zhi, presumably members of the Sakaravles tribe, who occupied this territory before the Yue-zhi migration into Central Asia.[65] Iconographically, these figures are very similar to representations on early coins with the archer on the obverse.[66] Such coins have mainly been found in the regions of Samarkand and Bukhara.[67] Yet, the warriors in chain-mail (Fig. 29) are very close to the horse riders on coins of the Indo-Scythian rulers (Azes, Asiles and others).[68] On a fragment of a wall painting from Dal'verzintepa, one can see the image of a warrior of the Khalchayan type. This fragment comes from the stratum preceding the general destruction of the site (i.e. before the nomad invasion).[69] In the Khalchayan reliefs we can thus distinguish two different and antagonistic ethnic groups, who were involved in a confrontation. Apparently, these Khalchayan scenes depicted events that took place during the second half of the second century BC, in any case before the visit of the Chinese diplomat Zhang Qian in 129/128 BC.[70] An important question is whether there are archaeological layers from the period of the Saka, who occupied the northern lands of Bactria before the arrival of the Da Yue-zhi.

Clearly, any layers of the Saka period must be situated directly underneath the Yue-zhi layers. Such layers have been found at Dal'verzintepa, one of the main Kushan sites in southern Uzbekistan.[71] Two remarkable fragments of wall paintings found in a layer that preceded substantial repair work after the destruction of a building are particularly interesting.[72] Indeed, the archaeological context attests to the presence of a population just before the Yue-zhi arrival in northern Bactria. The fragment from Dal'verzintepa shows a polychrome painting of a warrior with a helmet,[73] who resembles certain figures from Khalchayan. Iconographically, images of an armoured warrior (Fig. 30) can be linked to representations on the coins of Tanlismaidates, who was a local ruler.[74] The majority of these coins have been found to the west of Balkh.[75]

We have thus examined some of the Khalchayan reliefs. Figures with a demonic expression and very distinctive long whiskers also occur in terracotta plastic art. We know at present two figurines resembling the figures on the reliefs of Khalchayan. One of them was found at Old Termez in an archaeological layer dated to the second to first century BC,[76] representing a bearded head with large ringlets and long whiskers. The vertical lines on the neck clearly represent chain-mail armour. The other example is a hand-modelled figurine from Erkurgan (a major site near

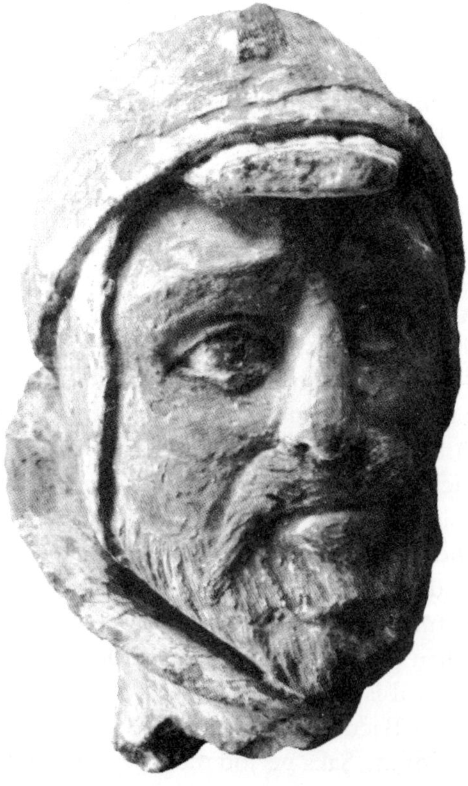

Fig. 30: Male portrait showing a Saka (Sakarauke) wearing a helmet and a high collar. Painted clay. Late 2nd century BC. H = 27 cm. (Institute of Art Research, Tashkent).

modern Karshi, in the Kashkadarya region to the south-southwest of Samarkand).[77] The representation is treated in a schematic manner, but there are some significant elements in its iconography. The terracotta figurine has a high armoured collar and long side-whiskers similar to certain Khalchayan figures.[78] It is dated stratigraphically to the second century BC.

Thus, both stratigraphically and in the figurative complex we can distinguish two types of the northern Bactrian population. The Khalchayan reliefs show us the scene of a battle between the Da Yue-zhi and Saka (Sakaraukes). It is possible to attribute the Khalchayan reliefs to the first century BC on archaeological basis, but the historical events reflected on these reliefs belonged to an earlier period – around the middle of the second century BC. In general, one could say that the Khalchayan complex forms a bridge between Hellenistic art of Bactria and Hellenized Kushan art.

In spite of the fact that the majority of images in the Khalchayan complex are evidently not of Greek appearance, the manner of modelling certain details is reminiscent of Hellenistic sculpture, some of which should be mentioned here. The headdress is a significant part of the iconography as it is one of the main features for the identification of style in a figurative complex. In this respect, the Khalchayan reliefs are of special interest. The presence of *putti* (garland bearers) on the reliefs of Khalchayan is also an unmistakable sign of Hellenistic influence.

In determining style, the minor personages are in my opinion the most informative. As a rule, the portrayal of minor personages reflects more closely portraits rather than abstract images. Here, in the modelling of the hair the sculptor was freer to choose coiffures that were in fashion at the time and familiar to him. Hairstyle reflects, to a certain extent, the period in which it developed, or became fashionable. Among the sculptures of Khalchayan, the images of a lute player and a harpist may serve as examples.[79] The hair of these figures is combed back over a relief band (Fig. 31), creating a protruding frame around the head. The hair is curled over the band in separate locks and in the centre, over the forehead; the relief band remains open. G.A. Pugachenkova considered this kind of hairstyle 'characteristic for all the other female representations of the Khalchayan palace'.[80] Nevertheless, as the analysis of the other heads shows, the hairstyle of the lute player and the harpist is clearly distinguished from that of the other female personages, even by the position of the diadem, which sits on the upper part of the forehead, covering the hairline. It should be noted that this latter feature is characteristic also of the male representations of the Khalchayan cycle and is, in all probability, an ethnic marker. Furthermore, regarding the hair twisted on the band, Pugachenkova states that 'such an arrangement of the hair is unknown in the complex of Greco-Roman

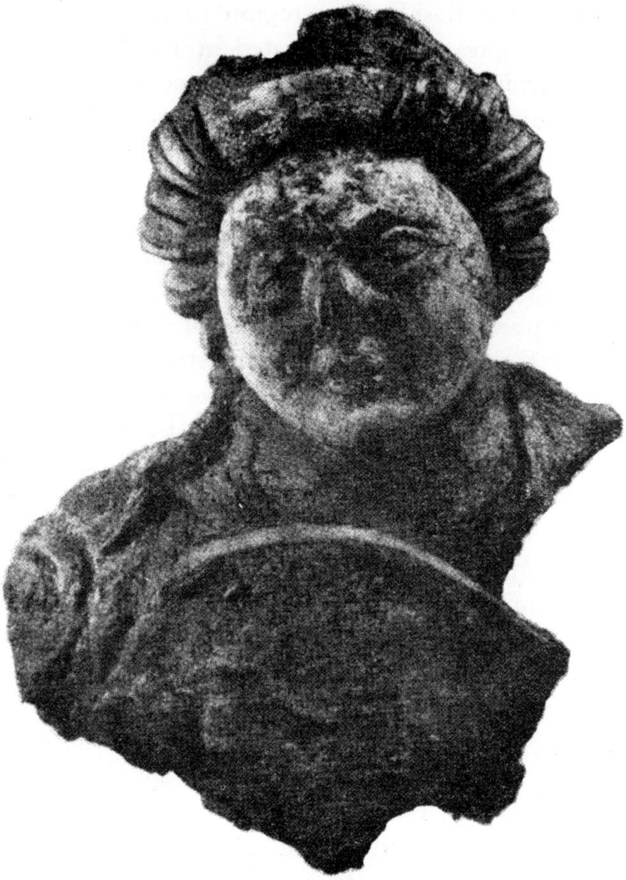

Fig. 31: Lute player. Khalchayan. Painted clay. Late 2nd century BC. H = 32 cm. (Institute of Art Research, Tashkent).

coiffures'.[81] As the Ai Khanum material demonstrates (for example, in an alabaster emblem showing a female bust[82]) here, too, the coiffure shows carefully arranged curls combed back over the band. Taking into account the higher artistic level of the Ai Khanum sculpture, the Khalchayan coiffure can be considered as a reflection of that found at Ai Khanum.

Finally, terracotta heads from Ai Khanum (Fig. 32) indicate the broad popularity of this same coiffure.[83] These heads can probably be dated to the second century BC, in any case not later than the first century BC. As evidence for the vast popularity of this coiffure there are many examples, geographically remote but chronologically analogous, including a female representation on a pendant sewn onto clothing from the royal burial at Pyatibratny no. 8 (Necropolis Elizavetinsky).[84]

As has been stated above, all individuals represented in the Khalchayan sculptures wear a forehead band (diadem) in a similar manner. Worn at the hairline, this style is essentially different from the Greek and even Greco-

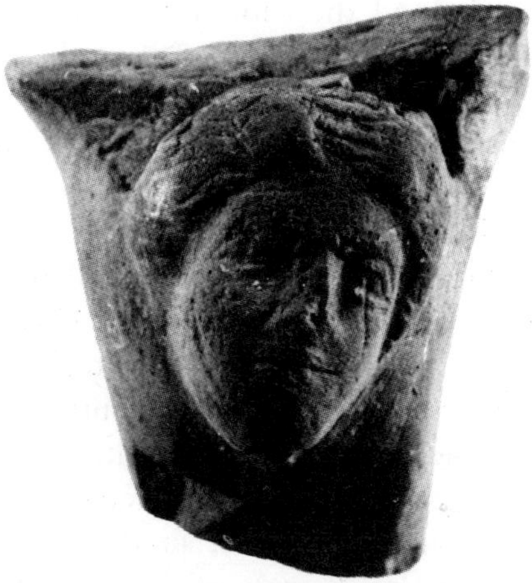

Fig. 32: Terracotta figurine (appliqué) from Ai Khanum, Afghanistan, with hairstyle similar to figures from Khalchayan. 2nd century BC. H = 3.4 cm. (National Museum of Afghanistan. Courtesy of B. Lyonnet).

Bactrian customs. As works of plastic art and coins demonstrate, the Greeks wore the diadem over hair that was carefully arranged in a row of curls.[85] This manner is especially clear on Greco-Bactrian coins. In this context, one can suggest that such a detail may be a reflection of ethnicity'. In any case, this element of the headdress on Khalchayan individuals appears to be under the influence of Hellenistic culture.

Another detail in the headdress of the Khalchayan sculpture should be noted. It is found on the representation of the so-called 'Prince of the Heraius Tribe'[86] and to a lesser degree on the head of a rider.[87] It concerns the coiffure represented as two large curls over the forehead, which are separated in opposite directions like two horns. The earliest example of this type of coiffure is the 'Portrait of Alexander the Great' by Lysippos.[88] It was to become one of the most popular hairstyles not only during the Hellenistic period, but also during the post-Greek period. As an example, we can cite the sculptural image of a youth from the necropolis of Ai Khanum. The head has not been preserved completely but on the upper left part can be seen curly hair, combed back, including a curl in the shape of a horn.[89] As another example, one can cite the representation of Dionysus on a *phaler* (metal plaque) found at Dushanbe.[90] Here, the hair is combed on both sides in the shape of up-turned horns and decorated with two rosettes. However, these two examples do not exhaust the analogies of this type of coiffure, which was widespread in the figurative art of the Hellenistic and post-Hellenistic East.

In spite of the complete difference from Greek dress, the costume of the Khalchayan figures, especially male costume, has some elements that resemble the Greek prototype. First, the cloak is usually worn fastened on the chest and draped behind the shoulders as it is often represented in Greek art (Fig. 33).[91] The nude figure of a youth from the Ai Khanum necropolis, mentioned above, is also shown with the cloak draped behind the shoulders.[92] This manner of cloak wearing is found on Bactrian terracotta figurines, for example, on a figurine representing a warrior from Kampyrtepa dated to the early Hellenistic period.[93] One can also recall the figure on the felt carpet from burial no. 5 of Pazyryk (Altai), where the rider in front of a deity seated on a throne is clad in a cloak draped behind the shoulders. Geographically and chronologically, this example is admittedly more remote.[94] However, it is necessary to mention that a cloak worn in this manner existed in the costume of the Central Asian population, particularly in Bactria, as far back as the Achaemenid period and was known as a *kas*.[95] Consequently, we cannot be certain that this garment was adopted from the Greeks, though the influence of the latter should not be entirely ruled out.

The influence of Hellenistic traditions on Khalchayan sculpture is observed not only in some attributes and elements of dress, but also in the facial details. For example, in the sculpture of the 'Elderly Man from the Heraius Tribe', the modelling of the eyes resembles very much that of Hellenistic art.[96] The carefully modelled eyelids, the large eyeball, and the slightly downward turned external edge of the eyelids all have parallels in the works of Greek masters.

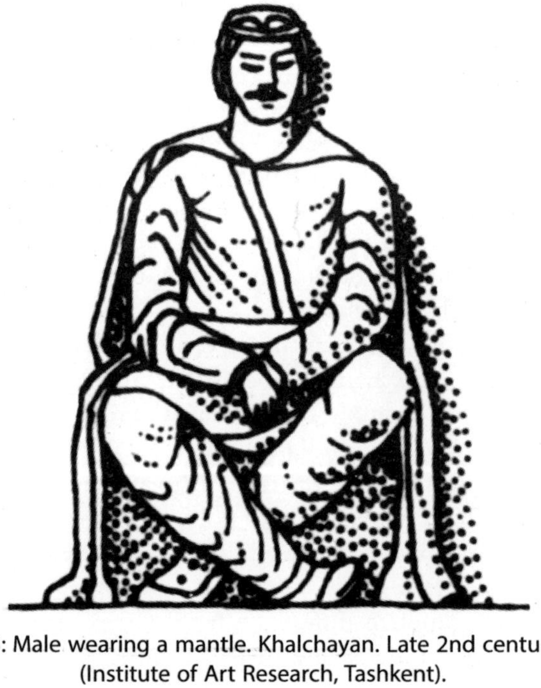

Fig. 33: Male wearing a mantle. Khalchayan. Late 2nd century BC. (Institute of Art Research, Tashkent).

The artistic quality of Khalchayan sculpture was certainly not inferior to that of early Hellenistic works and the dynamism of the previous period is still clearly felt in it. This characteristic, together with the inherent expressiveness and individuality of the figures, gives the Khalchayan sculptures brilliance and originality. This originality is present not only in sculpture, but also in certain architectural details. We have already mentioned finds of merlons and antefixes in the course of the excavations of Khalchayan. Some of the decorations of these pieces are typical of Greek architecture, as for instance the acanthus leaves of the antefixes. The quality of the design on the Khalchayan examples is lower than on those from Ai Khanum, which exhibit accuracy of proportions and elegancy of the lines. However, the Khalchayan area contributed an entirely new type of antefix in the shape of a male head[97] with a long horizontal moustache and a straight nose. The headdress consists of a high crown with an acanthus leaf motif. Aside from the Greek architectural system itself, one can thus trace a certain transformation in the ornamental details in the art of Khalchayan.

Many traits of Khalchayan sculpture that were undoubtedly created under Hellenistic influence persisted in the Kuevkurgan images of the subsequent periods. The absence of stamped details on the sculpture, for example, was typical of the Hellenistic art of Central Asia.

THE KUSHAN PERIOD

Surkh Kotal

While the Khalchayan reliefs correspond to an early stage in the pre-Kushan and early Kushan development of sculpture in which the Hellenistic art of the East can be perceived, the sculptural works of Surkh Kotal, albeit relatively few, demonstrate the flourishing dynastic art of the Kushans.[98] A dedicatory inscription to Kanishka the Victor found within the complex testifies to the dynastic character of the complex of Surkh Kotal.[99] The fire in the temple was connected, as correctly noted by the outstanding French scholar D. Schlumberger, not with the Zoroastrian tradition, but with a dynastic cult.[100] A close analogy for the temple is the shrine of Kanishka in Math (near Mathura, India).[101] The study of the Surkh Kotal sculpture also leads us to representations of royal personages at Mathura, but more essential in the Surkh Kotal figurative complex is the absence of motifs that could be related to Buddhist art. Does this absence of Buddhist motifs mean that Kushan dynastic art developed independently?

It is reasonable to scrutinize the material from Surkh Kotal[102] within the context of the general evolution of Bactrian plastic art. Here, we shall consider the few preserved fragments of sculpture, which, like the temple itself, were devoted to a dynastic cult. Much evidence speaks for the fact that these fragments represented royal individuals connected with the temple. However, before examining the sculptural fragments, it is necessary to describe the site itself briefly. This is important as the architectural decoration, according to Schlumberger, is distinguished by forms that are analogous to 'old Hellenistic traditions',[103] while the statuary bears all the signs of the new, non-Greek style.

The shrine was erected on the citadel as a rectangular structure enclosed by a fortification wall with towers. The peripteral temple was located on the top of a hill, surrounded by a court with a portico (Fig. 34). Terraces, whose different levels were connected by monumental stairs, preceded the eastern part of the temple. The width of the stairs was necessary for large processions during religious rites and festivals. Clay (mud brick) and stone were used to construct the temple. Stone was used mainly for facing and other decorative features of the buildings.

The preserved fragments of sculpture suggest that they were modelled in both clay and stone. They were placed in special niches. Of particular interest are the stone statues of royal personages, of which four have partly survived: three statues – two preserving only the lower half, the third a torso, and one high relief of a seated figure in rather poor condition.[104] The three statues were carved from a stone slab in low relief. However, it is likely that, following tradition, the heads of the statues were modelled in high relief (for example, the fragments of the head of a royal personage[105]). The cut and decoration of the garments are very close to the iconography of the Kushan kings, especially Vima Kadphises and Kanishka, known from coins.

The best-preserved statue wears a long caftan with fur trimming and

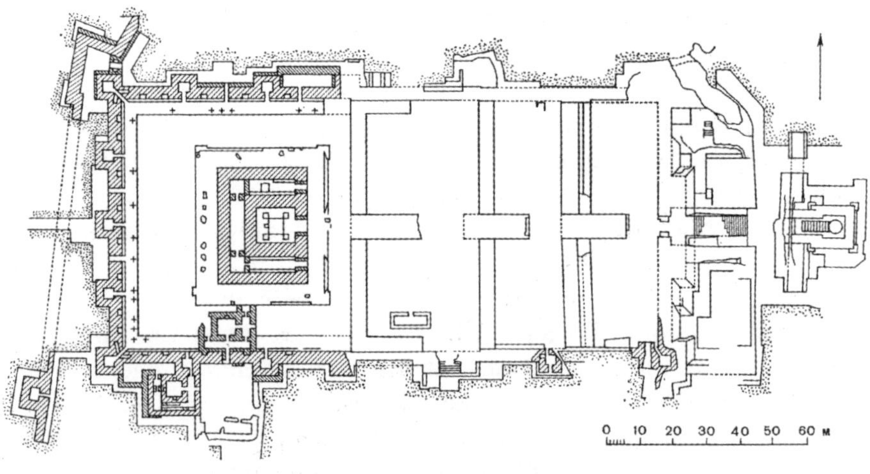

Fig. 34: Surkh Kotal, Afghanistan. Plan of the site. (After D. Schlumberger, 1985, fig. 48).

two circular plates (? fibulae), strongly resembling the dress of Vima Kadphises (Fig. 35). It is tempting to see in the royal statues of Surkh Kotal the images of both Kanishka and his ancestors, taking into consideration that the cult of ancestors was prevalent in Kushan religion.[106] Thanks to the discovery of an inscription from Rabatak (Afghanistan) we have knowledge of another individual from the Kanishka clan, namely Vima Taktu.[107] With this name, apparently, is associated the sculpture of a seated figure (Fig. 36) from Mathura, whose name V[e]ma Taksuma is mentioned

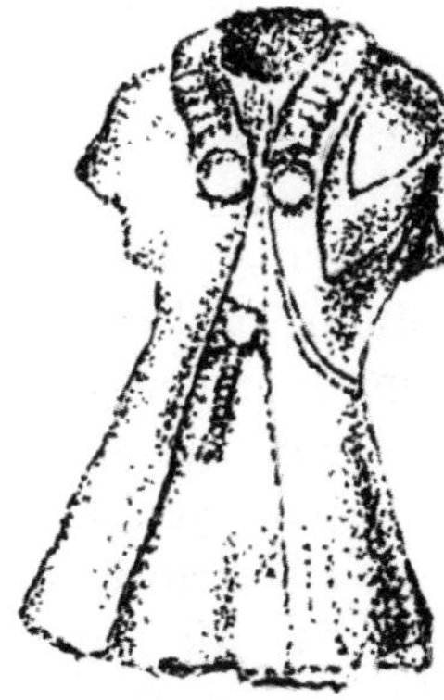

Fig. 35: Detail from statue of a royal individual wearing a Kushan style *kaftan*. Surkh Kotal, Afghanistan. 1st century AD.

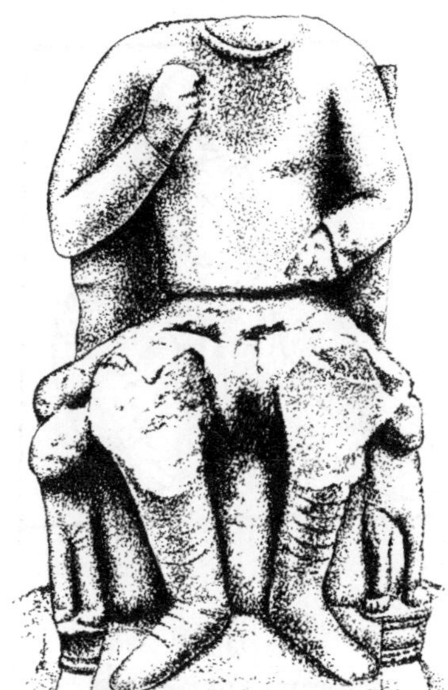

Fig. 36: Colossal statue showing an individual seated on a throne flanked by two lions (Vima Kadphises ?). Inscription reads 'Vima Tak. . .'. 1st century AD. Stone. (Scale not available) (Mathura Government Museum, Mat. India. Invent. no. 215. Drawing by K. Abdullaev).

in the Brahmi text engraved on the pedestal.[108] In light of the recently found inscription from Rabatak, the identification of this sculpture should be re-examined.

Returning to the Surkh Kotal sculpture, one peculiarity should be noted, namely, that it was executed in low relief. This technique was not typical for the previous period, nor was it typical for the Khalchayan complex and for the subsequent figurative complexes of the Kushan period. For example, the Mathura complex contained only sculpture in high relief, even in the round. Yet the technique of low relief was practised in ancient Iran; examples of such reliefs can be found in Achaemenid art and the later Sassanian period.[109] Between these two periods, however, is found the splendid figurative complex of southeastern Anatolia – in the kingdom of Commagene with its capital Samosata. The latter gained its independence from the Seleucids at the beginning of the second century BC. Among the abundance of sculptures and reliefs, the representation of a Persian nobleman from Nimrud Dag is the most significant for us.[110] However, it is not the low relief in which this figure is portrayed that matters, but the individual itself who wears a similar form of kaftan to the torso from Surkh Kotal (Fig. 37). The cut of the dress with fur trimming, the fastenings on the breast with round plates and with two descending cords, with slight variations all of these are present on the Surkh Kotal torso. It is interesting to note that this kind of *kaftan* with fur trimming is found also among

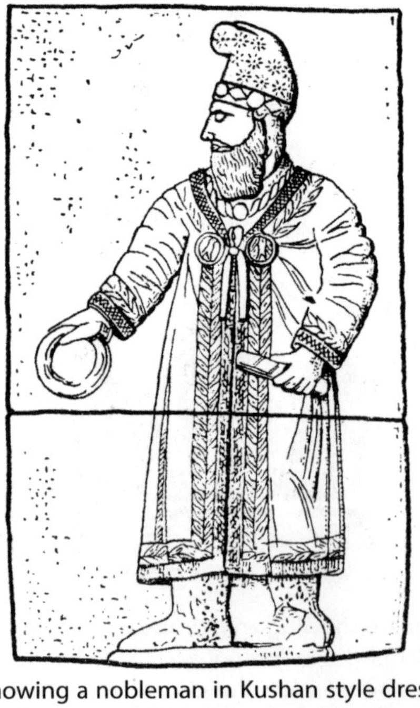

Fig. 37: Relief showing a nobleman in Kushan style dress. Commagene, Turkey. Stone. (Scale not available) (After D. Schlumberger, 1985, fig. 33).

the terracotta figurines of the Kushan period, bearing out its popularity in figurative art.[111]

The finds of sculptural, and especially architectural, details at Surkh Kotal and the neighbouring site of Old Termez clearly testify to their closely related figurative traditions in plastic art.

Old Termez

Old Termez (in Russian literature Stary Termez) was located on the strategically important crossroads to Balkh (Bactres), Chaganian, Sogdia, and Margiana. It is rare to find a Central Asian city having a port and water communication. This advantage of Old Termez is attested by both ancient and medieval sources which mention navigation along the Oxus (Amudarya) River (Fig. 38).[112]

Hypothetically, Alexandria on the Oxus, cited in Book 17 of Diodorus of Sicily, can be identified with Old Termez, more precisely with the oldest part of this site that is now called the *Kala* (citadel). The broad cultural layers conceal the true appearance of the ancient city. Archaeologically, it is difficult to trace the limits of the Hellenistic city of Old Termez. Only a few excavation trenches yielded levels from this period. These trenches are the only basis for the postulated location of Alexandria on the Oxus. Hopefully, future archaeological investigations in this area will provide a more solid scientific basis from which to study the history of this ancient city-site.

The concentration of monuments at Old Termez and its neighbourhood,

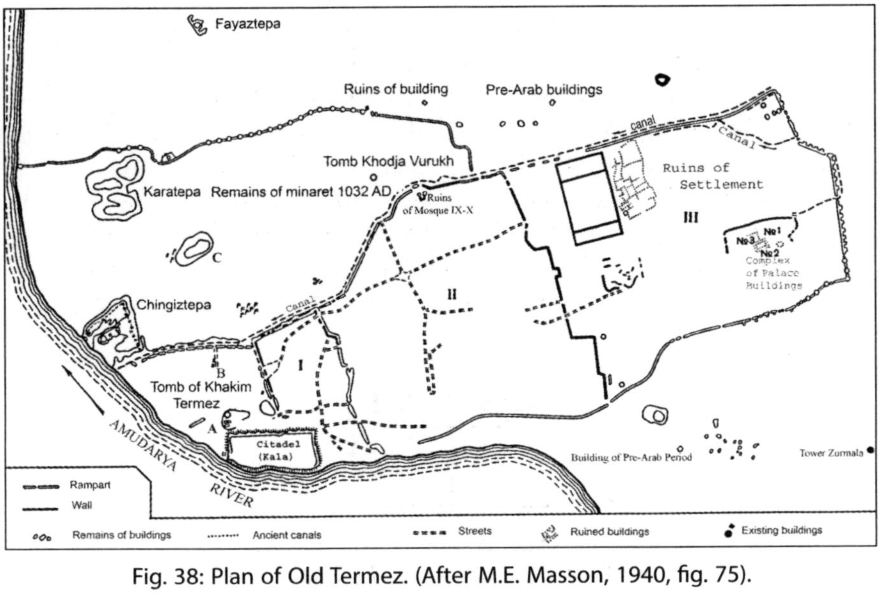

Fig. 38: Plan of Old Termez. (After M.E. Masson, 1940, fig. 75).

together with numerous finds of art objects, point to the existence of artistic schools and workshops inside the city. If these objects, which catered to the needs of the townspeople and nearby villages, were also being exported to distant regions, one could consider Termez as a centre of artistic culture not only in the distribution of its works, but also in its influence on the culture of neighbouring regions and settlements.

The most numerous items among the finds are column bases. The columns were made of local limestone and were turned on a special machine. The carefully executed details and the preservation of certain elements and proportions indicate the use of a model in their production. The most popular order of columns was Attic, resting on a square plinth with a profile of torus and cavetto (Fig. 39). Not infrequently one also finds at Old Termez capitals decorated in a pseudo-Corinthian style, sometimes including anthropomorphic and zoomorphic motifs.[113]

Old Termez has yielded a collection of sculpture executed in different materials and styles. In general, the plastic art represents one of the most developed genres in the artistic realm of the Bactrian region, and in particular of ancient Termez. Besides stone, the Bactrian masters employed clay, alabaster, and wood. However, due to its organic nature, wood rarely survived to the present time.[114]

As a rule, the multi-figured compositions typical of Buddhist art showing the Buddha in the centre surrounded by adorants demonstrate a remarkable understanding of the material from which they were worked. The ease of pose and gesture as well as the dynamic drapery underline the high skill level of the local sculptors. It should be noted that many pieces from the ancient part of the site were surface finds. However, until recently archaeologists had not identified any monumental constructions in this area. This may indicate that the pieces could have been transported from nearby Karatepa and Fayaztepa. In any case it is likely that they were reused by local inhabitants. There could also be other explanations for these finds. It is possible that inside the city there was a Buddhist temple (similar to that found at Dal'verzintepa), but given the current stage of research, this remains conjecture. Further archaeological work may clarify the situation. Recent discoveries at the Old Termez site on the Chingiztepa mound included some fragments of sculpture that probably came from a

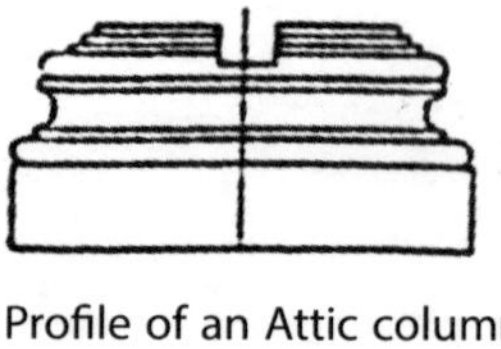

Fig. 39: Profile of an Attic column base. (Termez Archaeological Museum).

monumental building decorated with sculptural works.[115] The great quantity of architectural details gathered from the surface of Old Termez site consitutues the major part of the collections in the Termez Municipal Museum.

Architectural Decoration

The collection of architectural fragments in Termez Municipal Museum is distinguished by a richness of column bases and pilasters, capitals, cornices and other building elements (Fig. 40). In spite of the fact that the issues concerning architectural decoration have been discussed many times in scholarly literature,[116] research into the architectural decoration of north Bactria has not been pursued. Our knowledge in this field relies in most part on the results by G.A. Pugachenkova.[117] Although these are very valuable, numerous recent finds still require detailed study and systematization. The deceptive impression given by the absence of stone architecture in northern Bactria is dispelled when one looks at the accumulated material. The presence of the columns and their fragments, though comparatively few, proves the existence of stone columns in the architecture of northern Bactria. It should not be forgotten either that numerous stone columns have been found at Ai Khanum and other sites on the left bank of the Oxus River. For a better understanding of the evolution of architectural decoration in Old Termez, it is helpful to analyse architectural details found and studied by French colleagues.

French archaeologists and architects made great contributions to the understanding of architectural decoration. The value of studying such a site as Ai Khanum lies in the comparative analysis of the material from Greek city-sites. At Ai Khanum, we have a rare opportunity to trace peculiarities of Greek plastic art in a Central Asian context. This is of

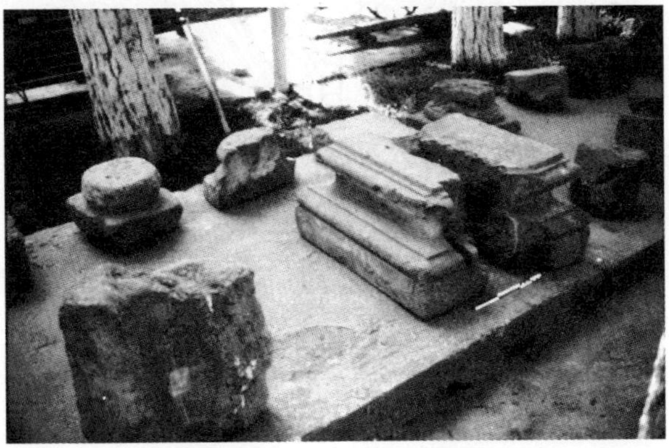

Fig. 40: The yard of the Termez Municipal Museum (old building) showing stone architectural details. (Photograph by K. Abdullaev).

special interest for the further development and transformation of Hellenistic cultural traditions in the pre-Kushan and Kushan periods. One important discovery at Ai Khanum was a large peristyle court of Rhodean type (measuring 136 × 108 m) with a hypostyle hall (measuring 27.60 × 16.80 m). The colonnades were executed in a whitish limestone, which had been quarried 50 km away near Imam Said on the left bank of the Oxus.[118] The enormous size of the Corinthian capitals was appropriate for monumental architecture. The capital, together with the upper part of the shaft, has a height of 110 cm and the capital itself a height of 92 cm.

The Corinthian capital consists of a vegetal basket with two rows of acanthus leaves (Fig. 41). On both sides of the calathos there are two caulicules. From each of these caulicules grows two volutes – a large exterior one and a smaller interior one. The acanthus leaves are arranged in two tiers; the lower row decorates the lower part of the capital, while the upper row reaches up to the middle of the capital. Out of the top of the caulicules grows a double acanthus leaf, touching the volute above. The capital is terminated by an abacus (measuring 14 cm in height, while the length of each side is 120 cm) and by ovuli. Paul Bernard observed the close analogies to the decoration of the Propylon of the Bouleuterion in Miletus and the Olympieion in Athens.[119] On the basis of analogies to

Fig. 41: Profile of a Corinthian capital from Ai Khanum. 2nd century BC. (After P. Bernard; drawn by J. Bernard, 1968, fig. 4).

Miletus (the dedicatory inscription of the Bouleuterion named King Antiochus IV Epiphanus), Bernard dated the capital to the second quarter of the second century BC.[120] Besides Corinthian columns, Ionic columns were also used at Ai Khanum. An Ionic capital was discovered during the excavation of the Temple with Indented Niches. The capital was carved in stone and wood.[121] Most scholars have dated the architectural decorations at Ai Khanum, including pilasters and column bases, and above all its peristyle court with the hypostyle hall, to the first half of the second century BC.

To the north of the Oxus we know so far of no monumental building that could rival the architectural ensemble at Ai Khanum. Nevertheless, in the archaeological layers of other sites one often comes across bases of columns or fragments of capitals, cornices, and various architectural elements. Frequently stone fragments from façade decorations were incorporated into later buildings. The material of these stone fragments – tertiary limestone, indicates that they had been re-used. One of the known quarries of tertiary limestone was *Orlinnaya sopka* (Eagle mound), located at the foot of the Babatag Mountains and extending to the right bank of the Oxus.[122] Curious in this respect is a large mortar (now in Termez Archaeological Museum) that was made from a column (despite the relative softness of limestone). Cannon balls for siege-guns were also made from columns. All these objects exemplify the re-cycling of spoils in subsequent periods for domestic and military purposes.

During the excavation of the citadel of Old Termez (Object D) numerous stone blocks were found *in situ* in later buildings. For the foundation of the walls, the residents used not only rectangular blocks, but also cut column bases, capitals, and bases of pilasters. These pieces had been repeatedly re-used throughout the period of occupation at the site. Old Termez best illustrates this practice, which was used in almost all regions in all times (Fig. 42). It should be noted that the majority of column bases, capitals and other objects without provenance in the Termez Museum came from the later layers. The column bases from Old Termez in the collection of the museum consist mainly of square plinths with a high, slightly flattened torus, which represents an earlier type of architectural decoration, not only in Bactria, but in the whole ancient Hellenized Orient (Fig. 43). As a rule, these plinths are huge in size and probably supported monumental columns for secular or sacred buildings.

The second most widespread order of columns was the so-called Attic order, which had square plinths with a double torus that was divided by a scotia and decorated on the lower and upper parts by listels (Fig. 44). The name 'Attic' is conditional here, because this order could have appeared under the influence of Hellenistic art and then developed in the context of the local sculptural tradition. The diameters of Attic bases vary from

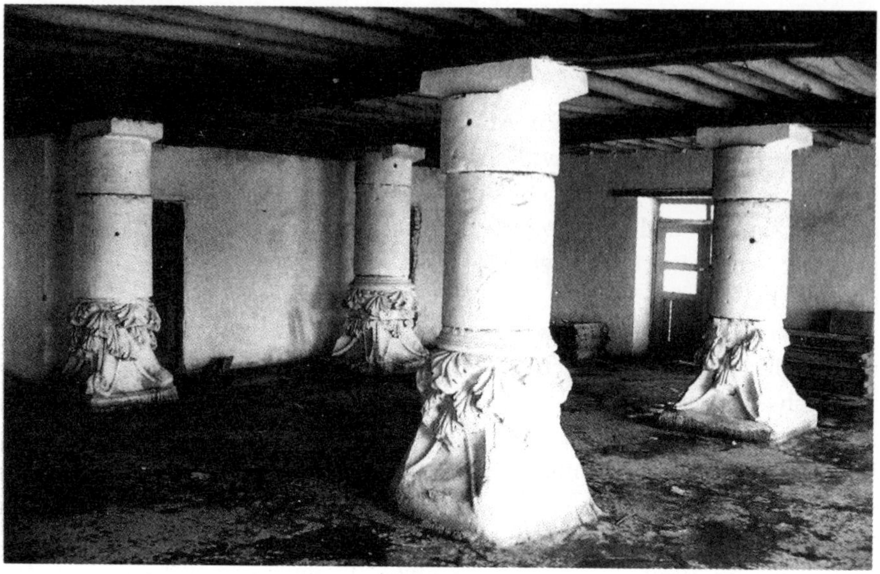

Fig. 42: Modern re-utilization of ancient architectural details. (Courtesy of R. Besenval).

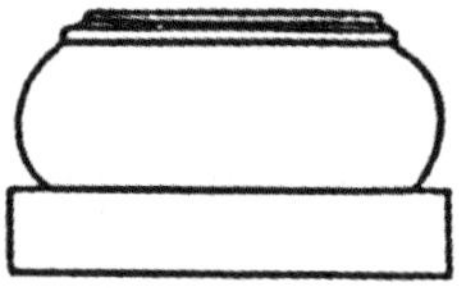

Fig. 43: Column base on a plinth and torus. Late Hellenistic period. (Termez Archaeological Museum).

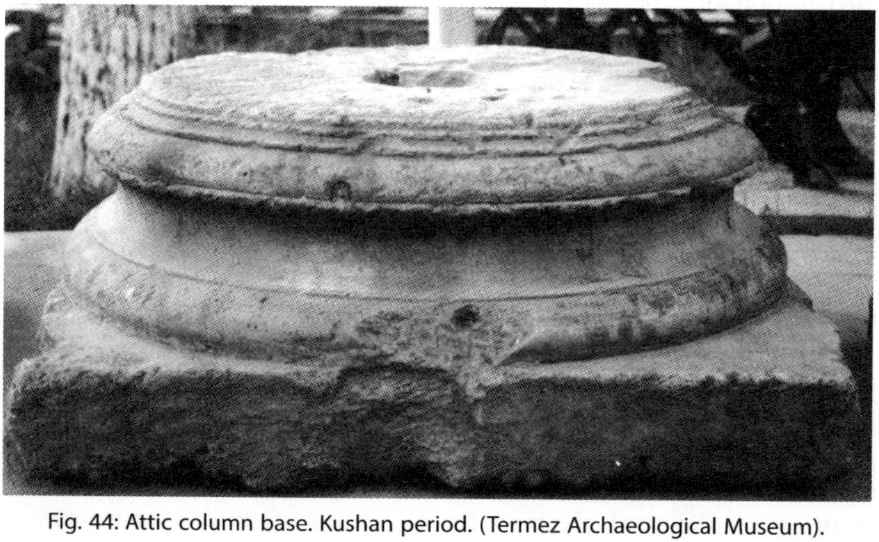

Fig. 44: Attic column base. Kushan period. (Termez Archaeological Museum).

large (60 cm) to small (35-50 cm). These variations speak for the popularity of this type. Similar profiles are also found on angular pilaster bases. The pilaster bases have normally three, or sometimes two, decorated sides. In many cases, traces of the stonecutter's tools can still be detected.[123] They are especially visible on the scotia, on which the long concentric marks were incised by an instrument, possibly a turning machine. Other indications of machine usage are the openings made on the lower and upper surfaces, in all probability to facilitate the turning and working of the stone with the aid of wooden supports. In some examples, the opening is drilled through the entire base.[124] Close analogies to the Attic bases in the Termez Museum can be found at Surkh Kotal.[125] Two kilometres to the east of Surkh Kotal, there is the so-called 'Platform of Statues',[126] dated to the period of Kanishka.[127] Although the main material for the building was clay, a soft white stone, possibly limestone, was used for the facing. The relationship of the fragments in the Termez Museum to the 'Platform of Statues' is attested not only by the presence of the carefully worked profiles of the bases, but also by the façade decoration of the building, which had pilasters with such bases. Relatively rarely, one encounters fragments of cornices at the Termez Museum. Some of these fragments are decorated with dentils, but most have a torus with one or two listels.

The capitals in the Termez Museum are mainly of the pseudo-Corinthian order. While some of them follow closely the Greek canon, others are disproportionate and are not up to the standards of their prototype. Besides, most of them have been considerably transformed under the influence of Kushan art. The capitals are decorated with predatory animals (Fig. 45),

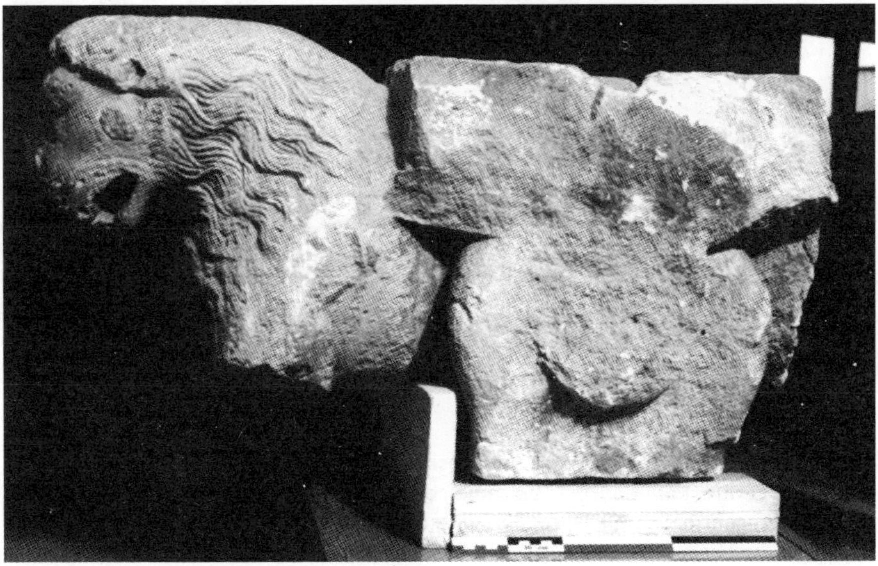

Fig. 45: Capital decorated with lion protomes. (Termez Archaeological Museum).

for instance, a lion's head with wide-open jaws. These examples gravitate more towards ancient Iranian types, as known from the architecture of Persepolis, Pasargadae, and other monuments of Achaemenid Iran.[128] Yet, the Indian figurative complex of the Ashoka period (dated to between 250 and 232 BC) offers close thematic analogies, including lion capitals.[129]

Another significant new tendency in the design of capitals in the Pre-Kushan and Kushan period was the decrease of the vertical proportions of the capital. The composition developed more horizontally. Thematic capitals include a lion with its front paws on the croups of two other animals (for example, a bull and a zebu from Karatepa or fantastic animals such as gryphons from Sham-Kala) gracing the upper part (Fig. 46).[130] The Termez Archaeological Museum has a fragment of a pilaster capital with a gryphon image resembling this composition (Fig. 46, d). For the Kushan period, vegetal motifs are also common capital decorative elements. In addition to the motif of the acanthus leaf, sculptors employed scrolls, fruits, and geometric patterns (Fig. 47), but used the volute sparingly. On the capitals of the early Kushan and Kushan periods the volutes are almost lost in the overall ornamentation.[131]

One of the new elements in capital decoration was the anthropomorphic image. Among the early specimens from Gandhara (Butkara) is a human bust on a vegetal background of acanthus leaves. During the first centuries

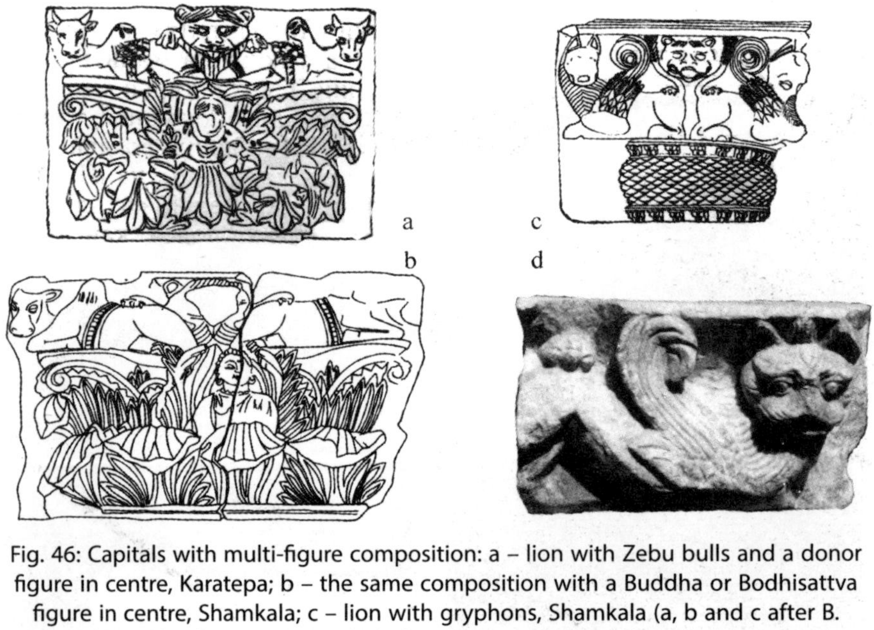

a c b d

Fig. 46: Capitals with multi-figure composition: a – lion with Zebu bulls and a donor figure in centre, Karatepa; b – the same composition with a Buddha or Bodhisattva figure in centre, Shamkala; c – lion with gryphons, Shamkala (a, b and c after B. Staviskiy, 1977, fig. 42); d – capital of a pilaster with a gryphon. Kushan period. 17.1 × 12 cm. (Termez Archaeological Museum).

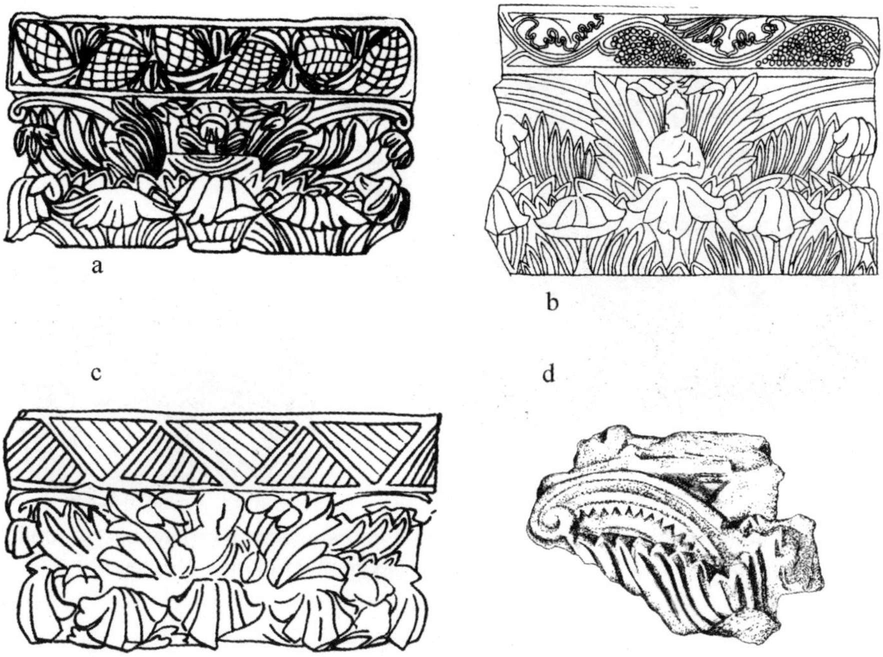

Fig. 47: Capitals of pilasters with vegetal and geometric motives: a, b and c – Surkh Kotal area near a Buddhist platform; d – fragment from Karatepa. Kushan period. (After B. Staviskiy, 1977, fig. 42).

AD, as part of the capital composition one can see a human figure in a gesture of adoration. Other capitals show the figure of Buddha in *padmasana* (for example the capital from Jemal-Garkhi, 1st–2nd c. AD).[132] The capitals from Old Termez display a variety of compositional schemes, which include a male figure reclining on acanthus leaves (Fig. 48). One of the peculiarities of the local masters was their treatment of certain details such as the inner edge of the volute in the shape of triangular dentils. Some of the capitals show the Buddha seated with his right hand in *abhaya-mudra* (Fig. 49). Many of the fragments preserve traces of gilding.

Besides the transformed details certain capitals nevertheless followed the 'classical' scheme. The most popular type of capital in the architectural decoration of the region included the essential elements of the Greek capital such as acanthus leaves and volutes, but in a simplified design.[133] Although the proportions lost their specific dimensions and the capital itself became shorter, the Greek scheme is still recognizable. Later, in the Kushan period, nearly all the classical repertoire was transformed (Fig. 50).

Oddly, Old Termez and neighbouring archaeological sites yielded mainly capitals of pilasters. Statistically, semi-capitals prevail over full ones. This may indicate that palatial and sacred buildings and constructions (such as the stupa at Old Termez) were decorated with pilasters. Hypothetically, we

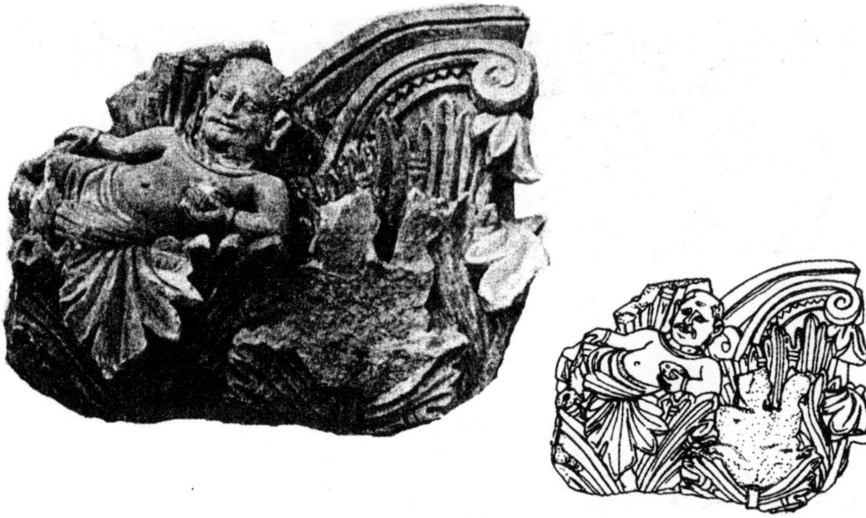

Fig. 48: Capital of pilaster with wrestling male figure against a vegetal background. Karatepa. Kushan period. (Museum of Oriental Cultures, Moscow).

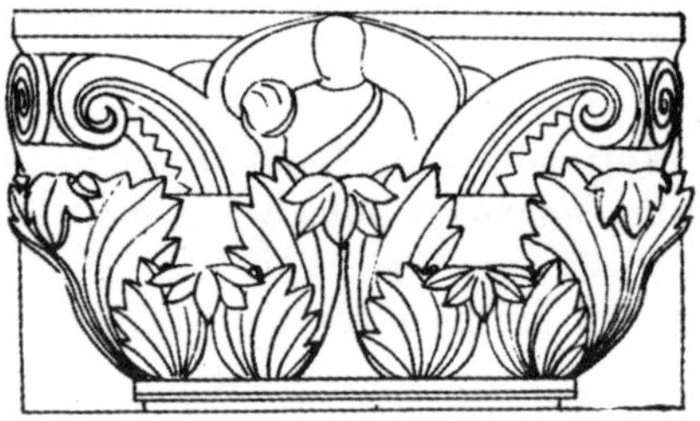

Fig. 49: Capital of pilaster with representation of a Buddha bust in *abhaya-mudra* gesture. Old Termez. Kushan period. (Termez Archaeological Museum).

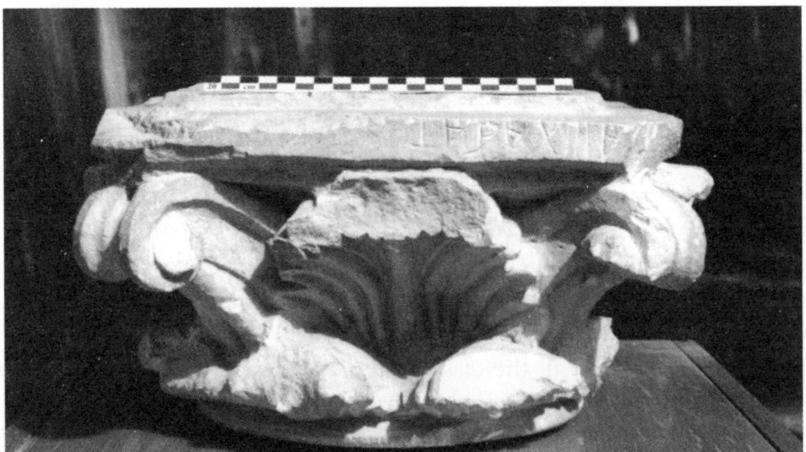

Fig. 50: Capital with volute and acanthus leaves. Old Termez. (Termez Archaeological Museum).

would like to propose that the relatively numerous finds of stone column bases (but less of stone capitals) can be explained by the existence of wooden shafts with wooden capitals, such as the Ionic capital from the Temple with Indented Niches in Ai Khanum mentioned above. The traditions in the sculpting of wooden columns continue from antiquity to contemporary architecture and should not be overlooked. These traditions could be observed, for instance, in a wooden zoomorphic capital from the Vaigal dwelling at the Kabul National Museum, decorated with animal figures.[134]

During the Kushan period, at the time of the development and flourishing of Hellenistic traditions in the architectural decor of Bactria, motifs and compositions appeared that are characteristic of a synthesized art, including anthropomorphic and zoomorphic representations, motifs of the lotus flower and other elements of the Buddhist figurative complex. One of the recent finds on the eastern part of the Old Termez citadel is a huge column base, evidently coming from the lower layers.[135] It indicates the former presence here of a monumental building.

Sculptural Works

There are a number of plastic works of the Kushan period that have a direct relation to Buddhist art. A stone relief with a double-tier composition (H. 42 cm) was a surface find at Old Termez.[136] The lower register represents a triad (Fig. 51). The seated figure of Buddha in the *padmasana* pose is placed in the centre of the composition. His hands are shown in the *dhyana-mudra* pose. He sits on a low horizontal throne with incised vertical wavy lines, symbolizing in all probability the lotus. The figure of Buddha is draped in a *sanghati* mantle with semi-circular pleats descending from the breast and stomach. Behind the head, the branches of a pipal tree with heart-shaped leaves form a wreath around his nimbus. Flanking the figure of Buddha are two kneeling figures. As their heads have been broken (? premeditated damage), it is difficult to identify them. Judging by the nimbus around their heads it is quite possible that they were divine personages. Both are nude from the waist up, except for a scarf flung over the left shoulder – in a combination of *paridhana* with *uttariya*.

The upper register of the relief represents a pentad. In the centre is Buddha, again in similar dress and in the *padmasana* pose. The position of his hands indicates *dharmachakra-mudra*. Judging by their prolonged shape, leaves of the *sala* tree surround the nimbus. The figure standing to the left of Buddha is most likely a *bodhisattva*. Three more figures are placed near the Buddha. The lower one is represented in kneeling pose, while in the background there is a smaller figure in a pleated garment with an attribute resembling a *vajra* (Vajrapani). Above these two figures is a third figure, difficult to interpret because of its poor preservation.

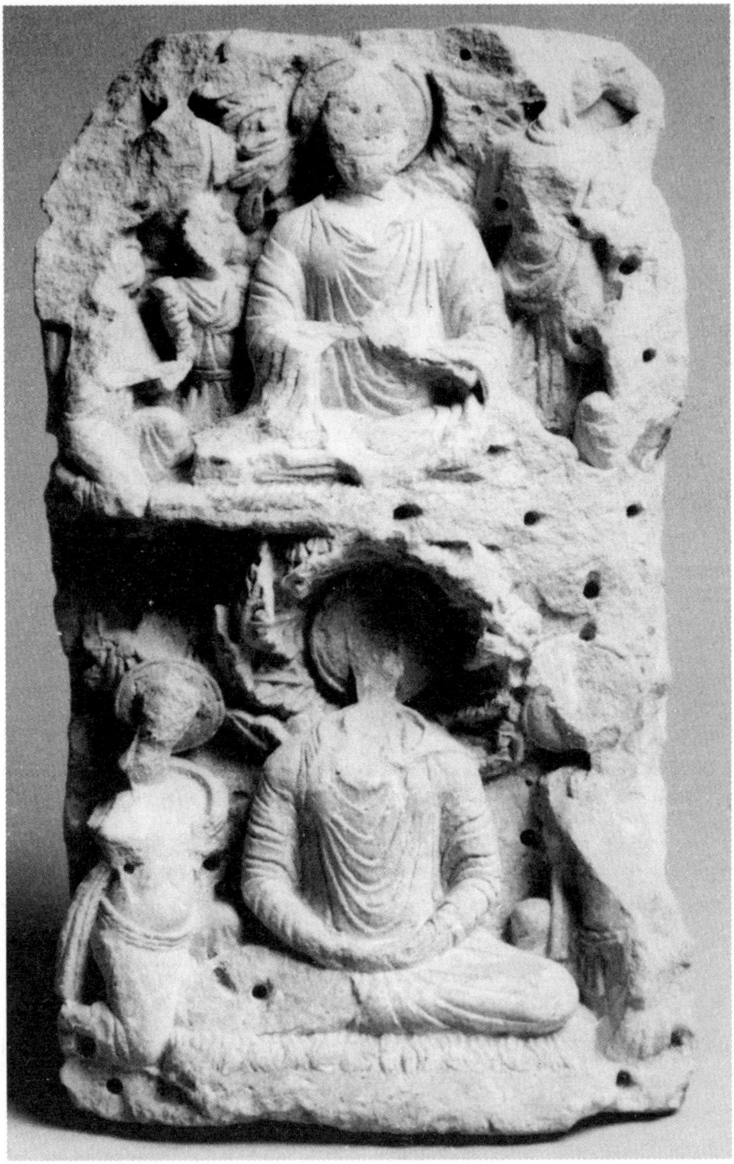

Fig. 51: Stone relief showing a scene of paradise from Old Termez. 2nd-3rd century AD. 42 × 25 cm. (Termez Archaeological Museum).

The multi-figured compositions on the relief from Old Termez just described and the triad relief from Fayaztepa[137] have many similarities with the art of the Gandhara School. It is necessary to distinguish certain local details, for example, in the treatment of the pleats of the *sanghati*. On the Termez pieces, the lines of the pleats are symmetrical, forming a triangular cut on the breast. Long pleats fall from the shoulder, where the material is gathered. The pleats form circular folds on the stomach. Such symmetry of drapery lines is not typical of Gandharan sculpture, where the pleats are typically grouped and concentrated on the right shoulder, or the right shoulder is bare and the pleats are concentrated on the left part of the figure. However, symmetry of pleating is characteristic for other centres of Buddhist plastic art such as Mathura. Indeed, one can see an analogous manner of modelling on the seated Buddha/*bodhisattva* statues from Mathura.[138] However, the composition in general resembles Gandharan multi-tiered reliefs with scenes of paradise, in particular, the 'Miracle of Shravasti' with Buddha surrounded by *bodhisattvas* and adorants.[139]

Another find from the neighbourhood of Old Termez can be associated with the Buddhist plastic art of the Gandhara School. This is a fragment of architectural decoration that we conditionally identify as entablature (Fig. 52). It was found near the *stupa* of Zurmala and is of marble-like limestone (42 × 38 cm), showing in relief on one side a multi-tiered decoration.[140] The lower tier displays a combination of lion heads with acanthus leaves. On the upper tier, a horizontal crossbeam divides the subsequent motif, at the same time forming the base of a balcony. Above the latter are ogival arches (of the Gandhara type) with half-length figures underneath them. Each figure holds in the right hand three lotus flowers. In the space between the arches (spandrels) there is also an object resembling a flower with two long leaves on either side and a bud in the centre on a thin stem. It is possible that this flower-like object represents a lotus. A

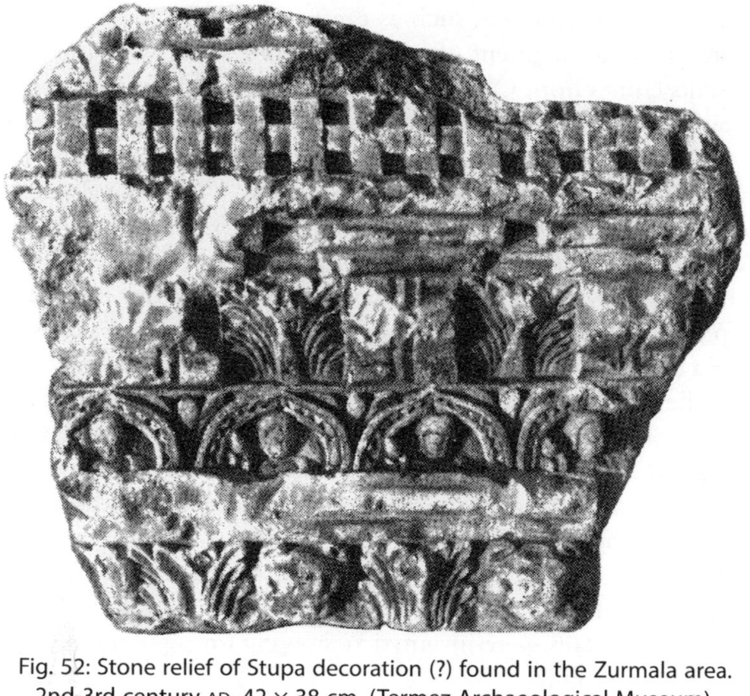

Fig. 52: Stone relief of Stupa decoration (?) found in the Zurmala area. 2nd-3rd century AD. 42 × 38 cm. (Termez Archaeological Museum).

thin line in relief separates this from the next tier horizontally. This decorative band is ornamented by fluted pilasters with a simple capital and two plinths (narrower below and wider above). The pilasters are combined with acanthus leaves. Above this ornamental band there is a pattern of lattice fencing, which perhaps imitates the railing (*vedika*) of the *torana*. Finally, the top of the relief is decorated with merlons. The relief can be dated to the second or third century.[141]

It is difficult to cite direct analogies for the whole composition, but similarities can be found for some of its details. Again we turn to Gandharan art. For example, one can find many common elements on a relief from the British Museum.[142] The relief shows a row of balconies with couples under the arches. The arches are semi-circular in form, different from the ogival arches on the Termez relief described above. Figures of eagles are placed between the balconies and are combined with lotus flowers. The individuals standing on the balconies each hold a bunch of three flowers. The London relief is more richly decorated than the Zurmala relief. On the London relief, the base of the balcony is draped with material, while the arches are supported by Corinthianized capitals. By comparison, the relief from Zurmala is simple and each of its registers is individually modelled in a graphic manner. Lion heads and acanthus leaves were also popular in Gandhara reliefs. Above all, the lattice crowning of the Zurmala composition was widely used in Gandharan plastic art. The lattice crowning served not only as gates and fences of sacred buildings, but also decorated other architectural elements, such as the bases of balconies.[143]

An architectural fragment of marble-like limestone with the depiction of elephants comes from Object D at Old Termez.[144] It was a corner facing and shows two elephants moving towards an object from either side. The object resembles a *stupa* and the composition itself represents a scene of veneration. Two elephants offer flowers to a *stupa*.[145] The animals are covered by a *chaprak* ornamented with relief circles (Fig. 53). Between the eyes of the elephants there is something resembling a *phalera*. The style of vegetation is in the shape of an acanthus leaf crowned by a flower. The relief with the elephants could have belonged to a *stupa*. There is a certain similarity with a fragment from the Lahore Museum, cited by F. Tissot.[146]

The reliefs discussed here show sacred and secular architecture. Often they represent historical scenes and events from the life of Buddha or other personages of the Buddhist pantheon. Did all the architectural elements represented on these reliefs actually exist in buildings of the time? That is a question that requires special study. The example from Old Termez (Fig. 49) confirms that during the Kushan period, classic Greek forms were successfully integrated (for example, the Corinthian order), while at the same time new details were invented, bestowing on the buildings a unique and peculiar appearance.

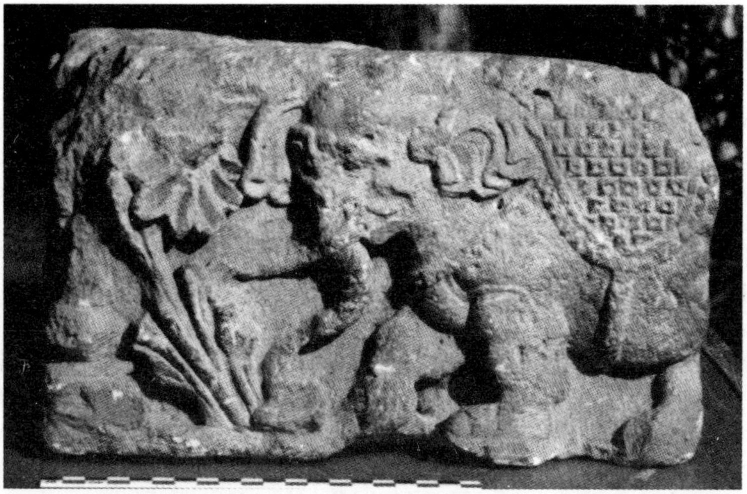

Fig. 53: Stone relief with representation of an elephant and acanthus leaves. Old Termez, trench D. 3rd-4th century AD. 31 × 18 cm. (Termez Archaeological Museum).

Buddhist Terracotta Plastic Art

Terracotta figurines are one of the most prominent categories of the Buddhist figurative complex. Their relative profusion in archaeological layers shows how far Buddhist plastic art had conquered the masses. The production of terracottas, being close to folk art, satisfied the cult requirements of both the urban and rural inhabitants.[147] Therefore such production reflects in full measure the more popular topics of religious iconography (Fig. 3). In general, small plastic objects imitate subjects and images of monumental sculpture.[148] Thus, one could postulate that the terracotta figurines of the urban and rural populations reproduced on a lesser scale the most venerated images of the time. Not by chance did clay serve as the basic material for both terracotta figurines and monumental sculptures by the Bactrian masters. In this respect, terracotta plastic art and sculpture were closely related. The following is a summary of the main types of figurines of northern Bactria.[149]

The dating of the terracotta figurines is based on the archaeological context within the total complex of finds. Only after analysis of these data is an iconographic study possible. This method is important as one can find the same types of figurines in different layers, which indicates continuing usage of the same moulds over different periods. Thus, methods combining the analysis of stratified layers with an account of iconographic particularities are the most effective for the study of terracottas.

If the terracotta images of Buddha, *bodhisattvas* and other personages of the Buddhist figurative complex repeated the iconographic scheme of the clay statues, then in some of these images discordance with the canonical principles of the Buddhist plastic tradition is evident. The terracotta plastic material of Bactria-Tokharistan comprises the following two types of a seated Buddha: (1) in the pose of meditation or *dhyana-mudra* and (2) in the pose of persuasion and protection or *abhaya-mudra*. These iconographic types developed in the figurative art of Bactria-Tokharistan were to become the most elaborate images in the Buddhist plastic complex. The figurines can also be divided into two groups according to their technique of modelling. The first group comprises figurines executed in high relief. The clay was stamped in a mould and then the leftover portions were cut away along the external edges of the mould. The second group comprises figurines imprinted in tile/slab moulds, often depicting Buddha sitting under the arch of a niche. The majority of terracotta finds of Buddhist character were concentrated in layers dating to the second to fourth centuries AD. In this period, the images show a rich diversity in dress, hairstyle, and pose. The examples of Buddhist terracotta plastic art described below came from different sites in the Surkhandarya region. They were predominantly surface finds, with only a small number recovered from excavations.

Terracottas from Old Termez and Neighbouring Areas, Including Fayaztepa and Karatepa

Terracotta figurines from Old Termez were usually surface finds, picked up on the site itself or collected by local inhabitants in the region during farming activities. Two figurines are exceptional in this case. They came from a stratified trench on the citadel of Old Termez.[150] Both figurines are broken at the neck. One of the figurines represents the figure of Buddha in *padmasana* pose with the hands in *dhyana-mudra* (Fig. 54). The dress has

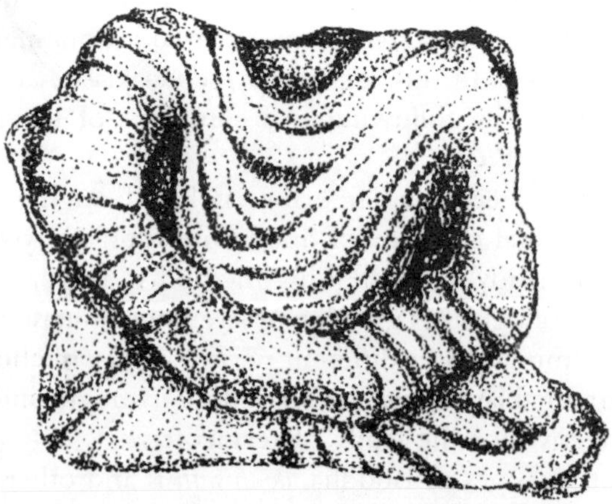

Fig. 54: Fragment of a Buddha terracotta figurine. Old Termez. H = 8 cm. (Termez Archaeological Museum).

thick folds rounded on the breast and stomach as well as short transversal pleats on the arms. The second shows the same posture and hand gesture as the first, and is seated on a base schematically resembling a lotus (Fig. 55). The drapery is distinguished in a different manner: the pleats cover the left shoulder and a large fold falls down between the legs. The arms are adorned with thick bracelets. On the breast, there is something resembling jewellery attached to the folds of fabric. The presence of jewellery indicates that this figure should not be identified as Buddha; most likely it is an image of a *bodhisattva*. Despite the fact that these figurines were found in an archaeological complex dated by a coin of Heliocles ('Barbarian' imitation),[151] their dating poses a problem. Although numismatically the first century BC is secure, it seems too early for an image of Buddha. Indeed, based on the numismatic evidence, Sh. Pidaev, the excavator of these terracottas, had first dated them to the first century BC, but later he completely changed his opinion without any satisfactory and convincing explanation.[152] T. Mkrtychev perpetuated this muddled dating of the Buddha and *bodhisattva* terracottas in his book on the Buddhist Art of Central Asia.[153]

The problem of the early dating of the Buddha representation is much disputed and different opinions have been put forward in numerous publications.[154] The majority of scholars are inclined to accept the dating of first to second centuries AD.[155] However, there is evidence to assign the image of Buddha to an earlier period. Coins of Kanishka I with representations of Buddha and Bodhisattva Maitreya no doubt copied statues.[156] If we date Kanishka's rule to AD 127, as proposed by H. Falk,[157] theoretically statues of Buddha could have already existed in the first half of the first century AD, or even in the late first century BC. Excavations by the Italian Archaeological Mission in Pakistan (Butkara), led by D. Facenna, have yielded material belonging to the last centuries BC.[158] In any case, although the date of the earliest Buddha statues has not yet been determined, the

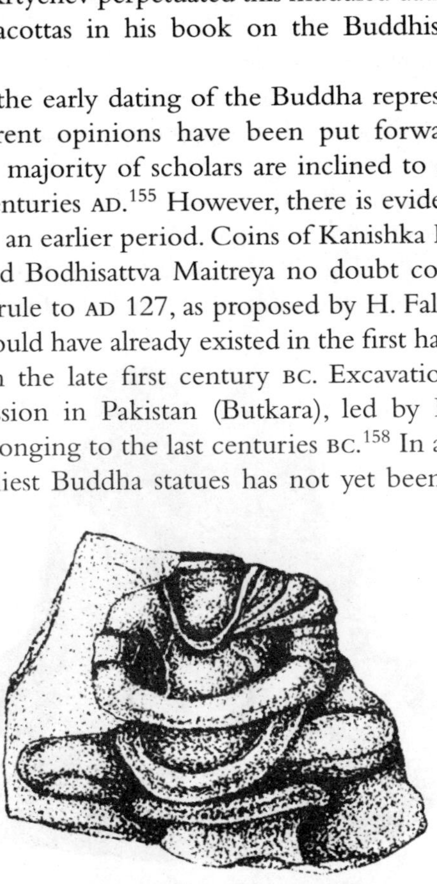

Fig. 55: Fragment of a *bodhisattva* terracotta figurine. Old Termez. H = 7.8 cm. (Termez Archaeological Museum)

material from Old Termez provides us with two important arguments. First, it offers us the rare case of an archaeological context that is confirmed by coins. Second, stylistically, these two stratified terracotta representations from Old Termez are very close to the Butkara style.

One must also take into account the fact that terracotta figurines are highly mobile artefacts. A statuette can be carried a long way in a short time and its duplication would not pose a problem for the masters of plastic art. Among the terracotta figurines found on the surface of Old Termez, there are representations of Buddha, *bodhisattvas*, *yakshinis* and donors,[159] all of which have been dated predominantly to the Kushan period.[160]

As noted, in terracotta plastic art two main types of the seated Buddha can be distinguished, in the pose of meditation – *dhyana-mudra* and in the pose of persuasion and protection – *abhaya-mudra*. A surface find from Karatepa can be associated with the latter[161] (Fig. 56). The figure, draped in heavy pleats, is shown in *padmasana*. Judging by the break on the right hand, it is in *abhaya-mudra*. The left hand rests on the knees. A terracotta figurine from Kampyrtepa provides an example with definite iconographic features.[162] Its right hand is in the *abhaya-mudra* and its left hand holds the pleats of the *sanghati* (Fig. 57). Iconographically, these terracottas are similar to a clay statue wearing red garments with traces of gilding found at Karatepa (see below) and dated to the second to fourth centuries AD.

Some fragments of terracotta figurines resemble the seated Buddha in the *bhumisparsha-mudra* (Fig. 58). In these representations, the left hand of the figure usually holds the folds of the mantle. Interestingly, the seated

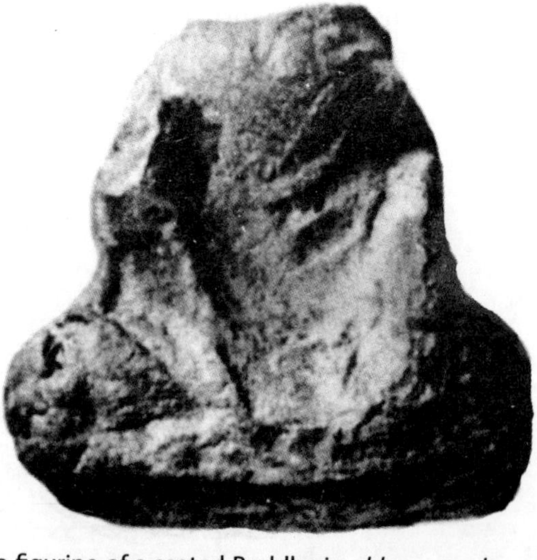

Fig. 56: Terracotta figurine of a seated Buddha in *abhaya-mudra* gesture. Karatepa. 2nd-3rd century AD. Surface find. H = 6.7 cm. (Termez Archaeological Museum).

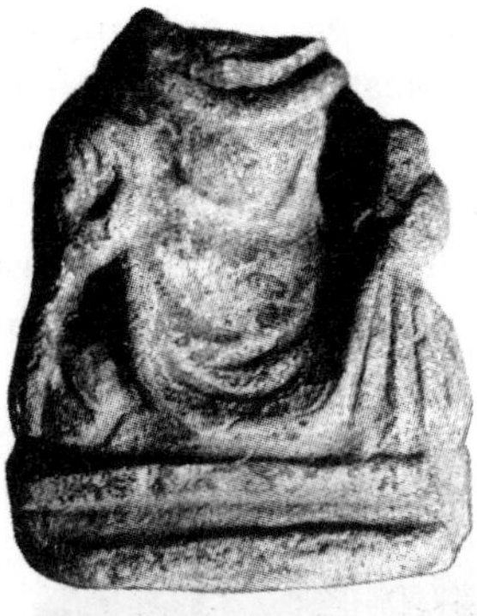

Fig. 57: Terracotta figurine showing a seated Buddha in *abhaya-mudra* gesture. Kampyrtepa. 2nd century AD. Surface find. 7.3 × 6.1 × 2.5 cm. (Institute of Art Research, Tashkent).

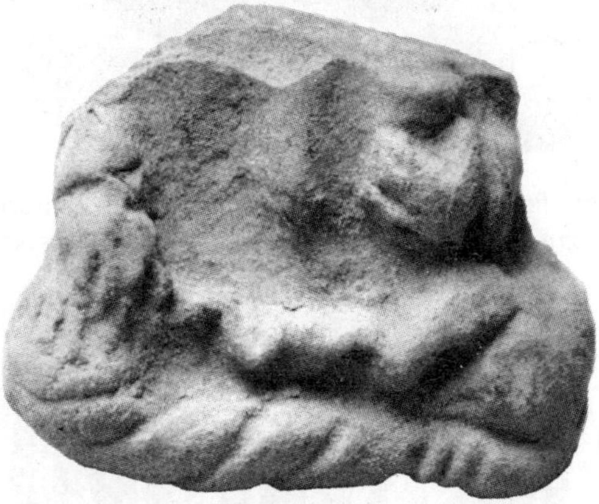

(a)

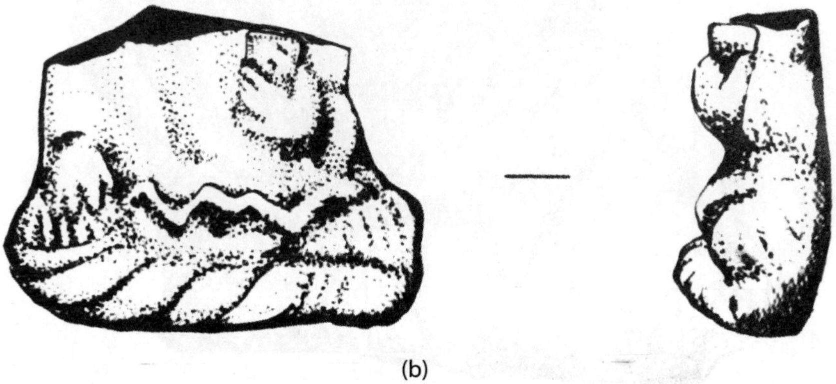

(b)

Fig. 58: Terracotta figurine of a seated Buddha in *bhumisparsha-mudra*. 3rd-4th century AD. Zartepa. 6 × 4 cm. (The State Hermitage Museum, St. Petersburg).

figure of a Buddha from Zartepa is holding a bowl in his right hand (Fig. 59). The same folds of pleated garment (*dhoti)* are seen on a figurine from Airtam (Fig. 60).

The seated Buddha under an arch or in a niche definitely imitates sculptural works that embellished Buddhist constructions (*stupas*) or the interior of temples. On certain specimens, the arch of the niche is projected

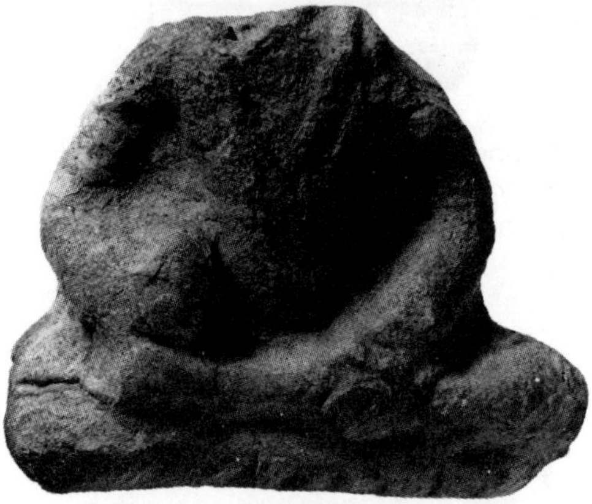

Fig. 59: Terracotta figurine of a seated Buddha. 3rd-4th century AD. Zartepa. H = 7.3 cm. (The State Hermitage Museum, St. Petersburg).

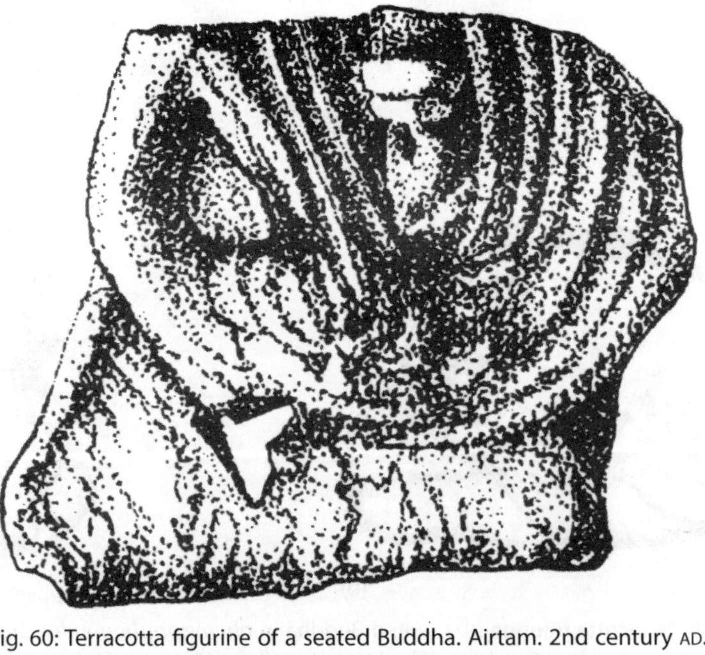

Fig. 60: Terracotta figurine of a seated Buddha. Airtam. 2nd century AD. H = 11 cm. (Institute of Art Research, Tashkent).

in relief, as on a terracotta tile from Karaultepa (Fig. 61), which shows the Buddha seated inside the niche. In all probability, the whole composition comprised statues of Buddhist personages, which were placed in wall niches. As we observed above, these reliefs are characteristic of the monumental cult sites of Karatepa and Fayaztepa (for example the triad reliefs showing the seated Buddha under the *bodhi* tree with a monk on either side). The Buddha on the terracotta plaque from Karaultepa wears a pleated garment and is in the traditional *padmasana* pose. The arms are modelled as a single horizontal relief, with frequent oblique pleats. Obviously the master tried to represent the *dhyana-mudra*. The hair of Buddha is shown in small round curls, represented in larger relief on the top (*ushnisha*). The arch of the niche has the shape of a keel. This terracotta plaque has an occidental character and was found on the surface of the site. It can be dated approximately to the fourth to fifth century AD.

A fragment of the upper part of a terracotta plaque from Talashkantepa II (in the Sherabad district of the Surkhandarya region) shows the head

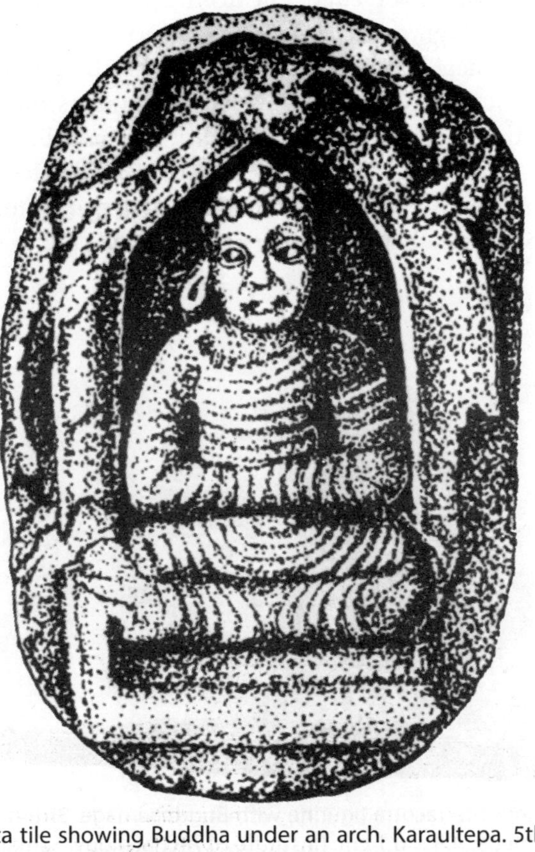

Fig. 61: Terracotta tile showing Buddha under an arch. Karaultepa. 5th-6th century AD. H = 14.5 cm. (Institute of Art Research, Tashkent).

of Buddha in high relief[163] (Fig. 62). The external edge of the plaque was precisely cut. The upper part of the plaque itself has a slightly pointed, hemispherical form. Whether the master was attempting to imitate an arch or a niche, we cannot tell. If we assume that it was a seated figure, it very possibly belonged to the Akkurgan type (see below). The head is somewhat lowered. The eyelids are typically slightly swollen and closed. The straight nose widens at the base and the chin is slightly foreshortened and rounded. The coiffure is high with an *ushnisha* on top; the ears have elongated lobes. The surface of the terracotta is covered by black slip. Everything, including the black slip, suggests that the terracotta dates from the third to fourth century.

Another Buddha image comes from Akkurgan (in the Surkhandarya region), stamped on an oval plaque and seated in the *padmasana* pose with the hands in *dhyana-mudra*. It is completely preserved and one can recognize the form of the dress, although due to the small size of the plaque its details are simplified. Nevertheless, one can note the round cut on the breast and the oblique folds falling down from the left shoulder. Two folds, spreading towards the lower edge, fall from each forearm (Fig. 63). The figure is seated on a high pedestal. The plaque was found in a late Kushan level and has been dated to the fourth or early fifth century.[164] The two folds are significant features in the drapery of Buddha's dress. Although it is difficult to find analogies in Gandharan art, it is possible to find similar elements in the sculpture of Mathura. Two seated Buddha/*bodhisattva* figures from the Calcutta Museum (no. N.S. 4143) and the Mathura Museum (no. A 65) demonstrate, albeit in higher artistic quality, this detail of the two

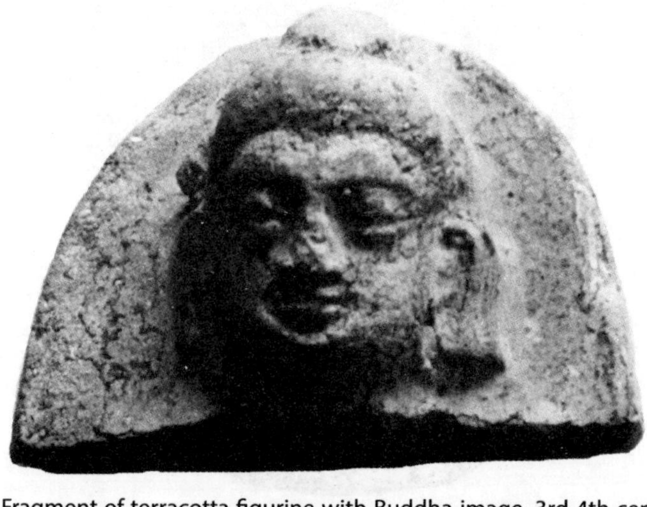

Fig. 62: Fragment of terracotta figurine with Buddha image. 3rd-4th century AD. Talashkantepa. 4.8 × 6.1 cm. (Institute of Archaeology, Samarkand).

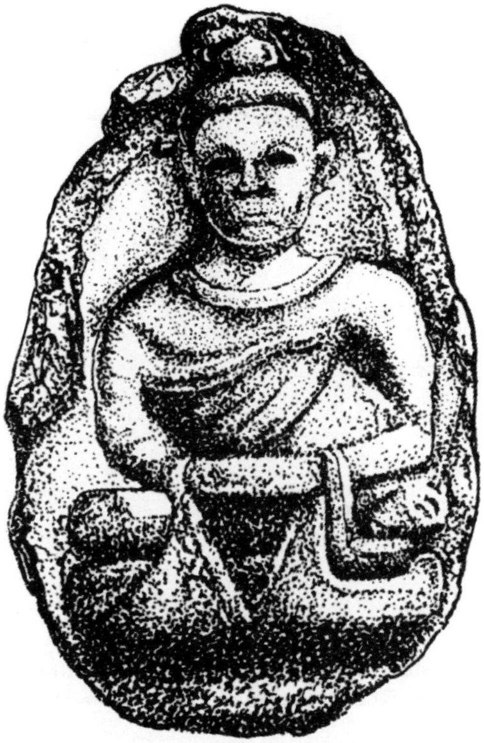

Fig. 63: Terracotta tile showing Buddha in *padmasana* posture and *dhyana-mudra*. Akkurgan. 4th-5th century AD. H = 11 cm. (Institute of Archaeology, Samarkand).

folds.[165] In the iconographic form of the Buddha in standing pose, his right hand is in *abhaya-mudra* and his left hand is holding the fold of the garment. He wears a long mantle (*sanghati*). This kind of representation undoubtedly copied the statuary popular in Gandharan art.[166] Two fragments from Zartepa exemplify this artistic phenomenon (Fig. 64).

Bodhisattva images in terracotta plastic art are more numerous and diversified. The earliest example, mentioned above (Fig. 55), came from an archaeological layer at Old Termez and is dated by a complex of finds, including a 'barbarian' coin of Heliocles. The hands of this terracotta figure are shown in *dhyana-mudra*; the forearms are adorned with bracelets and the figure wears a necklace. The *bodhisattva* is dressed in *ekanishka sanghati*, a sort of monastic habit, which covers the left shoulder. *Bodhisattva* images are sometimes shown seated with legs crossed in the so-called 'European pose'.

A remarkably modelled representation of a *bodhisattva* comes from Barattepa (Fig. 65). It was found by chance on the surface of the site together with other terracottas from the Kushan period.[167] The realism of the image is due to the careful modelling of the details. The unusual

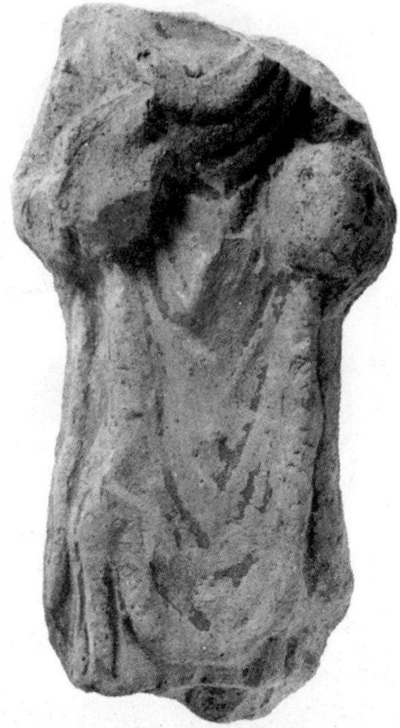

Fig. 64: Terracotta standing Buddha figure. Zartepa. 4th-early 5th century AD. H = 11.3 cm. (The State Hermitage Museum, St. Petersburg).

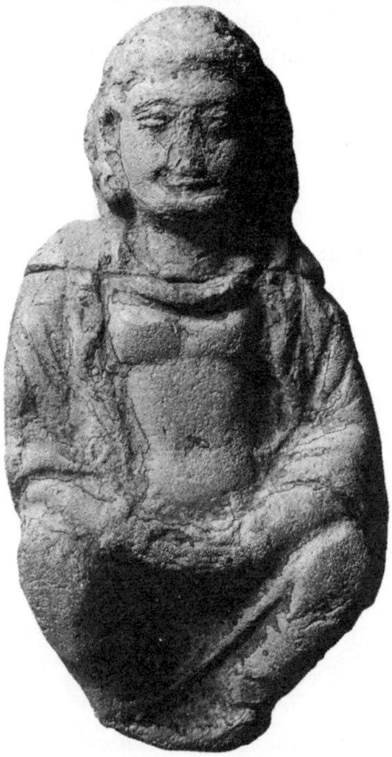

Fig. 65: Terracotta *bodhisattva*. Barattepa. 3rd-4th century AD. H = 12.5 cm. (Institute of Art Research, Tashkent).

position of the legs with knees apart is a tell-tale sign of the vulgarization of the Buddhist canonical iconography. The *bodhisattva* from Barattepa is similar to the sculptures of Gandhara art, where the *bodhisattva*s are represented in the so-called 'European pose'.[168] The collection of finds from Barattepa has been dated to the third to fourth century AD and the figurine representing *bodhisattva* can be assigned to the same period.[169]

All the characteristics of the Barattepa figurine are clearly visible. The hands are shown in *dhyana-mudra*. The necklace looks like a twisted cord. The breast is modelled in relief and the navel is shown by a depression. The drapery of the mantle is represented in an unusual manner, the material covering both shoulders symmetrically, revealing the breast and stomach. In Gandharan sculpture, the pleats usually cover the left shoulder of *bodhisattva* while the right remains bare with a bracelet on the upper arm. Certainly, this iconography is typical for the representation of *bodhisattva*s. However, as the Bactrian terracottas demonstrate, not all the elements of this representation follow exactly the canon of Buddhist iconography, and some of them are interpreted more freely. It is necessary to take into consideration the following peculiarity of terracotta plastic art: the original model, before its duplication by a mould, underwent a series of alterations by the potter.[170] It was relatively common for some significant iconographic elements to be lost during the duplication of an image. Simply, either the potter did not pay attention to these details or changed them according to his or her discretion. The piece from Barattepa reflects this process. We can trace the same phenomenon on three terracottas from Zartepa and Khaitabadtepa (two completely preserved and one headless).

In the *bodhisattva* images from Zartepa and Khaitabadtepa, the figures were moulded in high relief and coated with red slip.[171] A rather stout figure of the *bodhisattva* (from Zartepa) is seated cross-legged on a round

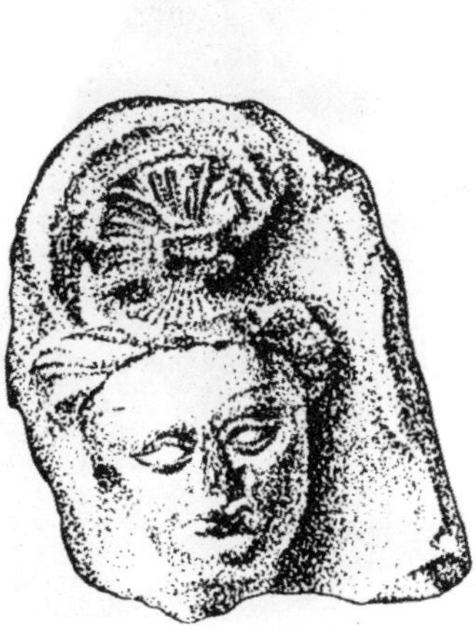

Fig. 66: Terracotta head of a *bodhisattva*. Ismailtepa. 2nd-3rd century AD. H = 4.8 cm. (Termez Archaeological Museum).

pedestal (Fig. 67). In the Khaitabadtepa example, the seat is in the shape of two parallel relief lines, apparently suggesting a double lotus form. The position of the hands is also unusual; they rest on the knees with the palms downwards. The *bodhisattva* wears a pectoral and large double earrings. Similar earrings can be seen on the terracotta figurine of a Mother Goddess at the National Museum in Delhi from the Maurya period, dated to the third century BC.[172] However, the terracotta from Zartepa must be dated much later; similarities with other finds of this type makes it possible to date it as late as the third to fourth centuries AD.[173]

It is difficult to find analogies to the posture of the Zartepa figurine.[174] A similar position of the legs is shown on a tile from *chaitya* with a Buddha representation in the centre under the *stupa*. The marble relief from Amaravati (Madras, State Museum) has been dated to the second century AD.[175] Another analogy to the position of the feet of the Zartepa representation is the figure of Buddha on the relief of a cornice from Nagarjunakonda, dated to the second century AD.[176]

The gesture of the Zartepa terracotta is rare in Buddhist plastic art. The hands with downward turned fingers are close to the *bhumisparsha-mudra* gesture calling the earth as witness. This gesture is shown on a Gandharan relief portraying a Buddha representation in the scene of the First Sermon from the Peshawar Museum[177] and is characteristic for Gautama and Akshobhya, one of the five Adi (primordial) Buddhas.[178] In any case, it is not a mistake to associate the Zartepa terracotta figurine with images of the Buddhist circle. The excavators dated them to the second to fourth centuries AD,[179] though according to the iconographic peculiarities a third to fourth century AD date is more preferable.

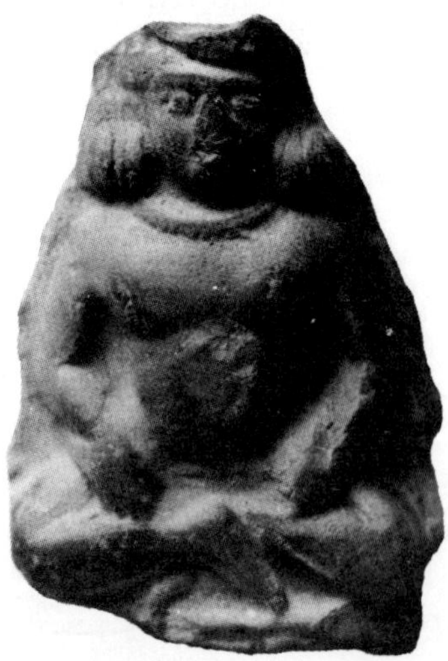

Fig. 67: Terracotta figurine of a *bodhisattva* figure, seated with crossed legs. Zartepa. 2nd-4th century AD. H = 6.5 cm. (The State Hermitage Museum, St. Petersburg).

The *bhumisparsha* gesture is more clearly shown on a terracotta fragment (only the lower part is preserved), also from Zartepa, that shows a figure in *padmasana*. The left hand holds the pleat of the mantle, while the right hand, with down turned fingers, rests on the tucked up leg (Fig. 58). This terracotta figurine reflects more or less the iconography of the Buddha on the relief from the Peshawar Museum mentioned above.

To the *bodhisattva* representations can be added a terracotta fragment representing the high headdress. It was found on the surface of Ismailtepa (in the Jarkurgan district of the Surkhandarya Region).[180] The *bodhisattva* has a round face with elongated eyes, his hair is gathered together on the top of the head and fastened with a precious inset of prismatic form; the upper part of the hairstyle is in the shape of a fan (Fig. 66). Such coiffures are known from Gandharan sculptures.[181] Stylistically, the Ismailtepa fragment can be dated approximately to the second to third centuries AD.[182]

A terracotta figure from Jandavlyattepa (in the Sherabad district of Surkhandarya region) is of special interest. The terracotta is executed in high relief and is relatively large (H. 14.2 cm, W. 6.2 cm; the proportion of head to body is 1:4). It is painted a dark red-brown colour. The figure was pressed in a deep mould on a thick clay slab, which was later cut from the figure (Fig. 77). The figure is frontal. The left hand is bent and rests on the hip; the right is lowered along the body with its palm turned toward the viewer. Apparently, the figure does not hold an attribute. The right leg is set slightly aside and back. Barely visible on top of the head is a strip indicating the *ushnisha*. The hairline corresponds to the lower part of the headdress that is decorated above the ears by barely visible rosettes in relief. The hair is shown as curls in relief. Rectangular pendants with pearls adorn the lobes of the ears. The eyes are shown as circular reliefs with a horizontally pressed line for the heavy eyelids – a characteristic of many terracottas of Buddhist type. The depressed corners of the mouth simulate a smile. The slightly increased relief of the upper lips with a barely inclined depression hints at a moustache.

Below the wide shoulders, the upper arms are adorned with armlets. On the breast, there is a necklace in the form of a wide strip and a pectoral, dangling on the stomach with a quadrangular pendant. On the wrists are bracelets. The dress of the figure represents the *uttariya* and *paridhana*. The *uttariya* is shown as two large folds running obliquely from the bottom upward (from right to left) and covering the left wrist. The ends of the folds of the garment freely hang down at the left to the level of the knees of the figure. Folds indicated by more frequent slanting lines pass at the left from the top downward. The hem of the dress (*paridhana*) is emphasized by parallel lines, possibly forming a border.

The identification of the Jandavlyattepa image is difficult because its details are rather vague.[183] The headdress in flat relief at the base and with two sockets on either side is reminiscent of that of a *bodhisattva*,[184] but is less ornate. The *ushnisha,* though, would speak in favour of a *bodhisattva*. The ear-pendants, in the form of threaded pearls, are also similar to the adornment of *bodhisattvas*.[185] Further supporting this reading of the image is the ornamentation and the form of the dress with its schematic *paridhana* and *uttariya*. The pose of the hands also follows the traditional iconography of the *bodhisattva*. If we take into consideration that the palm of the right hand with the fingers lowered is turned toward the viewer, this pose signifies *varada-mudra,* symbolizing grace or a boon.[186] However, this hand pose occurs relatively rarely in Buddhist figurative art. One example is the statue of an upright Buddha of the Gupta period at Sarnath Archaeological Museum, which has been dated to the sixth century AD.[187]

Among the terracotta figurines from Termez Municipal Museum there is a fragment representing the upper part of a female, dated to the Kushan period.[188] The face is round, with large eyes, arched eyebrows and a small, smiling mouth. The ears are adorned with large rectangular earrings and around the neck there is a massive necklace. The headdress, which is placed over the smooth relief representing the hair, has an interesting form. It is divided by vertical lines, which recall a *corona muralis*. Although thematically this representation can be related to the Buddhist figurative complex, a *corona muralis* is usually reserved for city deities; the protectors of the city and city walls (such as Tyche-Ardoksho).[189]

Yakshinis

One of the more popular images among the Buddhist terracotta figurines of northern Bactria are half-naked figures in the characteristic pose of slightly spread hands and legs. Figurines of this type have mostly the same adornments, comprising a necklace or pectoral on the breast and bracelets on the forearms, wrists and ankles (Fig. 68). Except for some details, these figurines represent the same iconographic type. The first of them was found at Zartepa and was interpreted as a 'dancer',[190] but these figurines should rather be associated with *yakshinis*,[191] which are very common in Buddhist art.

Yakshini figurines were found at Barattepa (Fig. 69) in the early Kushan layers, with one of them coming from the same layer as a first century coin of Soter Megas as G.A. Pugachenkova has mentioned,[192] although the layer of this stratum was most probably mixed. This group also includes a fragment from Tepai-Shah (in south Tajikistan), which was found in one of the rooms of a Kushan building.[193] Another stratified find of the same type was discovered in the passage to a room (dated to the Late Kushan period) during the excavation of Kurgantepa (Fig. 70) at Old Termez.[194] One can add two more figurines found on the surface of Old Termez, one of them discovered near the Stupa of Fayaztepa.[195] A second figurine

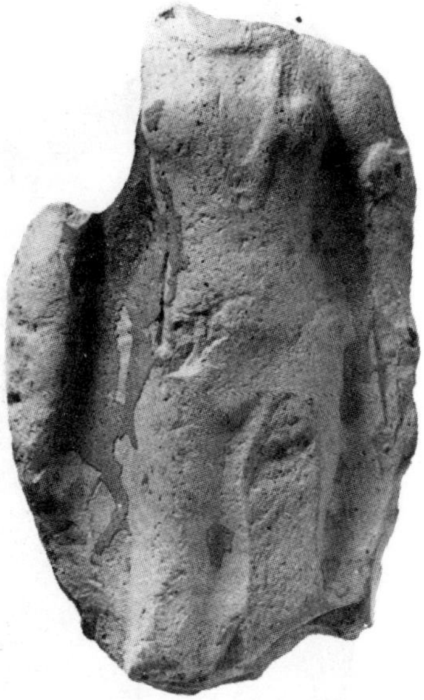

Fig. 68: *Yakshini*. Fragment of terracotta figurine from Zartepa. 3rd-4th century AD. H = 7.3 cm. (Termez Archaeological Museum).

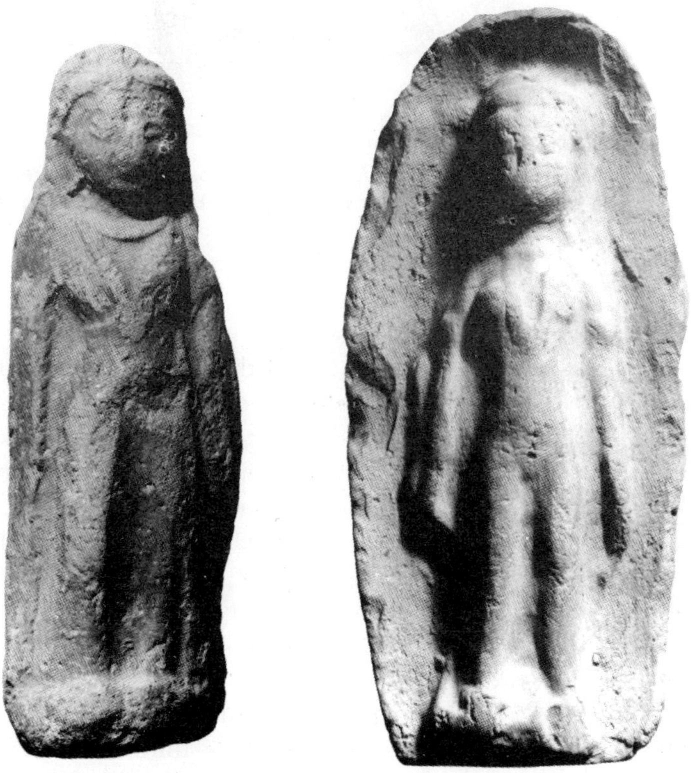

Fig. 69: Terracotta *yakshini* figure. Barattepa. 2nd-3rd century AD. H = 10.6 cm. (Institute of Art Research, Tashkent).

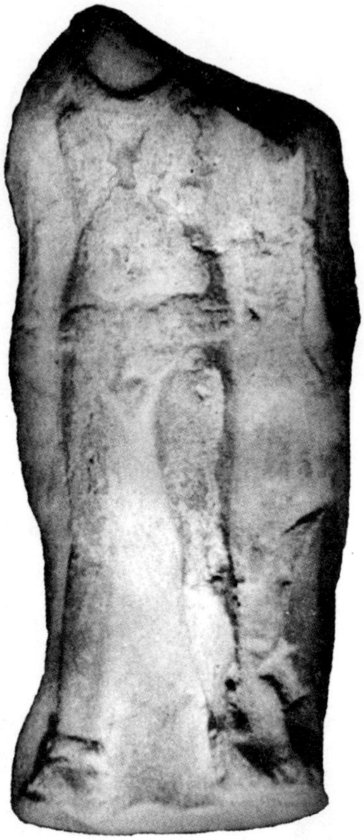

Fig. 70: Terracotta *yakshini* figure. Kurgantepa (Old Termez area). 3rd-4th century AD. H = 12.5 cm. (Termez Archaeological Museum).

(Fig. 71) of the same type very recently came to light in the Fayaztepa area.[196]

Two figurines from this group, from Kurgantepa and Tepai-Shah, are shown in *varada-mudra*: this feature makes them similar to the piece from Batyrabad and all three share the same meaning. The interpretation of this group of images in the plastic art of Bactria-Tokharistan is difficult for the simple reason that in the Buddhist figurative complex many personages have the same set of attributes. Whereas Indian sculptures and reliefs are expressive and dynamic, Bactrian terracottas are stiff, with strictly fixed positions of hands and legs. These images were initially interpreted as dancers but it seems more plausible to identify them as protectors of places of worship or *yakshini*s. These were often used as decoration in architectural monuments.[197] The archaeological circumstances of some of the terracotta finds (in Kurgantepa and Fayaztepa) would bear out their protective function. Chronologically, most of them date from the third to fourth centuries, while the earliest example was discovered in a layer dated to the second

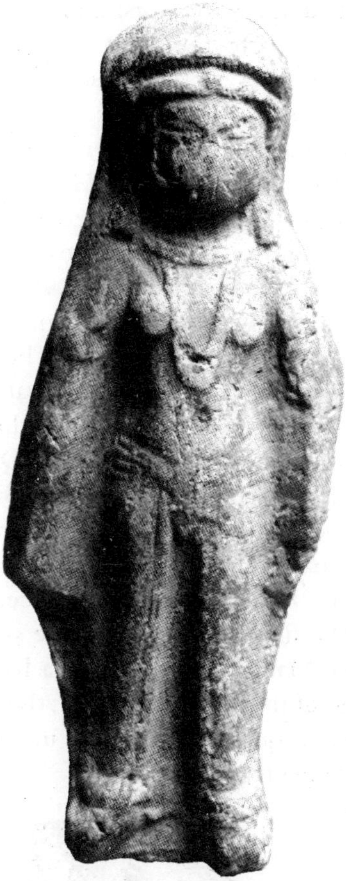

Fig. 71: Terracotta *yakshini* figure. Fayaztepa. 3rd-4th century AD. H = 13 cm. (Termez Archaeological Museum).

to third century. In general, it appears that in the late Kushan period terracotta figures of this type were dispersed all over Bactria and her neighbouring regions.

Adorants and Donors

Adorants and donors are popular images in the Buddhist figurative complex. This bears witness to their important role among the urban and rural strata of the population. Numerous works by Bactrian craftsmen are devoted to this theme, including relief compositions with the Buddha figure in the centre from Fayaztepa and Old Termez (see below). On these representations, the figures surrounding the deity have the appearance of indigenous people, both because of the fashion of their clothing, and also their features.[198] To this group can be added a fragment from Zartepa, representing a male figure in the position of adoration or worshiping – the so-called *namaskara-mudra*: both hands are pressed to the chest, palm to palm in the attitude of prayer.[199] An adornment covers the chest, and traces of long earrings hang down to the shoulders. A similar terracotta figure was found at Old Termez (Fig. 72). Both figurines, which were accidental finds, have been dated to about the first to third centuries.[200] However, there is clearly some doubt as far as their interpretation is concerned. Due to poor preservation, some of the details, including the hand pose, are not entirely clear. Iconographically, they could be close to a *bodhisattva* image in *dharmachakra-mudra*, but the original meaning of these figurines remains elusive.

Adorants with worshipping hands standing before the Buddha and *bodhisattva* occur very often in Buddhist art. Usually, the adorants appear in scenes showing the worship of the symbol of the Buddha, represented as a lotus flower, the Bodhi tree, Wheel of Law (*Dharmachakra*) or Stupa. Multi-figured compositions of *jatakas*, illustrating the Birth, the Enlightenment and the *parinirvana* of Buddha, show the main symbol in the centre around which the other personages are arranged. Tree branches, animals and architectural details are harmoniously interlaced within the overall composition. Later, in the first century, when the symbol representing the Buddha on the reliefs of Mathura and Gandhara had regenerated into the anthropomorphic image of the Buddha himself, the compositional scheme was not abandoned, but acquired a new life in plastic art and a strong impetus in the narrative genre of sculpture.

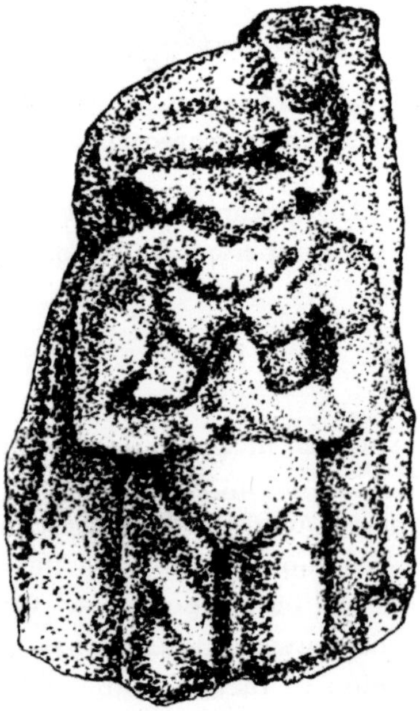

Fig. 72: Fragment of terracotta figurine (adorant or *bodhisattva*?). Old Termez. 3rd-4th century AD. H = 8.2 cm. (Termez Archaeological Museum).

Images of donors playing a subordinate role underwent the same development within the relief composition. Although the images of adorants and donors were very close to each other, the artist placed them in a hierarchical order starting from the central personage – in the foreground we can see standing or kneeling adorants and behind them, donors bringing flowers, fruits and vessels.

Among the terracottas from Bactria-Tokharistan are some figurines which can be identified as donors. The first of them was found during the excavations of Khairabadtepa.[201] The figurine was found in the lower layers of a room dated to the first and second centuries AD.[202] The terracotta was coated with a dark brown slip. It shows a standing male, draped in a long cloak that crossed over the left shoulder. In his right hand he holds a bunch of flowers, probably lotuses (Fig. 73), and in his left hand there is a rounded object, perhaps a vessel or the pleat of his cloak (?). There are many examples of this type among Mathuran and Gandharan sculptures,[203] but the closest is the fragment of a stone relief from the Buddhist monastery in Karatepa.[204] This fragment is related to the terracotta figurine from Khairabadtepa both geographically and chronologically.

Another type of donor is represented by a figurine from Zartepa, found in the late Kushan layers.[205] The terracotta was painted with red slip and its reverse was smoothed out after moulding. It shows a female figure

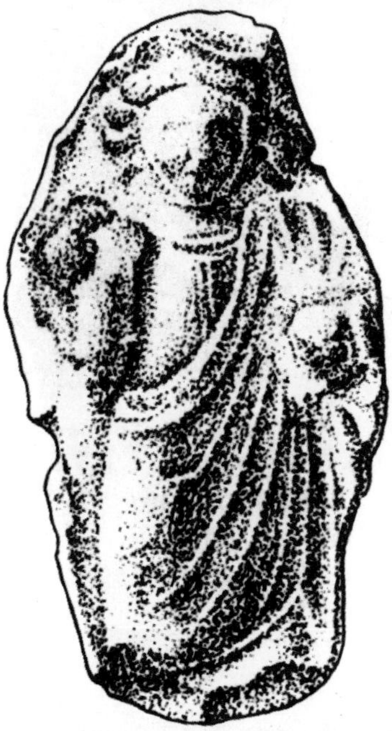

Fig. 73: Terracotta donor figurine. 2nd-3rd century AD. Khairabadtepa. H = 9.6 cm. (Termez Archaeological Museum).

holding a circular object in the left hand (Fig. 74), resembling fruit or a vessel. The head is slightly turned to the right and the hair style is prolonged with a cylindrical headdress. The female figure is clad in a tight garment reaching to the knees; embossed jewellery, comprising round pendants hanging from a necklace, adorns her bosom. A relief line parts her wide trousers and she wears soft shoes. As a whole, the figurine has shortened proportions in the lower part. It is noteworthy that a thick, rounded fold of the dress falls over the hands. The same element of attire is also conspicuous on the statue of the standing Buddha from Zartepa. The female donor finds an analogue in a terracotta figure from the same archaeological context at Akkurgan and dated to the late Kushan period.[206]

Iconographically, this type of donor is related to a donor statue from Shotorak (in Afghanistan), which has the same rounded ribbons, pleated wide trousers and soft footwear.[207] Similar costume is represented on a Mathuran sculpture (2nd-3rd century AD), which is attributed to the dynastic art of the Kushans.[208] The stratigraphic contexts of the terracottas

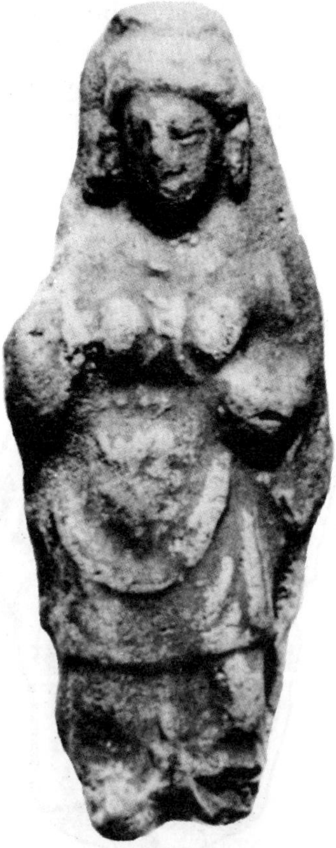

Fig. 74: Terracotta donor figurine. 2nd-3rd century AD. Zartepa. H = 12 cm. (The State Hermitage Museum, St. Petersburg).

and the analysis of the ceramics and coins found with the terracottas allow us to date these particular pieces to the fourth or the beginning of the fifth century, but this does not exclude the general use of this donor type in an earlier period.

Mithuna Figures

Within the category of adorants and donors belongs the 'amorous couple' or so-called *mithuna* group that was very popular on Indian reliefs of the Kushan period. In the monumental plastic art of northern Bactria it is difficult to find this specific subject, unless one sees it represented in the lower part of a stone sculpture from Airtam with a Bactrian inscription.[209] The fragment shows a couple with one of the figures clad in long drapery with anklets adorning the feet.

However, in terracotta we have two examples with a similar subject. One of them came from Batyrabad,[210] the other from Zartepa.[211] Both examples, of which only the lower part of the plaque is preserved, show the figures of a male and a female in low relief. The dress, the frontal representation, and the adornments are all elements that have many analogies in the art of both Gandhara and Mathura, and especially in the reliefs of Nagarjunakonda.[212] Both of these plaques can be dated to the third to fourth centuries. The first one was a surface found at Batyrabad (Fig. 75). Pugachenkova[213] connected its representation of a couple with an ivory

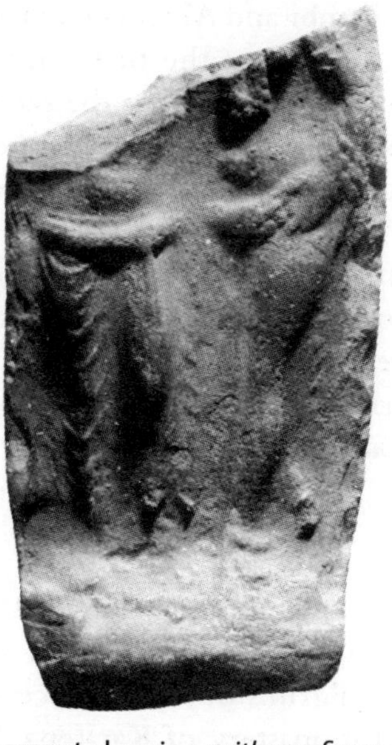

Fig. 75: Terracotta tile fragment showing *mithuna* figures. Batyrabad. 2nd-3rd century AD. H = 8.3 cm. (Institute of Art Research, Tashkent).

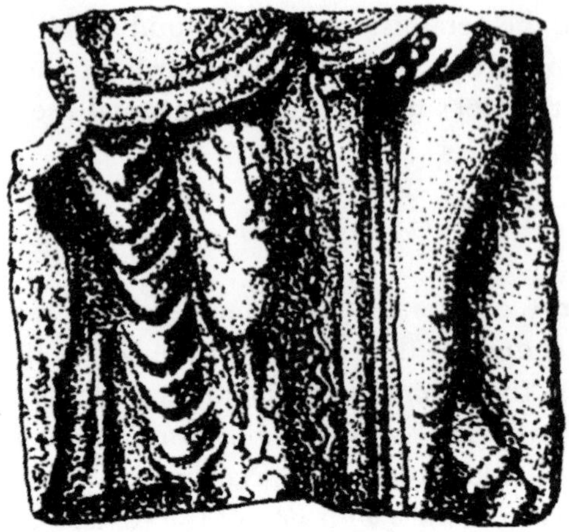

Fig. 76: Terracotta tile fragment showing *mithuna* figures. Zartepa. 3rd-4th century AD. H = 6.3 cm. (The State Hermitage Museum, St. Petersburg).

plaque from Begram.[214] The second fragment of a similar terracotta figure (Fig. 76) was found in compartment no. 23 in the late Kushan layers of Zartepa.[215] Both figures show the rather rare *mithuna* (amorous couple) in typically Indian clothes.[216] Beginning with the Shunga period, such reliefs of amorous couples decorated the pillars of the railings around *stupas*, for instance, on the reliefs of Mathuran and Gandharan sculpture.[217] The theme of the loving couple was widespread in the plastic art of India, and in the Bharhut,[218] and later the ornamental framing of the Buddha images. Among the material from Kaushambi and Ahichchhatra, there are many terracotta plaques with *mithuna* scenes from the first century BC,[219] yet the Central Asian objects belong to a later period, to the second to third centuries AD, and have some similarity with a fragment of stone statue from Airtam with a Bactrian inscription on the pedestal, dated to the first to second centuries AD.[220]

The archaeological material of the Kushan period in Bactria-Tokharistan also includes various other elements of the Buddhist religious complex, such as terracottas representing monkeys, sometimes in the place of handles of vessels, stamped ornamentation dubbed 'Footprint of the Buddha', ceramic models of *stupas*, and more.[221]

FAYAZTEPA

Fayaztepa, one of the most interesting sites of Buddhist art, is located on the modern road leading to Termez.[222] This site undoubtedly had an important meaning for pilgrims due to its accessible location on the way to the ancient city and monastery of Karatepa. More precisely, Fayaztepa is situated to the north-west of Old Termez and 1 km to the northeast of

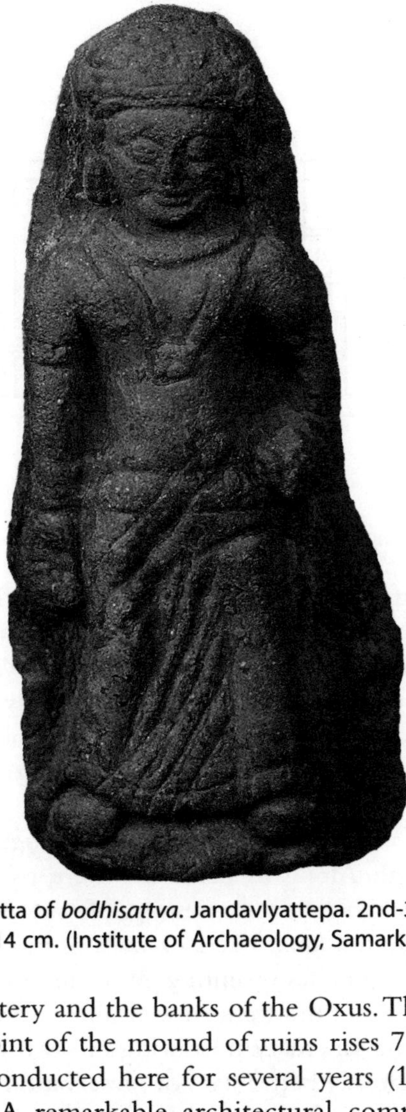

Fig. 77: Terracotta of *bodhisattva*. Jandavlyattepa. 2nd-3rd century AD. H = 14 cm. (Institute of Archaeology, Samarkand).

the Karatepa monastery and the banks of the Oxus. The site covers 1.5 sq km. The highest point of the mound of ruins rises 7 m above the plain. Excavations were conducted here for several years (1968-72), leading to brilliant results.[223] A remarkable architectural complex of a Buddhist monastery richly decorated with sculptures and wall paintings was discovered during these excavations. The complex represents one of the earliest monuments of Buddhist art and architecture in Central Asia.

Architecture

The dimensions of the Fayaztepa monastery testify to its monumental character and its primary function as a centre of activity for Buddhist society. Within the Fayaztepa complex, the *vihara* is one of the notable edifices. It was built using a combination of mud brick and *pakhsa* blocks,

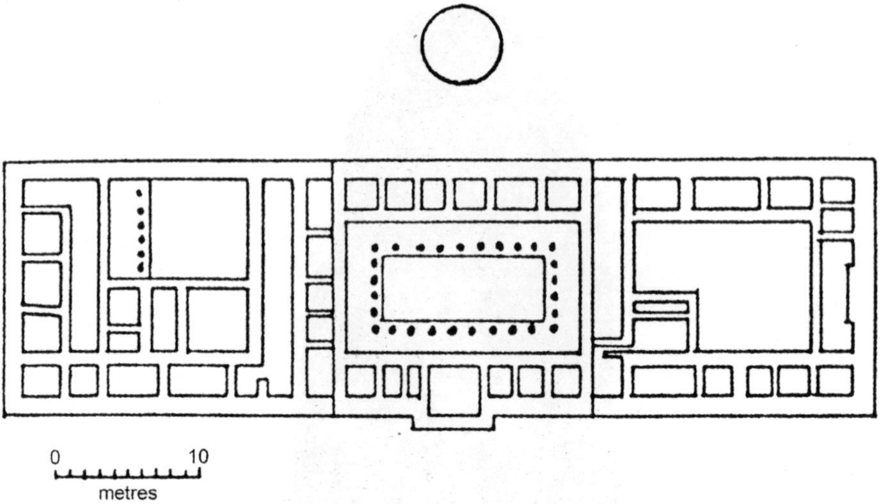

Fig. 78: Plan of Fayaztepa monastery (*vihara*). (After L.I. Al'baum, 1982, fig. 17, a).

the latter measuring 0.4-0.5 m in width. The plan had the form of an extended rectangle, with a length of 117 m and width of 34 m. The *vihara* was orientated north-west to south-east. The layout was divided into three parts. Aside from the temple in the centre, there was the monastery with a refectory on the north-west side (Fig. 78), and an isolated cult monument, a *stupa* with a cross-shaped plan, in the south-eastern section. A path led from the temple to the *stupa*.

The sacred space of the temple included a rectangular court measuring 20 to 30 m in length. Along its perimeter were twenty rooms opening onto the court. *Sufa*s (benches for resting, of various sizes) were placed along the walls inside the *iwan*. The rear walls of the *iwan* were decorated with paintings. Traces of these paintings were found on all four sides of the court. In the centre of the western wall, a doorway has been preserved that gave access to the sanctuary, measuring 6.0 × 6.1 m. In this area, the paintings are in a relatively better state of preservation than elsewhere. The walls of the sanctuary itself were also decorated with paintings.[224]

Sculpture

Sculptural pieces and fragments were concentrated mainly in the sanctuary. Here the well-known 'Triad' was found.[225] This 'Triad' can be considered a masterpiece of plastic art of Fayaztepa that fortunately has been well preserved. The relief represents the Buddha under a 'Gandhara' arch (Fig. 79). Directly under the apex of the arch, a round tree has been carved in the form of a hollow cylinder. It grows as a halo (nimbus) around the head of the deity. The branches, with leaves symmetrically sprouting on

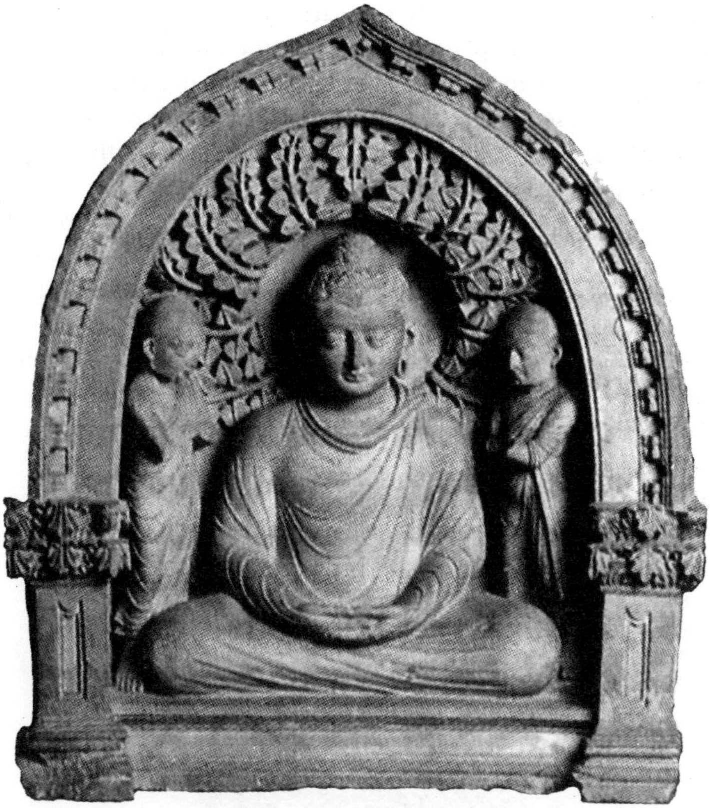

Fig. 79: Triad. Buddha under the arch. 1st-2nd century AD. Fayaztepa, shrine. Limestone. H = 75 × 62 × 28 cm. (Museum of History of the Peoples of Uzbekistan, Tashkent).

either side, are bent backwards to form a wreath. The heart-shaped leaves are like those of the sacred *pipal* (*Ficus religiosa*) tree in Buddhist art. A similar tree, though slightly transformed, is found on the relief of a *stupa* from Sikri in the Lahore Museum.[226]

The modelling of the Fayaztepa Buddha image follows the traditions of Gandharan art. The manner of representing the headdress of Buddha with the *ushnisha* on top is especially indicative of this. The texture of the hair is shown as smooth curving lines with a slightly dipped peak in the centre. Such rendering of the hairstyle is characteristic of many works of Gandharan sculpture.[227]

The Fayaztepa image is also similar to Gandharan sculpture in the modelling of the face, with carefully crafted details such as the heavy upper eyelids, the straight 'classical' nose, the sensitive mouth and the soft chin – features that ultimately derived from Greek sculpture. The Fayaztepa drapery too, with its gently separated long pleats of thin material, follows the pattern of the Gandharan masters. Finally, the carinated arch with all its elements occurs often in Gandharan plastic art and is sometimes called the 'Gandhara arch'.[228] Yet, in spite of the evident influence of Gandharan art, the 'Triad' of Fayaztepa was created by Bactrian artists who were trained in the native figurative tradition.[229] The adorants, in particular the traits of the worshipping monks, tie the piece to local Buddhist society.

Another Buddha head in alabaster is also important.[230] It represents one of the most outstanding finds from Fayaztepa. It is painted in white, but very possibly it was once gilded (Fig. 80). Apparently, the sculpture had been mounted on a base (podium), erected in the room in front of the stupa in the central part of the southern side. This base was of clay with a high admixture of straw. A very thin layer of alabaster covered the upper surface. Most of the sculptural fragments were painted in red. The surface of the sculpture was gilded.

The alabaster head of the Buddha was executed in the best traditions of Bactrian art. The face is white and contrasts with the long-arched

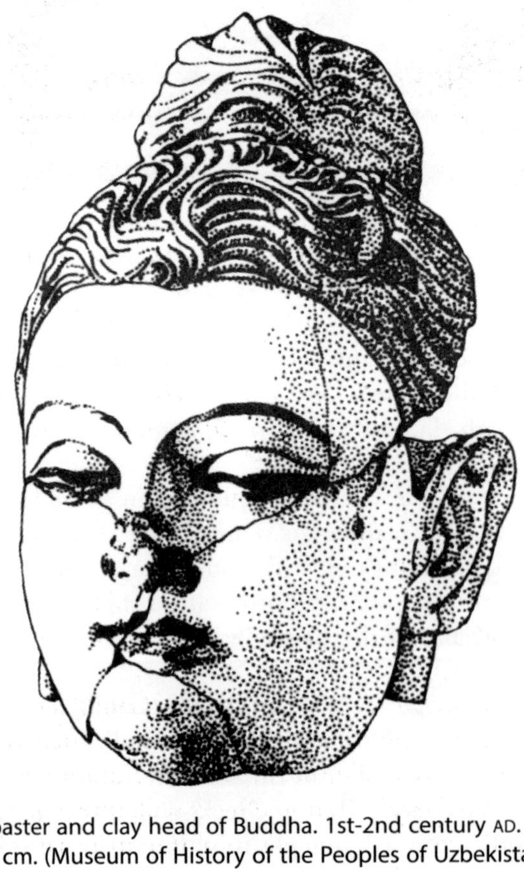

Fig. 80: Alabaster and clay head of Buddha. 1st-2nd century AD. Fayaztepa, shrine. H = 75 cm. (Museum of History of the Peoples of Uzbekistan, Tashkent).

eyebrows emphasized by thin black lines. The eyelids are semi-closed, lending a contemplative expression to the figure. The hair, combed in a sharp angle towards the middle of the forehead, is a detail that is characteristic of Kuevkurgan sculpture; but here, it is more subtle. Deep wavy lines render the texture of the hair. The plump face is characterized by the soft treatment of the delicately outlined mouth and chin. The ear with long lobes, elements of the hair, and other details were first impressed in a mould and then affixed to the sculpture. That this method was later practised at Kuevkurgan (during the 5th-6th centuries AD), demonstrates its continuity. Taking into account that the Fayaztepa complex is dated to the first century AD, it can be considered an early example of sculpture that used the combined technique of carving and applied details stamped in a mould.

Fayaztepa has yielded a rich corpus of small stone sculptures. These pieces were apparently carved on limestone slabs that decorated the bases of the statues and certain parts of the *stupa*. One finds semi-nude figures of donors represented in dynamic poses (Fig. 81). Most likely, they originally formed part of multi-figured compositions of *jatakas* or other scenes of Buddhist narrative. A stone relief from Fayaztepa showing the head of a youth (Fig. 82) deserves special attention. B. Staviskiy cited this fragment in his book on Kushan art.[231] The head is in high relief and has a hair comprising regularly arranged curls framing the round face with large eyes. Only the upper part of the bust is preserved. Below, there is a horizontal line showing architectural elements of a city wall. Within the frame, the background is decorated with projecting trapezoidal and triangular incisions together with upward pointing arrows. The latter correspond, in all

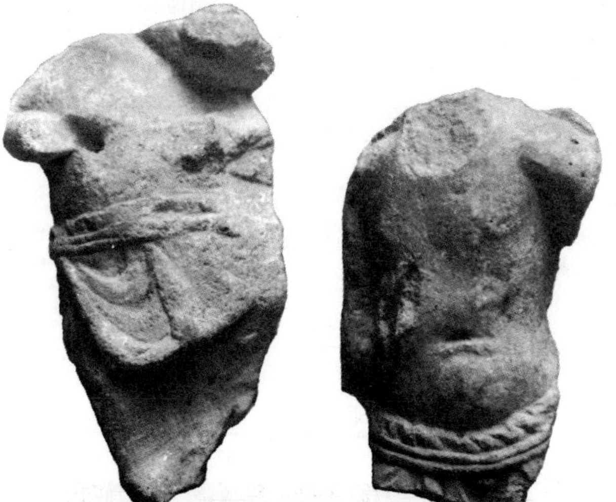

Fig. 81: Stone figurines of donors (?). 2nd century AD. Fayaztepa, shrine. On right: H = 8 cm; on left: H = 9.5 cm. (Termez Archaeological Museum).

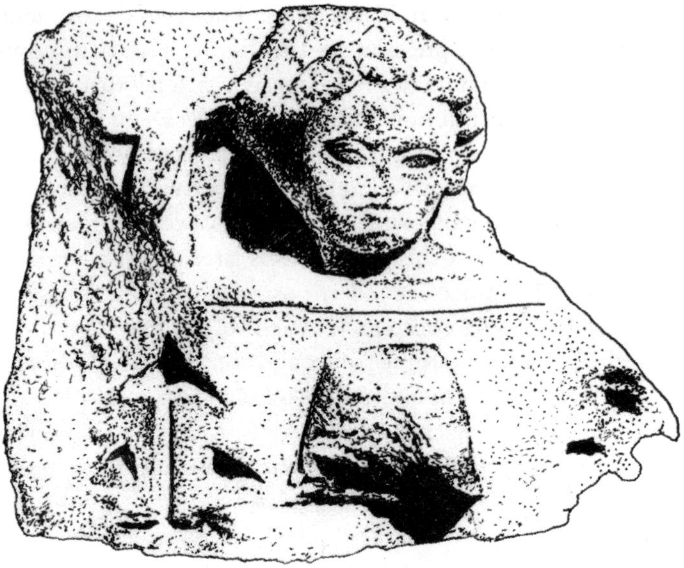

Fig. 82: Fragment of a stone relief showing a head and city wall. Fayaztepa. 2nd-3rd century AD. (Museum of History of the Peoples of Uzbekistan, Tashkent).

probability, to arrow-shaped loopholes (arrow-slits). Most likely, the relief represented a figure placed behind a fortification wall. Such elements as the projections and arrow-shaped loopholes would bear out the proposition that the youth was meant to be standing inside a city wall or fortress. The search for analogues brings us again to the art of Gandhara. Similar heads placed between the merlons of walls with triangular incisions representing loopholes are seen on a relief at Baltimore Museum (Fig. 83).[232] Another analogy from Gandhara is found on a relief from Mekhasandra (Fig. 84), depicting the departure of Prince Siddhartha from Kapilavastu.[233] A guardian with a spear is shown behind the fortification wall, which is decorated with rectangular and triangular incisions. It is interesting to note other

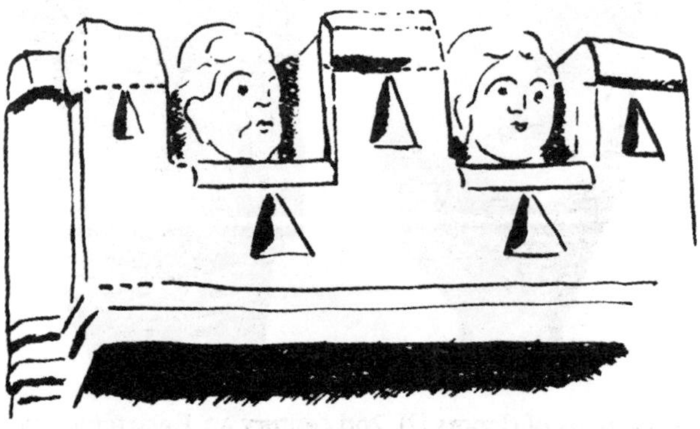

Fig. 83: Individuals on the city wall (*cf.* Fig. 82).
(Baltimore Museum of Art. After F. Tissot, 1985, plate I, 1).

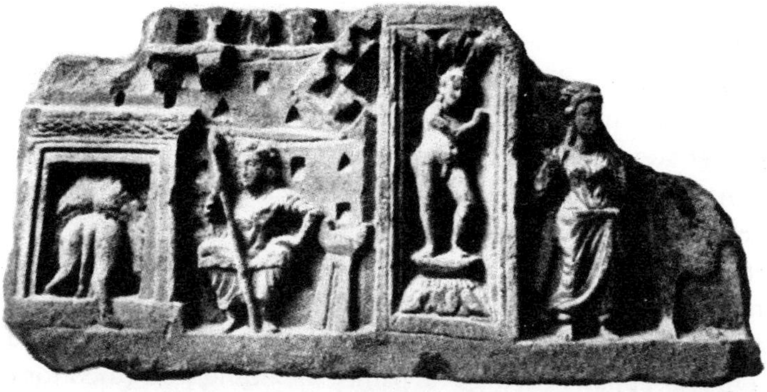

Fig. 84: Stone relief from Mekhasandra with scene of the Great Departure. (After G.A. Pugachenkova, 1982a, fig. 121).

details such as projections from the wall that most likely were intended to be supports for a ceiling. Two heads are looking over the parapet.

It should be noted that on the surface of the same site a terracotta figurine was found, which represents a *yakshini* in transparent dress (Fig. 85). This image was very popular in the figurative complexes of Buddhist character and especially amongst terracotta figurines[234] (see above).

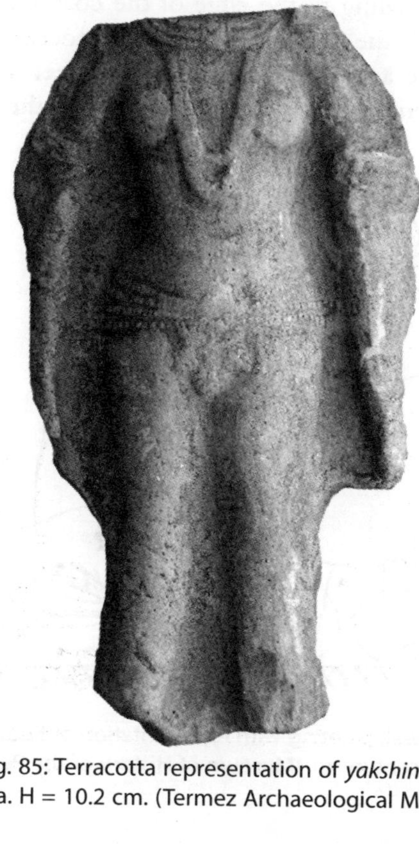

Fig. 85: Terracotta representation of *yakshini*. Fayaztepa. H = 10.2 cm. (Termez Archaeological Museum).

Painting

The other remarkable discovery at Fayaztepa is the wall paintings, which, together with the sculptures, decorated the interior of the Buddhist complex. The paintings were executed *al secco*. First, the rough plaster was covered with a thin, finely ground clay layer, and then primed with an alabaster admixture (also known as *ganch*). On this surface, the contours of the design were marked by black lines or by incision. The lines were then filled in with certain colours to represent the body, dress and other details. The paints were mainly inorganic in various shades of ochre, black and white. There were also, apparently, organic paints, including soot (used for carbon-black) and paints of vegetable origin (such as green). From the preserved fragments, one can conclude that most of the walls were decorated with multi-figured compositions such as scenes of adoration and offerings to the superior deities of the temple.

A composition showing two upright Buddha figures with halos around the head and the feet is interesting.[235] The figure of the deity is enveloped in a red mantle, falling to the shins (Fig. 86). On either side of this figure are two other figures in adoring poses. Judging by their costumes, they are women, each dressed in a mantle worn on the shoulders, without sleeves but with ties for fastening to the edge of the coat. On the coat, there are holes through which the ties are knotted.[236] Underneath the long mantle (*khalat*), one can see a long dress covering the feet. The numerous small pleats of this garment indicate the fine texture of the material. Over this

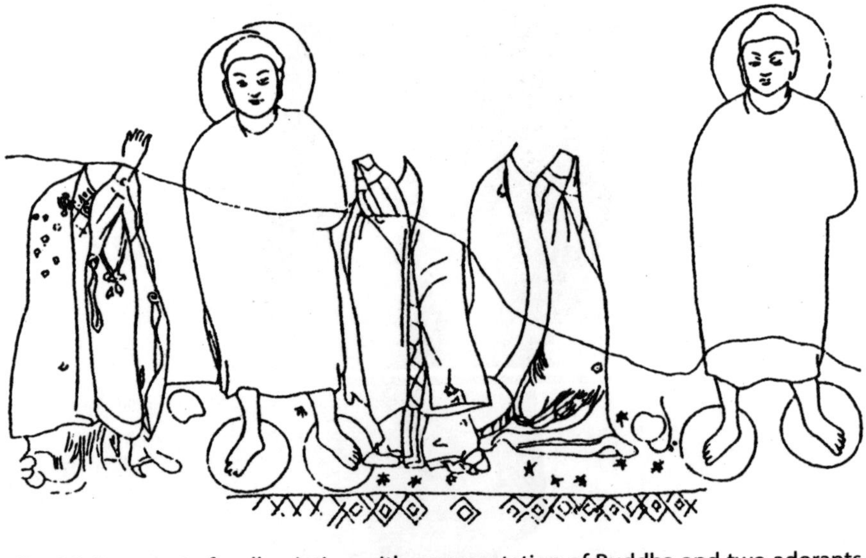

Fig. 86: Fragment of wall painting with representation of Buddha and two adorants. Fayaztepa. 1st-2nd century AD. (Museum of History of the Peoples of Uzbekistan).

is a shorter dress. It has a plain surface, without pleats, indicating a less fine material. A bell on a cord is hung around the neck. The cord falls below the level of the waist. The bell makes it clear that the women were pilgrims. Moreover, if they were representative of the local inhabitants, they can provide us with a glimpse of female dress in Bactria during the first century AD. It is interesting to note the similarity of the dress ensemble represented on the wall painting with that of terracotta figurines of the same period from Bactria, more precisely from northern Bactria (including such sites in Chaganian as Dal'verzintepa, Payonkurgan).[237]

A second extensive fragment of wall painting from the sanctuary shows a multi-figured composition with frontally standing male figures in garments of a secular character.[238] Evidently, it represented a group of donors (Fig. 87). This subject is typical for the Kushan period and is well documented in the statues of Kanishka from Math (near Mathura)[239] and Surkh Kotal (in northern Afghanistan).[240]

The composition comprises nine figures. Unfortunately, only the lower section has survived, limiting interpretation to the style of the dress. It consists of a long shirt falling to the knees, wrapped from right to left. The central figure wears an open *kaftan*, underneath which, in the centre, the hem of a long shirt can be detected. On some of the shirts there is ornamentation on the surface, but this is only just visible because of poor preservation. The shoes, and the manner in which they are worn, are also interesting. According to the fold lines on the feet, the shoes are soft, with cords on the ankles for fastenings. These cover the heel and ankle. On the inner side of the ankle is a circular decorative clasp (*fibula*).

On the better-preserved figures a belt with decorative plates can be seen. One of the figures holds an indistinct attribute, evidently an offering. The fourth figure from the right is shown in a characteristic gesture, with a finger pointing to the left, towards the central personage or deity. The same gesture is found on another fragment showing two figures, of which only the upper sections remain.[241] This fragment represents a remarkable

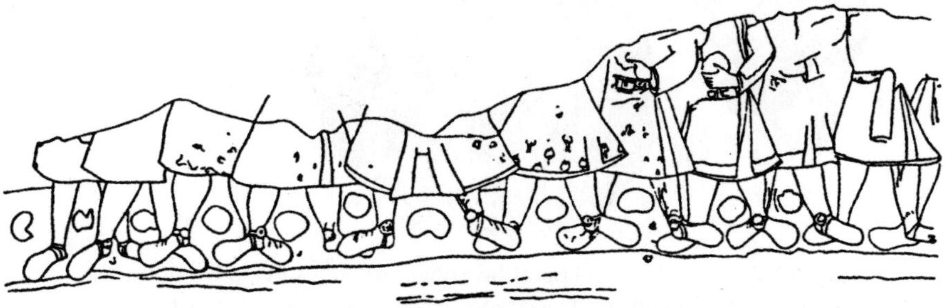

Fig. 87: Fragment of wall painting with representation of donors. Fayaztepa. 1st-2nd century AD. (Museum of History of the Peoples of Uzbekistan, Tashkent).

piece of artistic skill (Fig. 88). The harmonious but realistic images of donors with finely detailed profiles embody elegance and spirituality. A palette of brilliant colours was chosen with ability and taste. The upper bodies of the figures are represented frontally, but their heads are in profile. They supplement the previous fragment, demonstrating that, in spite of the *en face* position of the torso, the heads could be turned in profile. It appears that this was typical of the art of wall painting in northern Bactria during the Kushan period. The phenomenon is echoed in the numismatic iconography of the Great Kushans, for instance, in the coinage of Vima Kadphises and Kanishka.[242] It is especially prominent on the coins of Vima, where the figure is standing frontally and the head is turned to the left. Moreover, figures of deities were represented in the same manner. However, this peculiarity may have applied only to two-dimensional representations.

Returning to the representation of Buddha with flanking adorants, there is another unusual detail: the head of the Buddha as well as his figure

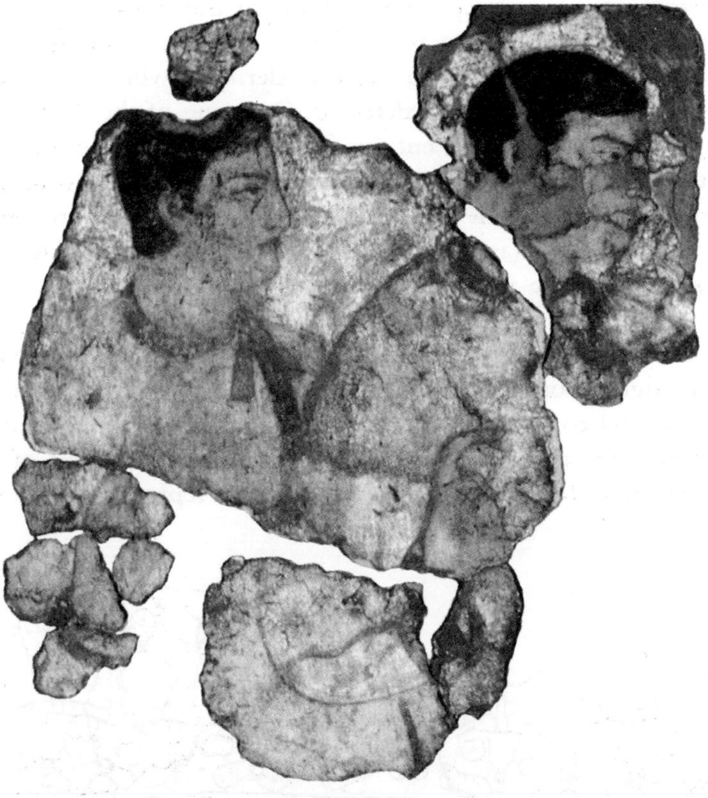

Fig. 88: Fragment of wall painting showing two individuals (donors) with pointing gestures. Fayaztepa. 1st-2nd century AD. 78 × 63 cm. (Museum of History of the Peoples of Uzbekistan, Tashkent).

represented *en face*, while the other figures are shown in profile. This peculiarity can be also traced to neighbouring Karatepa, as discussed below.

An inscription above one of the figures contains the name 'Pharro'. This has led some scholars to assume that it is a Zoroastrian deity receiving the offerings, though this is unlikely. It is more probable that 'Pharro' was simply the name of a donor. The Iranian origin of the name does not exclude the worship of Buddha.[243] The manner itself of inscribing the name above the personage is unusual. In figurative art, this was the custom in Greece and Rome, and their provinces where the traditions of the Greco-Roman world had penetrated. There are Greek vases and mosaics from Late Antiquity and the Early Medieval period, where often every figure had a name inscribed above.[244] In this aspect, Fayaztepa is actually a rare example in the Bactrian-Tokharistan iconographic context. Evidently, the representation of donors (usually rulers or noblemen) in Kushan art developed under the influence of the Greco-Roman world.

Another fragment supplements the missing parts of the dress of the previous personages (shown in the composition with nine personages) from Fayaztepa. It shows the upper part of the same mantle wrapped from right to left, with the cord on the left shoulder shown as a red band. The gesture of the finger pointing to the right gives a hint that these figures stood in the group on the left of the central and main personage. It is quite possible that they belonged to the multi-figured composition described above.

The composition of the scene with donors from Fayaztepa anticipates the multi-figured composition with donors on the wall painting of grotto no. 16 from Kizil (in eastern Turkestan), which shows bearers of swords and upright figures.[245] Although the wall paintings of Dil'berjin (in northern Afghanistan) (Fig. 89) would be a geographically closer analogue for the composition of Fayaztepa, it is chronologically much later.[246] The influence of Bactrian art, especially of the Buddhist figurative tradition, on regions along the Silk Roads during the Kushan and subsequent periods is borne out by different categories of finds including plastic art and wall painting.[247]

The chronology of Fayaztepa is based on excavated coins. The earliest coins are imitations of the coins of the Greek King Heliocles. Among the Kushan coins are those of Kanishka, Huvishka, and Vasudeva.[248] On the floors of the rooms were found mainly coins of Vima Kadphises and Kanishka.[249] Thus, the apogee of activity at Fayaztepa is believed to have taken place during the first and second centuries AD. If the abandonment of the site were caused by the Sassanian invasion of Central Asia, it would have happened during the time of Shapur I, at the same time as the devastation of Karatepa. However, the director of excavations L.I. Al'baum

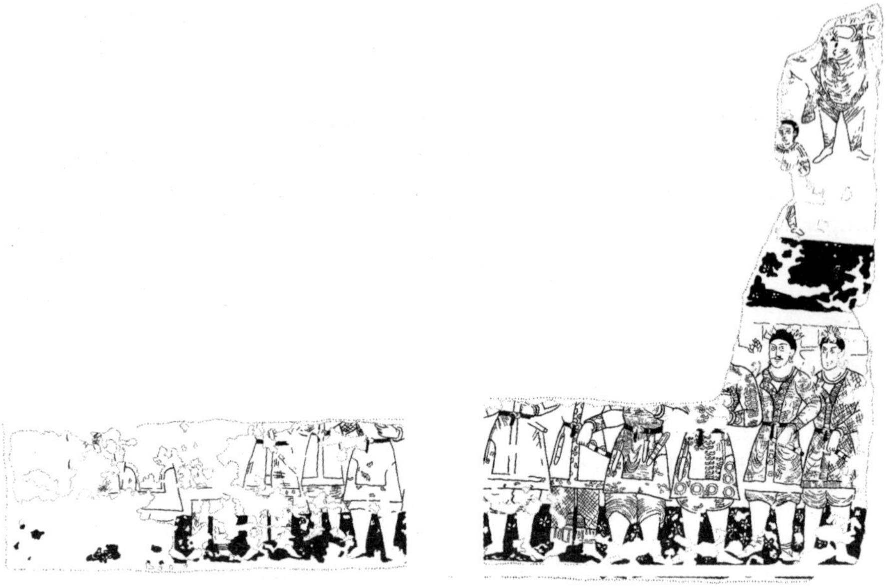

Fig. 89: Wall painting showing donor figures. Dil'berjin (Afghanistan). 3rd-4th century AD. (After I.T. Kruglikova, 1979, fig. 2).

disputes a third century AD date for the destruction of Fayaztepa, and prefers the early fourth century AD instead, which would have been the time of Hormizd I (AD 272-3).[250] It is more likely that the abandonment of Fayaztepa occurred under the Hephthalites (4th-5th centuries AD), when the entrances to the rooms were blocked.[251]

Karatepa

The most important monument of Buddhist culture to the north of the Oxus was the cult centre of Karatepa in the north-western part of Old Termez. In spite of its location outside the city walls, Karatepa was undoubtedly part of the city, and in its cultural aspect had a special meaning. Its location outside the walls is easily explained by its function as a monastery, built at a distance from urban life and mundane vanity. According to several inscriptions (four of the same content) on ostraca found during the exploration of this area, this Buddhist monastery was named *Khudevuka vihar(e)* – 'Vihar(a) of the King'.[252]

The first archaeological work at Karatepa was in 1924-7 under the leadership of B.P. Denike of the Museum of Oriental Cultures, and was continued by the Termez Archaeological Complex Expedition under the direction of M.E. Masson in 1936-7).[253] In 1937, a group of researchers from this expedition started to excavate Karatepa under E.G. Pchelina. Prolonged systematic excavations on this site followed under the leadership of B.Ya. Staviskiy in 1961.[254] The excavations were concentrated on the southern hill of Karatepa.

Architecture

More than ten cave temples and other rock constructions with cultic associations were discovered at Karatepe (Figs. 90, 91), in addition to courts, temples, and sanctuaries of separate Buddhist complexes above ground. A cave temple with a cella surrounded by four corridors and a court with colonnaded porticos similar to Central Asian *iwans* were characteristic for the majority of the complexes. The complexes also had numerous special rooms that were often connected with dwellings above, or an audience hall for lectures or with a stupa such as the one found in complex B. The *stupa* of complex B, located in the centre of the court, was similar to the *stupa* of Fayaztepa. Both had a cylindrical shape and a circular base decorated with lotus reliefs. However, the stupa at Fayaztepa was later enlarged as a

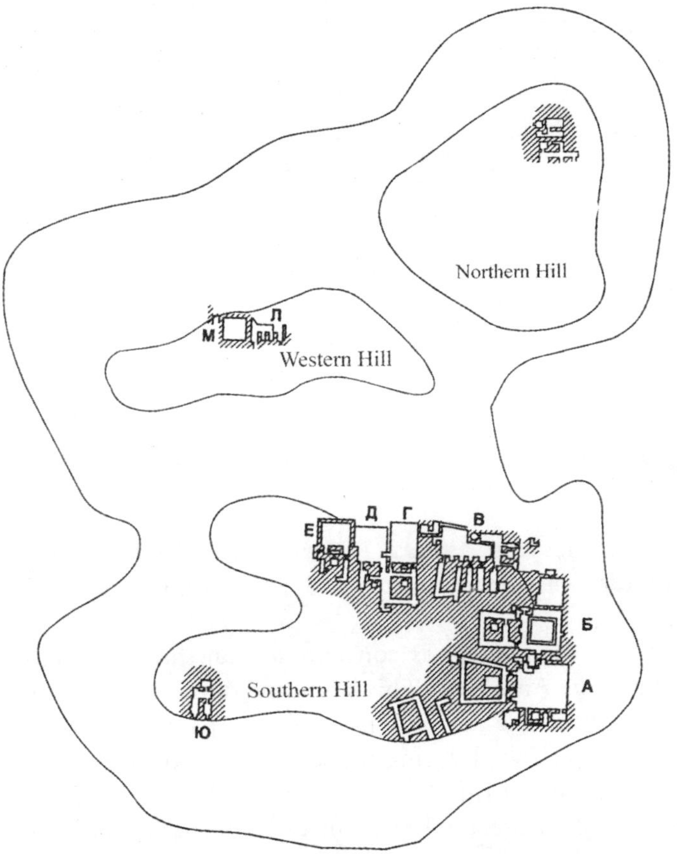

Fig. 90: Plan of Karatepa complex. (After B.Ya. Staviskiy, 2000, fig. 3b).

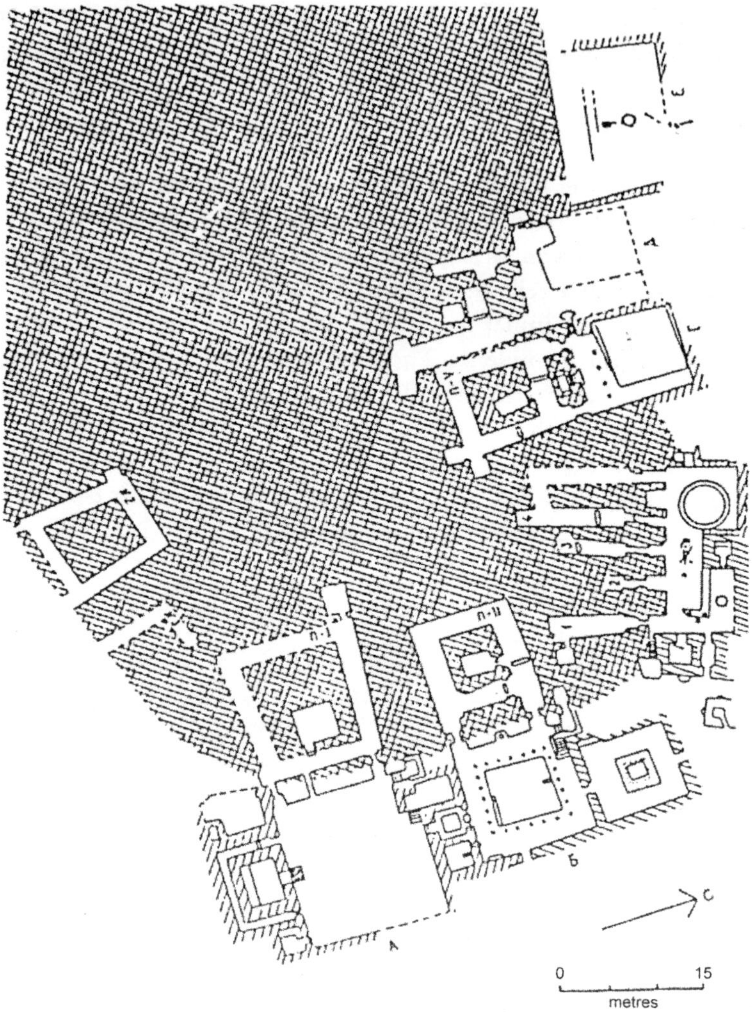

Fig. 91: Plan of excavated complexes of the southern hill of Karatepa. (After Sh. Pidaev, K. Kato, 2000a, fig. 1).

stupa with a rectangular base. As at Fayaztepa, the temples, courts and *stupa*s were decorated with stone, plaster and polychrome-painted clay sculptures.

The complex of Karatepa is concentrated on three hills situated close to the banks of the Amudarya. This landscape dominated the adjacent city, opening the view to the nearby *stupa* of Fayaztepa. Considering that these two complexes functioned during the same epoch, they must have formed the major cult centre of Buddhism in northern Bactria. It is not necessary to describe every architectural element of Karatepa, which consisted of a maze of cells within the caves and temples, in addition to a sophisticated layout of above-ground sacred buildings. The investigations of these features have been well published in the scholarly literature.[255] However, looking at certain objects found during the excavations of these sites, it is possible to observe some differences in the artistic style, for example, when comparing the sculptural objects from Karatepa and Fayaztepa.

Sculpture

The remarkable technique of clay sculpture is well demonstrated in the plastic art of Karatepa. The majority of fragments are in alabaster, clay and stone and are covered by polychrome paint and gilding. The figures of *bodhisattva*s and the Buddha are especially expressive, with their elaborate drapery showing both short and long cascading pleats in light-weight fabric. Iconographically, many images of Karatepa plastic art are related to Gandharan examples. However, in the figurative art of Karatepa there are peculiarities that derive from local traditions. These peculiarities were later incorporated in the art of Chinese Turkestan, disseminated along the Great Silk Road by Buddhist and other pilgrims, missionaries and artists, who spread these ideas and doctrines.

The most salient category of the figurative art of Karatepa was sculpture, an integral part of all Buddhist monuments. Its role was of great importance for the rituals of the Buddhist doctrine. The paintings, found throughout the complex, ornamenting the walls and niches of the cult rooms, were primarily decorative, though to a certain extent they served the propagandistic aims of the Buddhist religion. Yet, they were of a subordinate character. It was the sculptures of the Buddha or *bodhisattva*, placed in the centre or in a special space, with all their characteristic attributes, that were venerated. In this respect, the sculpture of Karatepa is especially significant. The intentions for the representation of the main personages of the Buddhist pantheon were very clear. The creation of the plastic spiritual image demanded accuracy and highly skilled sculptors.

Nevertheless, it should be noted that the most important object for veneration in the Buddhist cult complexes was the *stupa*. The *stupa*, among other aspects, symbolized the reliquary of Buddha's remains. In Karatepa, a *stupa* stood in every complex of the monks' cells, receiving daily rituals. In addition to the small *stupa*s, there was a large one, a kind of 'cathedral' stupa, for special ceremonies. Usually, it was richly decorated with reliefs depicting episodes of Buddha's life, narratives from his preceding incarnations (the *jataka*s) and symbols of the doctrine.

Indeed, the preserved fragments prove the high quality of the sculpture works of Karatepa. Almost all of them were executed in the same technique: branches, twigs and reeds served as the frame for the sculpture. The wooden base was covered with clay, after which the details were modelled in plaster and impressed in a mould. The next phase of modelling involved the touching up of the details as well as the whole sculpture, the surface of which was then primed with a thin layer of white plaster. Finally, the sculpture was painted, either in many colours or simply monochrome. Although sculptures coming from other sites were created by the same method, it is the various styles that set the different schools apart.

Among the sculpture fragments from Karatepa some heads deserve special attention. They are full of sensitive expressions and have been interpreted as the images of Buddha, *bodhisattva*s and *devata*s. The head of a Buddha from the Russian Museum of Oriental Cultures (Moscow) is modelled in the traditional manner characteristic of the Fayaztepa sculpture. However, here it possesses a vital energy. The features of the face with a straight nose, heavy eyelids and a repressed smile give the head an appearance of blessed conciliation (Fig. 92). The richly decorated halo (nimbus) was

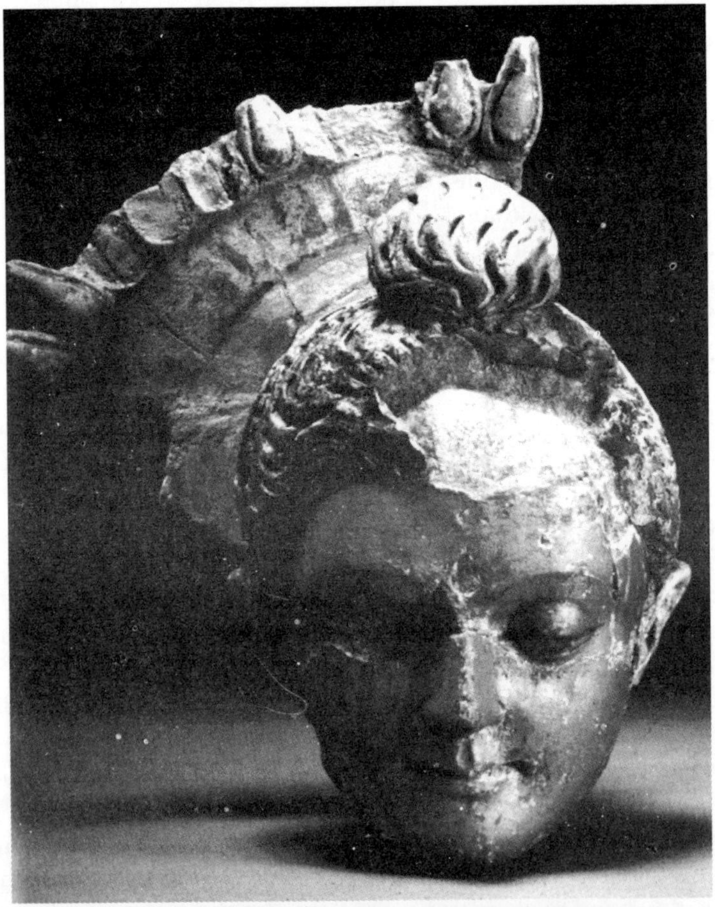

Fig. 92: Buddha with a painted and gilded halo. Karatepa. Piece P-V in the complex E. 2nd-3rd century AD. Clay, stucco, painting, gilding. (Scale not available) (Museum of Oriental Cultures, Moscow).

modelled as a row of tear drops in an extended relief, imitating the nimbus with radiating flaming tongues.

Another polychrome painted head represents an image of a *devata* with an elaborately curled hair style that was evidently impressed in a mould. The exquisite modelling shows the mark of an individual sculptor. The large eyes with arched eyebrows, the fine nose and slightly opened, sensitive mouth are all clearly distinguishable from the images of deities who are depicted in a canonical static manner. It is interesting that the images of minor personages in Buddhist plastic art are more dynamic and vital than the figures of Buddha or *bodhisattva*s seated or standing in a ceremonial fixed position that emphasizes the importance of their action or posture. While the divine images follow the canonical iconography, donors and adorants portray individuals, usually of the local nobility.

Among the sculptural fragments from Karatepa, the relief of a Buddha stands out. It was found in a layer covering the *sufa* in the south-eastern part of the court.[256] On the preserved part can be seen the garment, which consists of a tight-fitting mantle without folds. There are relief bands on both arms – on the shoulder and the elbow – in the shape of a plait. The hands are shown in *dhyana-mudra*. The representation of a tree in the same manner as on the Fayaztepa 'Triad', in this case as a wreath halo, is interesting. The elongated leaves distinctly resemble those of another sacred tree of Buddhist art, the *sala* (*Shorea robusta*) tree.

The Karatepa reliefs are not distinguished from those at Fayaztepa by the detail of the leaves alone. At Karatepa, the plastic modelling is simpler and rougher in comparison with the Fayaztepa reliefs with their finely modelled drapery. This roughness is not typical, however, of all plastic art of Karatepa; most likely it was caused by a different method employed by the sculptors. Another relief fragment from Karatepa showing a railing decorated by merlons has certain elements in common with Gandharan plastic art.[257] A similar decorative motif was noted on the stone relief above. A relief from Zurmala[258] is also decorated by merlons, similar to the railing on the relief from Karatepa.

The railing (*vedika*) on stone reliefs is an ornamental motif that was almost certainly inspired by the crenellation of sacred and secular buildings in both Gandhara and the entire Indian subcontinent. This architectural component was especially favoured on structures of Buddhist cult, for example, the *stupa*. Aside from the front gates (*torana*) that lavishly displayed reliefs illustrating the main events of the previous lives of Buddha (*jataka*s), the *vedika* was the most important part of the architectural decoration. The stone fragment from Karatepa with the representation of a railing probably came from a relief on the base of a *stupa* or other cult object. It should be pointed out that despite numerous finds of stone reliefs, the great statue of Buddha was executed in clay (using the technique that combined alabaster with clay). Although, to date, sculpted stone bases (pedestals) for statues have not been found *in situ*, it may be presumed that these fragments were used as decorations of such bases.

A sculpture from Karatepa demonstrates the high quality of Bactrian clay plastic modelling. It represents the figure of Buddha seated in *padmasana*. His right hand is held up in *abhaya-mudra*, whilst his left hand grasps the folds of his garment. The skilfully modelled drapery manifests a combination of oblique (diagonal) folds falling from the left shoulder and vertical folds (Fig. 93). The sculpture was covered with alabaster prime coating. Polychrome painting was executed over this prime coating and there remain traces of gilding.[259] The position of the folds resembles the relief with the Buddha from Fayaztepa mentioned above.

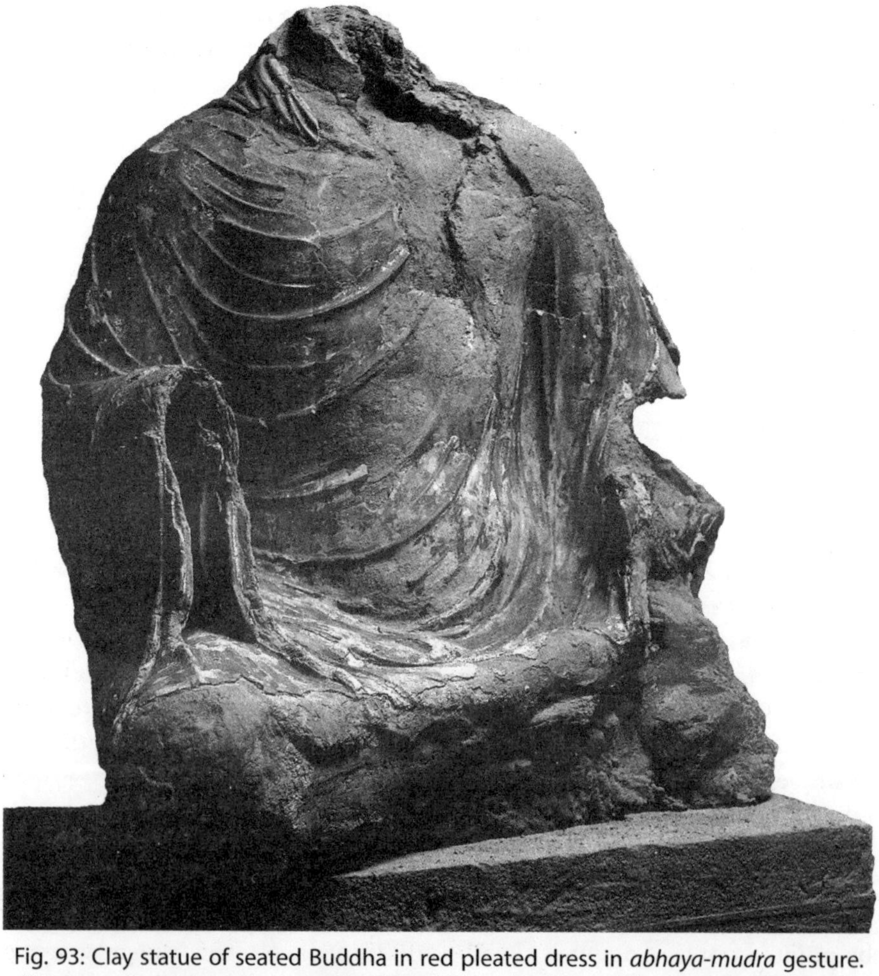

Fig. 93: Clay statue of seated Buddha in red pleated dress in *abhaya-mudra* gesture. Karatepa. 2nd-4th century AD. 97 × 59 × 84 cm. (Institute of Restoration, Moscow).

Donors and Adorants

Frequently, images of donors and adorants portrayed living persons or typified a specific ethnic community. In particular, the sculptor endeavoured to capture the traits of an individual who was making devout offerings to the temple or society. It is unlikely that a sculpture would immortalize a common donor. Probably, specific donors were members of the aristocracy or representatives of the authorities.

The recent excavations at Karatepa,[260] which concentrated on the northern and western hills, have unearthed new sculptures of Buddhist character (Fig. 94). In the northern part of the monastery complex, a large stupa was discovered (Fig. 95). Originally it had a two-stepped triangular

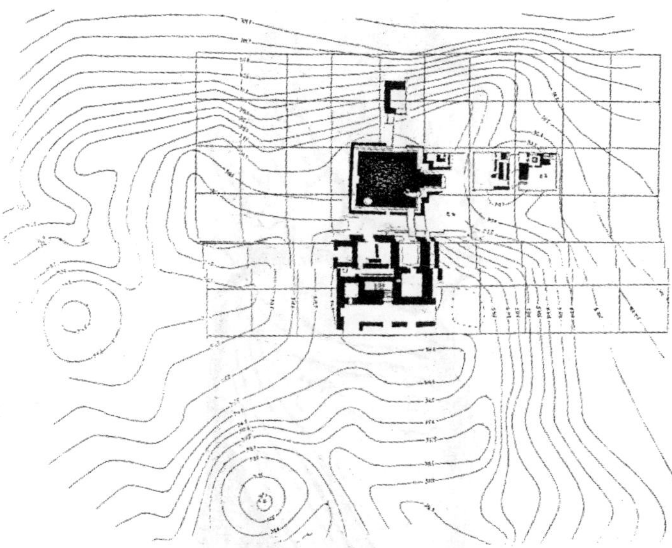

Fig. 94: Northern hill of Karatepa. Plan of excavation. (After Sh. Pidaev, K. Kato, 2000, fig. 3). Plan of Western hill of Karatepa. (After Sh. Pidaev, K. Kato, 2000a, fig. 4).

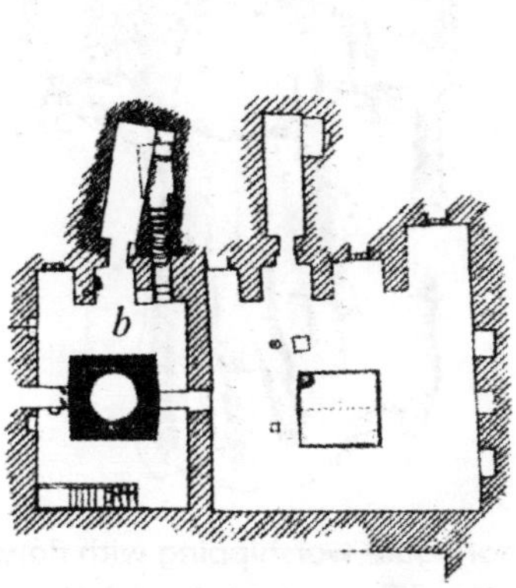

Fig. 95: Karatepa. Plan of western hill. (After Sh. Pidaev, K. Kato, 2000, fig. 2).

platform with the sides measuring in the east 14.67 m; south 22.39 m and west 14.38 m.[261] The perimeter of the *stupa* was surrounded by a corridor. Here, sculptural decoration included figures of female donors and Garuda, as well as other architectural details in stone.[262]

A pair of donors is shown in an identical pose of offering and worshipping. Their hands on their breasts are holding flowers in a gesture of veneration. The female figure wears a long dress in the local style, draped with a pleated scarf around the body (Fig. 96). The male figure wears a long shirt fastened by a black belt (Fig. 97). Another stone relief fragment was accidentally found in the area of the northern hill.[263] This relief represents the bust of an individual that, according to the hand pose, must have been a donor; the lower part of the bust is cut by a groove with a projecting

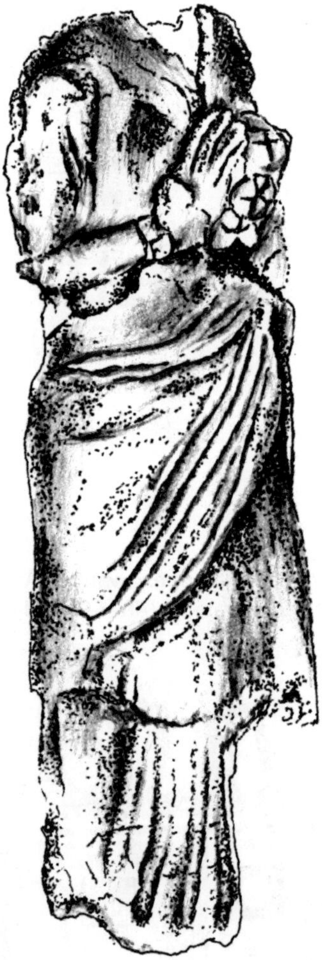

Fig. 96: Clay female donor figure worshipping with flowers in hands. Karatepa. 3rd-4th century AD. H = 35 cm. (Institute of Archaeology, Samarkand).

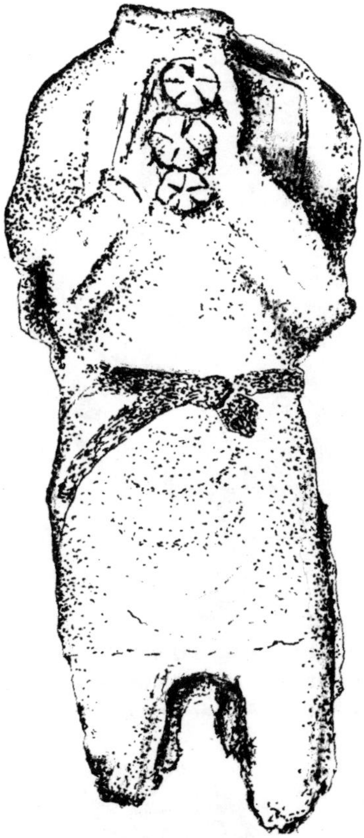

Fig. 97: Clay male donor figure worshipping with flowers in hands. Karatepa. 3rd-4th century AD. H = 30 cm. (Institute of Archaeology, Samarkand).

edge (Fig. 98). Apparently, the piece came from the spandrel of an arch with Buddha in the centre. A fragment of another figure could have belonged to the same type of decoration. It demonstrates an individual in a long-pleated dress with a pectoral on the breast (Fig. 99). Yet another small fragment (measuring 4.2 × 7.2 × 5. 7 cm) of a stone relief shows three zoomorphic heads, which have been published as the 'three lions' motif.[264] However, from their strange composition, a totally different conclusion might be drawn. The long necks with two vertical relief lines beginning just under the heads, and horizontally incised parallel lines on both sides of the latter, resemble serpent heads, perhaps cobras with hoods (Fig. 100). This element is above all associated with the Nagaraja, whose head usually is designed with a halo of 'standing' cobras.[265] Alternatively, the serpents can be an attribute of other personages related to Naga in Buddhist mythology. During a certain period (in his incarnation) before becoming Buddha, Shakyamuni was a Naga.[266]

Among the finds of plastic works is a fragment of a warrior in chain-

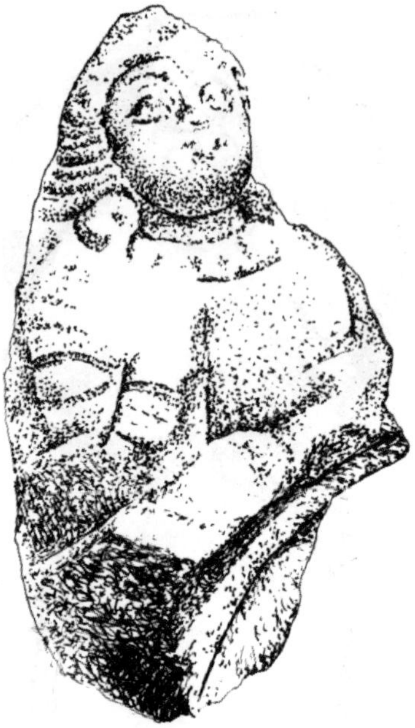

Fig. 98: Stone relief fragment showing a donor figure in the tympanis of an arch. Surface find. Karatepa area. 3rd-4th century AD. 10 × 17 cm. (Institute of Archaeology, Samarkand).

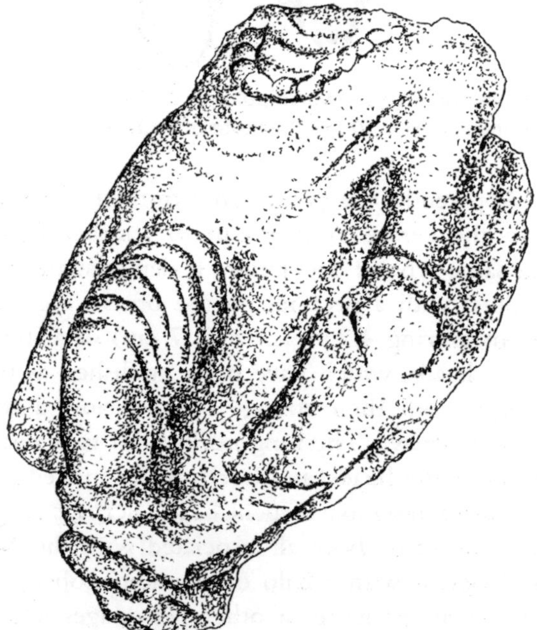

Fig. 99: Stone relief fragment showing a donor figure in a long-pleated shirt with decoration on the breast. Karatepa. 3rd-4th century AD. H = 18.5 cm. (Institute of Archaeology, Samarkand).

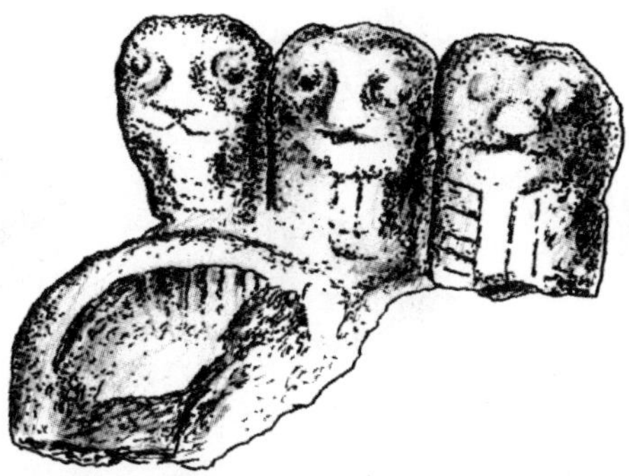

Fig. 100: Stone relief fragment showing three cobra heads (Nagaraja ?). Karatepa. 3rd-4th century AD. 4.2 × 7.2 × 5.7 cm. (Institute of Archaeology, Samarkand).

mail armour fastened by strips (Fig. 101).[267] There are also heads of distinguished personages including donors, *devatas*, *bodhisattvas*, and Buddha (Fig. 102) from scenes of the *jatakas* or other compositions of Buddhist iconography. A special find was a mould for casting the head of a Buddha.[268]

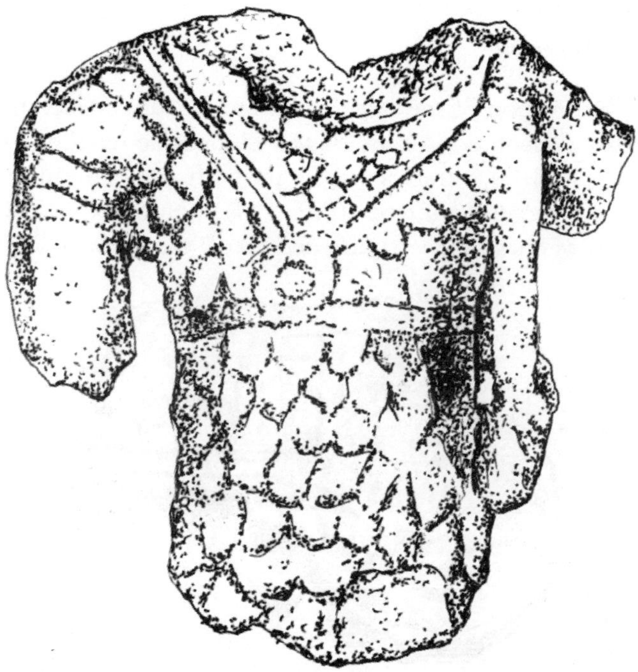

Fig. 101: Stone relief fragment showing a figure of a warrior. Karatepa. 3rd-4th century AD. H = 8.5 cm. (Institute of Archaeology, Samarkand).

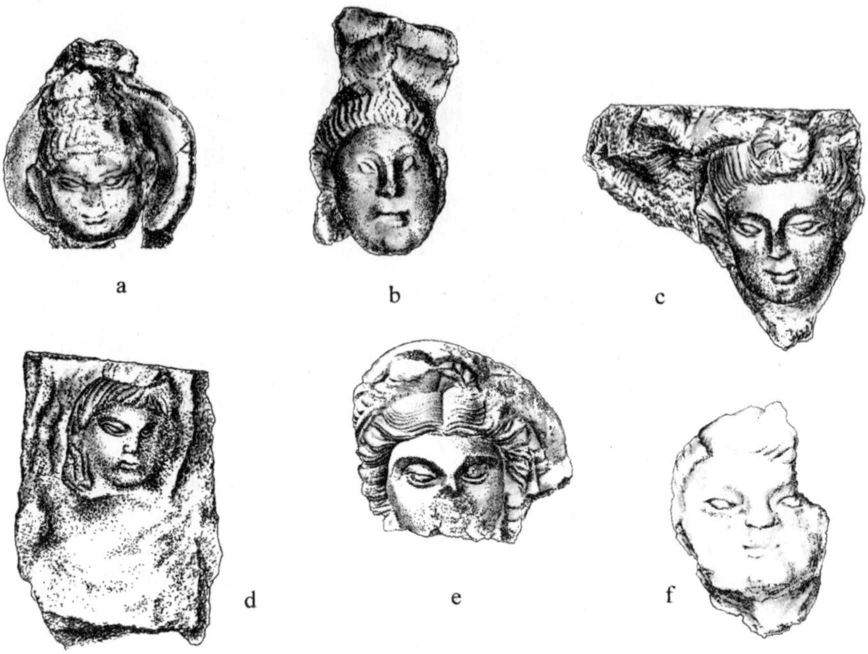

Fig. 102: Stone relief fragments showing representations of a - Buddha(?), b - *bodhisattva* (?), c, e - *devatas* (?) and d, f - adorants (?). Karatepa. 3rd-4th century AD. (Institute of Archaeology, Samarkand).

Architectural Decoration

During the excavation of the *stupa* much architectural decoration came to light. The stone decoration of the *stupa* included the relief of a tondo with an elephant (Fig. 103), a fragment of a portal frame entirely covered with geometric and vegetal motives (Fig. 104), column bases, and friezes. Obviously, all of these pieces once decorated the *stupa*. The sides of the

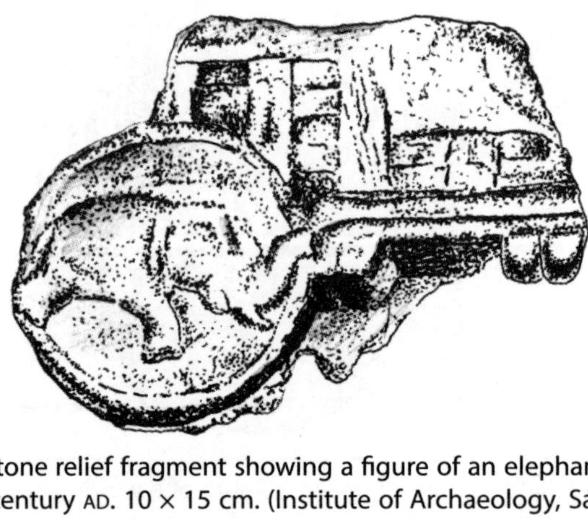

Fig. 103: Stone relief fragment showing a figure of an elephant. Karatepa. 3rd-4th century AD. 10 × 15 cm. (Institute of Archaeology, Samarkand).

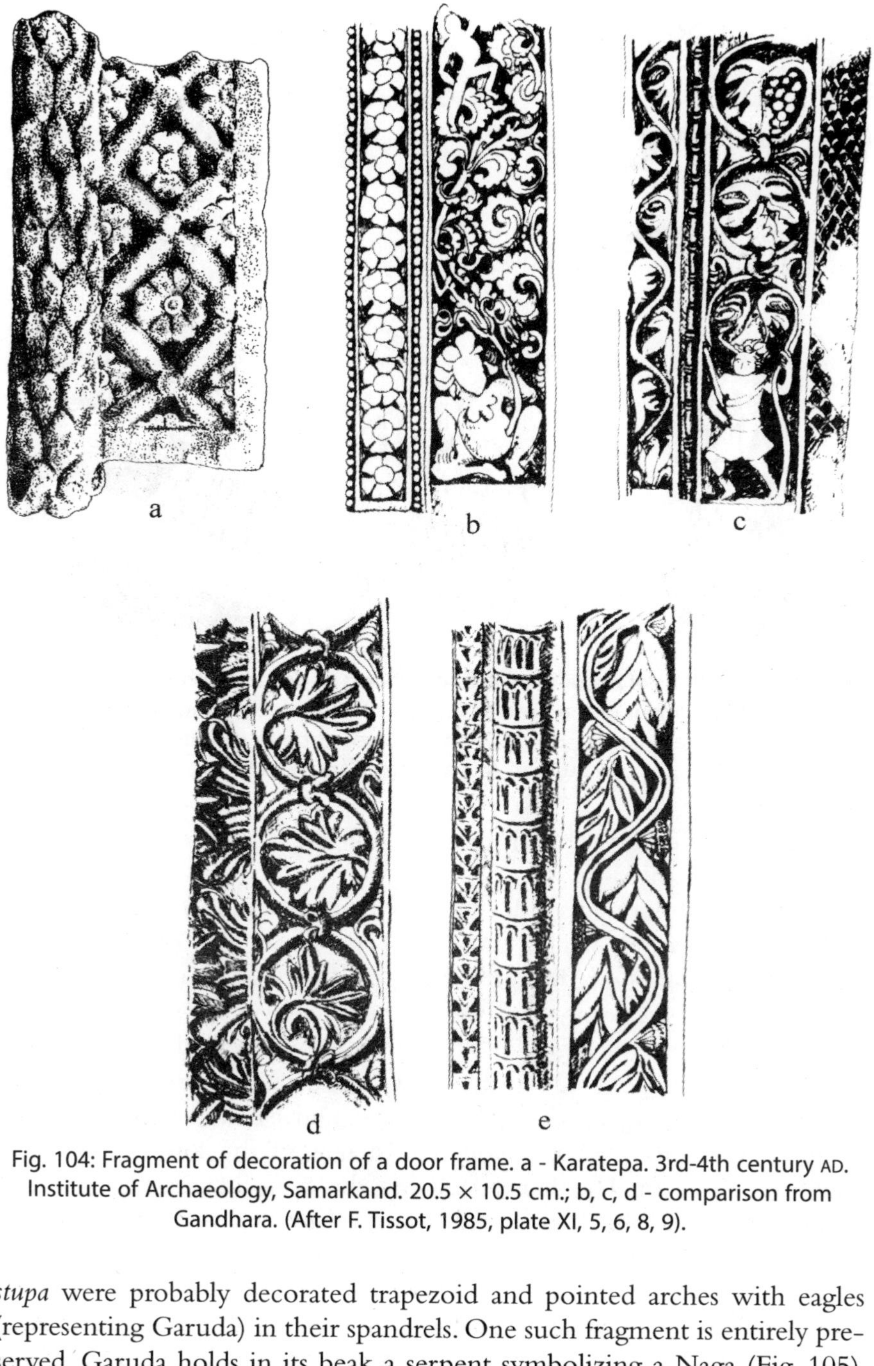

Fig. 104: Fragment of decoration of a door frame. a - Karatepa. 3rd-4th century AD. Institute of Archaeology, Samarkand. 20.5 × 10.5 cm.; b, c, d - comparison from Gandhara. (After F. Tissot, 1985, plate XI, 5, 6, 8, 9).

stupa were probably decorated trapezoid and pointed arches with eagles (representing Garuda) in their spandrels. One such fragment is entirely preserved. Garuda holds in its beak a serpent symbolizing a Naga (Fig. 105). Another *stupa* was discovered during the excavation of the courtyard. It had an approximately square plan with the north side measuring 19.67 m and the west side 18.74 m. In the north wall, there were three entrances

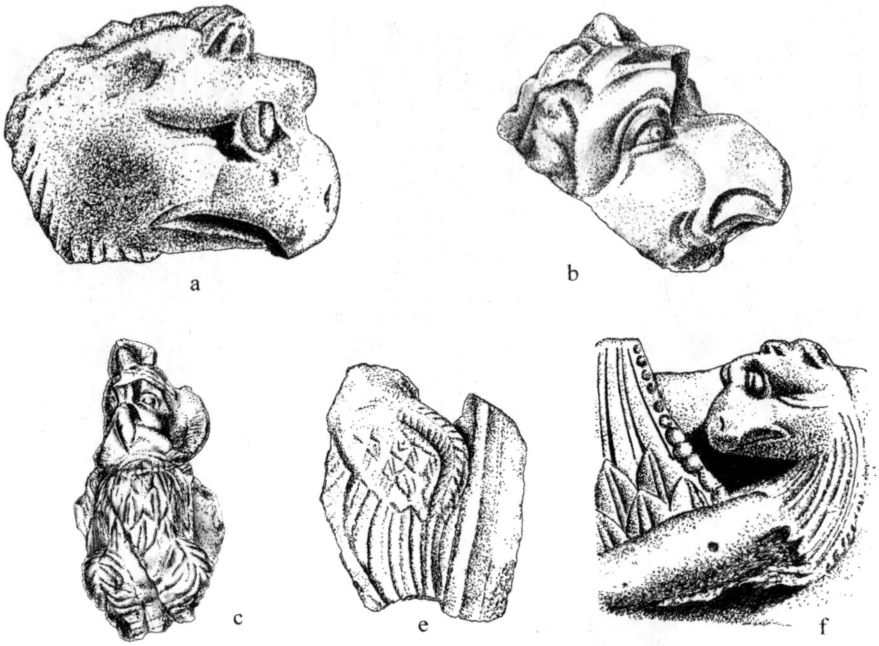

Fig. 105: Fragments of decoration: a, f - gryphons; c - Garuda with serpent in beak, H =15 cm; b - fragment of the head of Garuda, H = 9. 5 cm; e - fragment of a Garuda representation, H = 15.7 cm. Karatepa. 3rd-4th century AD. (Institute of Archaeology, Samarkand).

connecting the courtyard with the corridor. Eight bases of Attic columns were cleared in this area.

Room no. 11, located south of the southern corridor of the great *stupa*, is especially interesting. The entrance to the room was oriented to the courtyard of the *stupa*. In the centre of the room another *stupa* was discovered, of which only the two-stepped platform is extant. The latter forms a square measuring 2.70 × 2.60 m. It was erected using unbaked bricks measuring 32 × 32 × 12 cm. The platform was originally painted red and later, during a second phase, black. During the last period it was simply covered by plaster (*ganch*). The height of the lower step of the platform is 97 cm. The upper step has the same height with its sides diminished to 1.86 × 1.76 m and decorated by petals of lotus blossoms. Originally, the petals were painted in pink, but were later whitewashed.[269] The lower step of the platform was decorated by five niches under trapezoidal and pointed arches that rest on Corinthian pilasters with Attic bases. The arches were executed in clay and painted in red. The central arch was trapezoidal, flanked by two pointed arches. The insides of the niches were painted and under the central arch stood the figure of Buddha. In the lateral niches, there were figures of worshippers, who were turned

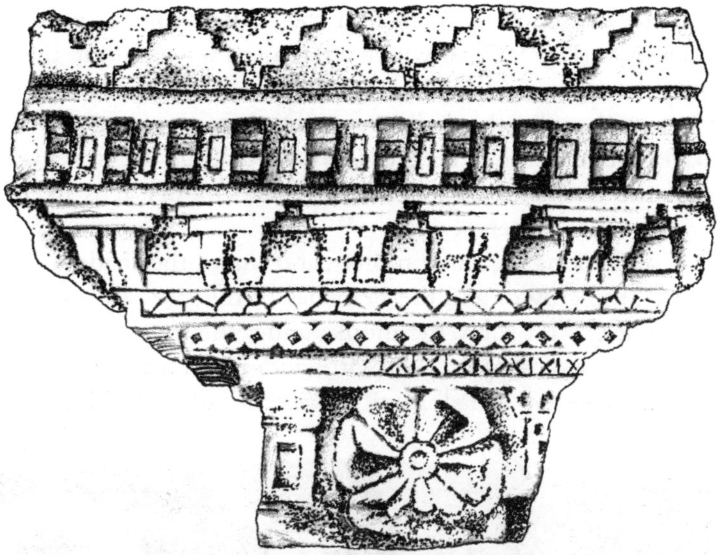

Fig. 106: Fragment of a *harmika* – element of *stupa* decoration. Karatepa. 3rd-4th century AD. 35 × 30 cm. (Institute of Archaeology, Samarkand).

slightly towards the main image of the Buddha. Another interesting detail of this composition is the birds present in the spandrels. The eagle-like birds resembling Garuda with open wings are very close to the Gandharan reliefs.[270] One of the most significant finds in this area was a fragment of a richly decorated *harmika* (Fig. 106), which belonged to the ornamentation of the upper part of the *stupa*.

On the western hill of Karatepa, complexes A and B were excavated. In this section a row of monks' caves (cells) was unearthed. As usual, there was a courtyard with a *stupa* and other cult objects. The *stupa* comprised a square platform (measuring 3.94 × 3.94 m) and a cylindrical body (whose diameter measures 2.25 m) which was covered by plaster (*ganch*) and painted red. The statue of a seated Buddha, a donor and other sculptural fragments were also found.[271]

The main period when all the recently discovered complexes at Karatepa were functioning has been dated to the Kushan and Late Kushan periods, including the time of Kanishka III. After the invasion of the Sassanian kings (between the late 3rd and the first half of the 4th century AD), the Karatepa buildings and caves were deserted and transformed into burials.

Wall Paintings

From the fragments that have come down to us, it is difficult to form an impression of the lost wall paintings from Karatepa and to comprehend their subjects. However, to a certain degree one can ascertain the methods employed by the artists. For instance, in the scene showing monks and Buddha under trees (Fig. 107), of which a fragment was found in the court of complex B, the figure of Buddha in *padmasana* is surrounded by a halo. The deity is seated under the *bodhi* tree, whose form is outlined against the dark background of the tree. Its leaves and fruits are schematically drawn. Given the brilliance and richness of the colours, it is likely that they were restored in a later period.

To the left of Buddha are three monks, also under the shadow of trees. Like the figures, the crowns and the branches of the trees are executed in a primitive manner.[272] Probably, the monks under the trees were originally repeated to the right of Buddha. Notwithstanding certain deviations, this fragment is similar to the 'Triad' from Fayaztepa with Buddha under the

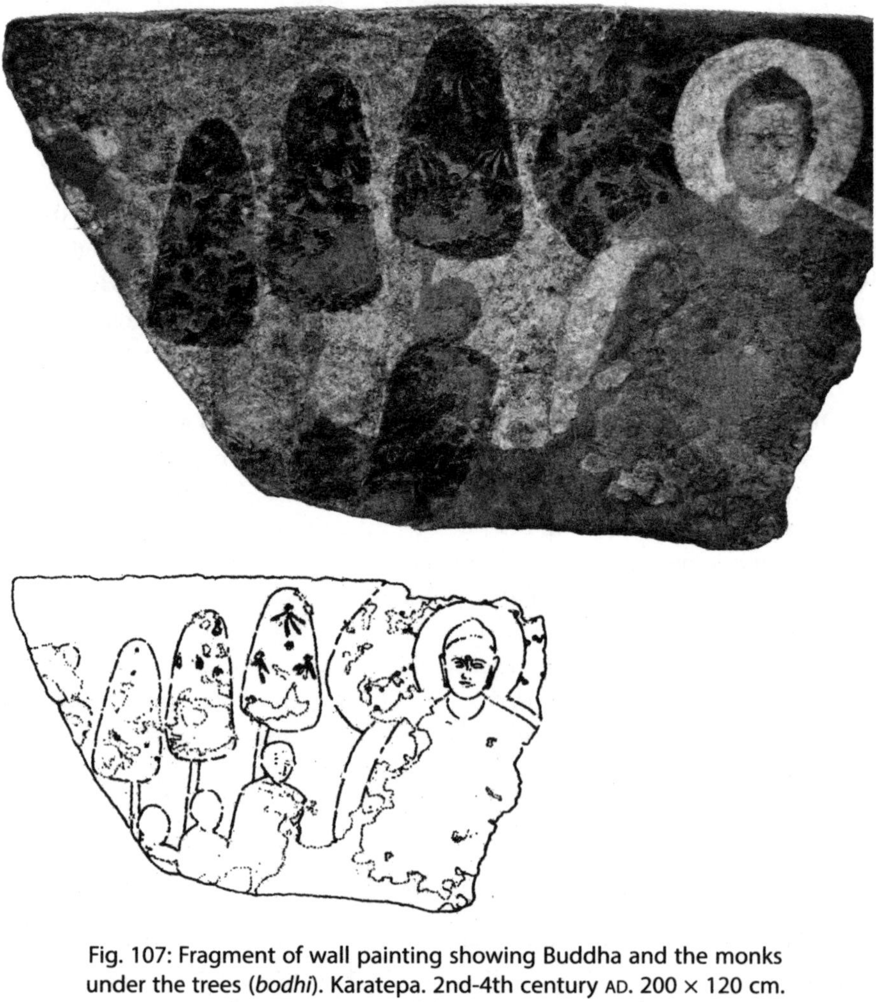

Fig. 107: Fragment of wall painting showing Buddha and the monks under the trees (*bodhi*). Karatepa. 2nd-4th century AD. 200 × 120 cm. (Russian Institute of Restoration, Moscow).

tree. Here at Karatepa, the artist tried to convey the inner calm of the main personage in meditation with slightly lowered eyelids and a fixed gaze.

The figure of the Buddha from the cave corridor of temple P-V in complex G is represented in a unique way, with the details carefully elaborated. For example, the folds of his long garment are more accurately portrayed (Fig. 108). They are finely draped and the garment has a round, low neckline. The hands are placed palms up on the crossed legs. The most interesting feature is the halo, composed of small sharp tongues of flames surrounding the figure. According to B.Ya. Staviskiy, this iconographic detail came from the traditional Buddha images by local artists.[273] Indeed, given the early date of the representation to the time of Kanishka and Huvishka, it would be difficult to find an analogy for this iconography elsewhere (in India, for example). Similar images of Buddha do occur in the art of eastern Turkestan, albeit during the later Early Medieval period.[274] This fact testifies to the influence of northern Bactrian art on neighbouring regions, where Buddhism found its adepts and was embodied in sculpture and wall painting.

For the reconstruction of the Karatepa wall paintings, it is helpful to discuss some other fragments which reflect the peculiarities of this region mentioned above in connection with the Fayaztepa wall paintings. These are the fragments from the southern wall of the southern *iwan* of complex B.[275] One of them shows thirteen feet that must have belonged to at least

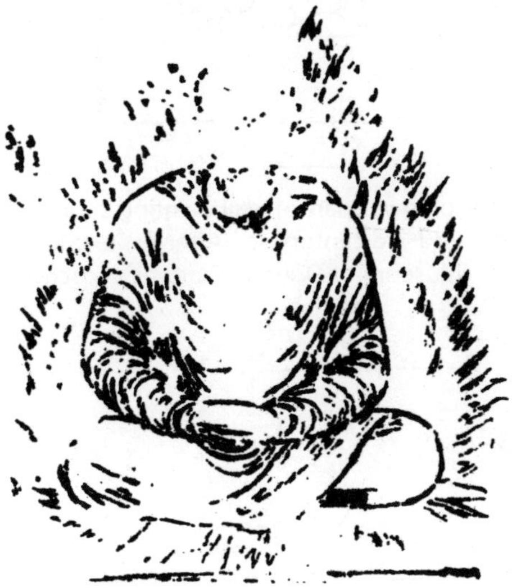

Fig. 108: Seated Buddha surrounded by tongues of flames. Fragment of wall painting in 'corridor room' P, complex G. Karatepa. 4th century AD. (Russian Institute of Restoration, Moscow).

six figures, plus an additional foot (Fig. 109). Apparently, the composition included four men and two women. The men's feet are turned outward and are wearing soft shoes with a clasp in the shape of a round buckle fastened at the inner ankle. The feet are clearly similar to those on the Fayaztepa fragment. The resemblance is intensified by the presence of two female figures wearing long dresses, whose feet are also similar to the Fayaztepa paintings (Fig. 110). The Karatepa composition most likely repeated the scene with donors as shown at Fayaztepa.

There is another distant analogy to the overall scheme of the Fayaztepa and Karatepa compositions. A row of frontally represented donors occurs on the wall painting from Dil'berjin, while at Karatepa a fragment of the wall painting from room no. 16 of the north-eastern cult complex depicts twelve standing persons, whose heads are also shown frontally.[276] The artistic style and form of the dress suggest a late Kushan and Kushano-Sassanian date for the paintings.[277]

Like the painting at Karatepa, the one from Dil'berjin had white priming over the clay plaster. Comparing the wall paintings of these two sites, in addition to the numerous common details, there is the most important subject of the figurative circle, namely the representation of Buddha. He

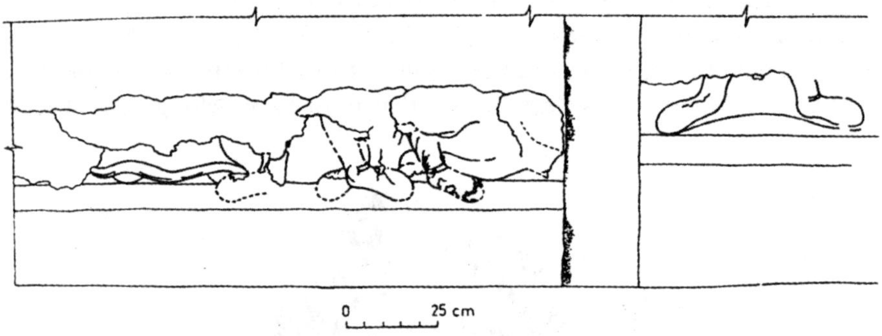

Fig. 109: Fragment of lower part of wall painting showing figures of donors. Karatepa. 2nd-3rd century AD. (After B. Staviskiy, 1979: 146) (Museum of Oriental Cultures, Moscow).

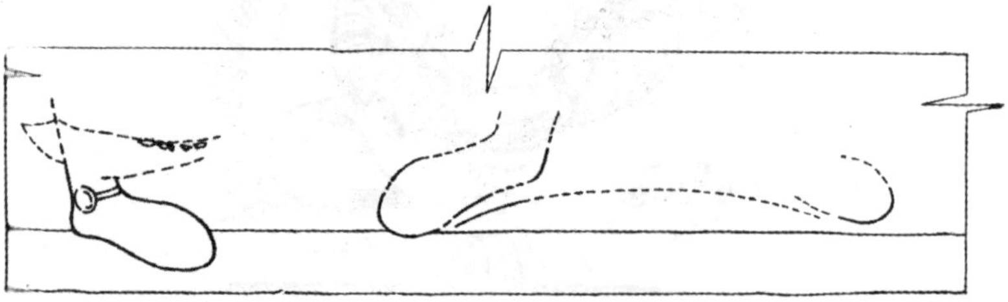

Fig. 110: Fragment of lower part of wall painting showing figures of worshippers and Buddha. Karatepa. 2nd-3rd century AD. (After B. Staviskiy, 1979, fig. 110) (Museum of Oriental Cultures, Moscow).

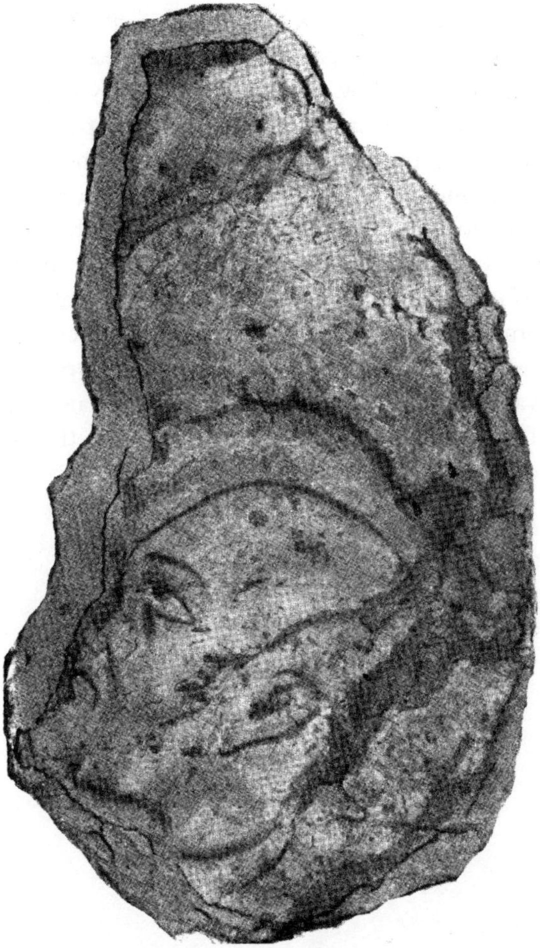

Fig. 111: Fragment of wall painting showing the head of a monk. Karatepa. 2nd-3rd century AD. (After B.Ya. Staviskiy, 1979, fig. 100) (Museum of Oriental Cultures, Moscow).

is represented as the central and main image, surrounded by monks, or a group of donors in Kushan dress, offering him gifts. Again, one can presuppose a frontal position for the figures, with their heads turned in profile. Indeed, one of the fragments seems to confirm this hypothesis. It shows the shaven head (Fig. 111) of an individual with upturned face.[278] Judging by the shaved head, this figure was probably a monk, like those on the Fayaztepa 'Triad' relief with Buddha in the centre.

Fayaztepa and Karatepa in the Cultural Context of Old Termez

Despite their outlying location, the complexes of Karatepa and Fayaztepa were nevertheless connected with the city of Old Termez and its cultural history, thereby forming an inseparable part of that city. Recent archaeological investigations at Old Termez, particularly at Chingiztepa and Fayaztepa, have supplied important new material for clarifying important issues. Archaeological excavation at Bol'shoy Chingiztepa (Big Chingiztepa) revealed a massive, well-preserved fortification system that had rectangular towers with rooms and an intra-mural passageway in the interior. On the basis of the archaeological finds, including ceramics, this structure has been dated to the first to second centuries AD, that is to say that it flourished during the Kushan period.[279] The fortified city wall ran from Maloe Chingiztepa (Small Chingiztepa) in a westerly direction. As subsequent archaeological work has verified, after reaching the top of the Chingiztepa mound this wall then turned sharply south toward the bank of the Amudarya.[280] Thus, the city wall of Old Termez left the Karatepa mound with all its Buddhist complexes outside the fortification system (Fig. 112).

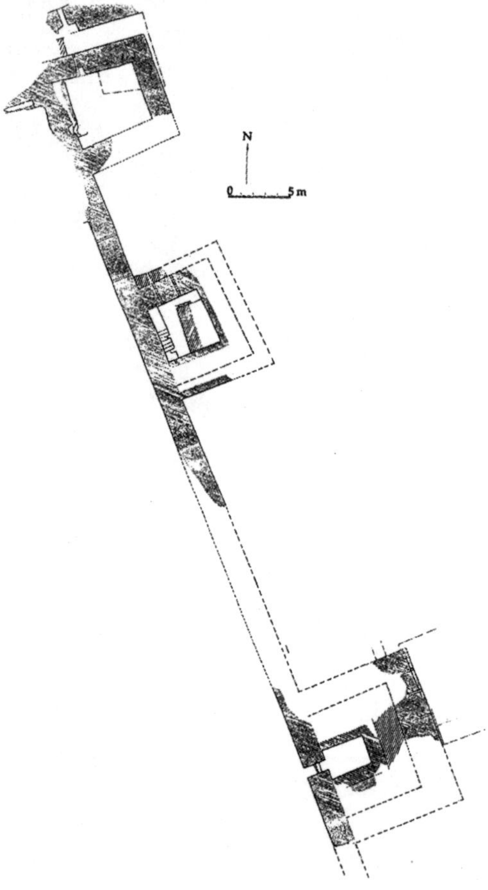

Fig. 112: Old Termez. Plan of the fortification system of the city walls. Section from the site Maloe Chingiztepa to Bol'shoe Chingiztepa with turning to the south (Amudarya bank direction). (After Sh. Pidaev and P. Leriche, 2003, fig. 1).

This fact deprives the site of Karatepa of its exclusive and privileged position, particularly in relation to Fayaztepa. Both of the Buddhist complexes – Karatepa and Fayaztepa – were located outside the walls of the ancient city.

One of the chief archaeological results at Old Termez was the discovery of a monumental building at the mound of Maloe Chingiztepa.[281] However, because of its ruinous state it is hard to reconstruct the original plan and elevation of the site. Stratigraphical research of this monument indicates three considerable reconstructions during its history.[282] The main rectangular room, aligned on a north to south axis, dates to the final phase of the late Kushan period. Only the eastern wall of this room is intact It was decorated with pilasters and *ganch* plaster. It would seem that the western wall was decorated in the same manner. A corridor ran along the hall on both the western and southern side. In this area, a limestone frieze was found with a representation of a Garuda. Schematically and stylistically, the relief of the eagle resembles again Gandharan examples. Another limestone relief is significant because of its composition, a fragment on which it is possible to make out the lower part of a human figure in a long dress with cascading pleats. To the right, there is a larger figure seated in *padmasana* pose (Fig. 113). Only its left knee is preserved, although neither the high throne nor any drapery is visible. Evidently, we have here a Buddhist composition showing a seated Buddha and flanking adorants, as in the 'Triad' from Fayaztepa and numerous analogies among Mathuran and Gandharan works.

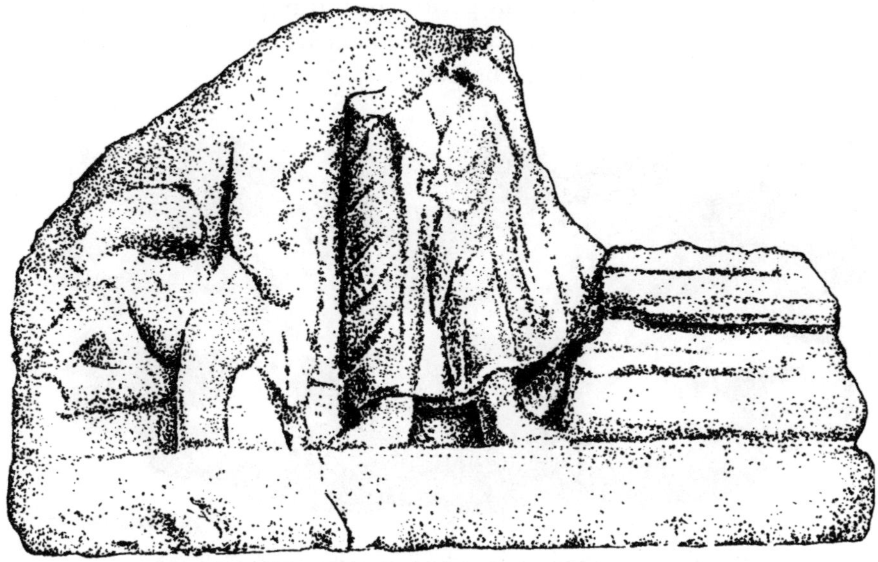

Fig. 113: Stone relief fragment showing a seated Buddha with an individual beside him. Old Termez (Maloe Chingiztepa). 2nd-4th century AD. (Termez Archaeological Museum).

According to the excavators, in its final phase, meaning 'not earlier than the late Kushan period and not later than Kushano-Sassanid time', this building could have functioned as a Buddhist temple.[283]

Another significant discovery at Old Termez was made within the western city wall. Here, under a nineteenth or twentieth-century dwelling, the base of a *stupa* was unearthed.[284] In spite of its complete destruction by medieval occupation it is possible to trace a square plan measuring 1.20 × 1.20 m, with a niche in the centre of each side. In the niche on the eastern side a fragment of sculpture was preserved. The pleats of a long dress indicate that it could have belonged to a Buddhist figure. The platform of the *stupa* was covered with *ganch* plaster. In this area, a lot of architectural fragments such as pilaster capitals and cornices were also found. In all probability, these fragments had once decorated a monumental building (a temple?). One of the pilaster capitals is typical of the architectural style of the Kushan period: a human figure with a gesture resembling *abhaya-mudra* is placed in the centre of the composition (Fig. 114). Below, on both sides, are acanthus leaves, while volutes with triangular dentils fill the upper part. This capital is very close to one cited by Staviskiy, also from Old Termez.[285] The compositional scheme on the pilaster capital resembles the reliefs on the Airtam friezes and is also reminiscent of the reliefs from Butkara (in the Swat Valley, Pakistan).[286]

Thus, based on the archaeological investigation of the area of Chingiztepa and along the western part of the city wall of Old Termez, it might be possible to propose the existence of a temple or other sacred structure (for example a shrine) in the Kushan period. In this respect, another example of an intramural temple comes to mind, namely Dal'verzintepa, with its remarkable sculptures discussed below.

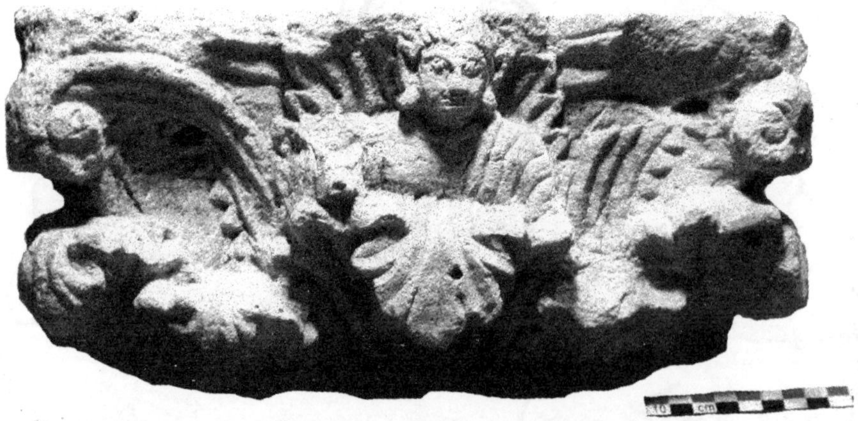

Fig. 114: Pilaster capital showing Buddha in acanthus leafs with *abhaya-mudra* gesture. Old Termez (Maloe Chingiztepa). 2nd-4th century AD. (Termez Archaeological Museum).

The recent excavations at Fayaztepa, which are still awaiting publication, provide new data for the original plan of the Buddhist monastery and its periodization. T. Annaev, who is in charge of the project, believes that the beginnings of Fayaztepa can be established from the ceramic complex found on the floor of the dwellings of the monastery.[287] These ceramics include cylindrical or conical goblets and vessels made of the so-called 'grey clay' that was in use between the first century BC and the first century AD. No less important were the finds of numerous ostraca inscriptions in Brahmi, Kharoshthi, and Bactrian, on the site. It is hoped that the deciphering of these texts will elucidate lingering questions about the relation of Fayaztepa to Karatepa and Old Termez in general. So far the archaeological evidence facilitates the assumption that the Fayaztepa monastery preceded Karatepa.

Leaving aside the still undeciphered inscriptions, the recent archaeological discoveries at Old Termez permit the following inferences about its Buddhist monuments: there are two great monasteries outside the city walls. Both seem to have flourished under Kanishka (2nd century AD). Topographically, the Fayaztepa Vihara was situated on the road approaching the city and the pilgrims would have visited it first, as with the modern traffic pattern, which more or less follows its ancient precursor. Clearly, Karatepa, with its location near the banks of the Amudarya, would have been more out of the way. Chronologically, on the basis of our current knowledge, Fayaztepa presents material from the first century BC to the first century AD, pointing to an earlier Buddhist foundation in this region than Karatepa. Its rich decoration also speaks for its privileged position in an earlier period. Hypothetically, there was also a Buddhist temple inside the city walls of Old Termez, the existence of which is borne out by numerous fragments of sculpture with purely Buddhist subjects.

Airtam

This site is best known for the discovery of remarkable reliefs showing busts of musicians and individuals with goblets, representing a banquet scene or images of donors. The first archaeological investigations at Airtam were conducted by the Termez Archaeological Complex Expedition led by M.E. Masson in 1933 and in 1939, and were of a preliminary nature (Fig. 115). However, even these early investigations comprised considerable material for the study of the history of the art and culture of the region. A reliquary, a square base possibly of a *stupa* and stone fragments of architectural details have been found here.[288] The Airtam reliefs, published many times in different editions, are central to the history of sculptural art of northern Bactria.[289] The Uzbekistan History of Art Expedition under the direction of B. Turgunov continued the excavations in 1964-6.[290]

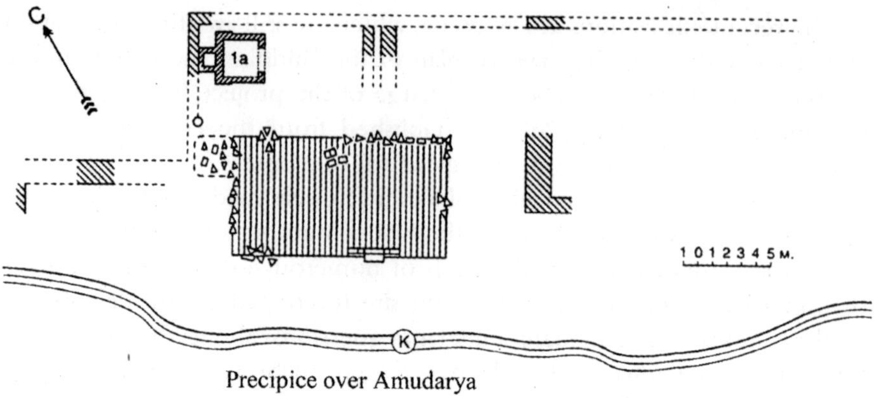

Fig. 115: Plan of Airtam. (After M.E. Masson, 1940a, fig. 1).

Airtam stood 18 km to the east of Termez on the Amudarya River and today comprises a group of separate hills of different dimensions and configurations.[291] During excavations, the remains of a Buddhist *stupa* were discovered (Fig. 116). The remains of the buildings have been dated between the second century BC and the first to third century AD.[292] However, the

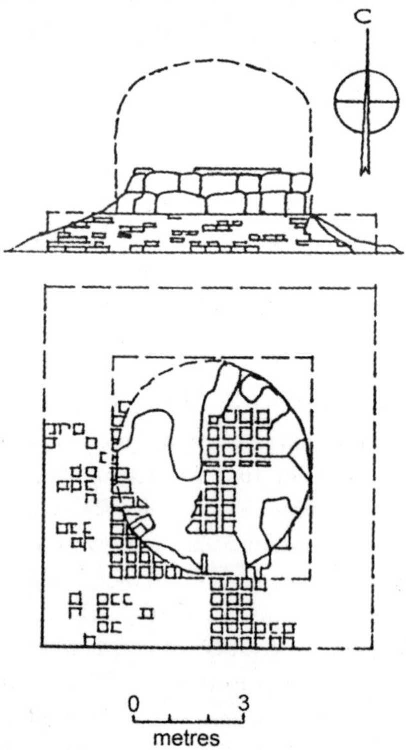

Fig. 116: *Stupa* of Airtam. 1st-2nd century AD. (After M.E. Masson, 1940a, fig. 2).

Airtam reliefs are the most outstanding monuments of this site. They were carved in high relief from a particular type of limestone. Their composition alternates between human half-figures and acanthus leaves (Fig. 117). In the foreground, there is a row of smaller acanthus leaves. The deeply carved veins of the leaves radiate from a central stem, creating contrasts of light and shade. The upper part of the acanthus leaves curls forward as if bent down. It should be noted that the contrast of light and shade lends the reliefs a certain dynamism. The human half-figures are almost lost among the huge acanthus leaves. The design is constant in both the smaller, lower leaves, and the larger, upper leaves, and manifests the same manner of modelling.

The human half-figures have different hair styles, dress, and jewellery, but share the same face modelling. The figure on the left holding a bi-conical percussion instrument has short hair, represented by separately curling strands falling on a broad, smooth forehead (Fig. 118). This individual has large eyes and arched eyebrows. The face is sufficiently impassive for a musician. There is only a faint smile represented by slight depressions at the corners of the mouth. The same can be said of the two other figures. In the centre of the composition is a figure draped in a shawl and playing a stringed instrument similar to a lute (Fig. 119). The forefinger and thumb squeeze a plectrum. The hair is shown under the shawl in the shape of circular curls.

The third figure from the right holds a harp (*harp angular*) against the breast and is distinguished from the previous two figures by its hair style. This consists of separate strands of straight hair combed down on the forehead, where they are twisted and cut in a fringe (Fig. 120). Above the middle of the forehead, there is a diamond shaped depression indicating the parting of the hair. From the lower point of the diamond shape hangs a cord with a pendant in the form of a heart.

The composition of half figures with acanthus leaves finds parallels in

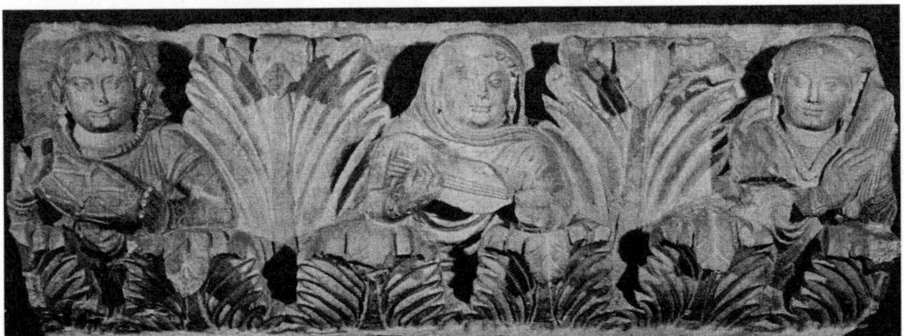

Fig. 117: Stone relief. Airtam. 2nd-3rd century AD.
(The State Hermitage Museum, St. Petersburg).

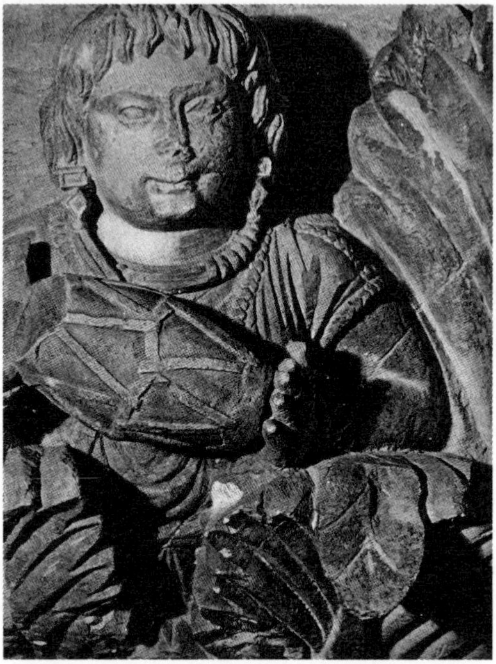

Fig. 118: Relief showing representation of a musician with biconical percussion instrument. 2nd-3rd century AD. Airtam. Limestone. (The State Hermitage Museum, St. Petersburg).

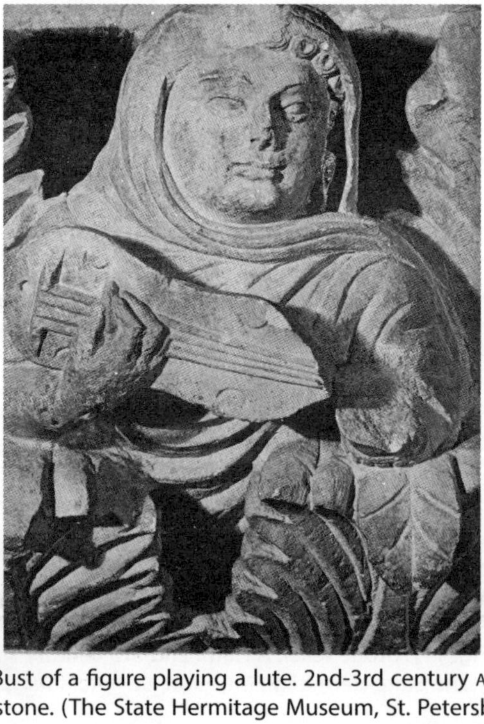

Fig. 119: Bust of a figure playing a lute. 2nd-3rd century AD. Airtam. Limestone. (The State Hermitage Museum, St. Petersburg).

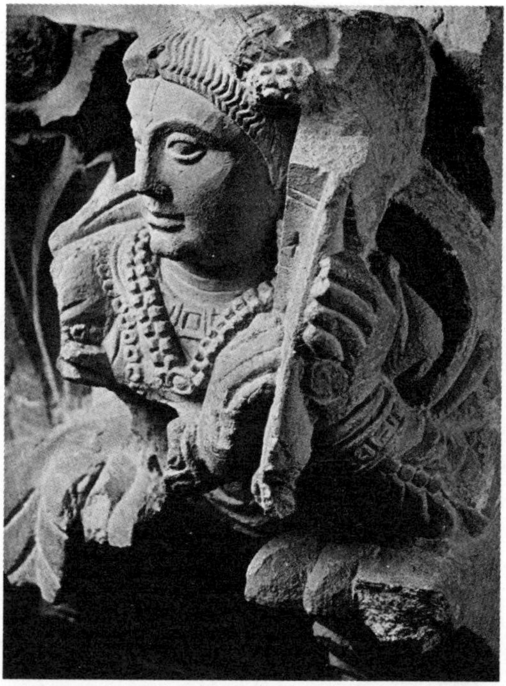

Fig. 120: Bust of a figure playing a harp. 2nd-3rd century AD. Airtam. Limestone. (The State Hermitage Museum, St. Petersburg).

the art of Gandhara. For example, on the frieze from Butkara dated to the period of Stupa no. 3 (first century BC–first century AD) is a relief of a couple, flanked on one side by an acanthus leaf.[293] Rosettes decorate the space between the figures and above them is an ornamental band with lions' heads combined with lotus flowers, flanked again on one side by an acanthus leaf. The relief from Butkara is superior both in artistic style and technique (bas-relief), but the combination of figures with a large acanthus leaf can be seen as a prototype for the later Airtam reliefs. In the Kushan period, as noted above, the vegetal motif is often employed as a background on scenes showing variations of this composition. The masters skilfully used the components of the orders of columns such as acanthus leave and volutes. A capital from Karatepa (in painted limestone) demonstrates how eclectic the pseudo-Corinthian style had become, with the inclusion of human figures and animals (a zebu bull).[294] Such free improvization as we have observed was characteristic not only of Gandharan art, but was also clearly mastered by the Bactrians. In any case, the distinctive appearance of the Airtam reliefs was achieved by combining well-known elements.

Among the terracotta statuettes found at Airtam is a figurine draped in a pleated dress and seated on a low pedestal. The position of the pleats and their scheme, in addition to the posture of the hands, resembles a Buddhist personage, maybe Buddha himself. The figure was found in a stratified context and the complex including this figurine is dated by the coins of Kanishka.[295]

DAL'VERZINTEPA

Investigation of this site has produced a wealth of material for the Buddhist plastic art of *Chaganian*. The striking and original character of the sculptural works of the Dal'verzintepa masters distinguishes this complex as an independent school of sculpture with its own peculiarities. From the outset of the excavations at Dal'verzintepa, archaeologists were surprised by the rich finds of wall paintings, sculpture, and terracotta figurines. Especially stunning was the unearthing of a hoard of gold objects of superb artistic quality, including gold bars with Kharoshthi inscriptions.[296] The excavation of the interior of the site, including the complex known as the 'House of a Rich Citizen', and also the temple and the crafts centre (Fig. 121), yielded

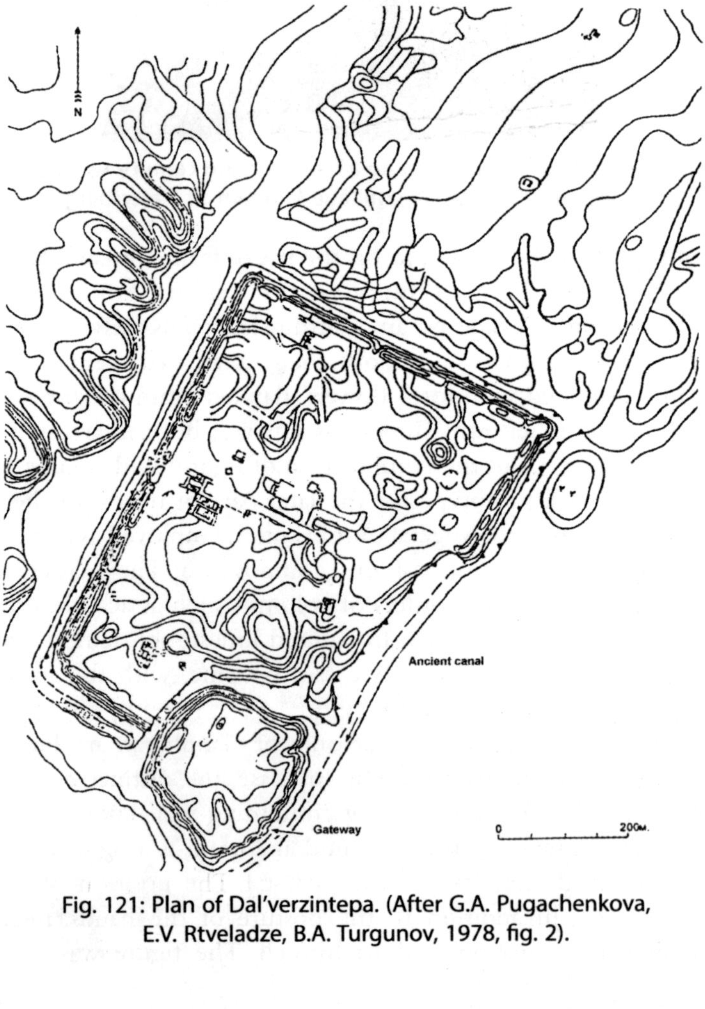

Fig. 121: Plan of Dal'verzintepa. (After G.A. Pugachenkova, E.V. Rtveladze, B.A. Turgunov, 1978, fig. 2).

large amounts of pottery, terracotta plastic art, sculpture, jewellery, and more.[297] During the 1980s, several sculptural masterpieces were discovered that had once decorated the Buddhist temple inside the city.[298] Their interesting archaeological aspects will be discussed below, but let us first summarize the general traits of the site and the main results of the excavations.

A Buddhist Shrine in an Urban Environment (DT-1)

For the study of the sculptural art of Dal'verzintepa, one monument situated outside the fortification system is exceptional.[299] The complex stands on a natural hill, 400 m to the north of the city wall (Fig. 122). It has been dated to the Kushan period, and it is possible that it was a sort of monastery or *vihara,* similar to those at Fayaztepa and Karatepa. The structure was cut from the rock (loess), preserving in the centre the shape of the base of a *stupa*. The surrounding floors were cut deeper than the level of the *stupa,* using at the same time the natural loess of the hill to form the walls. The central part (measuring 8 × 7-7.70m) was surrounded on three sides by long, narrow, inter-connected rooms. In the northern part of the complex (measuring 5.5 × 1.8 m) was a hall for rituals, as indicated by the finds of sculptures, including a large figure of Buddha and *devata*s. Numerous lamps were found here. A narrow passage connected the above-mentioned rooms with the western room (measuring 9.9 × 2.35 m) of the sanctuary, designated the 'Hall of the Kings'. It contained a group of sculptures of Buddha, monks, rulers and their retinues. The burnt clay and the lamp fragments indicate the lighting of fires here, possibly in veneration.[300]

The numismatic finds in the plaster of room no. 6 date the shrine to the time of the Soter Megas and Vima Kadphises mints.[301] According to the stratigraphic evidence, the destruction of the shrine took place in Late

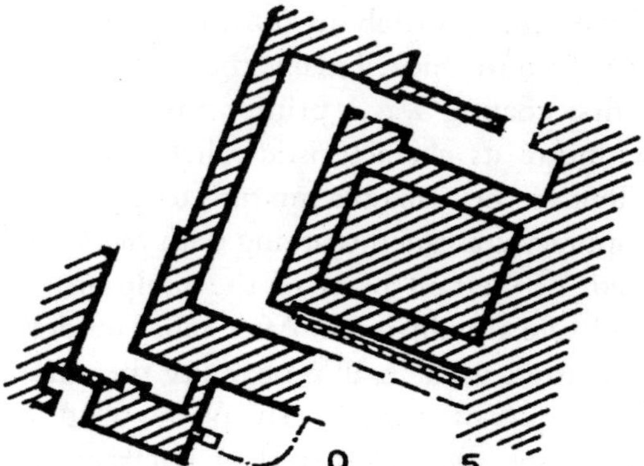

Fig. 122: Dal'verzintepa. Plan of the shrine outside of the city (DT-1). (After G.A. Pugachenkova, E.V. Rtveladze, B.A. Turgunov, 1978, fig. 60).

Antiquity (first century AD), when many statues of the divinities of the Buddhist pantheon were deliberately smashed. The figure of the Buddha in particular was vandalized. Only fragments of the headdress, the hands, and the feet are left. Figures of secondary importance such as donors or adorants fared better.[302] Archaeologically, the period of destruction and abandonment can be related to a 'mass grave'[303] occupying a small space (measuring 2.5 × 2 m) over accumulation layers (50 cm thick). The ceramic shards that were found *in situ* are dated from the end of the second to the third century AD.

Most interesting are the finds of alabaster sculptures that decorated the interior of the cult rooms. Near the northern entrance to the small 'Room of the Idols', excavators exposed a pit, 80 cm deep.[304] Here, fragments in red clay and alabaster as well as discarded parts of statues (mould-made fingers and drapery of the dress) were deposited. All of these pieces had been used as fill for the pit, which, after the completion of the sanctuary, was covered over by the plaster of the floor.[305] Evidently, even the defective parts of venerated sculpture were considered sacred; they were not thrown out, but buried in consecrated ground.

Traces of another structure connected with the Buddhist complex were found in the south-western part of the shrine, approximately 50 m away.[306] The architecture of this structure is poorly preserved, and only cultural layers have been found, containing ceramics from the Kushan period.

The sculptures found in the so-called Buddhist shrine of Dal'verzintepa consisted of numerous heads and other fragments. The majority of these were executed in alabaster mixed with clay and with traces of painting. The core of the sculpture was first executed in clay and affixed to a wooden frame. As the sculptures were hollow, they required the presence of wooden rods. The core was then covered with cloth rags and a plaster cast was taken from it. Onto this layer the finer features were modelled in alabaster. The drapery of the figure was about 5.8 mm thick, while the details of the head were 25-30 mm thick. Finally, the alabaster shell was coated in two layers. The first coating was a primer, the second a modelling layer that gave the sculpture its characteristic relief. Most likely, the sculptors added an ingredient to the alabaster mixture to slow down the hardening process – contemporary craftsmen working with *ganch* use a gum (vegetable glue) called *sheresh*.[307] Certain parts of the sculpture were modelled by hand, while some were mould-made. After relief modelling, the sculpture was painted. The masters used, in all probability, the same paints as for wall painting. The technique of using a clay plaster cast (alabaster) with an organic core is very specific and typical of Bactrian sculpture. Evidently, this combination had Bactrian origins. There is an early example in the Ai Khanum sculpture, dated to the third and second centuries BC.[308] The same technique of sculptural painting can be observed at Fayaztepa.

The excavators interpreted the Dal'verzintepa sculptures as Buddhist figures and their adepts, donors and adorants.[309] In the ceremonial room, fragments of a large statue were also found, which in all probability had been surrounded by adorants and devatas. A bare head, evidently of a monk (Fig. 123), is likely to have been part of the same image. The head was modelled in life size, with a characteristic smile on the lips.[310] Three heads of *devata*s were decorated with curls stamped in a mould (Fig. 124) and arranged in two or three rows. Another mould-made hairstyle has larger locks in various forms.

Approximately the same figural composition was found in the 'Hall of the Kings', where pieces from the great statue of Buddha have been preserved. Among these pieces we have fragments of the face of Buddha and part of the head with styled hair. All were scattered about the room. The other figures are in a better state. They were probably of a secular character (donors). The head of a prince with a high conical headdress adorned with pendants possibly belonged to a donor with richly ornamented attire (Fig. 125).

A fragment showing a lavishly dressed man standing frontally, G.A. Pugachenkova[311] has suggested, may have portrayed a royal personage, probably one of the donors. The ornamentation of the long shirt and narrow trousers with gold plaques (Fig. 126) were typical of the costume of the Kushan nobility whose garments were made of a delicate fabric and were decorated with golden pendants.[312] A third male figure is dressed

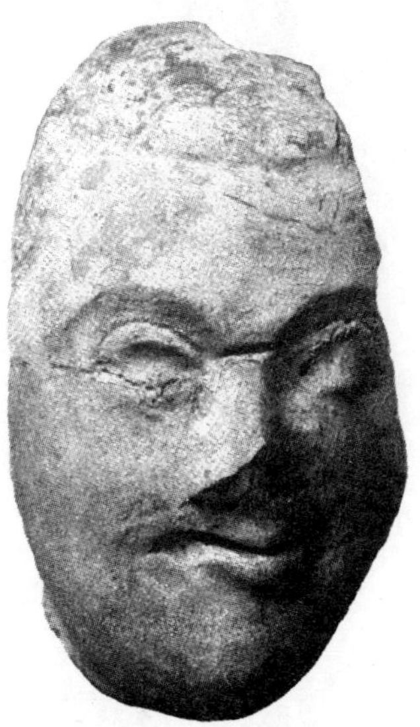

Fig. 123: Fragment of clay head of a monk from Buddhist shrine outside of the city (DT-1). Dal'verzintepa. 1st-2nd century AD. 20.5 × 10.7cm. (Institute of Art Research, Tashkent).

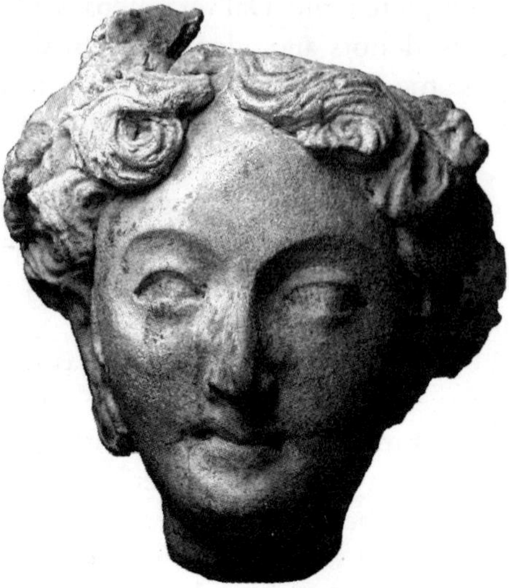

Fig. 124: Fragment of a clay head of a *devata* from the Buddhist shrine outside of the city (DT-1). Dal'verzintepa. 1st-2nd century AD. 21 × 20.5 cm. (Institute of Art Research, Tashkent).

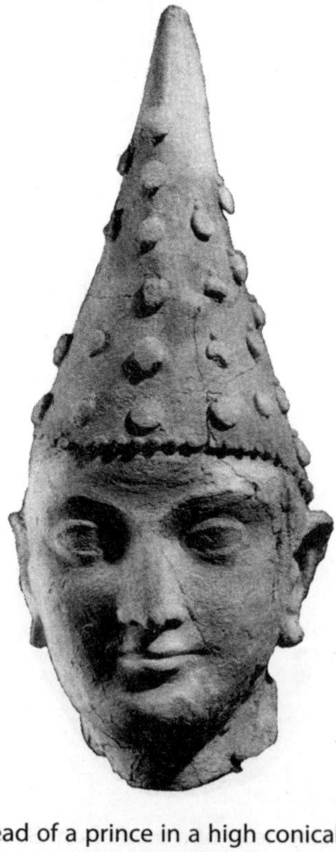

Fig. 125: Clay head of a prince in a high conical head dress from the Buddhist shrine outside the city (DT-1). Dal'verzintepa. 1st-2nd century AD. 49.5 × 19 cm. (Institute of Art Research, Tashkent).

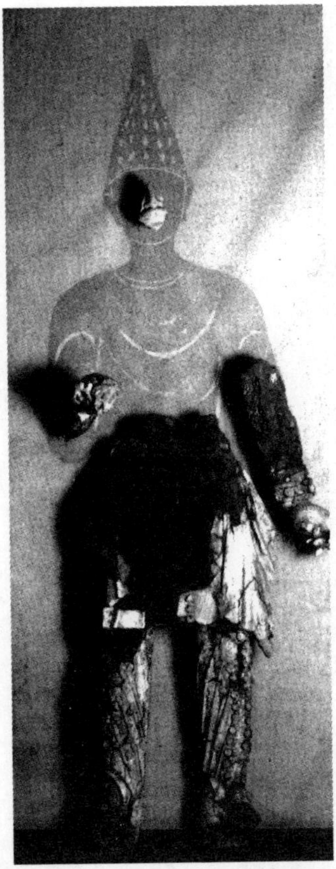

Fig. 126: Lower part of clay sculpture representing a nobleman (prince) in richly decorated dress (DT-1). Dal'verzintepa. 1st-2nd century AD. 87 × 39 cm. (Institute of Art Research, Tashkent).

modestly without any decoration (Fig. 127), wearing a long shirt and narrow trousers. A black belt fastens the long shirt, a kind of tunic. This costume is very close to that of the Karatepa complex (for example, the donor with flowers).[313] The scale of the statues varies according to their importance, with the largest size reserved for Buddha and *bodhisattva* images. Smaller figures represented the royal personages, while still smaller figures depicted relatives or other members of the aristocracy.

The technique of plastic modelling at Dal'verzintepa is similar to that of the Karatepa and Fayaztepa complexes, while its artistic style was influenced by the Khalchayan tradition. The complex, as mentioned above, is dated to the first to second centuries AD. There are certain similarities with the great sculptural centres of Gandhara and Hadda.[314] The cultural interaction and mutual influence between Gandhara and Bactria are indisputable. However, it is necessary to take into consideration the local traditions of the Bactrian region.

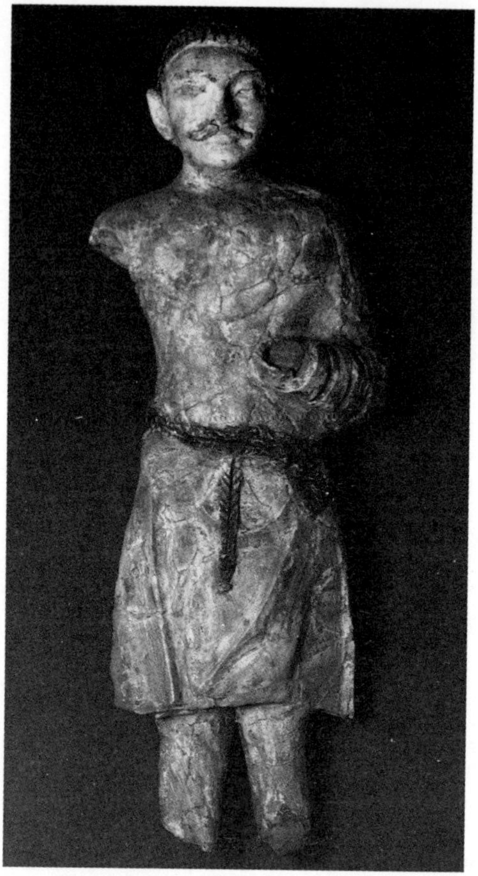

Fig. 127: Figure in long shirt (donor?) (DT-1). Dal'verzintepa. 1st-2nd century AD. Painted clay. 73 × 24 cm. (Institute of Art Research, Tashkent).

The Buddhist Complex in the Centre of Dal'verzintepa (DT-25)

The complex is located in the central part of the site to the north of the principal street and is visible as small mounds.[315] Following the contours of the site, a low linear rise can be traced surrounding the southern part of a small court. Here, about fifteen rooms were discovered. In some of them (nos. 2, 3 and 9) were numerous sculptural fragments (Fig. 128). The walls of the rooms were plastered very carefully and traces of wall painting were preserved. The main building of the Buddhist complex was erected in unbaked bricks (measuring 33 × 33-34 × 12-14 cm), while the dwellings were built in *pakhsa* and unbaked bricks (measuring 39-40 × 39-40 × 13-14 cm). A large hall or open courtyard formed the centre of the complex. In the southern part of the courtyard, where the wall is more intact, the beams show apertures, which might have been intended for consoles. In this area, more than twenty seated or standing Buddhist images were found.

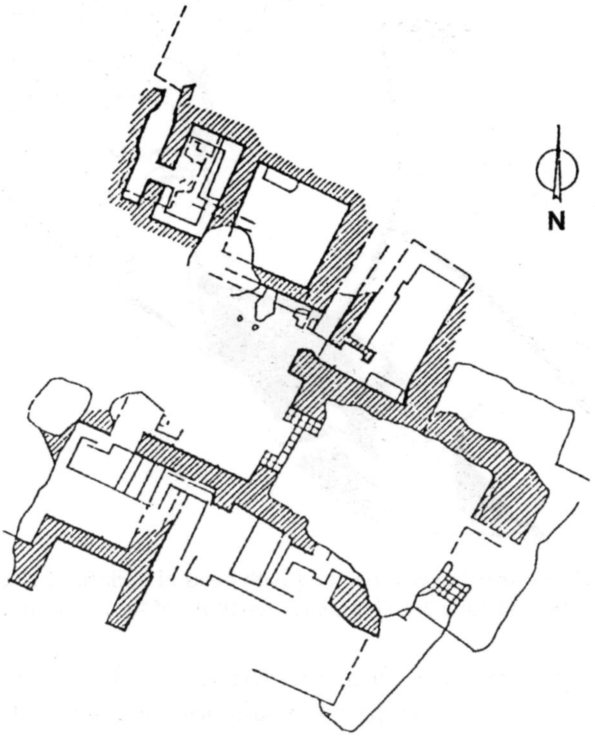

Fig. 128: Plan of the temple inside of the city. Dal'verzintepa, section 25. (After B. Turgunov, 1989, fig. 1).

The square courtyard in the centre would have had sculptures installed along three of its walls, alternating with niches and doorways. Along the northern, eastern, and southern walls, the sculptural groups and individual figures would have been displayed above the consoles and sufas.[316]

Wall Paintings

A considerable number of fragments convey aspects of Buddhism, above all an upper body fragment of the image of a Buddha (Fig. 129). The wall paintings were executed on a priming of alabaster laid over the clay plaster. Elements of plant motifs and borders were painted in dark red on a bluish background. Black and white pigments were also used.[317] Anthropomorphic representations were often painted against a white or rose background. The figure of Buddha is emphasized by a round halo, while a dark line marks the contour. The right hand is held up in *abhaya-mudra*. The head is portrayed in a simple manner without colour or shadows. Spaces filled in with specific colours play an important role. A clear-cut line beginning below its bridge, for example, indicates the nose. The nostrils are not represented in full, but are conveyed only by outline. The groove under the nose is shown by a

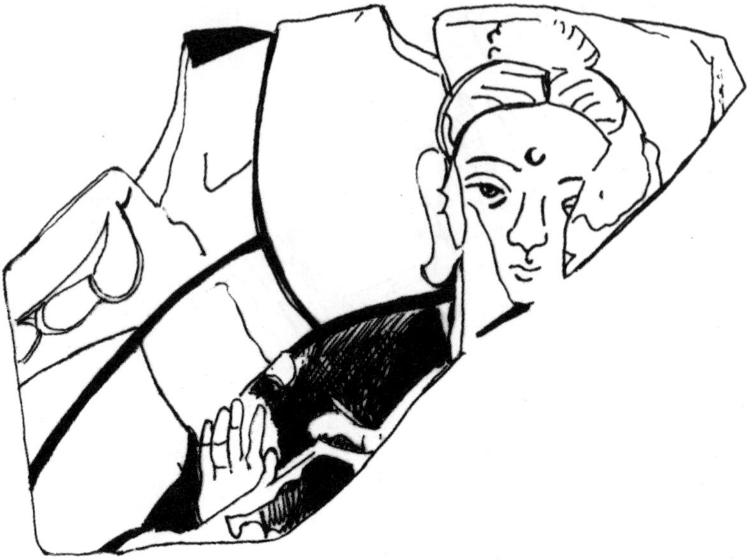

Fig. 129: Fragment of wall painting with head of Buddha. Dal'verzintepa, section 25. 2nd-early 3rd century AD. (Institute of Art Research, Tashkent).

circle. The lips are quite thin, and the mouth is relatively small. The lengthened and massive ears have long and rounded lobes. On the forehead above the bridge of the nose is an *urna*. The forehead is framed by a high hair style typical of the iconography of Buddha, and the texture of the hair is shown. The general form is emphasized simply by using thick lines. On the top of the head is an *ushnisha*.

Another fragment shows a more vital image of a young personage (Fig. 130), but this representation has some schematization in the modelling

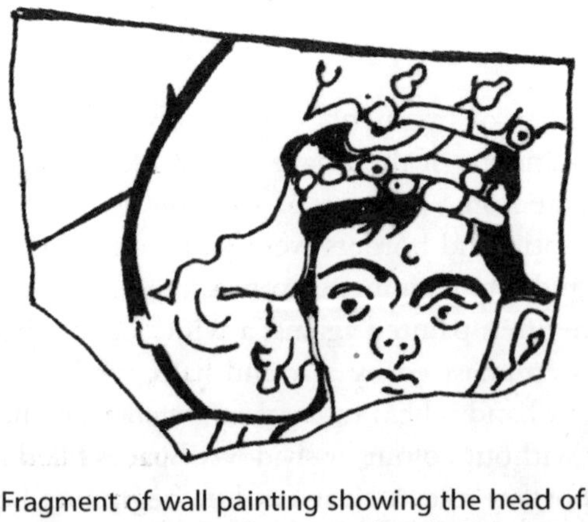

Fig. 130: Fragment of wall painting showing the head of an individual. Dal'verzintepa, section 25. 2nd-early 3rd century AD. (Institute of Art Research, Tashkent).

of details. Only the head with the thick line of a halo has been preserved. The tall elaborate headdress consists of three bands with decorative circles representing jewellery. The high forehead is framed by straight black hair and curls covering it. In the centre of the forehead is a mark in the shape of a teardrop. The large arched eyebrows continue from the bridge of the nose, but in thinner lines, curving to the level of the eyes. The nose itself resembles two commas. Two dots in the middle of the commas portray the nostrils. The eyes are wide-opened, looking sideways. The figure evidently has a secular character, representing an adorant from the local population. The headdress in the form of a diadem consisting of rows of circles has led to the speculation that this individual had an artificial skull deformation.[318] Given the fragmentary state of the painting, it is difficult to comment on this interpretation.

Clay Sculptures of Buddhas and Bodhisattvas from the Second Temple of Dal'verzintepa (DT-25)

The numerous fragments and some almost completely preserved sculptural figures from the Buddhist temple provide us with much information. Most of them were found in rooms 2, 3 and 9. The clay sculpture was executed over wood or reed frames. A thin modelling layer consisting of very fine clay that has kept its natural colour was then used to coat certain parts of the sculpture. Other fragments have another fine layer of alabaster that was typically covered with paint. Some of the sculptures were executed in gypsum, and had probably been cast in a mould. Certain details such as parts of the face, the ears, curls of hair or jewellery – including various rosettes and flowers – were stamped in a mould, using clay or gypsum. Some of the sculptures show traces of repair where the ancient restorers repainted discoloured parts of the sculpture. This fact is very interesting and important, because it sheds light on the poorly studied vicissitudes of the sculptures after their creation. It should be noted that this observation also applies to Kuevkurgan sculpture.

Among the sculptures from the temple, there are colossal figures of Buddha (Fig. 131) and *bodhisattva*s (Figs. 134, 135). According to the excavator, there were seven statues of Buddha, including two seated ones.[319] The head of one standing statue was broken off, but found on the floor near its feet (Fig. 132). Of four other statues, we have only the heads (Fig. 133). Five sculptures were executed in clay and two in plaster (*ganch*). The over life-sized figures are 2.50 m tall, but those of minor importance (like donors and adorants) were executed on a smaller (natural) scale. Images of the Buddha and *bodhisattva*s have the typical expression of tranquil contemplation and greatness. They embody the canon of Buddhist iconography. The artists effectively used small details of representation, for

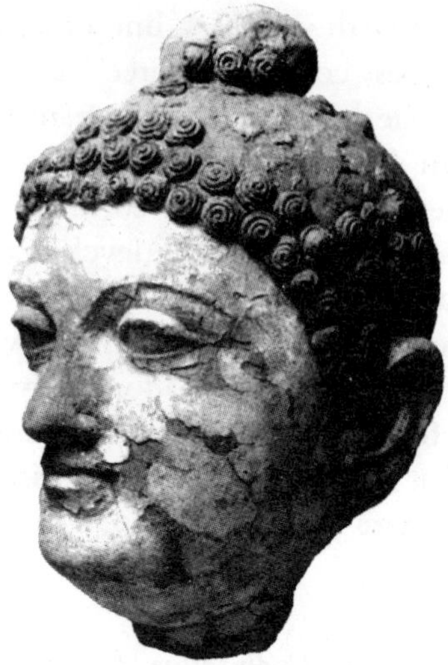

Fig. 131: Head of Buddha image. Clay sculpture painted in white with stamped black curls. Dal'verzintepa, section 25. 2nd-early 3rd century AD. 39 × 29 cm. (Institute of Art Research, Tashkent).

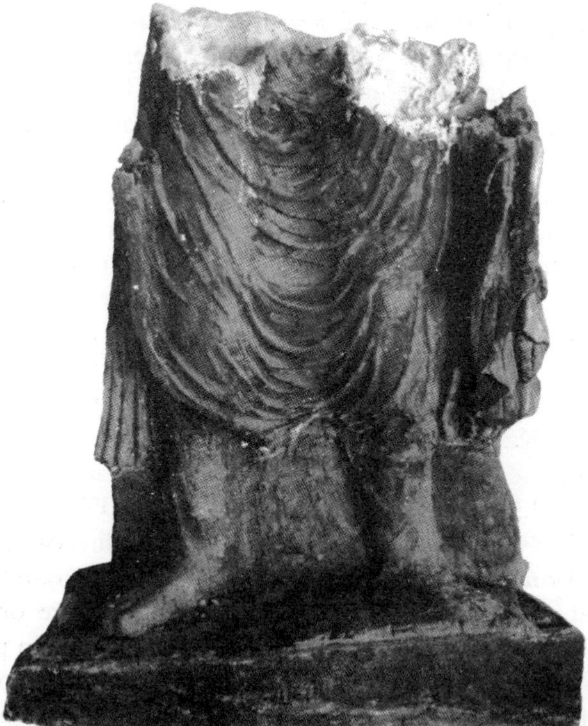

Fig. 132: Painted clay sculpture fragment of the lower part of standing Buddha. Dal'verzintepa, section 25. 2nd-early 3rd century AD. 96 × 75 cm. (Institute of Art Research, Tashkent).

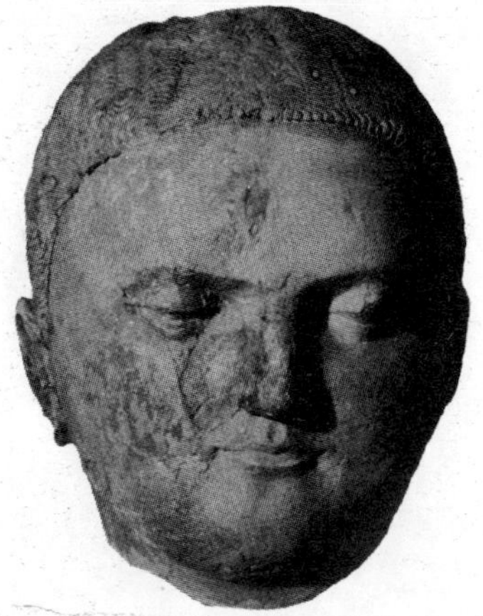

Fig. 133: Painted clay sculpture fragment of the head of Buddha. Dal'verzintepa, section 25. 2nd-early 3rd century AD. 28 × 26 cm. (Institute of Art Research, Tashkent).

example, the hair with a diversity of curls or ornamental motifs. All of this testifies to the free and easy manner of sculpting and high artistic quality.

The find of a stone mould for the duplication of decoration for the sculpture[320] helps to illustrate how this quality was achieved. Pliable material such as clay and gypsum was used for the combination technique of modelling. The moulds served for imprinting small details and also making parts of the hands and feet. A mould could even replicate such complicated elements as hands in certain fixed gestures, which demand a sophisticated method for their plastic representation. The smaller figures representing minor personages seem more vital and dynamic: obviously in their case the sculptor has employed hand modelling. Unfortunately, at the present time we do not have sufficient archaeological data for the reconstruction of the entire sculptural complex and composition. However, it is safe to assume that the clay figures decorated the interior of the court.[321]

Evidently, at the Dal'verzintepa complex the majority of the clay sculpture showed the same characteristics as the sculpture of Kuevkurgan, though the latter had a secular meaning. However, it is important to remember that the Dal'verzintepa complex belongs to an earlier period and anticipates many traits in the development of plastic art in Bactria-Tokharistan during Late Antiquity and the Early Middle Ages.

For the dating of the second Buddhist temple at Dal'verzintepa, we have numismatic evidence. Five coins were found: coins of Heliocles imitations and Soter Megas in the fill, and the others of Kanishka III and imitations of Vasudeva from the third to fourth centuries AD on the floor of room no. 2.[322] The latter point to the complex functioning in a late phase. The early period of the temple dates to the period of the Great Kushans, possibly to the time of Kanishka I, when the Buddhist society was engaged in building activities in northern Bactria. C. Silvi Antonini, in her article

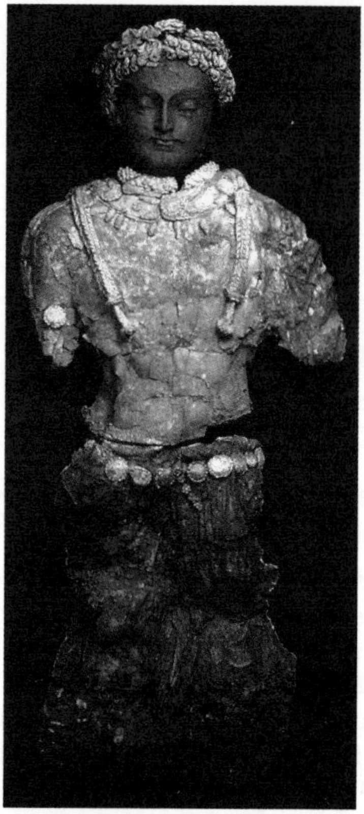

Fig. 134: Painted clay sculpture of a standing figure of *bodhisattva*. Dal'verzintepa, section 25. 2nd-early 3rd century AD. 218 × 89 cm. (Institute of Art Research, Tashkent).

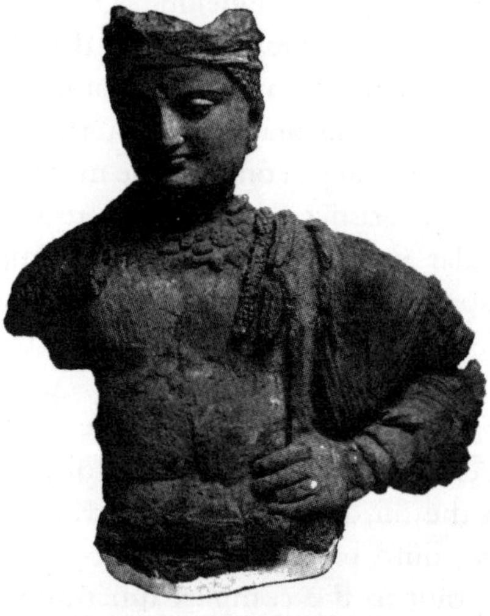

Fig. 135: Painted clay sculpture fragment of a standing *bodhisattva*. Dal'verzintepa, section 25. 2nd-early 3rd century AD. 96 × 95 cm. (Institute of Art Research, Tashkent).

devoted to the Dal'verzintepa temple sculptures, proposed an even later date, the fifth or sixth centuries AD, arguing that 'the 2nd-3rd centuries AD date for the Dal'verzintepa Buddhist temple 25 does not seem fully justified either from the numismatic and epigraphic data or from the stylistic analysis of the art works found in it'.[323]

Terracotta Figurines

Terracotta figurines were found both on the surface of the site and in stratified layers. A remarkable peculiarity of Dal'verzintepa should be noted. Considering the fact that there were two temples of wonderfully high artistic quality of Buddhist sculptures, it is surprising that terracotta figurines were missing. Sites in the regions surrounding Termez and Chaganian have yielded numerous terracotta figurines of Buddhist character, representing Buddha and *bodhisattvas* as well as other personages of the Buddhist pantheon, including adorants and donors,[324] whereas only a single example of a terracotta head of Buddhist character has turned up on the surface of Dal'verzintepa.[325] Among the large quantity of terracotta figurines, the majority of which can be dated by coins of Kanishka I and Huvishka to the second century AD, a female deity seated on a throne was the most widespread image. It is interpreted as the image of Nana, so predominant in the Kushan Pantheon.[326] A temple discovered on the northern part of the site was also attributed to the goddess Nana.[327] Such a situation speaks for the popularity of the cult of Nana among the ordinary citizens, while the more privileged adhered to the official Buddhist religion and worshipped in opulently decorated Buddhist temples.

Temple DT-9: Sculpture and Painting with the Representation of the 'Great Departure'

This fragment of a wall painting found during the early period of excavation of DT-9 is particularly significant. Topographically, the building, which has been interpreted as a temple, is of extraordinary appearance, given the fact that it stood in proximity to the potter's quarter.[328] The interpretation of the building as a temple is based on the ceremonial objects it yielded,[329] but there is no certainty about this. It was built on the high part of the potters' quarter in the north-western sector of Dal'verzintepa. The walls were erected with clay blocks (*pakhsa*) and have a thickness of 1.3-1.5 m. The building has a rectangular ground plan measuring 21 × 13 m. The so-called temple has been dated by objects and coins.[330] Between the first and second floors a barbarized coin of Heliocles and Soter Megas was found. According to G.A. Pugachenkova, the second construction phase belonged to the subsequent period of the Great Kushans and the first to the Kushano-Sassanids (i.e. to the end of the first to third centuries AD).[331]

On a *sufa* in room no. 1, fragments of two female figures were found.[332] These figures were executed in brown clay and wear long dresses with vertical pleats. It is possible that a combination technique was used, whereby the core of the sculptures consisted of clay within an outer shell of alabaster. Finally, on this alabaster form the fine details were modelled and painted. On the inner side of some sculptural fragments holes can be detected, indicating the use of wood or reed frames. It is difficult to judge the character of the sculptures on the basis of a few preserved fragments. In addition to the two female figures in three-quarter size, a figure of a boy and a girl were found. Again, according to G.A. Pugachenkova, one of the female figures could correspond to the main divinity and the other to the deity of a lower class.[333] The style and manner of the plastic modelling of these sculptures are analogous with the works of the Indo-Buddhist figurative complex.[334] This is confirmed by other characteristics of the finds from this building.

Painting

Judging from the preserved fragments, the paintings were executed on a white primer, which covered the wall. According to the description of G.A. Pugachenkova:

> The biggest fragment (72 × 95 cm) shows part of a slender male figure in a tightly fitting red garment (caftan) and wide, white trousers; the rear of a horse; and on the left side (to the right from the spectator) there are two floors of a building framed in the upper part by a white band and the lower part by sandal-red color band with a row of white circles. Two rows of females, shown from the waist up, are represented here. Their faces are modelled in profile or slightly turned in three quarter view. The women in the upper row are represented with black hair, while the women in the lower row have red hair, and all of them have a part in the middle. The shape of their eyes is horizontal; they have large noses (which are in profile), and a small chin. These profile views are analogous with the portrait of a woman from the Buddhist shrine Dt-1 and the head of a girl from the Khalchayan palace. The figures are dressed in rich red and yellow mantles with a white border. It is difficult to divine the subject. The images of the women have a clearly secular character. They observe the action before them to the left of the composition.[335]

In conclusion, G.A. Pugachenkova holds that, with regard to the figurative art of Dal'verzintepa, the wall painting from the vestibule DT-9 represented 'the departure of a hero (?)', who is watched by girls from a balcony. However, the question mark betrays her doubt.[336] Regarding the 'departure'

(Fig. 136), G.A. Pugachenkova focuses on the large male figure on the left wearing a jacket wrapped from right to left, that has a wide border on the edging and hem. This kind of costume strongly resembles the clothing worn by the figures of Fayaztepa that portray the local population. However, this figure is not the main subject of the composition. First of all, it is likely that he is not a horseman, but a pedestrian. This is apparent from his posture. The body of the figure is shown frontally, while the head is turned to the left in profile. A short section of the vertical line indicating the left (?) leg testifies also to the standing pose of the figure, as this line is symmetrical to the inner contour of the right leg. The left arm is bent at the elbow with its hand raised to shoulder level. Such a pose is not characteristic of a horseman holding a bridle. In fact, the raised left hand of the male is holding an object resembling a pole.

At thigh level, something has been applied to the figure that resembles a cover. A braid is visible on the upper part, which in the lower part is a bundle of straight lines. In our opinion, this braid is nothing other than the tail of a horse, twisted and tucked into a cover. This element of horse decoration was very typical for Central Asia, and many archaeological finds (for example, the Pazyryk burials[337]) and objects of figurative art (for example, the coins of Azes and the bone plates from Orlat[338]) illustrate

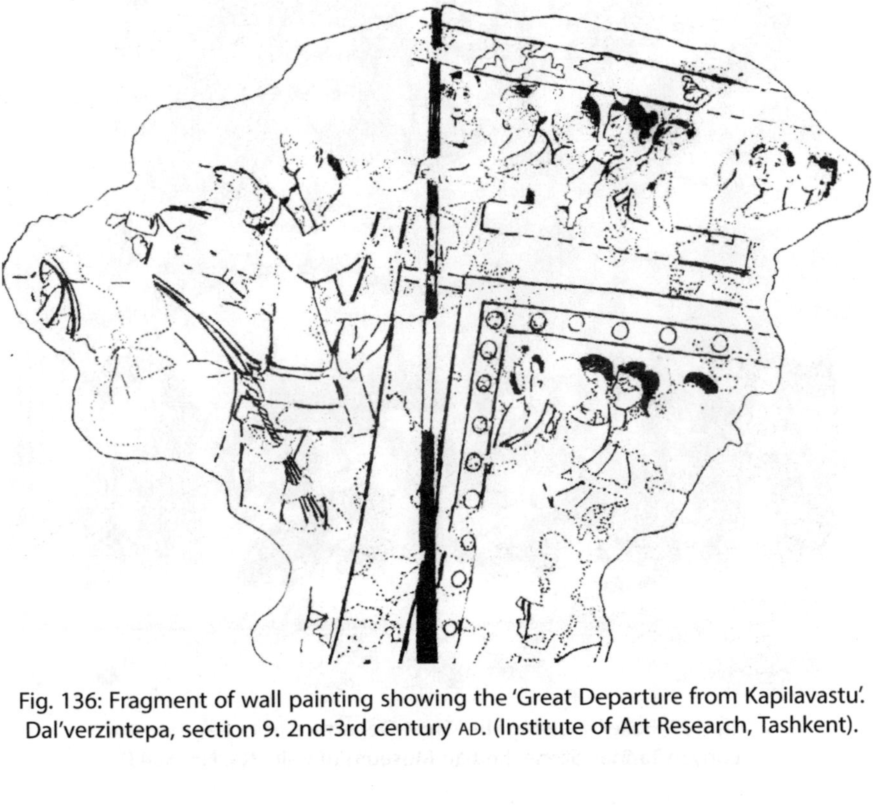

Fig. 136: Fragment of wall painting showing the 'Great Departure from Kapilavastu'. Dal'verzintepa, section 9. 2nd-3rd century AD. (Institute of Art Research, Tashkent).

this. The line from the cover descends in a sweep, forming, most likely, the rear of the horse. It becomes clear that the male figure does not sit on the horse, but stands beside it or follows behind it. This totally changes the meaning of the scene. We are convinced that the painting represents one of the favourite scenes in Buddhist iconography, the 'Great Departure of Prince Siddhartha from Kapilavastu'.

Gandharan reliefs exhibit close analogies to the Dal'verzintepa composition. We only need to consider one of them – the relief from Lorian Tangay in the Indian Museum of Calcutta.[339] If we compare the fragment from Dal'verzintepa with the completely preserved composition from Lorian Tangay, we notice many common elements (Fig. 137), but also differences, for example, in the way the figures are dressed. While the Lorian Tangay relief shows the Indian garment with its characteristic drapery, the Dal'verzintepa painter chose the local costume of that region. This circumstance is in keeping with the eclectic style of the Dal'verzintepa masters. The row of girls observing the scene from the balcony was, for instance, borrowed from Gandharan art. The male individual of the Dal'verzintepa composition should be associated with *Chandaka*, the bearer

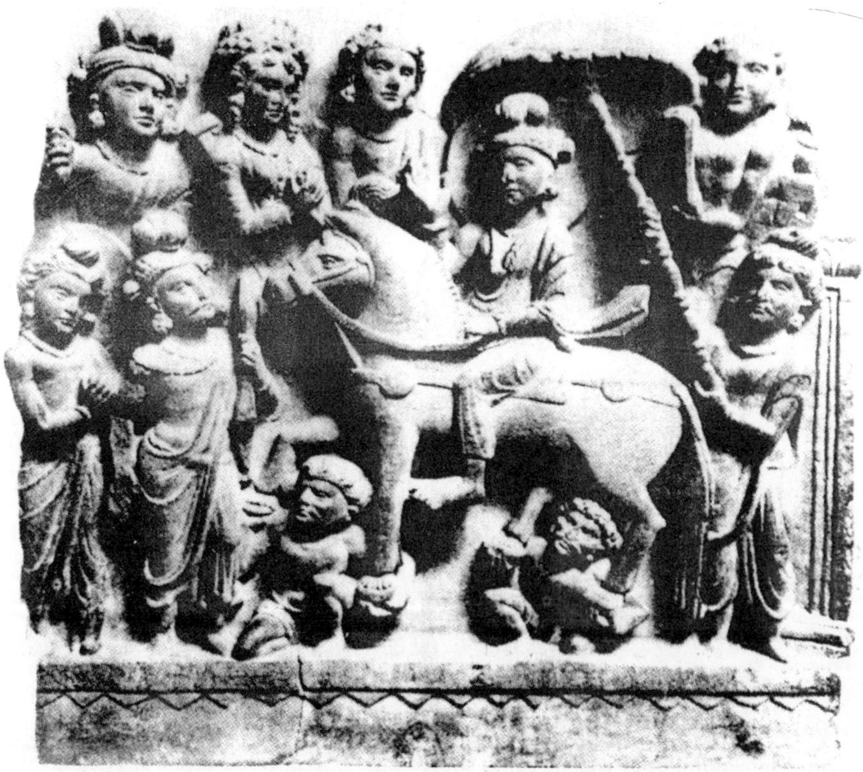

Fig. 137: Relief showing the 'Great Departure from Kapilavastu'. Loriyan Tangai. Stone. (Indian Museum of Calcutta. No. 5043).

of the parasol, who walks in the procession behind Prince Siddhartha riding on the horse *Kantaka*.

This interpretation implies that the scene with 'Prince Siddhartha leaving Kapilavastu' appeared here for the first time in the art of Central Asia, demonstrating how not only Buddhist subject matter, but also Buddhist multi-figured compositions had penetrated the art of Bactria. It is possible that earlier Bactrian reliefs of such scenes have not been preserved, because they were executed in organic material, so we cannot be sure that they did not exist in the repertoire of Bactrian sculptors prior to the creation of this image.[340]

Perhaps not by chance the same complex, DT-9, has yielded other objects whose representations are related to Indian art, for example, a bone hairbrush showing women at their toilette.[341] On the obverse, a scene with four female figures is engraved. One of the women (apparently the mistress), turning backwards, is seated in the centre on a padded chair and holds something in her hand. Four bracelets adorn her wrists, and she is also wearing hollow anklets. The upper part of the figure is nude, while the hips are draped in a complex manner. The other three figures, evidently maidservants, are placed at the corners of the composition. In the lower left corner, one is only partially visible. The heads of the other two figures are turned to the principal figure. One of these figures carries a bowl, perhaps holding bread or fruit.

On the reverse of the hairbrush, which is larger, the same ladies seem to be involved in another activity. One of the women moves impetuously to the left (Fig. 138). Her right hand is raised and points to a certain object, calling the attention of the others to it. Two figures are shown behind an elephant, as if they were seated on it. Between them is a goblet with a short stem, which resembles ceramic forms of Kushan Bactria.[342] A second identical goblet is placed between the seated figure on the left of the scene and the main personage. It is difficult to determine the relationship between the scenes on the front and back, apparently depicting episodes of the *jatakas*. In any case, these genre scenes are so vivid and realistic that their narrative character is unmistakable. There is a remote likeness in certain details of the hairbrush from Dal'verzintepa to the carved ivories of Begram. This likeness concerns the style of the figures, their attributes, their costume and headdress.[343]

In light of the above evidence, the statement of G.A. Pugachenkova that the 'absence of thematic analogies to the fragments of wall paintings from Dal'verzintepa in the ancient world – from the Mediterranean to India, testifies to local Bactrian traditions'[344] is not convincing. Without belittling the significance of the Bactrian figurative traditions, we think that in all probability they developed in intensive contact with other artistic centres, such as Mathura and Gandhara.

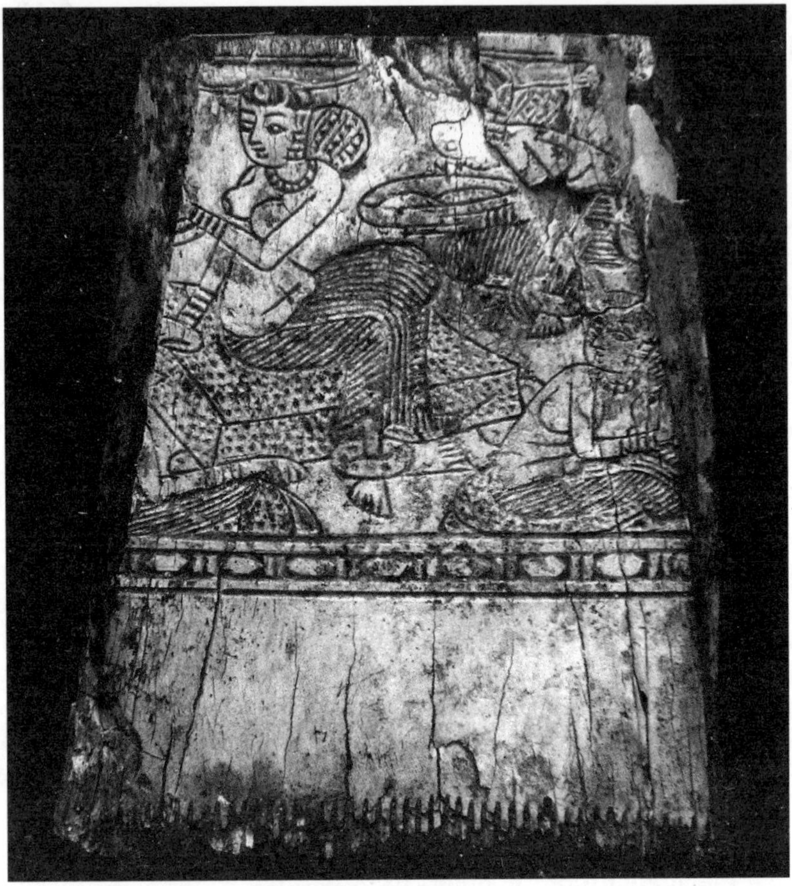

Fig. 138: Ivory comb with engraved compositions. Dal'verzintepa, section 9. 2nd-3rd century AD. 9.2 × 6.5 cm. (Institute of Art Research, Tashkent).

The Terracotta from Khatynrabat and the Problem of Jainism in Bactria

It has been maintained that one of the peculiarities of terracotta figurines that makes their identification difficult is their small size. They lack clarity of detail and this has led scholars to contradictory conclusions. A figurine from Khatynrabat (in the Surkhandarya region) is one such example.[345] Several archaeologists have given it a Jainist identity,[346] which has led to much debate.[347] Based on G. Pugachenkova's supposition,[348] V.A. Meshkeris interpreted this figurine as a Jaina image, although it is well known that one of the distinctive features in the representation of Jaina was nudity.[349] Further developing the idea of Jainist iconography in Bactrian terracotta plastic art – particularly in the images of Tirthankaras – Meshkeris alleged that Jainism had spread into this region. T. Mkrtychev in his monograph adhered to the same theory concerning the figurine from Khatynrabat.[350] Both scholars disregarded such an important detail as the relief line depicting the hem of the figure's clothing (Fig. 139). Furthermore, the hand of the figurine its palm turned toward the spectator, is characteristic of the *varada-mudra*, which is one of the essential gestures in Buddhist iconography. Conversely, all the standing Jainas are represented with hands clinging to the body and with palms turned inward. Yet another important argument against the idea of Jainism in Bactria is the absence of any inscription of Jaina character in Central Asia,[351] including the numerous finds from Karatepa and Fayaztepa. The interpretation of the Khatynrabat figurine as a Jaina image has caused only confusion in understanding the religious situation of Bactria. In archaeological literature, this terracotta has even been identified as a 'slave in shackles', setting off in earnest a debate on 'Slavery in Central Asia'.[352]

At the present time, there do not appear to be any literary sources concerning Jainism and its penetration into Central Asia, and in particular, Bactria. The numerous parables and legends about Kanishka, ostensibly the protector of Buddhism and Jainism, are biased and are at times doubtful, as, for example, the legend about 'Kanishka and the Jaina Stupa', cited by J. Rosenfield.[353] The legend from the so-called *Sutralamkara* collection relates that Kanishka, when crossing the plain on his return from his eastern Indian campaign, found himself in the darkness of night. He visited a *stupa* thinking that it was Buddhist. He dismounted and, taking off his precious

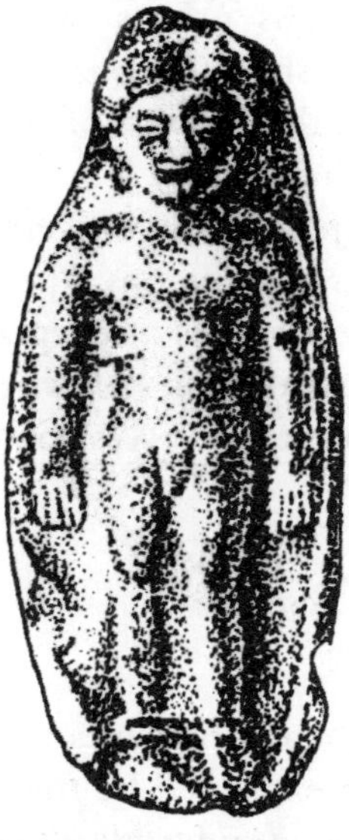

Fig. 139: Terracotta figurine of a Buddhist individual (*bodhisattva*?) in *varada-mudra*. Khatynrabad. 3rd century AD. 8.2 × 3.3 cm. (Termez Archaeological Museum).

hat, prostrated himself in prayer. But, suddenly, the structure collapsed. Kanishka was greatly concerned, but learned that it was a Jaina *stupa* and therefore did not deserve the honour of such a Great King – 'un âne ne porte pas la même charge qu'un éléphant'.[354] The episode concludes with a sharp reproach to the Jainas, who would not pay Kanishka due respect. Surely, the story has a hidden Buddhist message, and does not give us any reason to see Kanishka as a protector of Jainism. It is unlikely that all these legends and parables regarding Kanishka's leaning toward Buddhism, created later by adepts of this religion, have any real foundation. In any case, the religious pantheon on Kanishka's coins bears out the tolerance of the king toward different faiths. The propagandistic character of the representations on the coins does not require commentary, for these expressed the official position of Kanishka and other Kushan kings.[355] Indeed, the presence of deities of various religions on the coins of Kanishka demonstrates one of the most outstanding policies of this Kushan king. One recalls that besides Iranian gods such as Mithra, Mah and Wato (Fig. 140), there were images of Hindu, Buddhist, and Greek deities, as well as local ones such as Ardokhsho.[356]

Such tolerance can be associated with sovereigns who had great kingdoms, encompassing populations adhering to various religions and cults. One remembers the aspirations of Alexander the Great to embrace the local clergy, who represented a great political force, while he believed himself to be the son of the god Ammon. In this case, his actions were similar to the policies of the Achaemenid kings (prior to Darius), who tried to gain the support of the indigenous priests by introducing themselves as worshippers of Egyptian, Jewish, Babylonian, and other gods. The policy of tolerance stimulated both the growth of the idea of world supremacy and the stability of the empire.[357]

Therefore, finds of cult objects, including terracotta figurines, may testify to the dissemination of different religions. The use of these figurines by a religious community was completely acceptable. It is interesting that Buddhist figurines have been found on sites that had no sacred architecture (such as temples, shrines or stupas). We will return to these figurines shortly.

Objects of Buddhist Plastic Art from Neighboring Historic-Cultural Regions

We encounter Buddhist terracotta figurines not only in northern Bactria, where their presence can be explained by the spread of Buddhist culture, but also on sites located at a considerable distance from any cult centres of Buddhism. Below we shall discuss some of them.

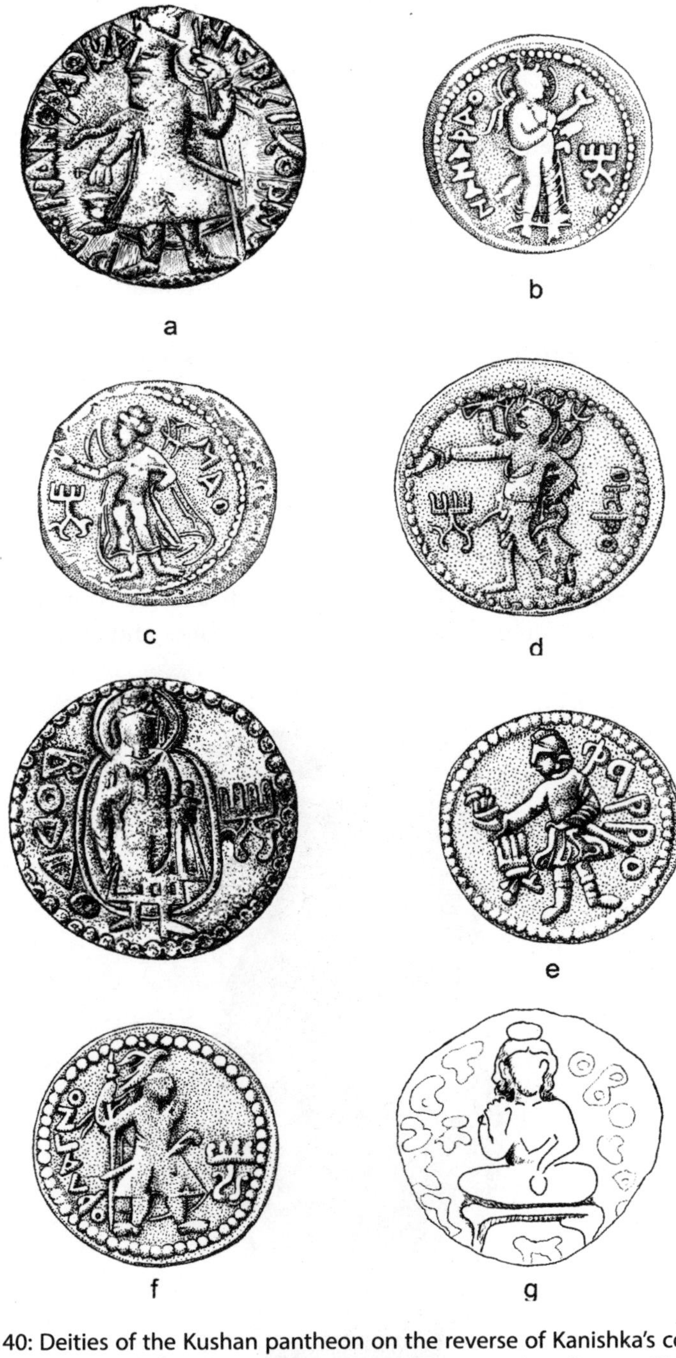

Fig. 140: Deities of the Kushan pantheon on the reverse of Kanishka's coins; a – obverse with Kanishka figure before altar, reverse standing figure of Buddha; b – Nana (Nanaia); c – Mao; d – Oesho; e – Farro; f – Orlagno; g – Maitreya. (B. Ya. Staviskiy, 1979: 64, 65).

Southern Sogdiana

During excavations at Erkurgan in southern Sogdia a terracotta statuette was found which is atypical for the plastic art of the region. In the scholarly literature it has been simply interpreted as a female figure.[358] On closer scrutiny, it seems that this figure has certain Buddhist features. The dark brown, almost black, slip is indicative of the third to fourth century AD. The terracotta has been impressed in high relief and shows a figure wearing a tall turban with rosettes. A decorative band extends from the centre of one of these rosettes (Fig. 141). The lower border of the turban is emphasized by a relief strip dotted with squares and rectangles. The figure has a plump face with swollen eyelids and tightly closed lips with a slight smile at the corners. The elongated lobes of the ears are adorned with hanging earrings. The personage wears a double necklace, one depicted as a simple relief line and the other as thick braided laces. Between the breasts, raised in relief, is a triangular fold. The arms are bent at the elbow and pressed to the stomach.

The treatment of the head, with its precise details of a complex headdress and the meticulous representation of the necklaces and a pectoral, masks

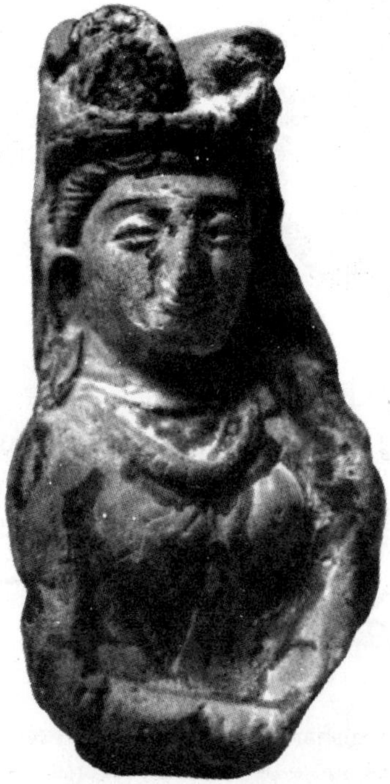

Fig. 141: Terracotta figurine of a Buddhist personage – *bodhisattva* (?). Erkurgan (Kashkadarya region). Accidental find. 3rd-4th century AD. H = 10 cm. (Institute of Archaeology, Samarkand).

to a certain degree the rather primitive modelling of the lower part of the figurine. Such adornments were very popular on Gandharan sculpture and on plastic work in Bactria, especially northern Bactria, as is evident at Dal'verzintepa.[359] While the triangular fold between the breasts plausibly conveys part of the dress, the rest of the torso from the shoulders downward loses all anatomical correctness. The shoulders and forearms are barely hinted at by narrow projecting reliefs with a rough surface. On the right arm – bent at the elbow and pressed to the stomach – the artist has not bothered to model the hand; instead the relief seems to prolong the elbow. The left hand appears similarly to be missing, but due to the poor preservation it is difficult to be sure. Most likely, the hands were meant to be folded at the stomach. The breasts are modelled in the same casual way. They are shown asymmetrically with the left breast smaller, and slightly higher than the right one. The hands and shoulders are carelessly depicted by irregular outlines. The contrast between the skilfully modelled head expressing conciliation and contemplation and the awkwardly executed torso is striking.

All these features speak in favour of the likelihood that the figurine copied an original, only available in a fragmentary state. Anyway, it seems indisputable that the upper part of the image and the lower part were made by two different artists.

On the basis of the complicated headdress with rosettes and bands and the modelling of the lower border of the turban with squares and rectangles imitating precious stones, it could be suggested that this form of headdress would be fitting for a *bodhisattva*, particularly Bodhisattva Avalokiteshvara. The modelling of the eyelids is definitely characteristic of Buddhist iconography. The adornment of the elongated ears with pendants and the double necklace is typical of many figures in Buddhist imagery. However, two details are particularly significant: the emphasized relief of the breasts and the pleat between them, for which there are close parallels on a female stone sculpture from Butkara (Fig. 142).[360] The Butkara sculpture is, however, essentially different in that its eyes are wide opened, while the Erkurgan figurine, with its heavy eyelids, resembles more the Bactrian Buddhist figures. Hypothetically, the image from Erkurgan could originally have represented a *bodhisattva*, but was subsequently transformed into another personage. It is possible that it is an example of the transformation of an artefact that stylistically belonged to the Bactrian terracotta school, but was later exported from Bactria to Erkurgan, where it underwent a change.

BODHISATTVA FROM ERKURGAN

In 1986, in room 8 at Erkurgan a small appliqué (H. 5.5 cm; W. 3.2 cm; H. of the relief 1.4 cm) was excavated. It was found in a layer above the

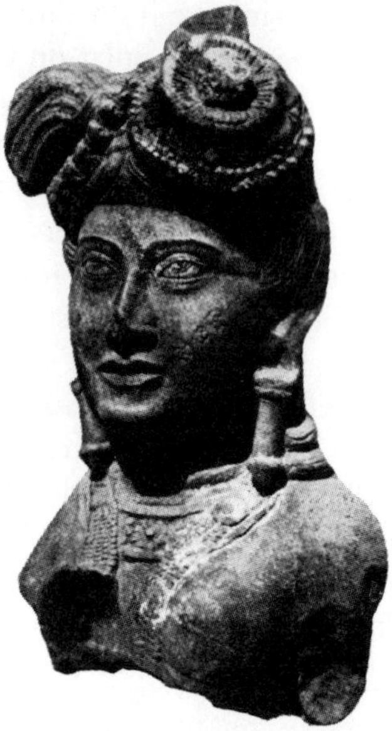

Fig. 142: Stone sculpture from Butkara (Pakistan) with female image (cf. Fig. 141). (After G.A. Pugachenkova, 1982b, fig. 95).

floor and according to the ceramic complex was dated to the fifth or sixth century AD. In his comprehensive monograph 'Ancient Nakhshab', R.H. Sulaymanov described this appliqué as 'a print of a bust from a tiny stamp'.[361] It is a gracefully modelled figure that represents realistically the face of an aristocratic young man, slightly turned to the left. He has a refined, elongated face with an extended moustache. On the head, over the combed back locks of hair, is a complex headdress, which can be interpreted as a tripartite crown with a conical tiara. On one breast can be traced the faint imprint of a thick necklace with the clasp in the centre.[362] Some details may be added to the accurate description of the author which may aid in its interpretation. First of all, the mould of the figure was appliquéd to another ceramic object. The edge of the appliqué was smoothed onto damp clay by a finger, and the concave form of the lower part suggests that it was the handle of a vessel (Fig. 143). During the potter's 'correction and attachment' of the appliqué, other details of the image were also smoothed out. This procedure of correction and attachment apparently accounts for the absence of the auricles (and their adornments) and the rounded relief below the neck, which initially represented a piece of jewellery, was moved downwards. The hair, which according to Sulaymanov is combed back, is actually protruding from under the headdress in the form of thin lines. The lines in relief extending to the nape, which have been understood as hair, are more precisely plaits, wound symmetrically back from both sides. The headdress in question is an intricate turban, of a type well

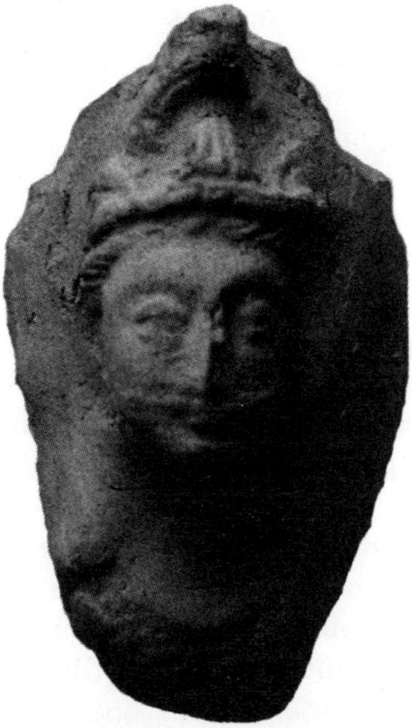

Fig. 143: Reused representation of *bodhisattva* image from Erkurgan. First (original) image can be dated to the 1st-2nd century AD. The second utilization as an appliqué can be dated to the 5th-6th century. Terracotta. H = 5.5 cm. (Institute of Archaeology, Samarkand).

known in Buddhist iconography, and in particular in Gandharan plastic art (Fig. 144).[363] The design of the headdress is similar to another terracotta image from Erkurgan, which has been noted above; the only difference being that on the present figure the turban has a depression at the centre

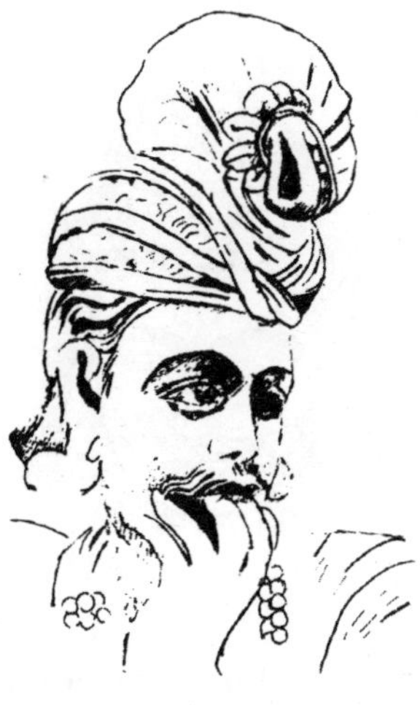

Fig. 144: *Bodhisattva* representation (cf. hairstyle in Fig. 143). Swat. (Museo Nazionale d'Arte Orientale 'Giuseppe Tucci', Rome, n. 1109. After F. Tissot, 1985, pl. XXX, 5c).

on the top. However, we have here the same form of the lower border of the turban with the drawn lines simulating a precious ornament; the tassel with the corrugated surface is more precisely shown. Unlike the beardless Erkurgan statuette, this figure has a moustache. Thus, here we can speak more confidently of an image of a *bodhisattva*, probably Avalokiteshvara. The expression with a relaxed smile and the heavy, semi-closed eyelids corresponds to a condition of contemplation, which recalls the best Gandharan examples (Fig. 145).[364] Obviously, the image of the *bodhisattva* was transformed on Sogdian ground and no longer functioned as a cult figurine, but as a decorative appliqué for pottery, possibly a vessel. Despite the fact that the appliqué was found in a layer dating to the fifth or sixth century AD, on stylistic grounds the image should be dated to the first centuries of our era.

These two terracotta figures of Buddhist character exemplify how images at a certain point of time could lose not only their cult function, but also their semantic *raison d'être*, being transformed on the whim of some potter into a decorative element or into a completely different personage. All that was needed was a change in some details, operations that a master could easily accomplish on the damp clay. From this 'new' type the master could then take a mould.

The archaeological material of south Sogdia includes two more terracotta plaques showing Buddhist subjects. The first image came from Saryktepa[365] (in the Kashkadarya Region) and represents a frontally standing figure (Buddha?) in a long dress and a pose resembling *abhaya-mudra*. Mkrtychev misinterpreted the feet of this figure as 'bird palms'.[366] This element of re-

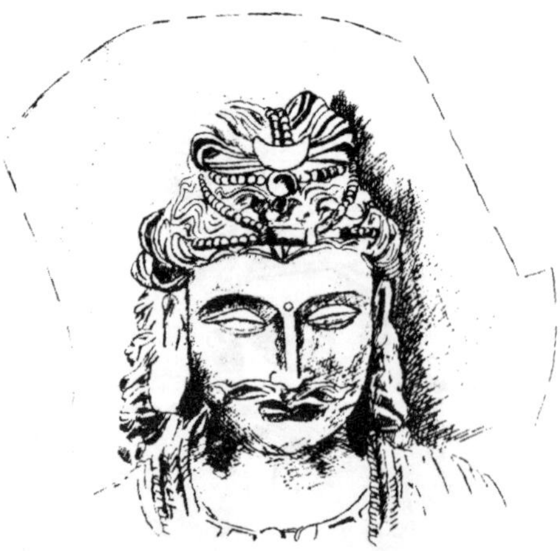

Fig. 145: *Bodhisattva* (cf. Fig. 143). Provenance unknown. (Allahabad Museum, India, n. 131. After F. Tissot, 1985, plate XXVII, 7).

presentation bears a strong resemblance to that of a figure from Khatynrabad (Fig. 139) which has also caused much confusion. In both cases, the horizontal relief line probably defined the hem of the garment (mantle?).

The second terracotta plaque from south Sogdia was found in the area of Kul'tepa and shows an image of *bodhisattva* on a high throne in *padmasana* with *dhyana-mudra*.[367] Both terracotta plaques can be dated preliminarily to the Early Medieval period, i.e. approximately to the fifth to sixth century AD.

Samarkand Region

Finds of Buddhist character are extremely rare in Sogdia and especially in Samarkand. For this reason the 'Buddhist' images published by V.L. Vyatkin in his book on Afrasiab[368] are of special interest. From the iconographic point of view, these finds have very subtle features, which can be associated with Buddhist terracottas. Some of the wall paintings from Pendjikent could also be related thematically with Buddhist art, particularly the painting from locus 28 (trench XXV) that is close to the image of the Buddha.[369] The find of a mould for a seated Buddha (Fig. 147) from the same site testifies to the degree Buddhist figurative tradition had penetrated the art of Sogdia.[370]

Isolated finds of Buddhist artefacts come from Samarkand itself. A gilded bronze statuette was discovered in the northeastern part of Afrasiab (Fig. 146). It represents a Buddhist, probably Bodhisattva Avalokiteshvara.[371] The statuette was unearthed in a layer of the tenth century, but stylistically belongs to the fifth or sixth century AD.[372] A small plaque was found in the south-western outskirts of Samarkand.[373] In spite of its small size (the height measures 32 mm), the figure reflects a high artistic level. In the centre, the Buddhist figure is seated on a pedestal in the shape of a lotus flower. The right leg hangs down from the throne, its foot resting on another smaller lotus. The right hand rests on the knee, while the left hand is pressed to the bosom in the gesture of *vitarka*. The figure wears a necklace and has additional breast ornamentation, together with a high conical headdress resembling *karanda-mukuta*. Stylistically, this image could be dated to the seventh to eighth century AD. There is no doubt that this terracotta plaque is similar to a *cretula* and that it was imported to Samarkand from Indo-Tibetan lands to serve as an amulet.

In 2005, on the surface of the ancient settlement of Kuldortepa (Urgut district, Samarkand Region), a small pendant (measuring 37 mm high and 10 mm wide) cast in silver was found.[374] It has the form of a standing figure *en face* draped in a long mantle falling almost to the ankles. The right arm is bent at the elbow and at the height of the shoulders the palm

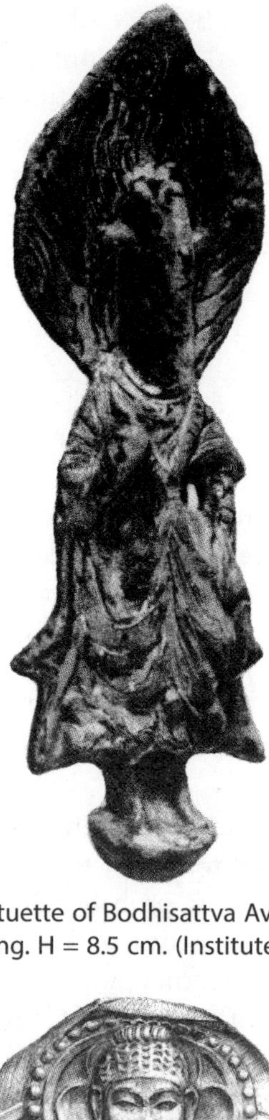

Fig. 146: Bronze statuette of Bodhisattva Avaloketishvara. Afrasiab.
Bronze with traces of gilding. H = 8.5 cm. (Institute of Archaeology, Samarkand).

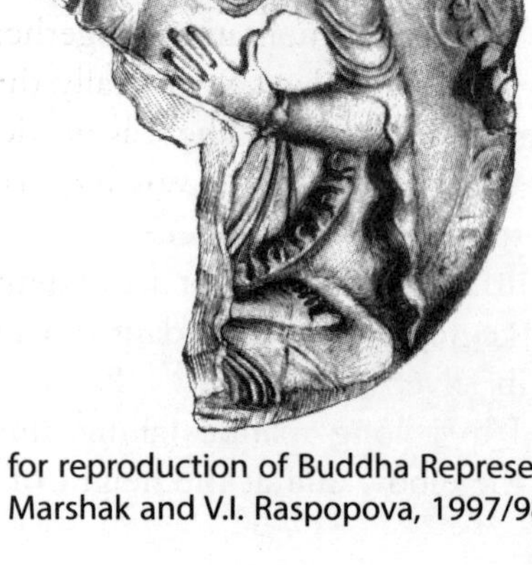

Fig. 147: Clay mould for reproduction of Buddha Representation. Pendjikent.
(After B.I. Marshak and V.I. Raspopova, 1997/98, fig. 2).

of its hand is turned toward the spectator. The left arm, bent and grasping the heavy folds of the tightly fitting mantle, is pressed to the left side of the body. One larger fold passes obliquely from the left shoulder downwards under the bent elbow. The lowest fold of the mantle is shown as a large rounded relief, underneath which the shins and a foot are visible. The figure seems to stand on a small base that tapers toward the bottom, where it is broken off. The head of the figure is finely modelled and the face is simply an oval with prominent eyeballs and cheekbones. A single continuous relief illustrates the forehead, headdress and nose. The eyes and ears are very poorly designed. The pupils of the eyes are perforated. The back of the figure is flat, although the smoothed contour of the figure is easily recognizable. It is unfortunate that many details of the suspension bracket have worn off due to friction from long use.

There is no doubt though that the suspension bracket shows the image of a standing figure of the Buddha, wearing a *sanghati* and in *abhaya-mudra*. The *ushnisha*, one of the *mahalakshana*s, the main attributes in the iconography of Buddha, has been pierced by an eyelet. This detail arouses suspicion. The fact that the *ushnisha*, an important element in the image of the Buddha incarnating wisdom and spiritual perfection, has been transformed into a practical device would have prevented the use of the figure as a cult object. If it served as an amulet, it hardly conformed to Buddhist orthodoxy. It seems likely that the figure became an amulet after it had lost its initial Buddhist meaning. For the interpretation of the figure as Buddhist, the tapering base might provide a clue, for an originally pointed end could have allowed it to be inserted in a larger composition. With its iconographic and stylistic features, the figure possibly dates tothe third or fourth centuries AD. However, as already noted above, the figure was in use for a long time, probably down to the Early Middle Ages and beyond.

B.Ya. Staviskiy investigated the site of Kuldortepa, on which a tiny Buddha figure was found in the 1950s. The archaeological evidence of the ancient settlement shows that the city flourished during the first centuries of our era. The superficial layers of the site covered the ninth to twelfth centuries.[375] A similar pendant representing the same person was found in the Talas valley in a burial that dated to seventh-eighth centuries.[376]

The dissemination of Buddhist objects across the territory of Sogdia possibly began in the Early Middle Ages. The apogee of the diffusion occurred during the dynasty of Wei and Tang, a period of regular diplomatic and mercantile relations. Archaeological evidence clearly shows the routes of various groups of missionaries, pilgrims, and merchants in Central Asia.[377] The exchange took place in two directions: on the one hand the Chinese colonization and expansion to the west sought to establish contacts with the culture of Serindia, while on the other hand a commercial colonization was carried out by the merchants of Central Asia. Amongst these merchants, the Sogdians were the most active and energetic. They penetrated far to the east, founding commercial cantons, as the biography of one Kang Seng-Hui, originally from Sogdia, makes evident. Born into a Sogdian family that had emigrated to India generations ago, he founded a monastery in Tsian (Nanjing) in AD 247 and translated a large number of Buddhist texts.[378]

The Chinese literary sources provide relatively little information about the fate of Buddhism in Sogdia. In the first half of the seventh century, these sources report Buddhist activities in two monasteries, which were in decline.[379] The inhabitants of Samarkand were hostile to the adepts of this religion and chased away the pilgrims with flaming torches. A passage of Hoi Chao, who visited this region a century later, confirms the decline of Buddhism in Sogdia. In Samarkand, Hoi Chao found only one monastery with a single monk dwelling in it.[380]

Even poorer is the archaeological evidence for Buddhist art in the neighbouring Ustrushana region. We do not know of any Buddhist objects from this region, aside from an oral communication that was given by the inhabitants of the Sangzar Valley to the archaeologist L.I. Al'baum in 1948. These people asserted that in 1933, during the leveling of a hill they came across mud brick masonry, column bases and bronze statues, including a figure with prolonged ears, and representations of animals.[381] There exists, however, one indubitable Buddhist image from Chach (modern Tashkent and Syrdarya regions), which came from Mingurjuk and shows Buddha on the lotus throne. It has been dated to the sixth to eighth century AD.[382]

Margiana

In contrast, the nearby Republic of Turkmenistan provides plenty of examples of Buddhist plastic art, including stone and clay sculptures as well as terracotta figurines. One terracotta figurine representing a *bodhisattva* was found at the Akkala settlement,[383] located on the middle reaches of the Amudarya. The excavators dated the statuette to the second to fourth centuries AD.[384] Margiana exhibits a remarkable Buddhist complex, indicating the infiltration of Buddhist missionaries in this territory. Two objects of Buddhist character – a *sangharama* and an isolated *stupa* – are located in the south-eastern corner of Gyaur-kala in Old Merv. The architecture of the *sangarama* has a layout comprising three parts: a court with a shrine, whose entrance is oriented to the north; the temple itself, which was decorated in the interior with wall paintings as well as clay and alabaster sculptures; and a dwelling area in the eastern part of the complex.

The *stupa* was discovered behind the eastern city wall on the same lines as the *sangharama*.[385] Its form of a square base with cylindrical trunk is similar to the *stupas* of Fayaztepa and Karatepa. Mud brick, *pakhsa* (clay blocks) and baked brick were used for its construction. On the basis of the numismatic evidence coming mainly from the base of the *stupa*, namely copper coins of Shapur I, the complex cannot be dated before the third century AD. Rather, the stone figurines, a Sanskrit manuscript (written in Brahmi) and several coins of Khosrow I Anushirvan that were found in the reliquary of the *stupa* would point to the sixth century AD. A finely modelled sculpture of Buddha and a musician (harpist) in black schist were evidently imported from Gandhara, as schist is more typical for that region and was very popular in the sculptural schools of Gandhara.[386] Another remarkable find from Old Merv was a colossal head of Buddha that represented the state of *parinirvana*.[387]

Chorasmia

A fragment of a terracotta figure from Kazakly-yatkan in Karakalpakstan on the territory of ancient Khoresm has been published as an image of 'Buddha or one of the Bodhisattvas'. Radio-carbon tests applied to the complex of finds to which the fragment belonged, narrowed its date to 39 BC–AD 69.[388] However, neither the pose nor the other indistinct elements allow a positive identification of the figure from Kazakly-yatkan with the image of Buddha or a *bodhisattva*.

The finds of isolated cult objects such as terracotta figurines cannot always warrant the spread of one or another religion. It is possible that they were used by individuals, who practised their religion privately, for certain Buddhist terracotta figurines were found on sites that did not possess any Buddhist sacred architecture such as shrines, temples, or the like.[389]

THE EARLY MEDIEVAL PERIOD (LATE FOURTH TO FIFTH CENTURY AD)

THE PROVINCIAL ESTATE OF KUEVKURGAN

The magnificent monument of Kuevkurgan, which stands on the plain beyond the Sherabad spurs, sets it apart from the numerous other sites located in the Surkhandarya province. Like the large ancient site of Zartepa, Kuevkurgan is situated 26 km to the north-west of Termez and 4 km to the south of the district centre Angor. The monument itself is located 300 m to the east of Zartepa and approximately 200 m to the west of the main Termez-Tashkent road. One can see its ruins from afar, majestically towering above the gardens, the golden loess contrasting with the green vegetation. The scale of the monument indicates, perhaps, that it served as the residence of a local prince. Behind it, in the distance, loom the ruins of Zartepa, made famous by the abundance of scholarly literature dedicated to the results of the protracted archaeological excavations there. Indeed, Kuevkurgan first received attention in a study on Zartepa and its surrounds.[390] Interest in the Kuevkurgan site began with the surface collection of ceramics, the analysis of which suggested an Early Medieval date. The ceramics of Kuevkurgan chronologically continued the ceramic tradition of Zartepa. It later became clear that life in Zartepa did not come to a standstill around AD 400, but continued, although not over the entire site, and overlapped with the last period of Kuevkurgan.[391] However, soon after, the whole area fell into decline.

Archaeological investigations of this area started by L.I. Al'baum at the end of the 1940s have yielded remarkable finds.[392] The study revealed the importance of smaller sites, whose rich finds were not inferior to those of the principal ones.

Architecture

The structure and plan of Kuevkurgan have been successfully identified through archaeological excavation. It was erected on an artificial platform constructed of unbaked rectangular bricks (Fig. 148). Prior to excavation, the site appeared as an oval mound 18 m wide, 20 m long and 5 m high. The initial site was probably almost a square. The monument was evidently two-storeyed (Fig. 149). This can be deduced from the height of the remaining external walls, which are higher than the presumed ceiling of

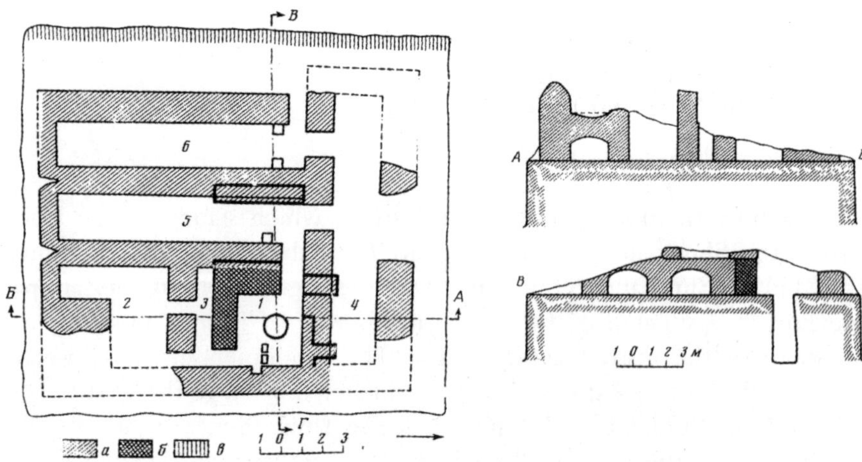

Fig. 148: Plan of Kuevkurgan. (After T. Annaev, 1984, fig. 1).

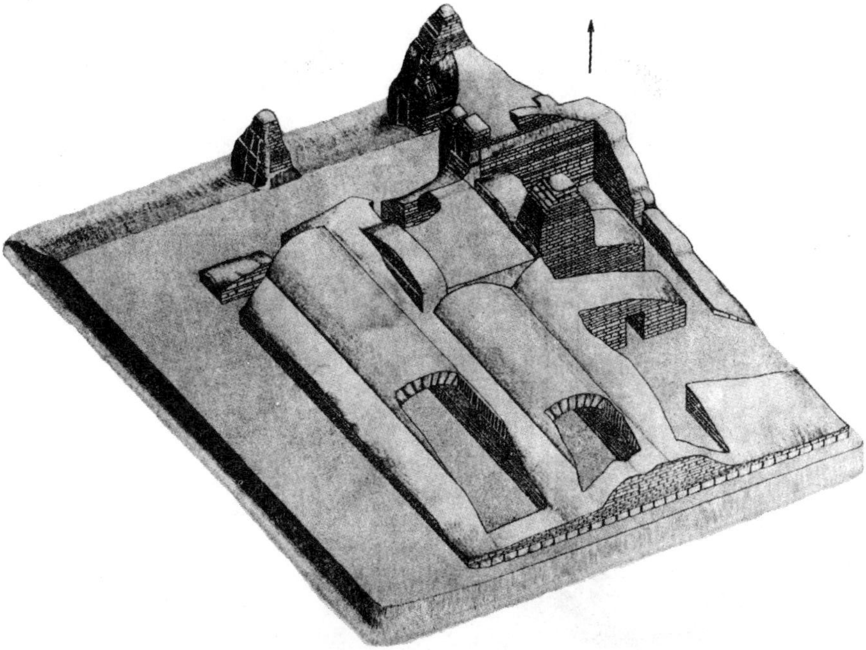

Fig. 149: Kuevkurgan. Overall axonometric projection. (After T. Annaev, 1984, fig. 2).

the first floor, and also from the proportions between the lower and upper layers.

The northern part of the monumental building included a long hallway (Fig. 150), which apparently served as a vestibule (room no. 4). Here, the walls are quite dilapidated and their plan considerably eroded. The western part has two long corridor-shaped rooms running parallel to each other (rooms 5 and 6). The eastern part of the monument has a more complex ground plan. All the rooms were raised above a clay platform or stylobate 4 m in height. In the western part, the stylobate projects forward by 3.7 m. It is quite possible that this was due to a major destruction during earthworks and originally the platform was meant to be more symmetrical. Of room no. 4, only the southern and the northern walls are extant. The wall surfaces were plastered with clay mixed with thick cut straw. A small vaulted niche had been hollowed out in the south wall, but was later filled in. A vault 1.8 m in height covered the supposed vestibule. It was constructed with inclined brick pieces, placed at an angle of 7-8 degrees to each other. The 30-40 cm wide space between the vault and the supporting wall was sealed by clay.

The diameter of the vault is equal to the width of the room. The masonry of the north wall is in the combined technique, coupling *pakhsa* with raw brickwork. Such construction techniques were quite widespread

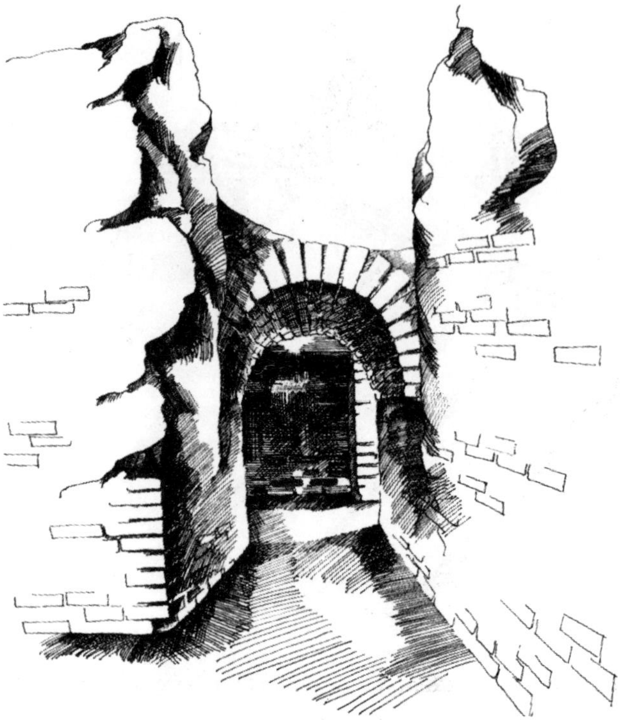

Fig. 150: Kuevkurgan. Entrance to an elongated chamber.
(After Sh. Pidaev, 1999b: 67).

in southern Uzbekistan and were already employed on some of the earliest monuments – an indication of the continuity of this building tradition.[393] The upper part of the wall is perforated by false arrow slits, measuring 60 × 20 cm, most likely serving a decorative function. The wall with the false decorative arrow-slits, together with the entrance in the central section, probably formed part of the ceremonial suite in the northern section of the building.

The eastern sector of the complex has two rooms, connected to each other by two doorways. The first entrance to room no. 2 was located in the centre of the north wall and was the main entrance to that room before the reconstruction of the building. At a later stage a large wall, in the form of an L, portioned off the narrow corridor no. 3. It seems likely that rooms 1 and 2 were square adjoining rooms with an entrance in the centre, for, as has already been pointed out, the intersecting wall was an addition to the original building. The new wall was probably needed as support for the second floor. It is partly wedged into the longitudinal wall of the corridor-shaped room 5 and into the walls of rooms 1 and 2.

The most important room was probably the well preserved room 1, the superb interior of which is discussed below. Initially, this room measured

5.15 × 5.45 m. In its north-eastern corner a well with a diameter of 1.1 m was exposed. From the modern level to the upper layer, the well was 2.4 m deep. Its walls were vertical, only slightly widening toward the bottom to a diameter of 1.35 m. The masonry was of clay bricks measuring 10 × 24 × 10 or 10 × 25 × 11 cm down to a depth of 4 m, at which point a sand layer was encountered. A moist layer of natural soil without any organic admixture filled the well.[394] The absence of any haphazard fill and ceramic fragments in the well proves that it was not a household pit, as Annaev asserts,[395] but rather a well. The careful masonry of the walls of the well also confirms this supposition. The bricks, despite being unbaked, were waterproof, thereby protecting the well from washout and landslide. In describing the interior features of the room, it is necessary to note a small niche (H. 80 cm, W. 50 cm, D. 40 cm) in the east wall. The bottom of the niche touches the floor and from its left edge, perpendicular to the east wall, runs a row of bricks to the well. These bricks measure 50 × 25 × 10 cm.

Another striking feature of the room was its sculptures, of which numerous fragments were discovered. There was a fill layer some 20-40 cm thick, which covered the entire area of the floor in this room, perhaps an aeolian layer accumulated during the abandonment of the building. Here, a few ceramic shards and animal bones, mainly goat and sheep, were found. Large pieces of *pakhsa* clay bricks with imprints of leaves and twigs were exposed in the upper layer (measuring 80-100 cm) of the floor. These might have fallen from above the roof beams, which would have been covered with clay packing. Such methods of roofing are known from the castle at Balalyktepan.[396] Apparently, the roof over the room in Kuevkurgan was very thick and had collapsed onto the sculptures, as clay pieces were mixed with fragments of sculpture. On top of this last layer was a loose layer of brick fragments that had formed after the monument was deserted.

The mud brick fill layer was cleared in the northern part of the room. Room no. 1, was connected with room no. 2 by means of a narrow corridor (no. 3), later blocked by another wall. Room no. 2 was L-shaped. Its south-eastern part was destroyed, but its western wall, the wall formerly shared by rooms 3 and 1, is still standing). The northern wall with two passages – in the centre and in the northeast corner – has also been preserved. The western wall measures 5.55 m, the northern wall 4.15 m and the southern wall 1.75 m in length. The height of the best-preserved section of the walls is 2.05 m. In the south-east corner, solid, heavy blocks of unbaked bricks have been exposed. It is possible that these blocks were shoring up the thick roof or the ramp (*pandus*) leading to the second floor.[397]

In the stratigraphy of the floor three layers could be distinguished. The bottom layer was 80 cm thick, consisting of loose soil with brick fragments.

Above this was a 15-20 cm thick layer containing small chunks of brick and some ceramics. This was in turn covered by a fairly hard layer of brick fill up to the modern surface. Room no. 3 was formed by the construction of the new L-shaped wall that cut across room no. 1. It has a longitudinal plan along the west-east axis, measures 4.2 × 2.1 m and has three entrances, one from room no. 2, one through the passage in the middle of the south wall (the north wall of room no. 2) and one through the passage in the south-east corner. The western part of the building consists of two elongated rooms (nos. 5 and 6), running parallel from north to south. The northern walls of these two rooms are adjacent to the entrance of room no. 4. Room no. 5 communicates both with room no. 4 (the passage is in the north-west corner and measures 1.3 m to 0.7 m), and with room no. 1 via the passage located in the north-west corner. Room no. 5 is about 2.4 m wide and 12.6 m long.

The south wall of room no. 5, shared by all rooms of the southern part of the monument, is 0.85 m thick. A square buttress of unbaked bricks was exposed in this room. The buttress measures 50 × 50 × 50 cm. The room is vaulted with inclined pieces of trapezoid bricks. The height of these bricks varies between 46 and 52 cm, the longer side measuring 26 to 30 cm and the shorter side 19 to 24 cm. The thickness of the bricks is 9-10 cm. The trapezoid bricks were laid in such a way that they were paired to form quadrangular blocks. Fragments of ceramics were found in the mortar between them, used, in all probability, for bonding. On the surface of some of the bricks mason's marks (*tamgas*) had been drawn by finger. The height of the vault is 1.8 m.

The ceramic complex found in room no. 5 may be divided into three groups. The ceramics of the first group were found predominantly in the masonry and in the plaster between the bricks, and mainly comprise large rim fragments. The ceramics found in the fill above the floor belong to the second group. A third group consists of fragments of cooking pots found on the surface of the floor.[398] As noted, room no. 6 in the western part of the building was parallel to room no. 5 and stretched from north to south. The western wall of this room was formed by the external wall of the monument. The room has two passages. One passage, with a width of 1.4 m was in all probability the principal one. It is located in the middle of the north wall and leads to the entrance room (no. 4). A second passage in the north-west corner of the room exits to the platform. In room no. 6, two cube-shaped pedestals were found next to each other. The same cubic structures were found in room no. 5, situated 1.15 m from the corner of the passage. The pedestals measure 50 × 50 × 50 cm and were built with unbaked bricks measuring 50 × 25 × 9-10 cm. Judging by the remains of the walls which are higher than the ceiling of the first storey, and also by their colossal size, the edifice no doubt had a second storey. Remains of the second storey have been preserved over rooms 1, 4, and 5. However, it is difficult to ascertain the dimensions of this second storey. It most likely occupied a smaller area than the ground floor.

The archaeological context of the monument suggests two consecutive stages of occupation. The first period of its existence was connected with the construction of the building on the original architectural plan. The lodgings and, perhaps, official spaces were in rooms 1 and 2; the first room most likely had a ceremonial character, while the second served as the living quarters, being the inner apartment of the country-seat. Apparently, sculptures were installed in these two rooms only. It is impossible to imagine the aspect of the second floor during this first period. However, considering the fact that the more powerful and monumental external walls (rooms 4 and 1) of both storeys were erected simultaneously, it can be taken for granted that from the very beginning there was a second storey. The long corridor-shaped rooms of the western part of the building are intriguing. It would be logical that they fulfilled a domestic purpose. However, the pedestals in these interiors would be hard to reconcile with such an interpretation, especially if they supported sculptures. It is still not possible to solve the question of the function of these rooms.

During the second stage the building underwent reconstruction, which altered its plan. The changes affected mainly the eastern part of the complex, specifically room no. 1. A thick wall now screened off the small corridor-shaped room no. 3, where the new entrance in the north-east corner replaced the primary entrance from room no. 1 to room no. 2. Most likely, the well in room no. 1 already existed before and remained there, partitioned off by a small wall. The main room, which can be conditionally termed a hall, probably had a high ceiling. However, during the second construction phase, this ceiling was removed for the sake of the new floor level of the second storey. Hardly anything remains from the beams. These beams were fixed at 2.1 m above the ground floor. The excavator, T. Annaev, supposes that the upper storey above room no. 1 was only built in the second period.[399] In principle, this does not contradict the hypothesis that the construction of the thick wall was intended as a support for the second storey. But another circumstance should be taken into consideration: from the outset the façade of this building appears to have been conceived as two-storeyed. The width and height of the exterior walls testify to this, regardless of the fact that some of them have no traces of additional brickwork or superstructures. The idea that some of the sculptures were placed on the second floor makes no sense. An additional fact should not be ignored. If, as is generally accepted, the sculptures were connected with a dynastic cult of ancestors, the observances of which involved water, it is unlikely that such a room would be located upstairs. A better choice for the interior decoration of the second storey would be wall painting, as noted by the excavator.[400] Judging by the fragments of plaster exposed in the fill, wall paintings might indeed have adorned the upper rooms. A more serious problem in the presence of sculpture on the second floor would have been the weight, not to mention the small size of those rooms. Wall paintings were thus better suited as decorative elements on the second storey, taking up no space and having no weight.

The building was erected with unbaked rectangular bricks; its walls plastered with clay 1-3 cm thick. In all rooms with a vault, the clearing of the brickwork revealed that the trapezoid bricks were used only for the construction of the arch. The walls of the main rooms had been especially thoroughly plastered, no doubt in preparation for murals. Perhaps these rooms were also decorated with sculpture.

The Site and the Search for Analogies

In terms of plan and chronology, Kuevkurgan is closely related to Kuchuk castle.[401] Kuchuk is located just to the south of Kuevkurgan, towards Termez, and near the Central Asian railway on the land of the former V. I. Lenin collective farm. The similarity of the two sites is evident in the general layout of the plan, which resembles a square (Fig. 151). The size and construction of the platforms further strengthens this similarity. The Kuchuk castle platform measures 26 × 26 × 3 m, thus it was slightly higher than that of Kuevkurgan; it was erected in *pakhsa*. The difference in height of the platforms could have been a result of the respective terrain, but was

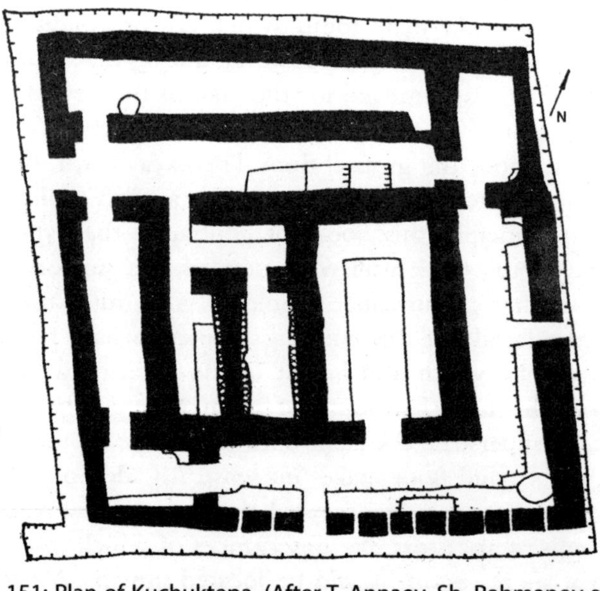

Fig. 151: Plan of Kuchuktepa. (After T. Annaev, Sh. Rahmanov and A. Bobohodjaev, 1988, fig. 1).

not crucial for their function. Kuchuktepa is oriented slightly off east; this slight deviation was also present at Kuevkurgan. Much conformity in the architectural design of both monuments would point to a common source, which would probably also clarify the reason for their analogous construction techniques. The narrow vestibule with a doorway located midway is relevant in this regard. There are two parallel rooms in the western part of the Kuchuk monument. The central part, slightly displaced to the east, consists of a complex of rooms around the main hall (room no. 5). Long corridor-like rooms accompany the main hall along the perimeter (rooms 7, 8, 9). The presence of wells in the interior of several rooms (nos. 7, 9, 1) is curious. Certainly, these must have benefited the inhabitants of the castle. As the excavators have noted, the second storey was directly located above the vaulted rooms 4, 6 and 9. The existence of a second storey, probably the main kitchen above room no. 11, has been established on the basis of potsherds found in the destruction layer on the ground floor. The main entrance to the upper storey, a staircase, was along the south wall of room no. 13.[402]

The Cult Character of Some Elements of the Kuevkurgan Interior

The presence of the well in room no. 1 can be explained in two ways, each a real possibility. According to the first explanation, the well was essential for the activities of the inhabitants and was to supply them with water in the event of a long siege. As a rule, the enemy would attack the irrigation systems of a town, settlement or castle. There are many such incidents known from history, particularly connected with nomadic invasions, which aimed at gaining the wealth of the town and not the town itself. In short, the construction of the well within the house was dictated by practical and physical necessity, and additionally, independence in the case of siege.

The second supposition is of a spiritual nature and is associated with a cult ceremony. The scriptures of the Zoroastrian Holy Book, the *Avesta* prescribe the worship of a divinity as one of the obligatory rituals of an elaborate cult.[403] In this respect, the well can be regarded as being located in a sacred area reserved for cult ceremonies. The meaning of the well as a sacred place, a reservoir of moisture – is borne out by the archaeological context, which strongly confirms the concept of purity in this location. The well did not become a household pit or rubbish heap. Nothing had fallen into it, not even by chance. This suggests that the well was regularly cleaned to maintain its 'purity' as a sacred place. The cult of water is discussed below. The point to be made here is the specific location. The sanctity of this location was emphasized by the brickwork, which screened the well from the entrance to room no. 2. Moreover, the *in situ* discovery of numerous sculptures and sculpture fragments corroborates the cult character of the well and room no. 1 as a whole. These sculptures seemed originally to have been placed only in this room.[404] Written sources also confirm the connection of sculpture with the well.[405]

Unfortunately, the question concerning water reserves, both man-made and natural – including wells, ponds, springs and rivers – has not been thoroughly studied. Each of these reservoirs was considered sacred and had its own ritual and ceremonial peculiarity and proper place in the architectural plan of a monument. However, it is important to stress that despite its almost secular appearance the sculpture of Kuevkurgan had a sacred meaning. The first written source concerning the sacred well and water is the inscription on a stone from the dynastic temple of Kanishka at Surkh Kotal.[406]

> This acropolis is a temple [dedicated to] Kanishka the Victor, by which the Lord King honored Kanishka. And here, when the [construction] of the acropolis was finished, inside the containers for the water were dry; as a result the acropolis remained without water. And when because of intense summer heat a drought came, the gods were taken away from [their] abode [places?], [i.e.] their [?] divine images and sculptures. And the acropolis was deserted, when in the thirty-first year of ruling, in the month Nisan, Nokonzok the Governor, favorite of the king, the most beloved [?] to the king, excellent, untiring to do good, being full of virtues, pure of intentions toward all creatures, visited the temple. Then he walled [?] the acropolis, dug a well, drew water, faced [the well] with masonry in order that the people on the acropolis might not feel any lack of water and in case of a drought from intense summer heat the gods should not be taken away from [their] abode, and the acropolis should not be deserted. And a windlass for the water [buckets] was constructed over the well [and] also a reservoir was built. And thanks to this well and thanks to this reservoir all at the acropolis prospered.

A second inscription comes from Airtam, a site situated on the right bank of the Oxus River 18 km to the east of Termez. The six lines in Bactrian script are carved into the pedestal of a sculpture representing a couple. The inscription is dated to the second century AD:

> King Huvishka in the fourth [or: fortieth] year of his rule, when [the king?] the city [. . .] [King [?] granted to sangha [?]. Founded by Shudiya, descended from [. . .] who put the temple in order [or: decorated]. And gave the name of. . . . And, besides, at the acropolis Shudiya built large gates [?]. . . [for] the gods and built dams in the flowing water [or: river] the way it was needed for worshipping [gods]. And [brought] both deities here, and they were. . . . This was inscribed by Mirzad on the order of Shudiya.[407]

These two inscriptions bear out not only the utilitarian character of the wells, but also the relationship of the water contained in them with the veneration of the cult images.

The site of Takht-i Sangin attests to the existence of temples devoted to river deities.[408] In addition, an inscription on a votive object mentions the deity of Oxus.[409] It is also interesting in this respect that a figurine of Marsyas was related to the River Meander in Asia Minor. The Greeks who came to Bactria continued to hold water divinities and water elements sacred. The representations of marine creatures such as tritons, Cupid on the dolphin, and the hippocampus in the repertoire of the Bactrian masters, as well as of the subsequent Sako-Yuezhi and Kushan periods (for example, at Tillyatepa[410]) mirror this tradition.

However, among these minor creatures with mythological connotations, the river-god Oxus held a supreme position. Personal names with the root 'Oxus' were probably derived from this river divinity. For example, at Ai Khanum two such names appear in inscriptions – Oxubazes and Oxeboakes;[411] other names containing this same root include Oxiart, Oxaphr, Oxubag (a variant of Oxuboakes?). These names were popular in the Iranian-speaking regions, especially among the population inhabiting the valley of the Amudarya (Oxus) River. The importance of this river cult was probably greater than we imagine.

It is most likely that certain rituals took place during the construction of an irrigation canal or a similar project involving the waters of the river.[412] Apparently, sacrifices were offered to the river divinity at the ceremonial opening of a canal or the branching off of an arm of the river and so on. Water cults in the context of the archaeological data would be a rewarding topic for future research. The *Avesta* devotes a special *Aban Yasht* to water, underlining the significance of the element and its worship.[413] In the *Avesta*, water is venerated under the name *Apo*, indicating the names of deities bestowing moisture on the earth and the creatures related to it. One of them is Apam Napat – the Grandson of Water. An essential female divinity of the Avestic Pantheon, Ardvisura Anahita (strong, virginal Ardvi') is also tied to the cult of water. Her beautiful feminine image is associated with the Amudarya that is overflowing into a great number of branches, giving fertility to the earth, animals, and peoples.

One of the ancient deities connected with the phenomenon of nature cycles is the star Tishtrya (hypothetically Sirius). Tishtrya, in the image of a white horse, fought with the demon of drought, Apaosha, and defeated him, while demanding help from Ahura Mazda. Following this, Ahura Mazda ordered the people to venerate Tishtrya. And from the Lake Vorukasha the wind (Vato) brought the clouds and the rain began to fall on the earth. Thus, the well in Kuevkurgan may be associated with sacred water. If the popular cult of water and the existence of temples devoted to the water divinity (the temple of Takht-i Sangin) are taken into consideration, we can postulate that, aside from its practical purpose, it also had a spiritual meaning.

The Sculpture at Kuevkurgan

All the sculptural fragments recovered during the excavation of Kuevkurgan were executed using the same technical and artistic methods, and represent a single figurative and plastic complex. As it is difficult to reconstruct the original arrangement of the figures, it is possible only to speculate that some of them formed part of a group while others were displayed individually, as the finds of pedestals would suggest.

HEADS AND FRAGMENTS OF HEADS

A. *Complete Heads*

1. Female head (Fig. 152)
   This example was found near the south *wall.* The head has been sculpted in relief and, in all probability, was attached to a wall (of a niche?), which served as background to the whole composition. The back and sides of the head are shapeless clumps of clay, which probably helped to prop up the sculpture.
   The framework of the head was an oval blank, made of finely pounded clay with some pieces of reed. The clay is of a grey-yellow colour. A

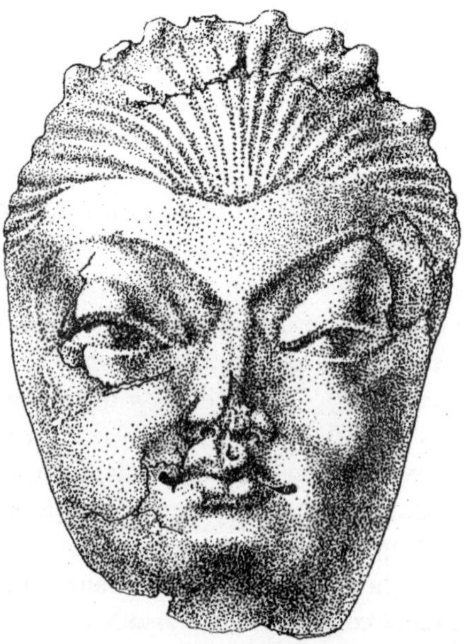

Fig. 152: Female head with straight hair and a pearl diadem. Kuevkurgan. Clay sculpture. 5th century AD. H = 19 cm. (Museum of History of Culture and Art of the Peoples of Uzbekistan, Samarkand).

very thin layer of clay was on the surface, tinged with grey and without any additions. The thickness of this clay layer differs: it is about 6 mm thick in the lower part of the face and on the forehead up to 25 mm. A 1 mm layer of plaster – covered the clay surface. This plaster was then painted. The polychrome nature of the plaster emphasizes the facial features and details of the hair. The height of the preserved section of the head is 18.5 cm from the base of the chin up to the wreath; the width is 13 cm across the forehead and temples and about 8 cm across the cheeks. The head is badly cracked, the right cheek is considerably damaged, and in many places the colour has disappeared.

The image was strictly frontally portrayed. The regular features have been carefully modelled (Fig. 152). The priming of the face is white with touches of colour selected from the usual palette, including different gradation of ochre from yellow to red, black, white and blue, distinguishing the lips and other details. Barely visible traces of tinged pink remain on the tight, well-defined lips. The thin, arched eyebrows, the eyelashes, and the external corners of the eyes (possibly expressing the contemporary ideal of beauty) are outlined in black. The hair is straight and black, and the forelock is distinguished by black paint on the middle of the forehead. The crown is gilded and has a row of round pearls.

The face of the head with its harmonic proportions symbolizes spirituality. The first feature to attract attention is the manner in which the eyes are modelled. They have large and heavy lids, slightly lowered over the iris, and the impression is one of concentration and self-contemplation. However, unlike in the canonical sculpture of the Buddhist school, in this case, the sculptor lifted the eyelids a little, thereby creating a slightly arched lower line of the lid. This can be compared with a sculpture from Gandhara, where the eyelids of Buddha and *bodhisattva*s are represented in an almost horizontal line across the lower edge, conveying the state of meditation and self-contemplation[414]. The manner of the modelling of the eyebrows is peculiar. It is not done in relief as usual, but by a smooth plastering of the surface above the eyelid, forming an edge along the lower line of the forehead, which is then traced with a thin black line to stress the broad arches of the eyebrows.

The fine, straight nose has been carefully modelled: the depth of the nostrils was achieved, most likely, with a tool. In the same way, a small perforation below the nose has been executed by the gentle pressing of an instrument. A similar perforation is found in the corners of the clearly delineated lips, however, in this instance, the depression is slightly deeper. The expression of a faint smile is given by these perforations in the corners of the lips. The straight, combed-back hair, dispersing like a fan from the middle of the forehead, is shown as deep furrows. The hairline is approximately parallel to the lines of the eyebrows. A pearl-studded crown covers the top of the head.

2. Female head (Fig. 153)
The execution is in high relief, and the technique is the same as for the head just described. However, on this example the plaster coating is considerably better preserved and traces of paint remain. Unfortunately, the head has been severely damaged: the nose is partly broken off, while the left eyebrow, the top of the head, the left ear, the chin, and part of the right ear are completely missing. The remaining height is 17 cm, the width 9.5 cm across the temples and forehead and 6 cm across the chin.

As with the previous head, the details have been carefully crafted, and the soft finish of the face as a whole, with clearly distinguished nose, eyes and lips, is characteristic. The extreme high relief of the sculpture allows it to be seen both in full view and in profile. This makes us wonder whether the head had its place in the foreground of a larger composition. The face is round, but slightly foreshortened towards the chin. The half-closed eyes give the impression of full concentration. The bright paint, emphasizing the features, contrasts with the priming in white plaster. The eyebrows, eyelashes, and the pupils are painted in black while the corners of the eyes are tinged dark blue; barely visible traces of pink-red paint are on the lips. The heavy, down cast lids are

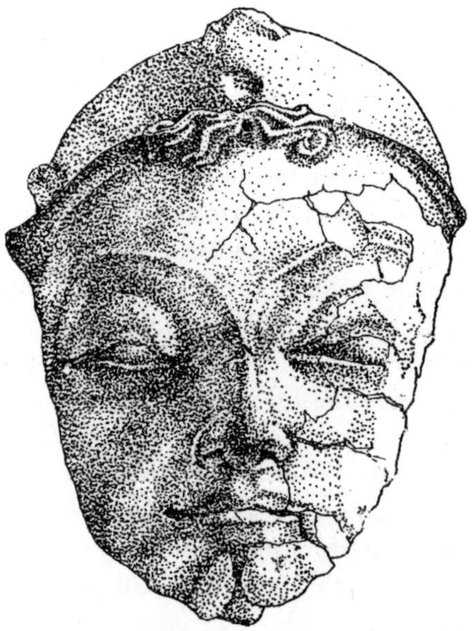

Fig. 153: Female head with black hair and a pearl diadem. Kuevkurgan. Clay sculpture. 5th century AD. H = 21.5 cm. (Museum of History of Culture and Art of the Peoples of Uzbekistan, Samarkand).

indicated by a rather thick relief, and for this reason the external corners of the eyes are somewhat drawn out. A thin line along the edge of the upper lids defines the eyelashes. The irises are marked by a black spot, almost hidden under the lids; the pupils are not discernible. The lower lids are slightly swollen. The eyebrows are distinguished by their relief and are accentuated by a thin black line, which meets at the bridge of the nose. The lips are soft and full and together with the dimples at the corners give the impression of a faint, scarcely perceptible smile. The high forehead is framed by short curls, arranged identically in a row consisting of a double wave followed by a circular outline. The external side of the ear was finished off in detail and painted in white.

The method of shaping repeats, on the whole, that of the first head. The rendering of the hairstyle on the current sculpture is interesting. Some details have been depicted in paint, for example, a curl on the temple, which is rendered by a thin black line as on the first head. The lower row of the hair, which is only preserved on the right-hand side, consists of moulded/stamped curls. Here, the curls are combed slightly backwards. This hair style is familiar from monuments of Buddhist sculpture in northern Bactria, such as Dal'verzintepa[415] and Ajinatepa,[416] and to the south of the Amudarya River, notably at Dil'berjin[417] and Tepe Sardar.[418] It was also widely employed by the Gandharan sculptors.[419] It is interesting to note that this hairstyle is still absent on the Khalchayan sculptures, and therefore appears to have been imported with the Buddhist sculptural tradition into north Bactria-Tokharistan.

3. Small head (Fig. 154).

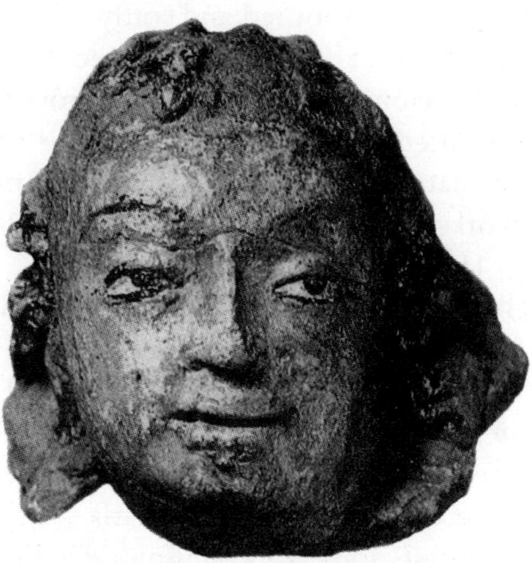

Fig. 154: Head of a male personage with stamped ringlets. Kuevkurgan. Clay sculpture. 5th century AD. H = 11.5 cm. (Museum of History of Culture and Art of the Peoples of Uzbekistan, Samarkand).

The method of sculpture resembles that of those described above. The head has been executed in three dimensions and was located, very likely, in the foreground of the composition together with the previous sculpture. A circular wooden trunk, which was the frame of the sculpture, has been preserved; it is 13 mm in diameter. The head is 11.5 cm in height. It is reasonably well preserved, except that the right ear is chipped and the upper part of the hair somewhat damaged. The combination technique was used for the hairstyle: the curls were stamped separately in a mould and were then affixed to the head; afterwards the remaining part of the hair was manually finished. The black paint of the hair has been applied carelessly and, in part, beyond the relief of the curls.

The head differs from the previous one in several details. The sculptor has modelled the head slightly tilted to the right. The general colour of the face is yellow-pink. The plump oval form of the face is characterized by distinguished features. The sculptor tried to render the statue a portrait, as is obvious from details and also from the appearance of the whole. The eyes are coarse with thick, black lines underneath the plump, heavy eyelids. The lines extend beyond the corner of the eyes. The iris, marked by a black dot, is clearly distinguished on the white background of the eyeball. The forehead is rather high, slightly retreating, and is framed by a richly defined hairstyle, but unfortunately preserved only incompletely. The upper part of the hair consists of radial streaks in relief with rectangular furrows between them. The hair framing the forehead was finely executed, with large, untidy, curls.

The thin arches of the eyebrows continue the line of the delicately executed nose. The corners of the lips are slightly lifted, and the mouth is barely open. The chin is smoothed and softly curves into a short thick neck. Despite the fact that the sculptor used the same method of modelling as for the previous sculptures, here he strove to infuse dynamism into the statue. The tilted head, upward fixed stare and slightly opened, smiling mouth animate the statue, which could not be said of the aforementioned works with their expressionless, aloof faces.

4. Female head (Fig. 155).

This head, modelled in high relief, is badly damaged: the sides, part of the chin and the left cheek are broken. It is 18 cm high; 11 cm wide across the temples, and 7 cm wide across the chin. The general colour of the face is white, due to the thin plaster. The eyebrows, eyelashes and hair are black. The adornments, represented as projecting beads, are white, simulating the colour of silver or pearls.

The oval face manifests some carefully modelled details. The eyes are represented as narrow slits with sharp corners. The thick edges of the eyelids are emphasized by a narrow line. The large, heavy eyelids are lowered, reflecting a sense of equilibrium and concentration, as if in a

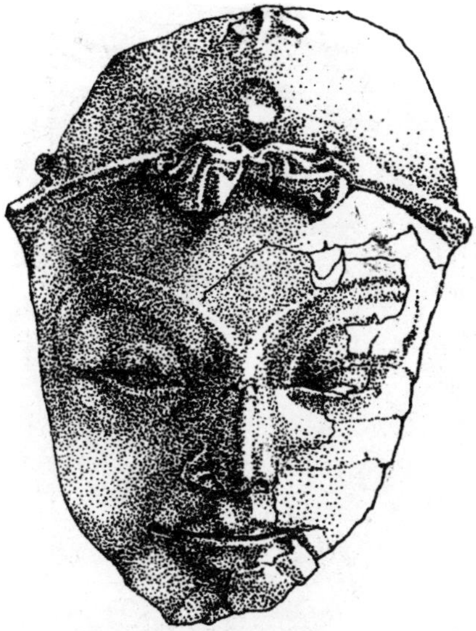

Fig. 155: Female head with hair separately stamped in a mould and a diadem in shape of pearls. Kuevkurgan. Clay sculpture. 5th century AD. H = 18 cm. (Museum of History of Culture and Art of the Peoples of Uzbekistan, Samarkand).

state of meditation. The semi-circular eyebrows are rendered in an unusual manner by cutting away a considerable amount of plaster from the upper part of the eye socket. The clean-cut edges of the eyebrows meet the bridge of the nose, continuing its fine straight line. The orifices of the nostrils are perforated with an instrument. The corners of the lips of the small mouth are slightly raised.

The rather high, somewhat retreating, forehead is framed by a hair style represented as a relief strip. In the centre is a line indicating a parting between two symmetrical halves of the hair. The curls have been stamped in a mould. The rest of the hair forms a smooth surface, painted in black. Traces of a diadem are found in a strip, preserved a little above the curls and in a small section on the right of the head. The remains show circular projections, painted white, representing, most likely, pearls, which perhaps formed a straight row, as on the first head. The remains of the adornment are widest at the midpoint; probably the compound central part of the crown was fixed there. The head is a vivid example of the conventional method of sculpture, where features of the Buddhist canonical tradition can be vaguely seen. Here, the confident hand of the sculptor is reflected in the plastic modelling, which gives the sculpture consummate finesse.

5. Head of a male statue (Fig. 156).

This is the largest of the heads, measuring 23 cm high, 11 cm across the temples, and 8.5 cm across the chin. It has been worked in the

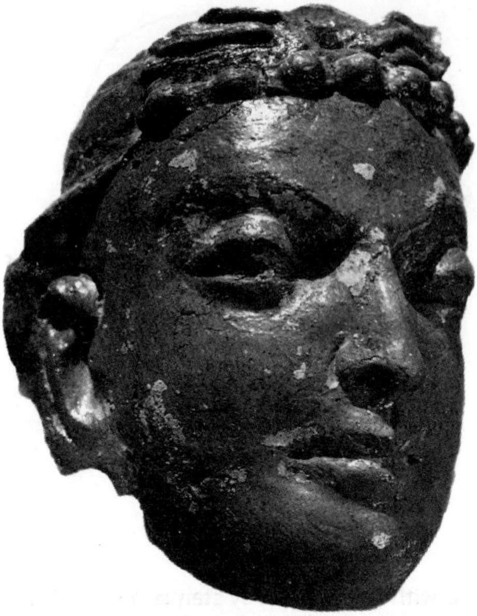

Fig. 156: Male head wearing diadem. Kuevkurgan. Clay sculpture. 5th century AD. H = 19.5 cm. (Museum of History of the Peoples of Uzbekistan, Tashkent).

round. The background colour of the face is white. The same colour was used for the ornamentation of the headdress. The hair and eyebrows are black. The edge of the lower eyelid is outlined with blue paint. The lips are distinguished by pink, traces of which remain on the upper lip. On the whole, the manufacture repeats the technique of the previous examples.

The thorough rendering of the details of the sculpture is reflected in the individuality of the features. The sculptor evidently tried to achieve a portrait. The face is oval,the forehead is not high, and slightly retreating, the nose is thin and aquiline. Small recesses, emphasized against the background of the rather plump cheeks, distinguish the nostrils. The lips have soft contours with a small dimple in the upper corners, giving the face an almost imperceptible smile. The round, smoothed chin has been gently modelled. The eyebrows have been worked in a peculiar way; they are different from the previous sculptures in that they sharply meet the bridge of the nose as if in a frown. The thin line of the eyebrows gives expression to the face. The eyes have large heavy lids, especially the upper lids, which are modelled in high relief. The deep recesses in the corners of the eyes push the eyeballs out. The upper edge of the eye is shown as a semi-circle rather than a horizontal line, as is commonly the case. It conveys a look of frankness and directness. The round eyeball has been painted blue along the lower eyelid. Traces of paint in the iris are absent and the pupils are slightly projected. The eyes are asymmetrical, the right one being opened wider. The external edge of the ear is large, although only the right one with thoroughly worked details has been preserved.

The hairstyle seems to have been made using a combination of techniques, blending handmade work in places with the relief of mould-made curls. The surviving curls behind the outer edge of the ear are traceable only by the remains of black paint. The hair of the upper part of the head is also black. The way in which the head adornments are worn deserves special attention. Pearls adorn the hairline on the upper part of the forehead. The pearls are rather large: eight of them in the centre are particularly distinguished. They are covered with white plaster, rendering either the colour of the pearls themselves or their metal imitation. Above the diadem are traces of the clasps by which the diadem was apparently affixed. It is interesting that the custom of fastening the crown on the upper part of the forehead along the base of the hairline was reserved for male figures. A similar method is shown on many Gandharan sculptures (for example, on *bodhisattvas*[420]), while on the female figures (for example, head no. 1) the string of pearls was placed on the top of the head. The face is represented in all its grandeur: the sculptor had caught even the subtle shades of a psychological state and has created a complete and harmonic plastic appearance.

6. Small head (Fig. 157).

This is the smallest head, 9 cm high and 5.5 cm wide. The hair is completely lost; the ears, the central part of the forehead, the neck, and lower part of the chin are broken off. The paint is barely preserved. The

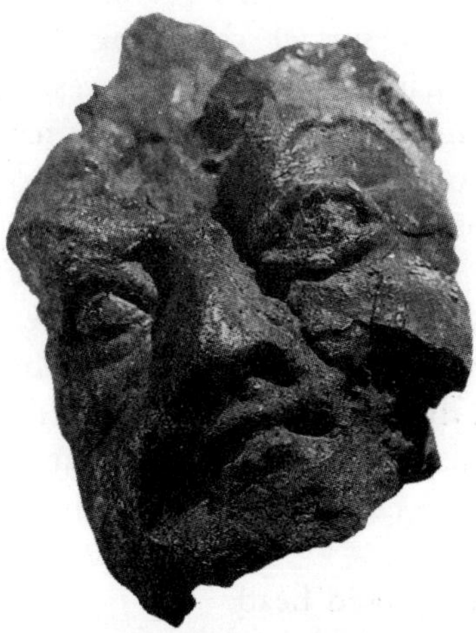

Fig. 157: Fragment of small sculpture modelled in grotesque manner. Kuevkurgan. Clay sculpture. 5th century AD. H = 11.5 cm. (Museum of History of the Peoples of Uzbekistan, Tashkent).

head was modelled in high relief, and the technical methods repeat those on the heads described above.

The exaggerated features of the statue give it a grotesque appearance. The low forehead, the clean-cut, angled eyebrows, and the aquiline nose with deep nostrils compound this expression. The eyes are wide open, the upper and lower lids in high relief. The eyeballs are distinguished by deep recesses in the corner of the eyes and are painted white, while sunken pupils underscore the black spots representing the iris. The mouth is open, the upper lip arched. The face is red. The hair, or more exactly what remains of it, has traces of black paint, while the eyebrows and eyelashes have also been painted black.

The face is full of expression, its dynamic character reinforced by the asymmetry of its features, especially the rather disproportionate position and size of the eyes – the left is slightly smaller than the right. These features lend an almost demonic appearance to the sculpture. Judging by its size, it had a subordinate meaning in the composition and possibly portrayed a secondary figure. In Buddhist multi-figured scenes showing legends or other stories, as a rule, the secondary characters accompanied a central group of heroes. Grotesque sculptural aspects are vividly present in the material of Hadda.[421] The quantity of finds from Hadda suggests that it was one of the main centres of plastic art. In Central Asia, grotesque images are found in the wall paintings of Afrasiab[422] and Penjikent[423] and also in terracotta plastic art.[424]

B. *Fragments of Heads*

1. Fragment of a large head.

   Only the left ear and part of the hair remain. The ear was painted red, judging by the traces of surface colouring. Above the ear and at the back of the head the hair is rendered as waves. On the top of the head, the hair is plastered in relief strips divided by narrow furrows. Traces of black are preserved on the hair.
2. Fragment of a sculpted head.

   The fragment is 15 cm in height. The upper part of the ear is painted white. The hair, in thin furrows from the forehead to the back, is black. There is a badly preserved stamped curl on the back of the head. As on the other heads, the hair has been plastered using the combination method of manual shaping with details separately produced in a mould. On the temples, some curls have been painted by brush over a thin plaster background.
3. Small fragment of a sculpted head.

   Parts of the upper external edge of the ear, a cheek and part of the hair are preserved. The hair above the ear has been finished off with relief stripes, divided by several furrows. The face is white, the hair black. The curls at the temples, rendered as circular locks, have been painted black. Judging by the fine lines, the colouring was executed by brush.

4. Fragment of a head of a statue.
   The extant height is 18 cm, the width in the middle is 11 cm; the surfaces, except for small fragments of the cheeks and hair, and a crown, have been lost. The head clearly shows the same modelling method as above.
   The core of the statue is oval-shaped, made of rough clay with considerable vegetable temper. The second, plaster layer was directly applied to this core, the plastic modelling in relief being 0.8 cm thick in this case.
   The face was primed with white plaster. The hair is shown in black. The upper part of the hair is rendered as a smooth surface without any relief work. The lower part of the hair has curls, the contours of which are emphasized with small perforations. Above the forehead, at the hairline, sits a pearl-studded crown. On the temples, in front of the ear, a curl has been painted in black, similar to the example described above (no. 5).
5. Fragment of a sculpted head.
   Part of the temple, the hair with adornments and the upper part of the outer edge of the ear have survived. The paint layer is damaged. The hair above the ear is in relief. Three rounded projections or pearls are shown on the side, forming a row. They are fragments of a lost diadem.
6. Fragment of a sculpted head, similar to no. 11
   Part of the hair and one of the large ears are extant. Traces of painting on the hair and the rendering of curls on the temple can be seen here and there.
7. Fragments of a female sculpture (Fig. 158).
   Two large fragments from the upper part of a female figure have survived that include the bust and shoulders with forearms. The figure is in a yellow dress. Below the shoulders, the arms are draped with a scarf thrown behind the back. On the right arm the scarf is shown as a piece of triangular cloth with oblique folds continuing behind the shoulders. On the left arm there is less drapery of the scarf and its cloth is modelled in relief, partly covering the forearms. Under the pleats of the scarf, a row of rosettes can be traced. Although only one is still intact, the others can be distinguished by traces of petals. The rosettes probably formed a band around the upper arm. The small vertical pleats below and above the breast indicate the fine, transparent material of the dress, which has a broad, round neckline. A necklace is shown on the bare chest, consisting of slightly flattened circular elements, perhaps portraying pearls or small silver beads. The necklace and the lower neck are painted white. It is interesting to note that on the torso there is a very thin layer of pink

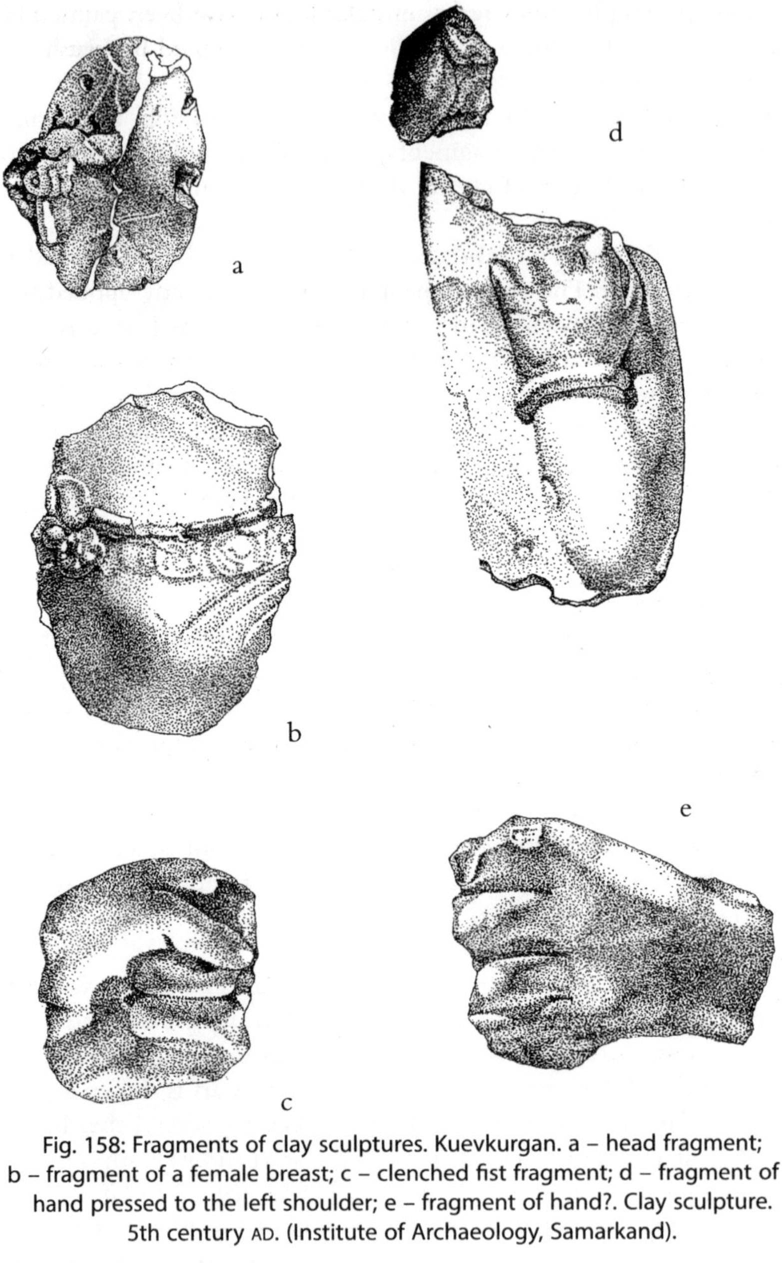

Fig. 158: Fragments of clay sculptures. Kuevkurgan. a – head fragment; b – fragment of a female breast; c – clenched fist fragment; d – fragment of a hand pressed to the left shoulder; e – fragment of hand?. Clay sculpture. 5th century AD. (Institute of Archaeology, Samarkand).

clay (ochre?) above the ordinary clay layer, which is not found on other sculptures. White paint covered this layer of pink clay. Fragments of black curls can still be seen on the right shoulder. They are held together (?) at the edges of the shoulders. These elements point to the originally rich hairstyle of the figure. The fragment is 23 cm in height and 35 cm in width.

8. Female bust (Fig. 159)
   A large fragment of the upper part of a female torso in *bas-relief*. The naked part of the chest, limited by the large semi-circular neckline of the dress, has a thin plaster layer. The cut of the dress can be deduced from the sunken lines along the upper part of the relief of the breasts. The dress is of fine cloth, painted blue, with the chest distinctly showing through the material. The small pleats of the dress are marked on the upper and lower part of the breasts. The nipples have been damaged; very likely, rosettes or round, flat disks similar to the previous sculpture (no. 13) had covered them. The adornment is of great interest: it consists of a torque and a richly decorated necklace hanging down between the breasts.

The torque is in relief, with a round transverse section similar to a rope. The centre was accentuated by a jewel, possibly a gemstone. The torque is yellow, very likely conveying the colour of gold. The necklace has three pendants: the upper two are in the shape of rosettes with a central relief, surrounded by eight beads on the upper pendant and ten on the middle

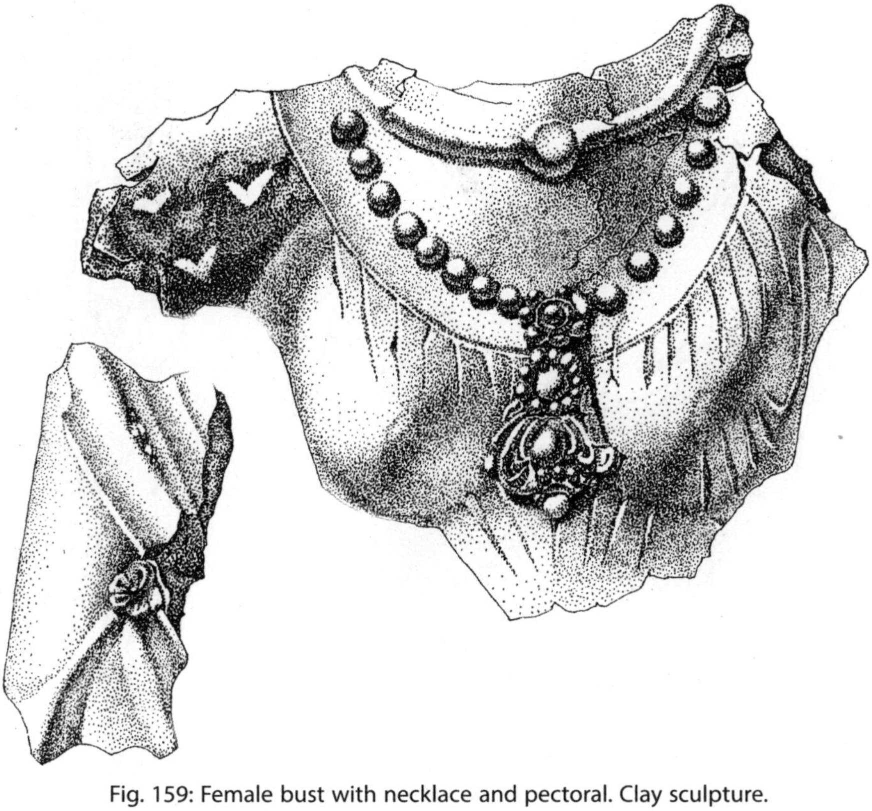

Fig. 159: Female bust with necklace and pectoral. Clay sculpture. 5th century AD. H = 24 cm. (Museum of History of Culture and Art of the Peoples of Uzbekistan, Samarkand).

one. The lowest and largest pendant is a large oval relief surrounded by vegetal motives. The central part of this medallion is painted in yellow, simulating gold. At the same time, the beads around the upper two pendants have traces of red paint, perhaps imitating semi-precious and precious stones.

In addition to the above listed fragments there are many small ones of hands, feet, faces, hair and elements of dress, occasionally with ornamentation (Figs. 160, 161). Thus the plastic art of Kuevkurgan demonstrates the tradition of a local school of sculptors. Their style of plastic modelling is very close to Buddhist art and also similar in certain other methods. At the same time, the iconography can be associated with secular art. This situation highlights two important aspects of Bactrian-Tokharistan art. On the one hand, we can be certain that the masters of Kuevkurgan were acquainted with the Buddhist plastic style and worked under its strong influence. On the other hand, we have proof for the dominating role of Buddhist art in this region.

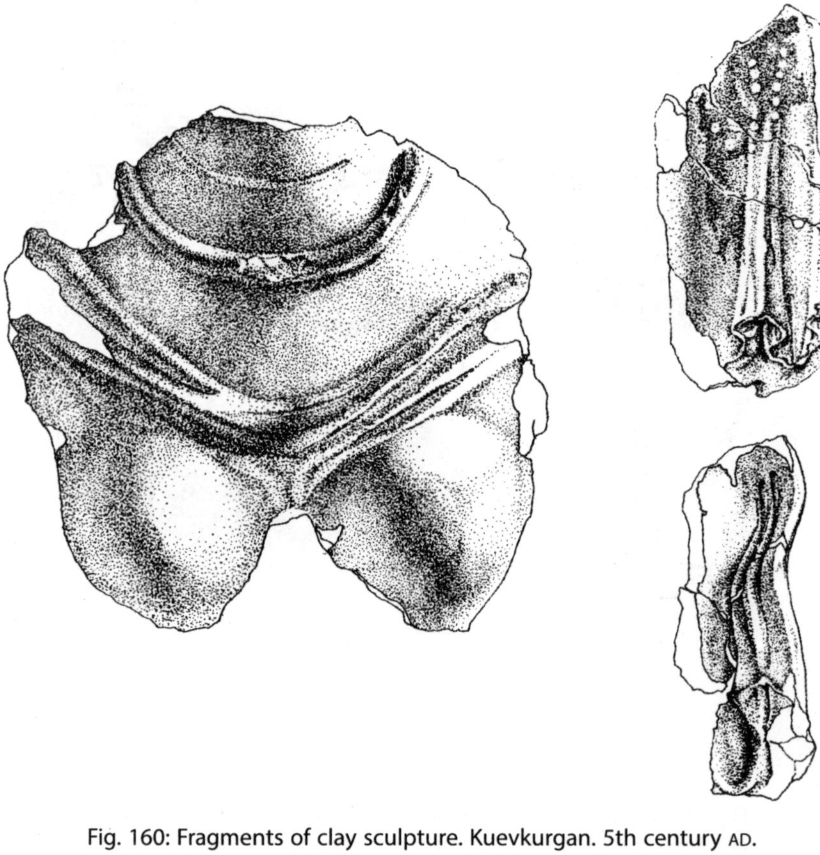

Fig. 160: Fragments of clay sculpture. Kuevkurgan. 5th century AD. (Institute of Archaeology, Samarkand).

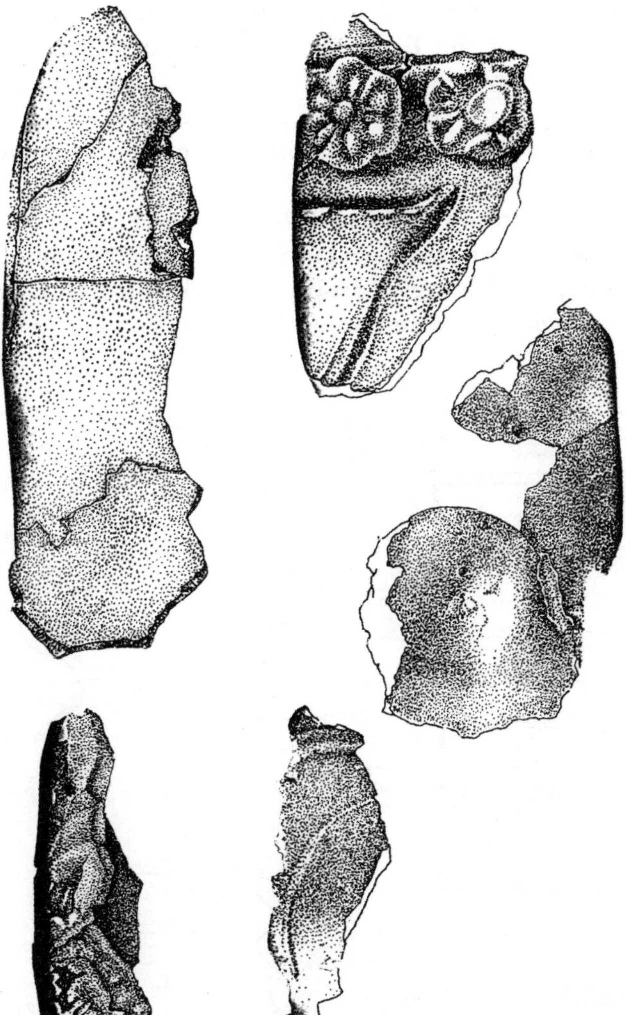

Fig. 161: Fragments of clay sculpture. Kuevkurgan. 5th century AD. (Institute of Archaeology, Samarkand).

The Ceramics of Kuevkurgan

The ceramics of Kuevkurgan are conventionally categorized as tableware and cooking pots. To the first group belong vessels such as jars, jugs, mugs, *tagora* (basins for dough or other preparations), bowls, red-slip pots, or *oinochoes* (wine jugs with a trefoil rim for pouring). Jars with double handles on both sides have a diameter of 10 to 15 cm. The clay, as a rule, has a yellowish colour on the outer surface and is reddish inside. Some vessels have a small projecting ridge below the rim. The vessels were manufactured in fine clay. Mugs with double ring-shaped handles are typical of the ceramic complex of the Early Medieval period (Fig. 162: 3).[425] They obviously copied metal vessels.[426] The mugs have a straight neck emphasized by a projection or incised line, with a rim diameter of 12-13 cm. They were made of fine clay and covered with a clear slip, sometimes of a yellow colour.

Jars come in a variety of forms. They represent about 30 per cent of the entire ceramic corpus of Kuevkurgan and are divided into two groups. The first group is characterized by high-necked jars (Fig. 163: 1-9, 13, 14).[427] These high-necked jars were of fine clay and have a rim diameter

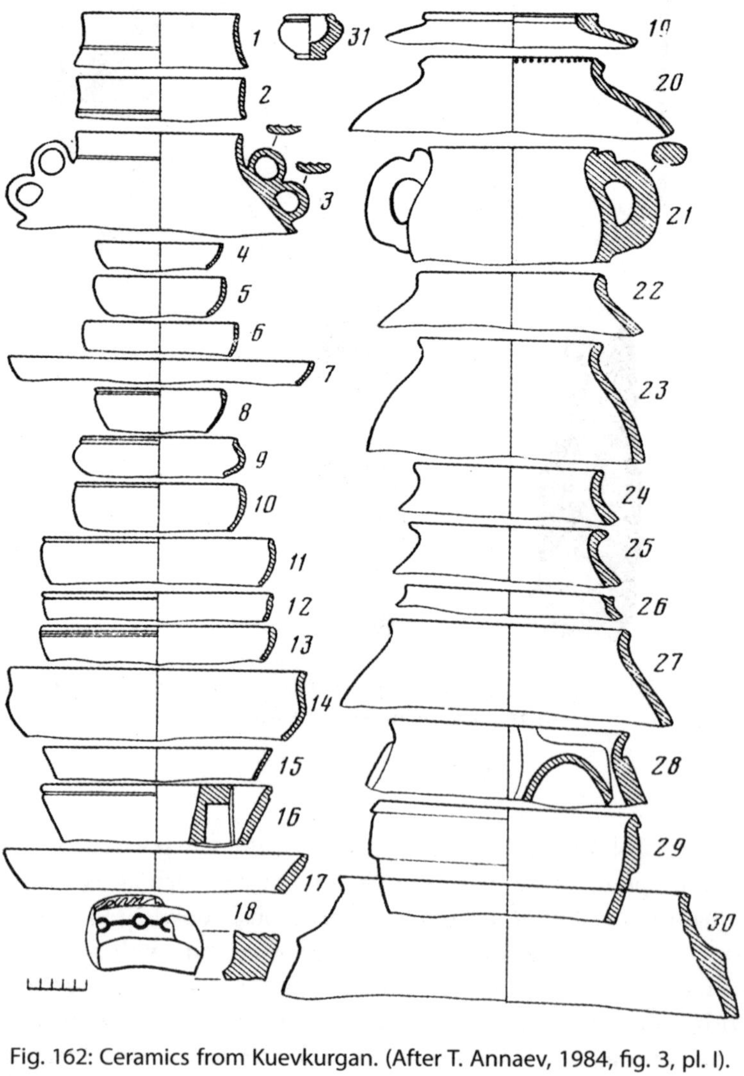

Fig. 162: Ceramics from Kuevkurgan. (After T. Annaev, 1984, fig. 3, pl. I).

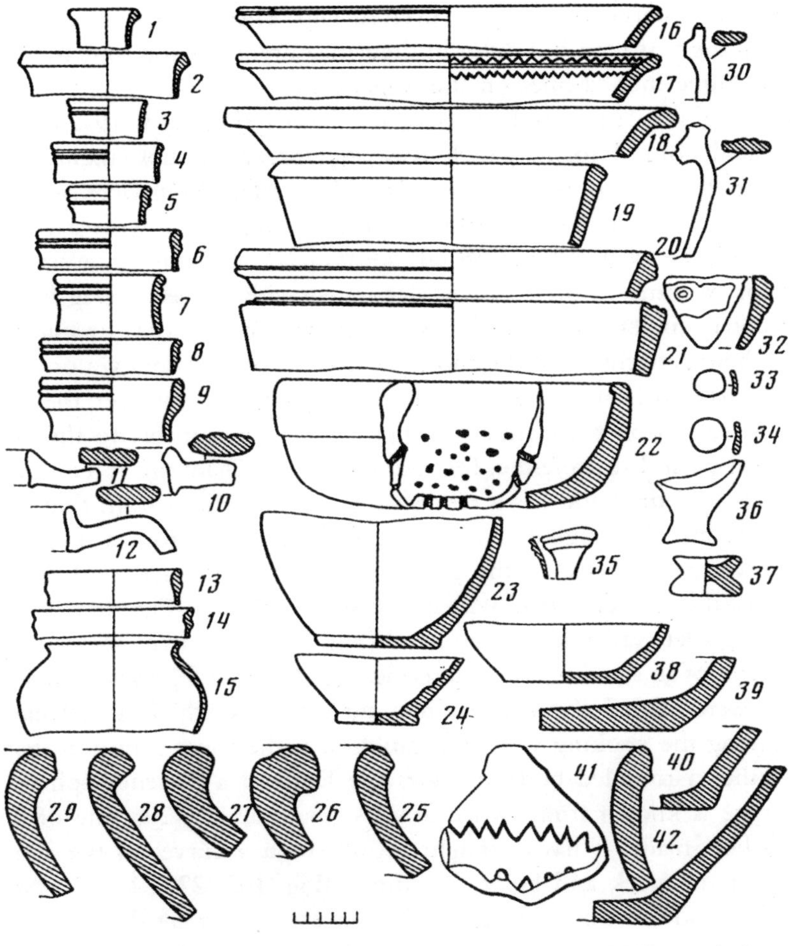

Fig. 163: Ceramics from Kuevkurgan. (After T. Annaev, 1984, fig. 4, pl. II).

between 4 and 12 cm. They are covered with a white or red-brown slip. On the exterior, there are two incised parallel decorative lines under the rim. The second group of jars is distinguished by a more massive form and thickness of wall. The rim diameter is between 6 and 12 cm. The exterior surfaces are covered by a clear slip (Fig. 163: 5, 3-9), and sometimes a brown polishing is visible (Fig. 163: 15, 23, 24).[428] The jars in this second group have quite massive handles attached vertically or curving at an angle (Fig. 163: 10-12). The lower parts of the jars are egg-shaped, with an enlarged, saucer-like circular foot (Fig. 163: 23, 24).

The bowls (Fig. 163: 16-18) have a rim diameter from 18 to 24 cm and are represented by two forms. The first has a triangular rim. On some examples, shallow incised lines can be traced on the upper part of the bowl. These bowls are covered by a red slip and sometimes have a polished neck. The second form has an everted rim. These bowls have the same form as the first type, but differ in their measurements and sometimes have one to three incised lines on the upper part.

Among the larger table vessels, the basins (Fig. 163: 19-21) have a truncated conical form, which was widespread in subsequent periods, although the form of the mouth and the decorative motifs were continually changing. For the Kuevkurgan corpus, basins (*tagora*) with a diameter measuring between 32 and 38 cm are typical. The rims are everted. The interior of some of the basins is decorated with incised zigzag lines and concentric circles. Together with small indentations or dots executed by a pipe, these patterns form the most popular decoration motives on pottery of Bactria – Tokharistan during the Kushan period. However, the origins of this decoration reach much further back,[429] presumably to the Greco-Bactrian period (manifested, for example, at Ai Khanum).[430] This type of vessel is well fired and has a reddish slip and was made from fine clay.

There are also fragments of two goblets. Judging from a fragment of the lower part of one of the goblets it had a stable, massive foot and a cylindrical-conic cup that widened toward the top (Fig. 163: 37). The second goblet was modelled by hand (Fig. 163: 36). There are also several fragments of an *oinochoe* shaped jug (Fig. 163: 35). All of the vessels described above were of fine clay, evenly fired and covered with thick red slip.

Among the cooking ware, the cauldron is the most common shape. It has either a rounded body or takes the form of a flattened sphere. The first type is known from two examples (Fig. 162: 19, 20), one of which was wheel-made. It has a straight mouth with a curve on the shoulder between the neck and body. Cauldrons (Fig. 162: 22, 24-7, 30) with a rounded body can be distinguished from each other by the form of the rim, which is normally slightly everted. They have pushed up lug-handles, some of which may have been purely ornamental (Fig. 162: 28, 30). The majority of these are handmade. They are grey or reddish in colour and the clay is coarse with sand and chamotte inclusions.

The ceramic corpus of Kuevkurgan, despite its relatively small size, illustrates the peculiarities of pottery production during the functioning of the site. While most of the shapes did not undergo considerable change, some new forms with new elements of decoration were introduced that continued into the Early Medieval period. For example, double-handled mugs were a completely new addition to the ceramic corpus. Such forms, or their prototypes, were absent in earlier layers at neighbouring Zartepa. The complexes of the upper layers are dated between the third century and the first half of the fourth century AD.[431] These levels are absent from other sites located in the vicinity of Kuevkurgan (such as Karatepa, Fayaztepa and Dal'verzintepa).[432] The closest parallel to the Kuevkurgan double handled jug was found in a burial chamber at Kukhnakala. This example is decorated with similar ornamentation and has a single handle. The complex is roughly dated by coins that range from the second to the fourth century AD.[433] Similar mugs, but with two handles, were found in the ceramic material of Aysarytepa, dated to the third to fifth century AD.[434]

Handmade bowls with spouts were found in the upper layers of Akkurgan, dated to the fourth century AD. Cauldrons with a spherical body were uncovered in layers 3-4 at Challyatepa, which has been dated later than Akkurgan.[435] Earlier examples were unearthed at Dal'verzintepa (Dt-6) in the so-called 'House of a Rich Man' in a layer together with coins of Vasudeva II.[436] The conical cooking *tagora* (bowls) continued, as noted above, the tradition of the previous Kushan period into the late Kushan period, and even until the beginning of the Early Medieval period.

Cups with concave rims were found in the upper levels of the floor of a room at Hayrabad, in the same layer as a Hephthalite silver coin of the fifth century AD.[437] Geographically more distant analogies come from sites in southern and central Sogdia, particularly Erkurgan and Penjikent, whose complexes have been dated to the fifth to sixth century AD (for Erkurgan)[438] and the fifth to seventh century AD (for the lower layers of Penjikent).[439]

Dating

From the material described above, it can be concluded that the ceramic complex of Kuevkurgan chronologically followed the late Kushan complexes of northern Bactria, inheriting certain of their elements for which Zartepa represents the closest connection. The ceramics of Kuevkurgan can be dated to the fifth, or perhaps the very early part of the sixth century AD. Most probably, the Kuevkurgan sculptures should be dated to this period too. More problematic is the establishment of an initial date for the sculptures. This is rendered difficult by their restoration and their possible transport from another site, such as Zartepa. The latter hypothesis requires additional evidence and will be discussed in more detail below.

If we propose to date Kuevkurgan in the fifth to early sixth centuries AD, this period would serve as the *terminus ante quem* for the sculptural complex. Regarding the *terminus post quem*, there arise questions related to the durability of the sculptures. Essentially, how long could a clay sculpture serve as interior decoration and as an object of worship? As we have already pointed out, some fragments show traces of repair and even restoration. The issue of the durability of the statues brings us face to face with one of the lesser-known aspects of the plastic art of Bactria. It is not an exaggeration to say that issues such as the duration of the life of sculpture, particularly clay sculpture, and its future destiny, have so far not been studied in Central Asian art.[440] For this reason the dating of the sculptures remains relative.

Interpretation

Due to its poor state of preservation, the sculpture of Kuevkurgan is difficult to interpret. There is no possibility of reconstructing the original compositions. The exposed pedestals in certain rooms could be interpreted as bases for sculpture. However, this suggestion remains hypothetical, as there is no proof for this (for instance, there is no decoration in relief or painting on the pedestals). If we assume that the figures were displayed on these pedestals, then their function changed, because on each of these pedestals only a single sculpture could be installed. In this case, we would no longer be able to speak of a multi-figured composition. Yet the character of the sculptural fragments of Kuevkurgan suggests a unified programme. Among the figures one can distinguish major and minor heroes, the main image was most probably placed in the central part of the composition, while the minor ones were gathered around this personage.

The male head no. 5 is conspicuous because of its pearl diadem, resting below the hairline. Above the forehead, there are two curls combed back in opposite directions. The curls schematically resemble wings, but could also represent two up-turned curls as on one of the heads from Khalchayan (according to G.A. Pugachenkova, this is the head of a prince of the Heraeus clan[441]). Evidently, they were part of the headdress; however, the state of preservation does not allow clarification of this detail. The plastic modelling of the face can be better evaluated. The face with its majestic calmness and dignity has a remote likeness to that of the Khalchayan prince noted above. However, this likeness is purely external and loses its force when compared in detail. The eyes of the Kuevkurgan sculpture, with their heavy upper lids and slightly swollen lower ones, gravitate towards the Buddhist tradition of sculpture. The smooth manner of modelling without elaborate facial muscles and the faint smile visible at the corners of the lips, where drilled orifices executed by an instrument are visible, are also characteristic of Buddhist images.

Such a manner of modelling is characteristic, as observed above, for the entire Kuevkurgan sculptural complex. The influence of the Buddhist tradition is particularly manifest in the modelling of the helix of the ear, which was stamped by a mould. The straight nose, the rather heavy, rounded chin, the sleek forehead, and the large eyes with heavy eyelids are all features seen in images of Buddha and *bodhisattvas*. If it were not for the diadem and elements of the headdress, one could accept this image (no. 5) as Buddhist. Judging by the relatively large size of this head, it may have belonged to one of the main figures of the composition and represented a royal individual in the circle of his relatives. Evidently, he formed a pair with the female figure (no. 1), who also wears a diadem of a single row of pearls. Her straight hair is combed back; the texture is shown by deeply incised lines, radially separating from the hairline, that dips slightly in the centre of the forehead. It is interesting to note the ethnic features: broad, with some Mongoloid traits such as the widely placed narrow eyes, the slightly protruding cheek-bones, the short nose with flared nostrils, and the thick black hair falling on the forehead.

Hypothetically, we can attribute to this head a separate female bust (no. 14), whose dress and jewellery deserve special attention. First there is the fine, transparent material of the dress, with vertical pleats descending from the round neckline as shallow incised lines. Below the breast, these pleats are treated somewhat differently, forming darts radiating from the stomach. There is a heart-shaped pattern on the dress, preserved on the right shoulder. Most probably, the hearts signified gold plates sewn onto the dress, a style of ornamentation abundantly represented in the previous Kushan period. One can see various forms of gold pendants, including heart-shaped ones, on the Sako-Yuezhi dress from the burials of Tillya Tepe (Afghanistan).[442] The garment of a 'ruler' from Dal'verzintepa was also adorned with sewn on pendants (first century AD).[443] The torque with an oval plaque in the centre was also popular in Kushan Bactria. The oval plaque probably represented an engraved gemstone, as the pectoral from Dal'verzintepa suggests.[444]

Torques occur frequently in Kushan art. A sculpture representing a Genius from Hadda with similar adornment comes to mind.[445] This sculpture is related also in another detail typical of the Kuevkurgan sculptures, in its hairstyle of moulded curls with concave ends. The piecefrom Hadda has been dated to the third to fourth centuries AD.

Another analogy to the jewellery described above is found in wall paintings, for instance on the central personage from the Dil'berjin composition.[446] In all probability, the wall painting represented a female divinity in armour, such as the Greek Athena. On Kushan coins, a similar deity bears the name of Rishto.[447] Around the neck of the deity from Dil'berjin there is the same jewellery as at Kuevkurgan. I stress here two particularities of the Kuevkurgan representations: the round cut of the neckline of the dress, discussed above (no. 14); and the temple curl with twisted ends of the headdress. The curls on the temples of Kuevkurgan sculptures are shown not in relief as the rest of the headdress, but in black paint (nos. 5, 10). The Dil'berjin wall painting with the representation of the warrior deity is very close in appearance to the late Kushan or Kushano-Sassanian figurative complex. The search for pearl-studded jewellery leads to the same period.

The pearls have a rather uncommon spherical form and, perhaps, are not typical for the early Kushan complex. There are rare exceptions, such as the necklace of large, rather flat beads on the figure of a princely donor from Mathura.[448] It is not certain whether the sculptor wanted to depict pearls. Another example of this unusual spherical form is found on the Surya figure from Khair Khaneh.[449] Spherical beads are rare in the Parthian figurative complex. A few spherical bead necklaces are found in the decorative complex of the funerary statues of Palmyra, for example, on a relief from the Damascus Museum dated to the second to third centuries AD.[450]

The jewellery described above characterizes the works of figurative art most popular in Sassanid Iran. It is no coincidence that the motif of a pearl-framed medallion with an image in the centre spread far from Iran, becoming one of the preferable ornamental motives in different genres of art and crafts, including glyptic, toreutic, textile, wall painting and relief sculpture. Some examples with representations of spherical beads may be cited. Beads adorn the figure of Anahita on the relief from Naqsh-e Rostam that shows Narses' investiture.[451] The same monument depicts the victory of Shapur over Valerian, where the king himself and the minor figures are wearing such beads.[452] Monumental sculpture representing King Shapur from Bishapur also displays a similar form of beads.[453] The same kind of jewellery is shown on reliefs of later Sassanian kings including the investiture of King Bahram I, dated to the later third century AD, the hunting scene of Bahram II from Sar-Meshhed, where in the third century AD both the king and his wife wear spherical beads,[454] and the scene of investiture of Ardashir II, dated to the fourth century AD.[455] Among toreutic works, one can cite a silver plate from the Tehran Museum with the scene of a royal hunt,[456] where the king wears a necklace of spherical beads (the plate is dated to the 4th century AD). The same form of bead jewellery is represented on gems (intaglios). For example, on a gem from the private collection of Farukhi, there is a female figure with royal attributes including spherical beaded jewellery.[457] Another gem from the State Hermitage Museum represents a Sassanian ruler (4th century AD) with a necklace of round pearls.[458]

Finally, we should address the numismatic iconography. The analogies to the above-described jewellery are found on coins of the Sassanian rulers: Shapur I, Khormizd I, Bahram III, Khormizd II, Shapur II, Yezdigerd I, Bahram V, Peroz I and Kavad I.[459] Sassanian art shows that the necklace of spherical beads was worn by both male and female personages as shown, for example, on a plate from Baltimore with a banquet scene, where the couple wears spherical beaded necklaces (the plate is dated to the fifth-sixth centuries AD).[460] All of these instances (of which only a small number could be listed) analogous to the adornments of the Kuevkurgan sculptures contain certain Kushano-Sassanid elements. These in turn indirectly set the earliest possible date for the sculptures to the fourth century AD.

The decorative complex of the sculptural fragments of Kuevkurgan betrays their local origins. Among the sculptured heads of Kuevkurgan, there is a small one that attracts attention for its grotesque manner of modelling (Fig. 157). Despite the poor preservation, this fragment reflects an expressive mode of representation that distinguishes it from the calm, majestic faces of other Kuevkurgan figures. On the one hand, the grotesque manner very much resembles certain figures of the Khalchayan cycle,[461] which, however, date from an earlier period. On the other hand, this grotesque manner of modelling is similar to figures of Buddhist character – the so-called images of Mara's warriors (see a relief at the Central Museum of Lahore and reliefs from Butkara).[462] As an analogue to these images, one can cite the head from the Buddhist temple of Kuva (Fergana Valley) that was destroyed during the Arab invasion.[463] Although chronologically this head is far removed from the Kuevkurgan example, to a certain degree it nevertheless reflects the stable Buddhist tradition in the figurative complex. With regard to Buddhism in the Fergana Valley and Kirghizia during the Early Medieval period, most likely we have influences from the opposite direction, from Chinese Turkestan, where Buddhism was firmly rooted. Here, numerous schools and artistic centres of plastic art were formed, spreading their works towards the west.[464]

The Sculpture of Kuevkurgan and the Cult of the Ancestors

It has been mentioned that the sculpture of Kuevkurgan was not religious. This means that it did not belong to a figurative complex subordinated to canonical methods of representation. Again, the emphasis here is on the strong influence of the Buddhist figurative tradition, reflected in different artistic fields of Early Medieval Tokharistan. But is it possible to ascribe a purely secular character to the sculpture from Kuevkurgan? The monumental sculpture in particular embodied a concept of veneration.

In the architecture of Kuevkurgan it is also possible to trace ritual elements such as the sacred well. There is no doubt that the sculpture of Kuevkurgan was part of the interior decoration of the buildings. Another important aspect is the individualization of features – the sculpture as a portrait. In spite of the fact that certain sculptural methods are almost the same as those of Buddhist modelling, some of the works surely portrayed historical personages. For example, the head with a diadem (no. 5), full of dignity and serenity, can be compared with some figures from the Khalchayan reliefs.[465] The dress and ornamentation also testify to the secular character of the sculpture. Unfortunately, it is impossible to hypothesize about the context of the Kuevkurgan sculptures, due to their poor preservation. It is very possible that the head with a diadem (no. 5) belonged to a large composition of enthroned figures, which were represented according to their social hierarchy. The cult character of the personage can be more confidently judged. The cult of the ancestors held a dominant position in Central Asia. This is proven by two inscriptions from Afghanistan, namely the inscriptions of Kanishka from Surkh Kotal[466] and Rabatak.[467] Although these inscriptions exalted his dynasty, at the same time they propagated the cult of his royal ancestors. However, this subject has been poorly researched in the history of Central Asian states.

The well-known monuments of temple architecture were tied to dynastic cults. Surkh Kotal is an example of this. One of the more interesting peculiarities of the rituals was the altar for the holy fire. The significance of fire in Kushan religion can be traced in the numismatic iconography, as for instance on the obverse of coins of the Kushan kings.[468] The representation of the king with outstretched hands held above the sacred fire can be interpreted as a protective gesture, and testifies to the veneration of the sacred fire. Despite various images of non-Iranian deities on the coins of the Kushan kings, preference was nevertheless given to Iranian deities. Furthermore, the portrait of the king on these coins is often accompanied by a representation of flames behind his shoulders.[469] On one hand, this flame could be seen as a symbol of royal powers and divine sanction (*hwarna*, *pharro*), but on the other hand, it cannot be ruled out that in the cult of ancestors, one of the central actions involved fire. One remembers the unusual fire altar in the dynastic temple of Kanishka.[470] The cult of ancestors was also very strong among the nomadic tribes, as recounted in Greek and Chinese sources.[471]

Kuevkurgan and Zartepa

Kuevkurgan and Zartepa had close connections especailly during the final phase of functioning of the Zartepa citadel (early fifth century AD). As the sculptures of Kuevkurgan show signs of restoration, it might mean that at some point they were moved from their original place, and it is possible that they were transferred to Kuevkurgan from nearby Zartepa, where urban life was in decline. At Zartepa, layers synchronous with Kuevkurgan were found only on the citadel, indicating a relatively short period of habitation. The Early Medieval housing on the citadel was modest with only small rooms[472] which were not suitable for the rich kind of decoration befitting the seat of a ruler. Unfortunately, it is not possible to discuss the original plan of the Zartepa citadel, as it has not been excavated, but we can assume that in the beginning it was a residence worthy of a king (Fig. 164), with amenities that included a heating system or *kan*.[473] Excavations at Zartepa showed a complicated stratigraphy for the late Kushan city with rich evidence for the material and spiritual culture of its inhabitants.[474]

It should be noted that Zartepa (Fig. 165) is one of the largest sites of the Kushan period in southern Uzbekistan, comprising 16.9 ha, surpassed

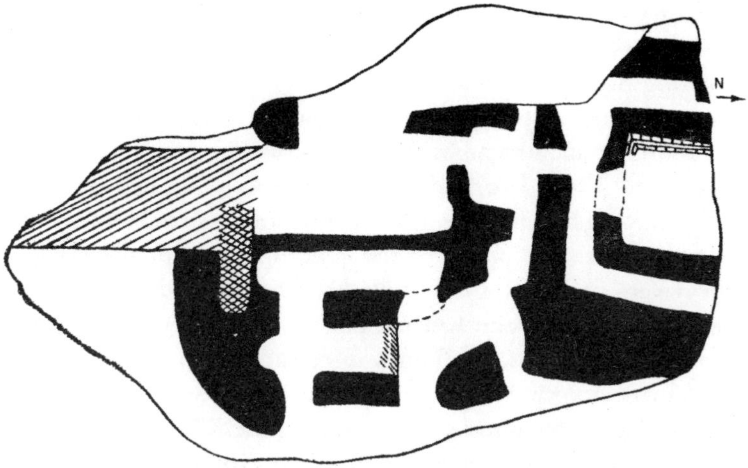

Fig. 164: Plan of the citadel of Zartepa. (After K. Abdullaev, T. Annaev, 1990, fig. 1).

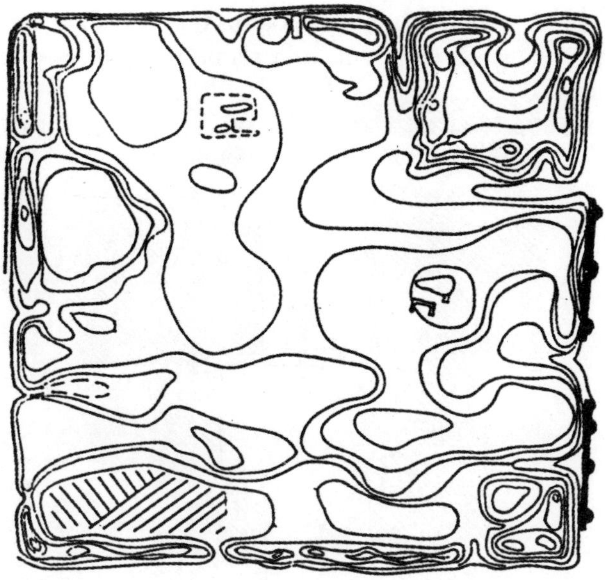

Fig. 165: Topographic plan of Zartepa. (After V.M. Masson, 1976, fig. 6).

in size only by Old Termez and Dal'verzintepa. The foundation of the city has been dated to the Yuezhi period (first century BC–first century AD).[475] Zartepa was square in plan, with its cardinal points oriented slightly to the west. Excavations revealed a massive fortification wall flanked by semi-circular towers as well as a rampart and moat. A trench excavated in the north-western corner of the site revealed thick cultural layers (5 m in depth). The city flourished during the Great Kushan period in the second to third centuries AD, but from the second half of the third through to the fourth century AD the city was possibly under the control of the Sassanian Kushan Shahs, as the numismatic material and other archaeological objects show a strong Sassanian influence.[476]

The excavations of the upper cultural layers unearthed the foundations of several monumental structures, including a building with a four-columned hall measuring 13 × 9.3 m, and a larger twelve-columned hall measuring 17.6 × 9.2 m.[477] The entrance was on the southern side of the complex with a large court. The shafts of the columns are not preserved - most likely they were of wood. Only their Attic bases survive and these are of the type widely used in the Kushan period. The bases with a profile of a scotia between two torus mouldings were turned on a lathe, as is evident from the square hole in the upper surfaces used for fastening the timber of the lathe. The high plinths are quadrangular. The bases and all other architectural details were made of limestone. Among the finds were also pseudo-Corinthian capitals showing careful modelling of acanthus leaves and protruding volutes.

In trench no. 2, which was later recognized as revealing part of a shrine (Figs. 166, 167),[478] small fragments of a statue with traces of gilding were

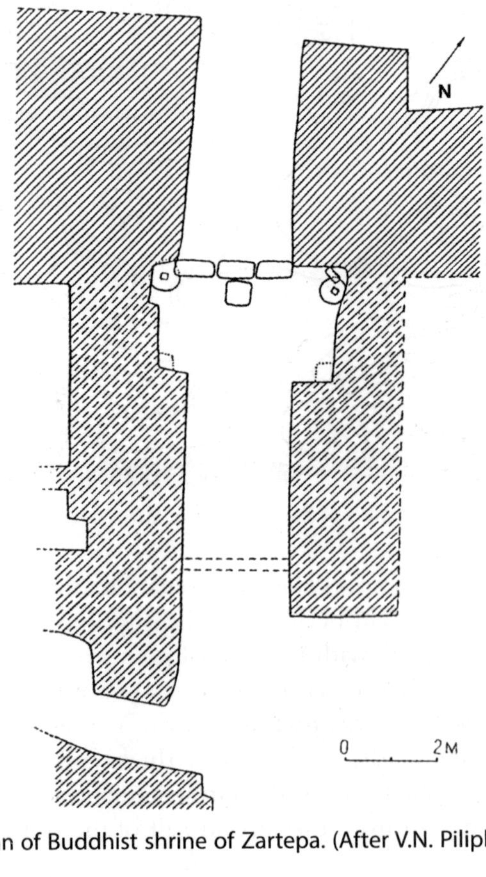

Fig. 166: Plan of Buddhist shrine of Zartepa. (After V.N. Pilipko, 1976, fig. 1).

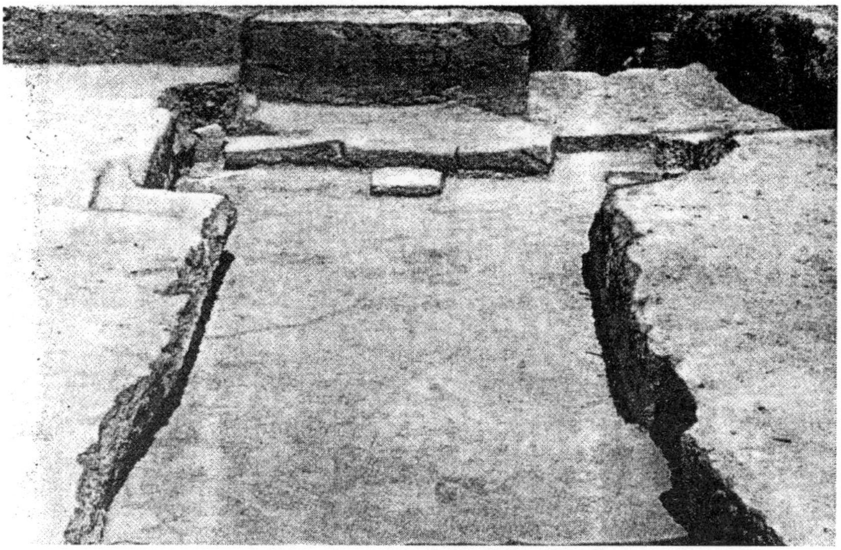

Fig. 167: Photo of Buddhist shrine of Zartepa. (After V.N. Pilipko, 1976, fig. 2).

found in a burnt layer. The head (H. 15-18 cm) of a Buddhist figure was found *in situ*. Hypothetically, the head may be interpreted as the head of Buddha himself, with a hair style comprising round, mould-made curls (Fig. 169). Only two rows of curls are preserved, together with an *urna* in the form of a circular incision on the bridge of the nose. The statue was made in clay on a wooden frame. Unfortunately, it is difficult to reconstruct the sculpture because of its poor preservation.

Some art objects discovered during excavations at Zartepa have a Buddhist character and seem to point to the past existence of a Buddhist temple. At the least, they demonstrate the worship of Buddhist divinities by the inhabitants of Zartepa. This hypothesis is supported by a small round structure discovered in the area, interpreted as a Buddhist stupa (Fig. 168). An alabaster head of Buddha modelled in the best tradition of plastic art should be noted (Fig. 170). It either came from a single sculpture or a multi-figured group. The head preserves traces of gilding similar to Buddhist figures in the territory of Central Asia that were influenced by traditions from Pakistan and India. However, gilding can also be seen in earlier sculptural complexes, for example at Takht-i Sangin.[479] In any case, the extensive use of gilding receded with the penetration of the Buddhist figurative complex in northern Tokharistan, and generally in Central Asia.

The style of the terracotta figurines found in the late Kushan layers may be associated with Hellenistic art. These include, for example, two heads with fluffy hair, a thick beard and a moustache, the ends of which are turned down. The mouth is slightly open. The nose is wide with well-

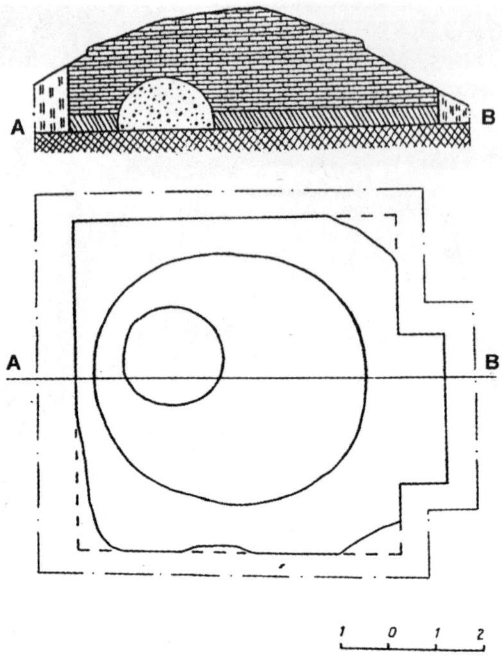

Fig. 168: Plan of *stupa* in the area of Zartepa. (After B.Ya. Staviskiy, 1998, fig. 44).

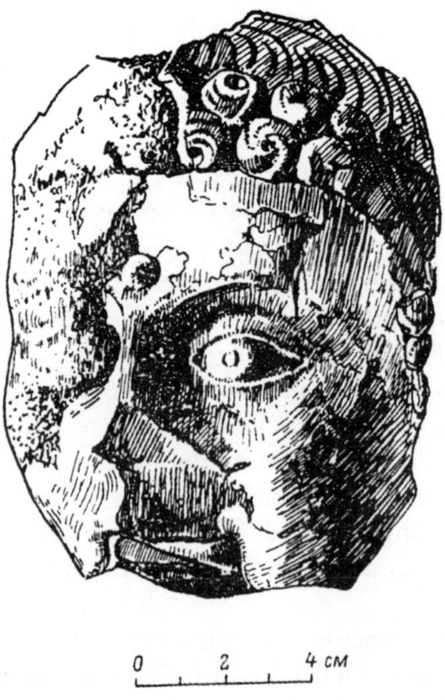

Fig. 169: Clay head of Buddha from the Zartepa shrine. Sculpture. 4th century AD. (The State Hermitage Museum, St. Petersburg).

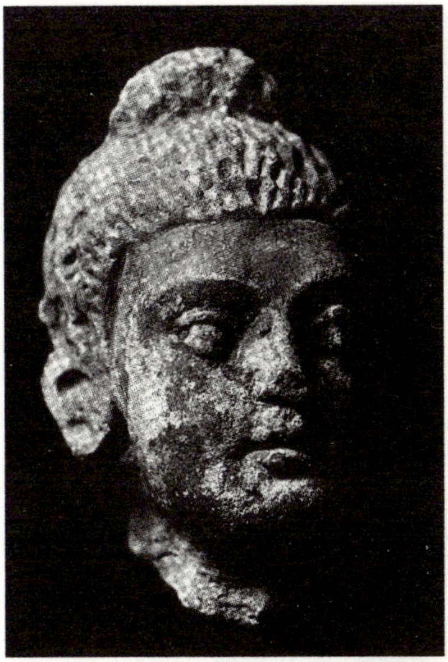

Fig. 170a: Moulded and gilded alabaster head of Buddha (photograph). 4th century AD. H = 8 cm. (The State Hermitage Museum, St. Petersburg).

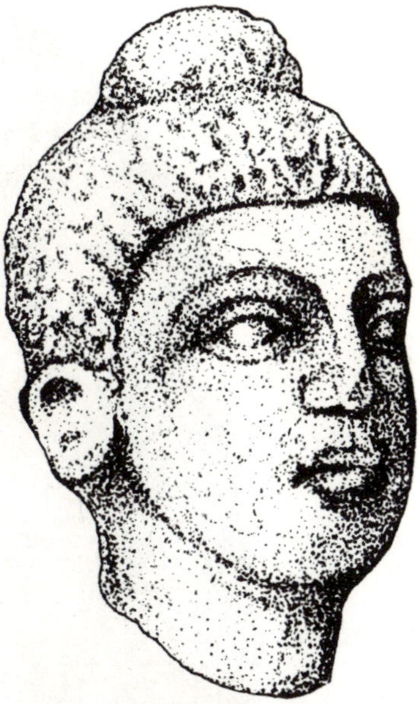

Fig. 170b: Moulded and gilded alabaster head of Buddha (line drawing). 4th century AD. H = 8 cm. (The State Hermitage Museum, St. Petersburg).

modelled flared nostrils. The image resembles Heracles, but the pointed ears are reminiscent of a Satyr (Fig. 171). Another interesting find was a terracotta tile showing a relief of a young man with a beardless face and short hair, wearing a sleeveless chiton. He holds a Pan flute with both hands (Fig. 172). An identical statuette was found in the Hellenistic layers (second to first century BC) of Kampyrtepa, located not far from Zartepa.[480]

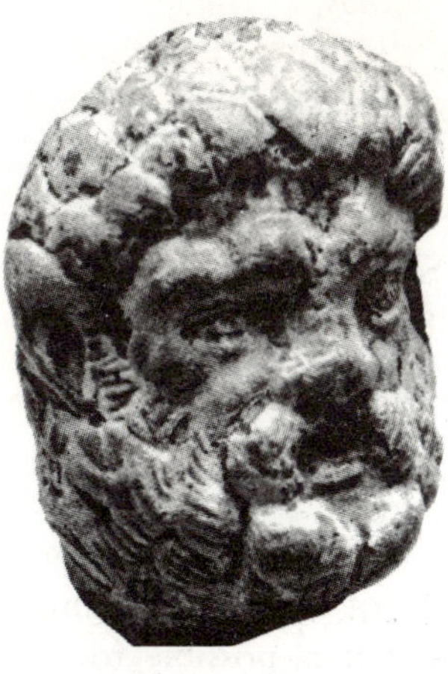

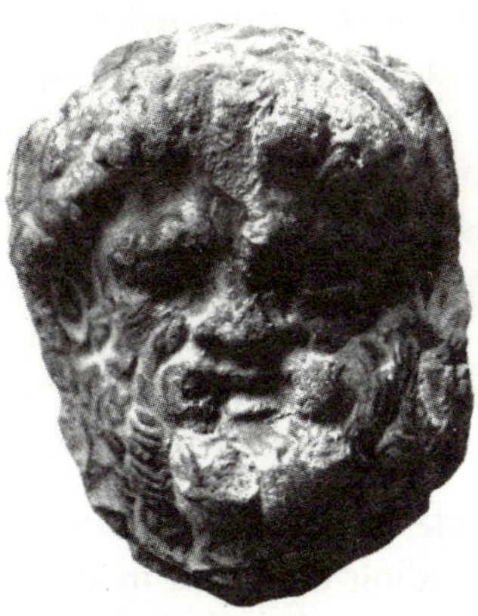

Fig. 171: Terracotta heads of bearded individual – Heracles (Satyr?). Zartepa. 1st century AD. H = 6 cm. (The State Hermitage Museum, St. Petersburg).

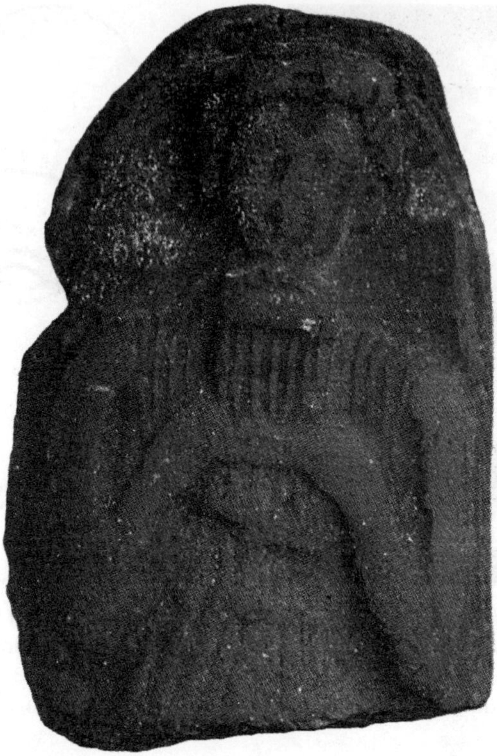

Fig. 172: Terracotta figurine. Flute player. Found in levels dated to the 3rd-4th century AD. Zartepa. H =14 cm. (The State Hermitage Museum, St. Petersburg).

Among the figurines of Buddhist plastic art one can note the representation of Buddha in *padmasana* pose and a figure of Buddha in the *abhaya-mudra* wearing a long pleated *sanghati*. There are also images of *bodhisattvas*, *yakshinis* and donors. One of these representations, namely, a female donor holding a posy, resembles a stone relief from Karatepa.[481] All these Buddhist terracottas have already been discussed above. Elements of Buddhist symbolism can be also traced in ceramic ornamentation. The representations of a lotus, the 'footprint of Buddha', terracotta models of *stupas*, *swastikas* and other symbols show how deeply the Buddhist figurative complex had pervaded the life of the urban population during the Kushan period.

The Tradition of Buddhist Art in the Early Medieval Periods (Ushtur-Mullo and Ajinatepa)

The stable tradition of Buddhist plastic art was mentioned above. As one of the leading traditions in the figurative art of Bactria, its influence was felt for a long time. It has been shown that it is possible to detect the Buddhist manner of plastic modelling in the secular Kuevkurgan sculpture.

Buddhist art developed successfully in the subsequent Early Medieval period. The discovery of two significant sites in Tajikistan, Ajinatepa and Ushtur-Mullo, manifests the continuity of this tradition. A special monograph has been devoted to Ajinatepa, including the wall painting and sculpture.[482] A series of articles have been published on the results of the excavations at Ushtur-Mullo.[483]

Ushtur-Mullo

The ruins of this Buddhist monastery are located in the Kobadian oasis, on the southern side of the Verbluzh'ya Gorka (Camel Hill). The plan of Ushtur-Mullo is typical of Buddhist monasteries (Fig. 173). A series of rooms opened onto the *stupa* in the middle of the interior court (Fig. 174). The temple had a flat roof, supported by a wooden pillar (diameter = 25 cm). The cella walls were plastered with a mixture of clay and straw, covered by another thin layer of alabaster. According to the excavator, one of the walls had been prepared for painting.[484] The painting covered only a section to the right of the entrance in the eastern corner of the room.

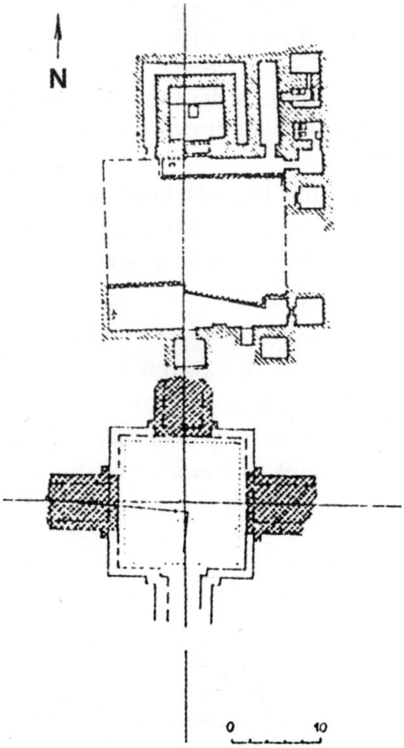

Fig. 173: Plan of Ushtur-Mullo site. Tajikistan. (After T.I. Zeymal', 1988, fig. 2) (Excavations sponsored by The State Hermitage Museum, St. Petersburg).

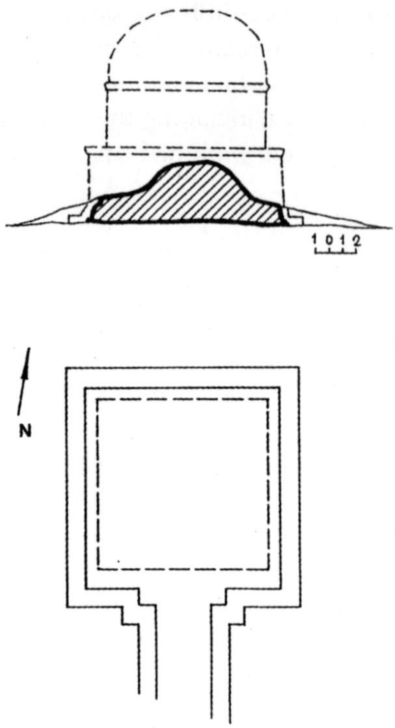

Fig. 174: Plan of *stupa* of Ushtur-Mullo. (After T.I. Zeymal', 1981, fig. 1) (Excavations sponsored by The State Hermitage Museum, St. Petersburg).

The painting is fragmentary and has not been well preserved, despite the fact that it was protected by bricks. The remains show the lower part of a composition preserving the feet of four standing figures, separated from each other by column bases (Fig. 175). Soft shoes are worn on the feet. The creases on the surfaces of the shoes are rendered with parallel strokes. On the inner sides of the ankles are round plates. Usually they covered the ties of the straps, serving at the same time as an ornament. This detail was characteristic of Kushan costume, and is manifested in works of plastic art, wall paintings and even coins. A barefoot figure in the centre wearing a long red mantle evidently has a cult character, and, in all probability, was

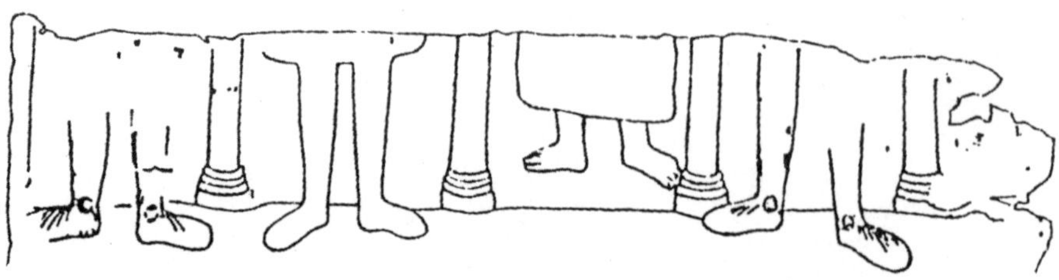

Fig. 175: Lower part of composition of wall painting with figures (donors?). Ushtur-Mullo. (The State Hermitage Museum, St. Petersburg).

an image of Buddha. The overall composition of the scene is typical: the Buddha figure in the centre flanked by adorants or donors. Analogies to this composition are found on the fragments of wall paintings from Karatepa and Fayaztepa and later at Dil'berjin. On the basis of the archaeological material, the complex of Ushtur-Mullo can be dated to the third to fourth centuries AD. The monastery functioned during the entire fourth century and its destruction was connected to the expansion into these territories by Sassanian Iran in the later fourth century.[485] In any case, Ushtur-Mullo demonstrates the continuity of Buddhist architectural and figurative traditions of the previous period.

Ajinatepa

Ajinatepa was discovered in 1959 under a mound, measuring 100 × 50 m, which had the typical appearance known from other sites in the Vahsh Valley of Tajikistan. From 1960 onwards, the South Tajikistan team of the Tajik Archaeological Expedition explored this area under the direction of B.A. Litvinskiy.[486] The archaeological investigation of Ajinatepa revealed an architectural compound with dwellings and a Buddhist monastery (Fig. 176). The monastery, located in the south-eastern part of the site, consisted of a square courtyard (19 × 19 m) that enclosed various buildings (Fig. 177). Wall paintings and sculptures were unearthed at the site. On

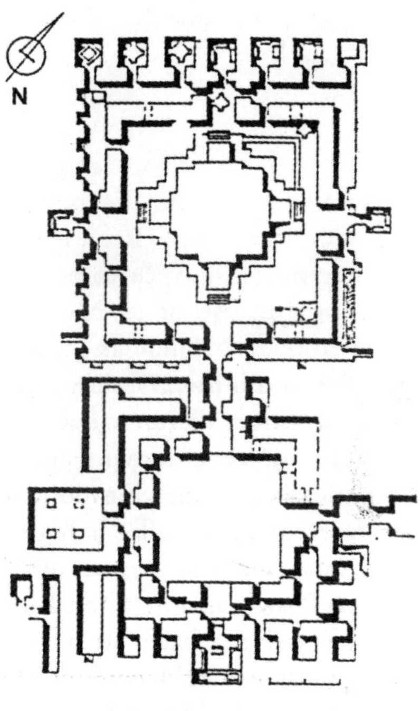

Fig. 176: Plan of Ajinatepa, Tajikistan. (After B.A. Litvinskiy and T.I. Zeymal, 1971: 27) (Excavations sponsored by The State Hermitage Museum, St. Petersburg).

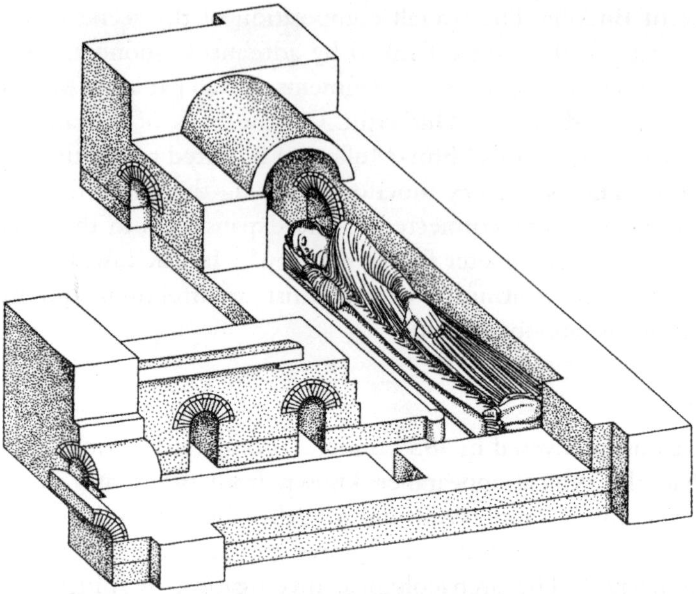

Fig. 177: Axonometric view of the temple with Buddha in *parinirvana*. Ajinatepa. 7th-8th century AD. (After B.A. Litvinskiy and T.I. Zeymal, 1971: 72-73) (Excavations sponsored by The State Hermitage Museum, St. Petersburg).

the basis of numismatic and other finds the complex of Ajinatepa can be dated from the second half of the seventh to the first half of the eighth century AD.[487]

WALL PAINTING

The bulk of the sculptural and painting fragments were concentrated in the monastery area, including the shrine. Rich decorations were found in room no. 1. One of the fragments shows a seated figure turned to the left. This fragment is interesting because of its background, which is richly ornamented with vegetal motives.[488] There are numerous poorly preserved fragments (for example from room no. 27), showing Buddhist figures with the Buddha image mostly in three-quarter view.[489] A large fragment from room no. 31 portrays an offering scene showing personages in local dress.[490] According to the drapery, the sleeves were worn loosely around the shoulders and tightly around the forearms. The collar is high and round (Fig. 178). The donors are holding vases and a large plate or bowl filled with fruits or flowers. The figures are shown against a red background. The borders dividing the scene are executed as a black stripe with white dots.

A fragment of a wall painting once decorating the ceiling of room no. 27 represents a multi-tiered composition with figures of Buddha (Fig. 179). The figures are painted on a dark (brownish-black) background, and are surrounded by a nimbus (*mandorla*). The garment is draped in numerous

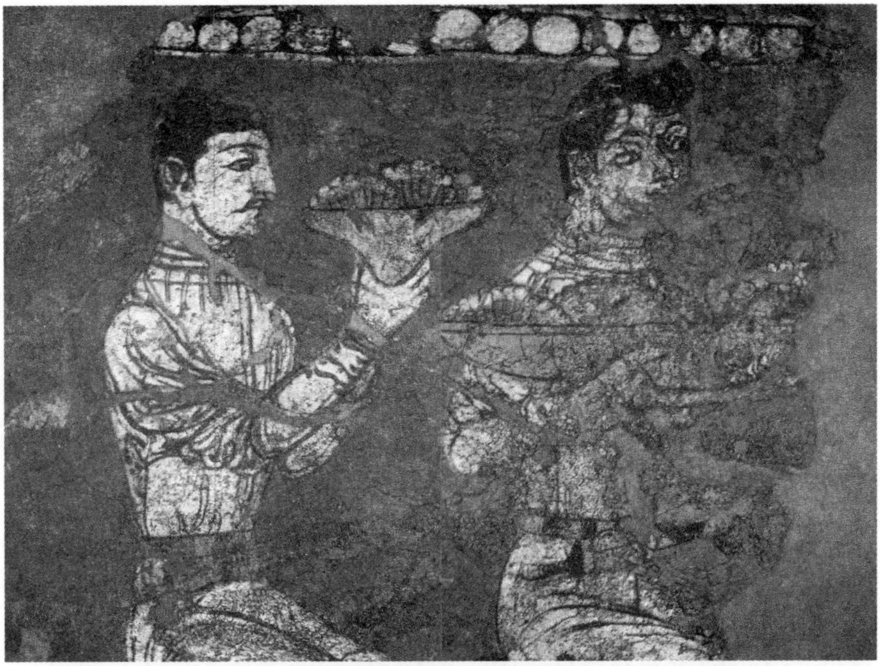

Fig. 178: Fragment of wall painting showing individuals with offerings. Ajinatepa. 7th-8th century AD. 75 × 50 cm. (The State Hermitage Museum, St. Petersburg. Inv. V-1666. S).

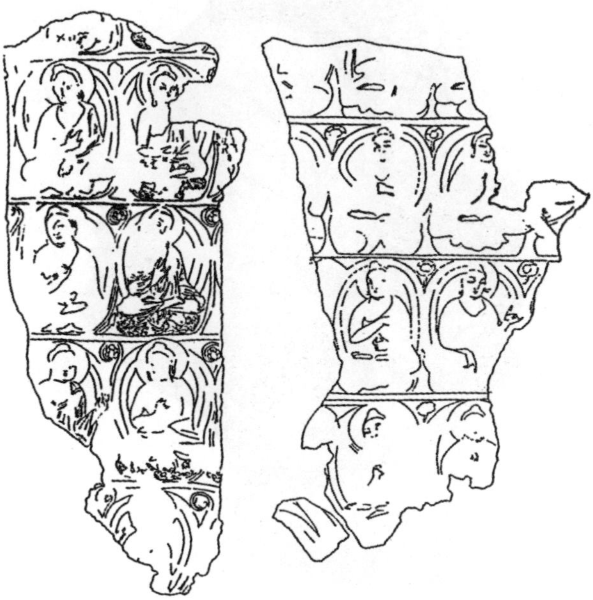

Fig. 179: Multi-register composition of wall painting with Buddha images. Ajinatepa. 7th-8th century AD. 200 × 180 cm. (The State Hermitage Museum, St. Petersburg. Inv. V-1714).

pleats and has a traditional reddish-orange colour. As a rule, the Buddha is seated in the *padmasana* position and his hands are in the *dharmachakra-mudra* or *abhaya-mudra*.

SCULPTURE

Sculpture and sculptural fragments from Ajinatepa were found mainly in room no. 1 (the shrine) and inside the niches there, where they had been formerly placed on pedestals. The sculptural technique continued the traditions of the previous periods. The masters used the same set of colours for both sculpture and wall painting. The heads and fragments of Buddha were more numerous here and distinguished by their larger size. Certain details were stamped in moulds, such as the curls of the hair. The curls were arranged in rows consistent with the hairstyle of Buddha and *bodhisattvas*. However, there is another type of hair style, rendered by deeply incised lines (as seen, for example, on the head of a *bodhisattva* from room no. 27).

The compositions of the Ajinatepa sculpture are conventional. Essentially they repeat the subjects of the above-mentioned Buddhist complexes: in addition to the Buddha (Fig. 180) and *bodhisattva* (Fig. 181) figures there

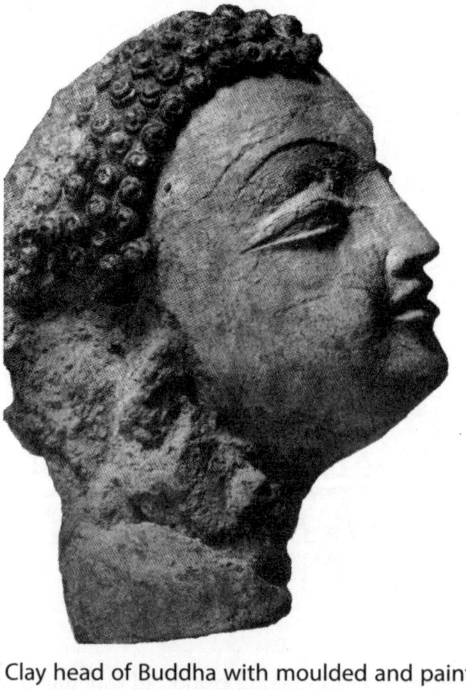

Fig. 180: Clay head of Buddha with moulded and painted hair. Sculpture fragment. Ajinatepa. 7th-8th century AD. H = 19 cm. (The State Hermitage Museum, St. Petersburg. Inv. V-1614).

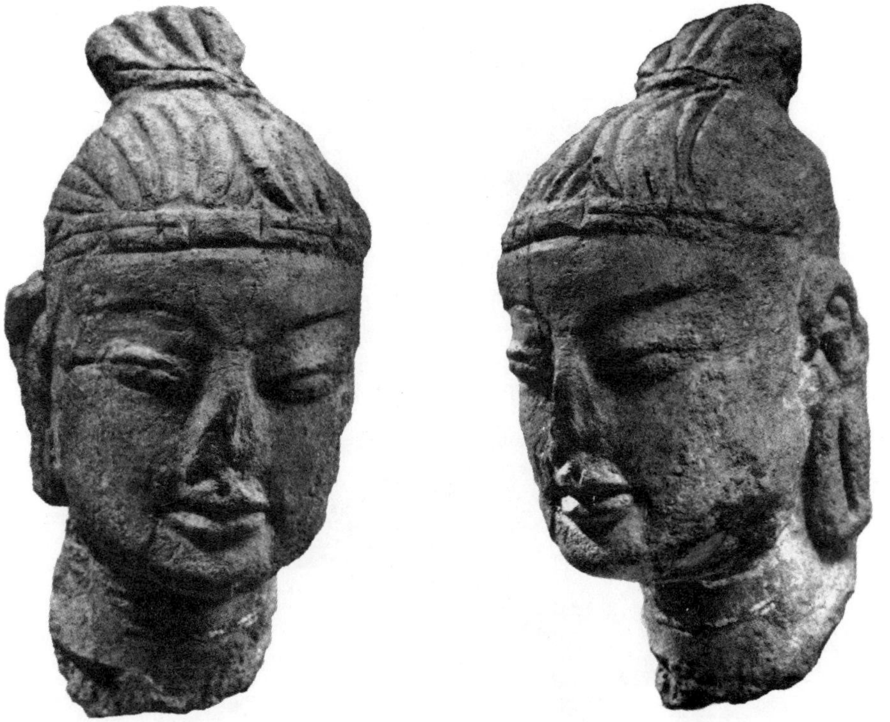

a b

Fig. 181: Clay head of a *bodhisattva*. Sculpture fragment. Ajinatepa. 7th-8th century AD. (Scale not available) (The State Hermitage Museum, St. Petersburg).

were heads of devatas (Fig. 182) and, evidently, male and female donors. However, the sculpture of Ajinatepa reflects a new method that was not typical for earlier Buddhist plastic art such as that of Karatepa, Fayaztepa and Dal'verzintepa. The modelling of certain details also distinguishes the Ajinatepa representations from the earlier sculptural complex of Kuevkurgan. The sculpture of Ajinatepa is distinct, for example, in the modelling of the facial features – the manner is heavier and at the same time laconic. The eyebrows are marked by deeply incised lines; the eye sockets are cut over the eyeball, which is modelled in high relief. The eyelids are usually executed more coarsely. The headdress and hair texture[491] are modelled almost without nuances (Fig. 183). The strands of the hair are rendered by roughly incised lines, for example, on the warrior of Mara (Fig. 184). On the other hand, certain methods employed in the modelling of the face are very close to those of the Kuevkurgan sculptures. For example, there is the same type of smooth forehead shown without the relief of the eyebrows, which are merely indicated by a deeply incised line and by paint. The expression of a faint smile on some Ajinatepa sculptures is enhanced by subtle depressions at the corners of the lips, for example on the head of a *bodhisattva* (Fig. 185). This method was also characteristic for many heads at Kuevkurgan.

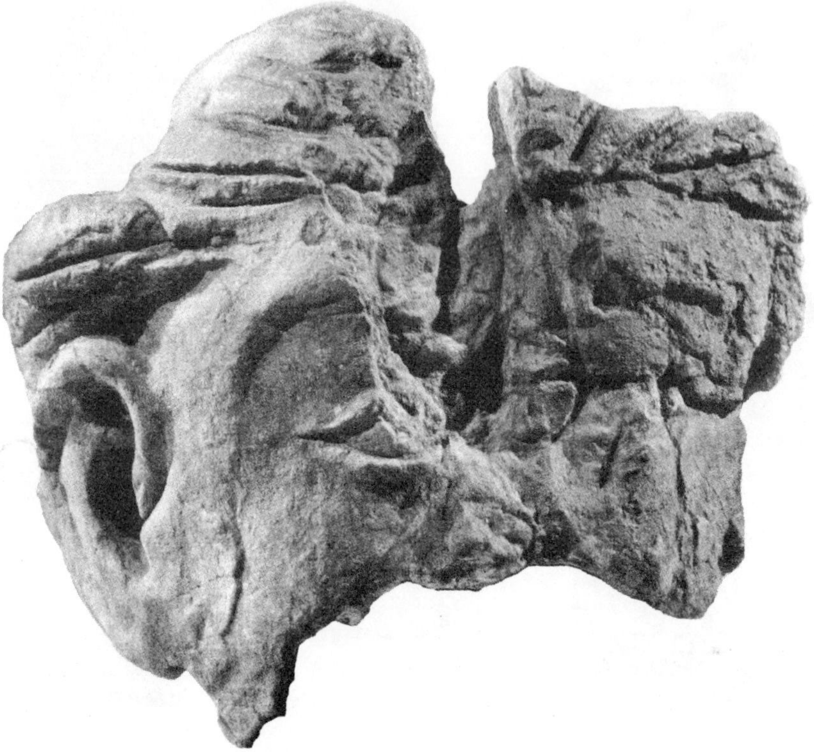

Fig. 182: Clay fragment of a *devata*. Sculpture fragment. Ajinatepa. 7th-8th century AD. 14 × 16 cm. (The State Hermitage Museum, St. Petersburg. Inv. B-1480).

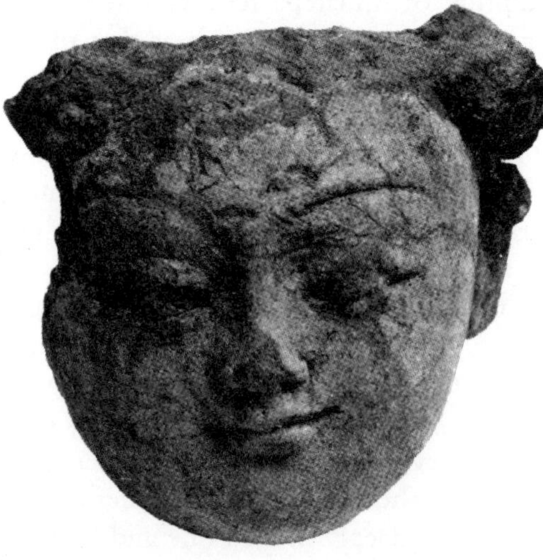

Fig. 183: Clay head of a divinity. Sculpture fragment. Ajinatepa. 7th-8th century AD. 10.5 × 10.5 cm. (The State Hermitage Museum, St. Petersburg. Inv. V-1669).

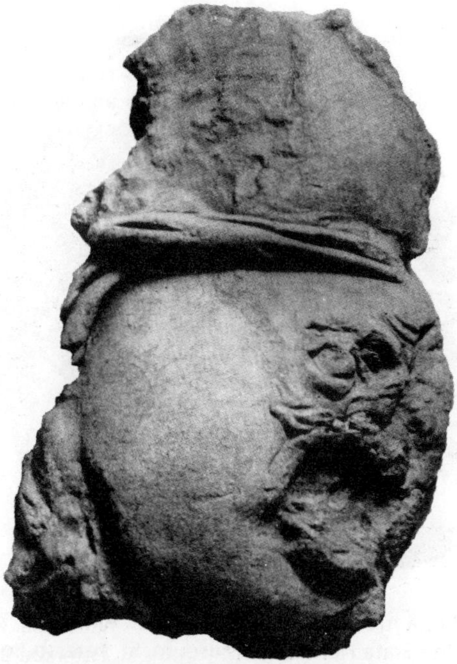

Fig. 184: Clay fragment of a representation (Mara's warrior?). Ajinatepa. 7th-8th century AD. (scale not available). (The State Hermitage Museum, St. Petersburg).

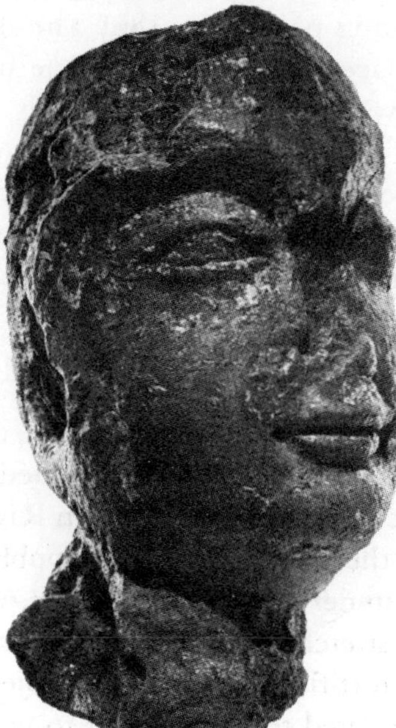

Fig. 185: Clay head of a *bodhisattva* (?). Sculpture fragment. Ajinatepa. 7th-8th century AD. 28 × 14 cm. (The State Hermitage Museum, St. Petersburg. Inv. V-1673).

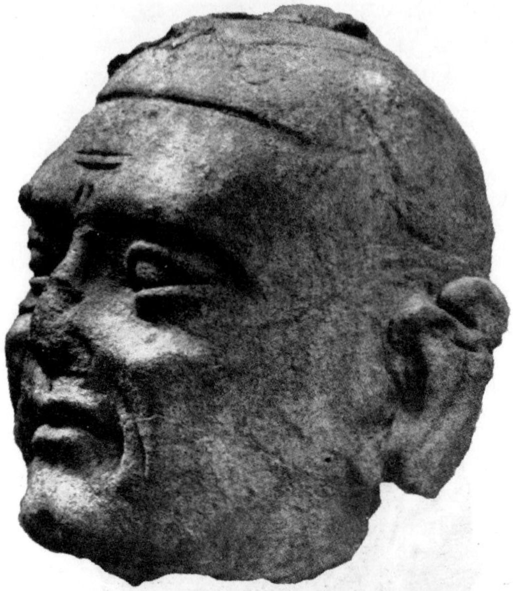

Fig. 186: Clay head of a monk. Sculpture fragment. Ajinatepa. 7th-8th century AD. 14 × 13 cm. (The State Hermitage Museum, St. Petersburg. Inv. V-1668).

It is interesting that in addition to the traditional schematic representation of the divine images, some heads have been treated as individuals. The head of a monk is a case in point (Fig. 186). The sharp features with deep incised lines make his face very expressive. One might say that the head looks like that of a native man. As we have already observed above, besides the canonic images of Buddha, *bodhisattva*s and other members of the Buddhist pantheon, the secondary figures (donors, adorants) bear more realistic features and even approach individual likenesses, apparently drawn from the local population.

Kalai Kafirnigan

Another site in south Tajikistan, Kalai Kafirnigan, demonstrates the spread of Buddhism in Tokharistan during the Early Medieval period. The site is located on the middle course of the Kafirnigan River, about 80 km south-west from Dushanbe, the capital of the Republic of Tajikistan. It was excavated in 1974-80 under the direction of B.A. Litvinskiy.[492] The site had an elongated plan stretching 275 m from north to south (3.5 sq ha) and was protected by a fortification wall with projecting towers. The upper layer of the site can be dated to the seventh to eighth century AD. In the most prominent location of the site, a richly decorated building was unearthed that is believed to have been an aristocratic palace. The building had a central hall surrounded by corridors. Inside the hall, there were benches along the walls and in the middle of the hall there was a stone altar. Near this building stood another structure that sheltered a small Buddhist temple (Fig. 187) in its northern part. The square shrine was located in the centre of the temple. In a niche of one of the walls a seated Buddha figure was found. In the corridor, a pedestal displayed another figure of a seated Buddha. Among the sculptural fragments from this locus, the painted clay head of Buddha with the traditional features of his plastic image is remarkable (Fig. 188). The walls of the corridor were covered with murals. On one of these fragments is an image of Buddha seated on the lotus throne. The lower register of the painting depicts a row of human figures bringing offerings and worshipping the deity (Fig. 189).[493]

An unprovenanced piece from Tajikistan is a terracotta mould for replicating an image of a human face. The image is clearly related to Buddhist plastic art. The mould-made impression has a circular form with a diameter of 15.5 cm. The tondo with the bust of the personage is framed by a string of simulated pearls in round relief between two concentric relief lines (Fig. 190). The face has elongated eyes and long arch-shaped eyebrows. The headdress is shown as two rows of crescent-shaped incisions emphasized by a relief line below them. On top of the hair, there is a trapezoid-shaped relief apparently representing the *ushnisha* (?). Underneath the chin, there is a row of identical reliefs representing a necklace. On the

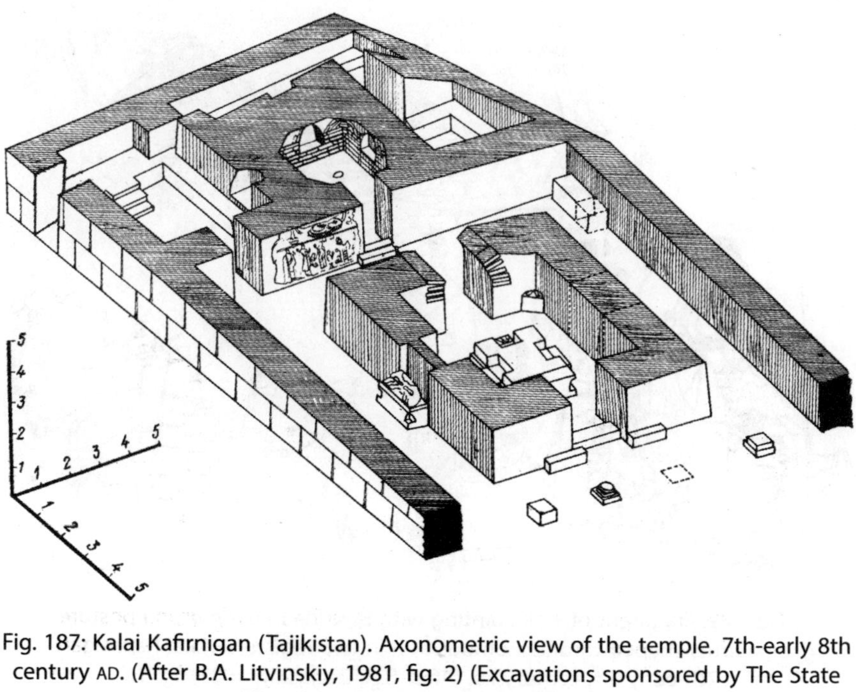

Fig. 187: Kalai Kafirnigan (Tajikistan). Axonometric view of the temple. 7th-early 8th century AD. (After B.A. Litvinskiy, 1981, fig. 2) (Excavations sponsored by The State Hermitage Museum, St. Petersburg).

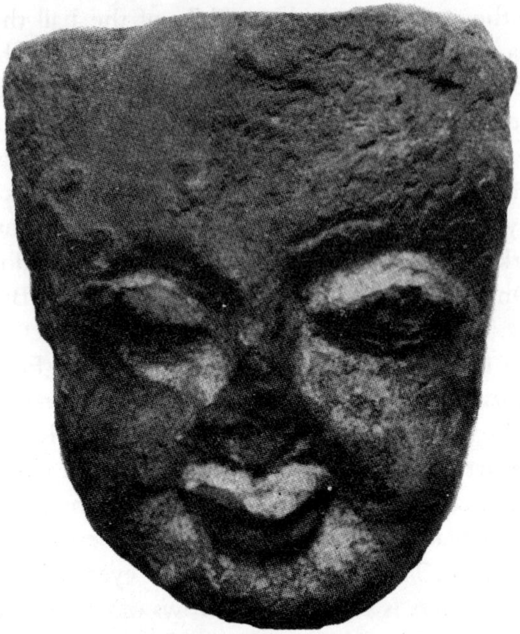

Fig. 188: Head of Buddha. Kalai Kafirnigan. 7th-early 8th century AD. 37 × 27 cm. (The State Hermitage Museum, St. Petersburg).

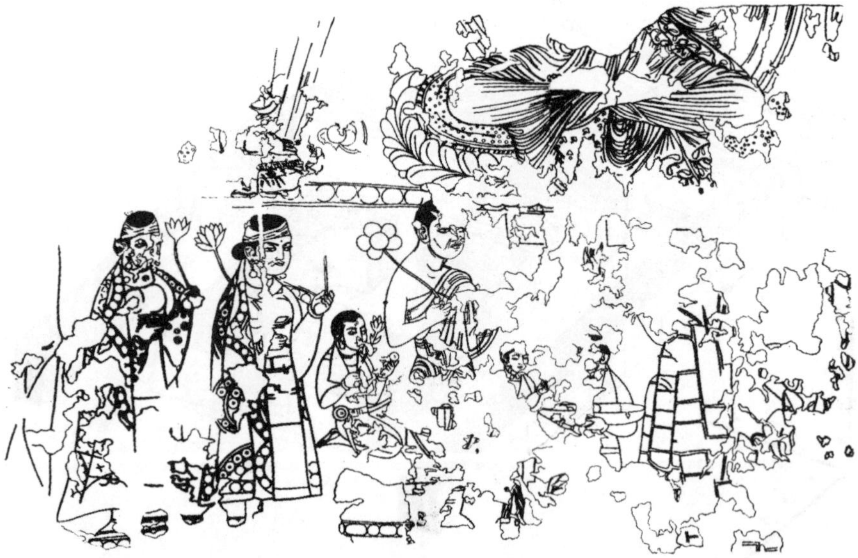

Fig. 189: Fragment of wall painting with Buddha in *padmasana* posture on a lotus-shaped throne. Composition in two registers. Kalai Kafirnigan. 7th-early 8th century AD. (After B.A. Litvinskiy, 1981, fig. 1). (The State Hermitage Museum, St. Petersburg).

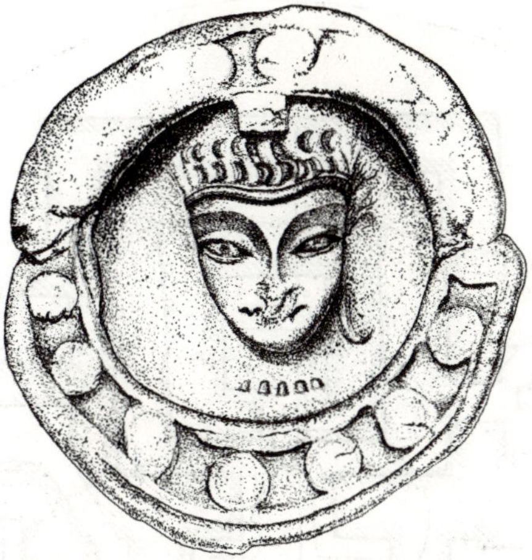

Fig. 190: Modern impression of an ancient mould reproducing the head of *bodhisattva*. 7th-8th century AD. Tajikistan. Provenance unknown. 15.5 cm. (Institute of Archaeology, Samarkand).

left side of the head there is a relief line showing the long lobe of the ear. The scroll line continuing the mouth evidently conveys a thin moustache. The image is very close to representations of *bodhisattvas*, particularly of Ajinatepa. The preliminary dating of the terracotta mould is seventh to eighth century AD.

Hisht-tepa

This archaeological site in Tajikistan has yielded many works of plastic art. Hisht-tepa is located in the Hovaling area in the territory of medieval Huttal.[494] Excavations of the mound (measuring 60 × 50 m) have brought to light an Early Medieval Buddhist monastery with about twenty rooms built in mud brick and clay blocks of *pakhsa* (Fig. 191). The main entrance between two pylons was from the east. The sanctuary (room no. 12) and room no. 20, where a votive *stupa* was found, were the most decorated in the complex. In the sanctuary, the altar was flanked by columns with round bases ornamented by vegetal motives. The front of the altar was painted red. The wall painting comprised basically vegetal and geometrical motives. The corridors around the sanctuary were also decorated.[495]

In the corners of room no. 20, where a *stupa* with cruciform plan was placed, pedestals were unearthed which in all likelihood had been destined for statues. The fragments of clay sculpture found here speak in favour of this.[496] Other important finds from Hisht-tepa include more than sixty votive clay *stupa*s (Fig. 192), whose form imitates actual *stupa*s. Nearly half of these votive *stupa*s contained clay tablets (Fig. 193) inscribed in Brahmi with the ritual text *dharma-paryaya*.[497] The dating of Hisht-tepa is based

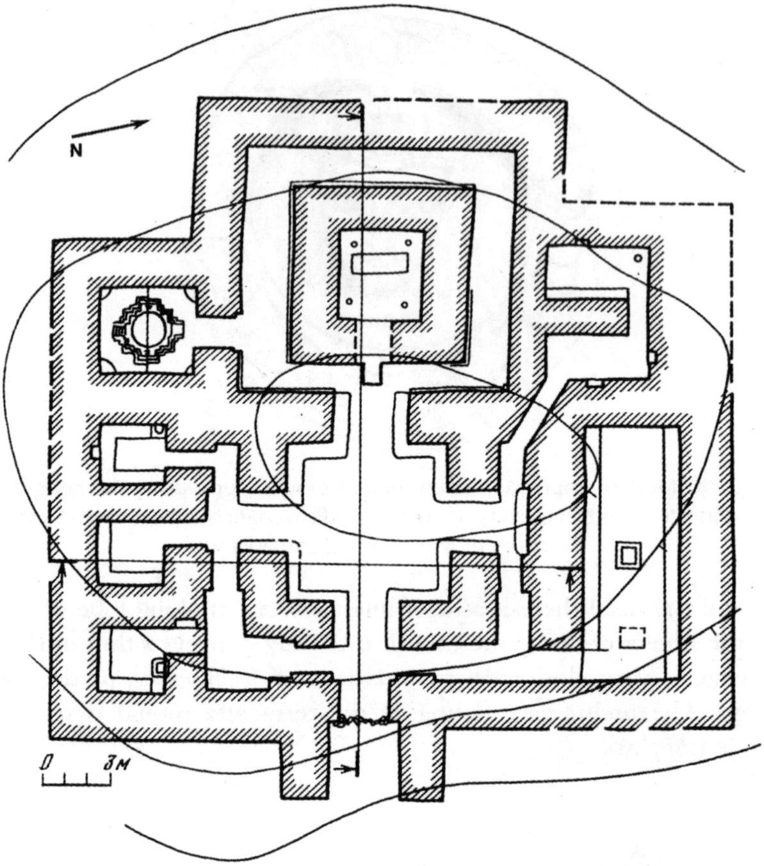

Fig. 191: Plan of Hisht-tepa (Tajikistan). Second half of the 7th-first half of the 8th century AD. (After M. Mullokandov, 1990, fig. 1).

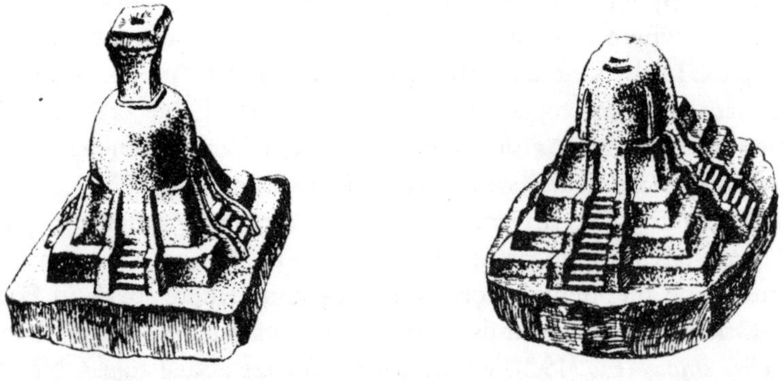

Fig. 192: Clay models of votive *stupa*. Hisht-tepa (Tadjikistan. Second half of the the 7th-first half of the 8th century AD. (After M. Mullokandov, 1990, fig. 3).

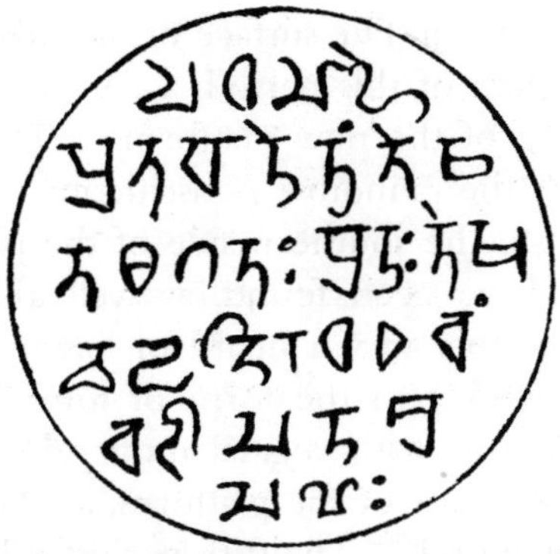

Fig. 193: Tablet with Brahmi inscriptions hidden in votive *stupa*. Hisht-tepa (Tajikistan). Second half of the 7th century-first half 8th century AD. (After V. Vertogradova, 1990, figure 1).

on the numismatic finds. All the coins including Arab-Sassanian, Sogdian, and Tokharian coins with Sogdian legends belong to the second half of the seventh century AD. The destruction of the monastery was caused by the Arab invasion and the conquest of Huttal in the middle of the eighth century AD.[498]

Buddhist Monuments in Margiana

The discovery of archaeological material at Gyaurkala in Turkmenistan points to the north-western extent of the distribution of Buddhist culture in Central Asia. The Buddhist architectural complex of ancient Merv was first investigated in 1960 under the direction of M.E. Masson.[499]

The *stupa* and *sangharama* located in the south-east corner of the site were the focus of excavation. These structures were orientated north-south with a small deviation to the east. The cylindrical body of the *stupa* is 10 m in diameter. It stands on a platform 3.5 m high, and 14 × 13 m^2 with stairs on the northern side. Traces of black and red paint were found on the stairs.[500] According to the excavators, the *stupa* functioned over five periods. The first is characterized by a monolithic construction 4 m in diameter which was set on a platform 2.5 m high. The dating of this construction is based on the find of five coins of Shapur II (AD 307-79) at the foot of the platform. The excavators connect the second period with a repair to a buttress on the western side of platform. The dome of the initial *stupa* also underwent repair during this period, with the re-laying of rectangular half bricks, and with a thick layer of clay (40 cm) placed on its surface. The dome of the *stupa* was transformed into an oval outline, but retained its height of 6 m from the base of the platform. During the third period, an essentially new *stupa* was constructed. The platform was raised by 1.5 m with the creation of the new dome, which now became almost hemispherical in form. The surface of the dome was covered by an alabaster layer. In the plan of this period, a corridor 1.4 m in width ran along the western edge of the new platform.[501] The excavators connect the fourth period with the grandiose construction of a new *stupa* on the ruins of the old one. On the southern side of the platform, traces of red, blue and black paint have been found, as well as fragments of plaster. During the cleaning of this area, a hoard of Sassanian copper coins was found. A plated gold buckle in the form of four-petal sockets was also found in the hoard. A gem with vegetal motif was found at the base of the stupa. In the western part of the platform, an Aramaic inscription on a pottery fragment was found.[502] The fifth period, relating to the cessation of functioning of the stupa, saw it filled and blocked. During this process, the head of a huge statue of Buddha was immured. A painted vase containing manuscripts was found, together with a reliquary, in the general area of the *stupa*.

On the basis of the stratigraphy of the *stupa*, the excavators consider that 'finds of coins of Shapur II in the platform of the first period'[503] have made it possible to date the construction of the first *stupa* not earlier than the mid-fourth century AD. The presence of coins of Kavad I in a layer above the platform of the cylindrical tower dates the fourth period in the life of *stupa* to the end of the fifth or the beginning of the sixth century AD. It is, therefore, probable that during the reign of Khosrow Anushirvan (AD 531-79) the fifth period began. This period was connected with the blocking of the *stupa*.

The second important structure of the Buddhist complex at Gyaurkala was the *sangharama*, which was located 4.35 m to the south of the *stupa*. The *sangharama* was built using mud bricks and *pakhsa* blocks (clay); in certain sectors the combination of these two techniques was used. Under a burnt layer were found coins from a Sassanian mint dated to the fifth to sixth centuries AD, together with small fragments of plaster with traces of wall painting, and pieces of a clay sculpture. The total area of construction of the *sangharama* was 140 m^2. Thirty-two rooms were excavated, allowing the monastic and temple sections of the building to be precisely allocated.[504]

Comparing the architectural plan of Fayaztepa with that of the Buddhist complex of Old Merv, it is possible to note a regular pattern in the spatial layout of the cult complex. The authors of the publication of the complex in Merv take as the central 'axis' of the complex a square courtyard on the perimeter of which stand all the architectural features.[505] In my opinion, the 'axis' on which parts of the whole ensemble were built was the sanctuary and the *stupa*. Coordination of these two important elements of a Buddhist cult complex determined the general plan, which was subordinated to this principle. Sanctuaries both in Fayaztepa and in Old Merv were built strictly on one axis with the main *stupa*, as a rule, supporting the general line of the *sangharama* (*vihara*). The exit of the sanctuary was aligned with the *stupa*. Put more simply, a person seating in the sanctuary and looking through the door could have a clear view of the main *stupa*, even if it were some distance away. The line of sight passed not only through the door of the sanctuary but also through a door in the courtyard on the opposite side.

According to G.A. Pugachenkova and Z.I. Usmanova, 'the composite idea of a sanctuary surrounded by corridors' and an *iwan* in a courtyard, are characteristic of Achaemenid architecture. This tradition is later reflected in the cult architecture of the Kushans.[506] This form became known in almost all Buddhist monuments, and was found further east, and was the most popular in east Turkestan.[507]

During the excavation of the Buddhist complex at Gyaurkala, fragments of Buddhist sculpture and terracotta figurines were found, as well as the monumental head of Buddha mentioned above. Clay tablets were found close to a reliquary, with the stamped image of a *bodhisattva* figure in the centre, seated on a circular plinth which rose from the form of a lotus. To the right of the figure was a design representing a *stupa*, on the left a standing figure (a donor?). An inscription follows on the four sides of the composition. As Pugachenkova and Usmanova have noted, features characteristic of the figurative tradition of the Hephthalite period can be traced in the iconography of the *bodhisattva*. These Hephthalite traits are especially clear in the manner of decorating the crown in the shape of three semi-circles and also the set of decorations.

Based on numismatic finds, the period of use of this Buddhist complex is dated by the excavators to the fourth to sixth centuries AD. However, there is some debate regarding this dating. In particular, G.A. Koshelenko, on the basis of the same numismatic data and on some unpublished coins, offers a Parthian date for the beginning of the complex.[508] In addition to the complex at Gyaurkala, another Buddhist monument has been discovered 600 m to the south-east of the east gate of the ancient settlement.[509] A tower-shaped hill appears to represent a Buddhist *stupa*, similar in size to stupa no. 1 (the main *stupa* located in the south-east corner of the site), with a platform measuring 13 × 13.3 m. Remarkable finds from this monument include a clay vessel which contained four stone and one ivory figurines. A small hoard of Sassanian coins belonging to the period of Khosrow Anushirvan (AD 531-79) and a Brahmi manuscript were also found. The stone figurines were executed in dark schist – the traditional material for Gandharan sculptures – and represent characters of Buddhist art executed in Gandharan style.[510]

KUVA

In the Early Medieval period, Buddhist monuments spread far beyond the borders of Bactria-Tokharistan. For instance the discovery of a Buddhist temple at Kuva in the territory of Fergana is evidence of the eastward movement of Buddhist culture. Kuva is located not far from the modern city of the same name in the extreme eastern district of the Fergana region on the Andijan-Margelan road. The site itself is square in form with a citadel rising 10 m above the *shakhristan* (the territory of the city-site proper) and *rabad* (suburbs). Kuva was situated on the ancient trade route that linked the Fergana Valley with Kashgar in Chinese Turkestan.

The 1950s excavations by V.A. Bulatova in the area of the *rabad* yielded densely built housing of the craftsmen and a Buddhist temple dated to the seventh to eighth century AD (Fig. 194). Clay sculptures were some of the remarkable finds from this site.[511] Among the sculptured images were heads with grotesque features. Widely opened eyes and mouths as well as coarsely emphasized eyebrows give their faces a demonic expression. One of the heads was identified as the 'Head of Mara's Warrior' (Fig. 195).[512] Another fragment with ruffled hair above a low forehead (Fig. 196) and wide-opened eyes has been associated with the Bodhisattva of Wisdom, Manjushri.[513]

The Kuva figurative complex offers another fragment of sculpture, where the face is modelled in the distinct plastic manner that gives to it the

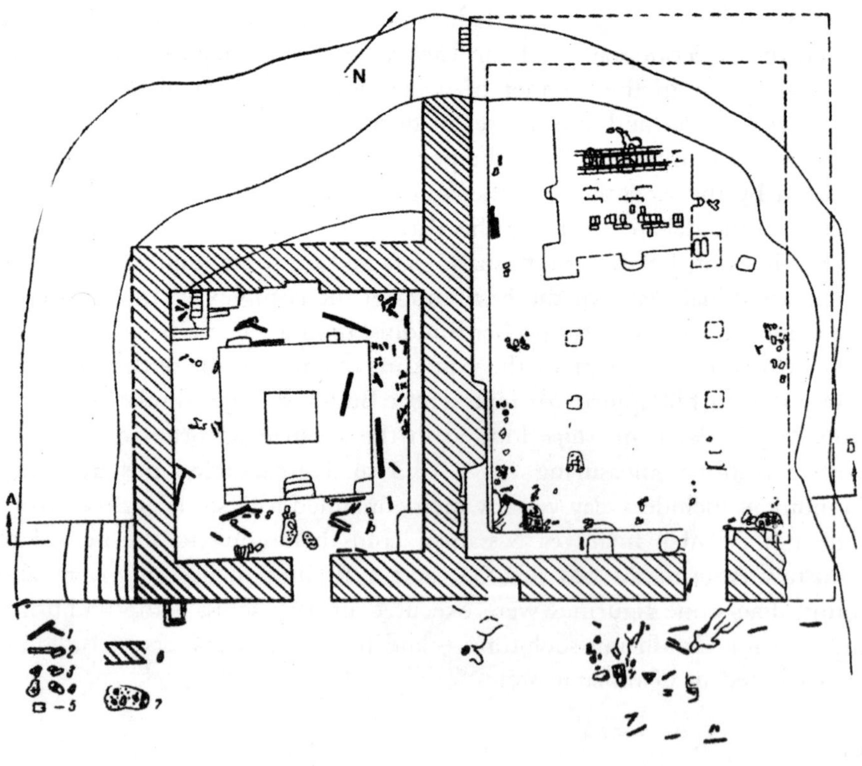

Fig. 194: Plan of Kuva temple with location of the sculpture fragments. (After V.A. Bulatova, 1972, fig. 1).

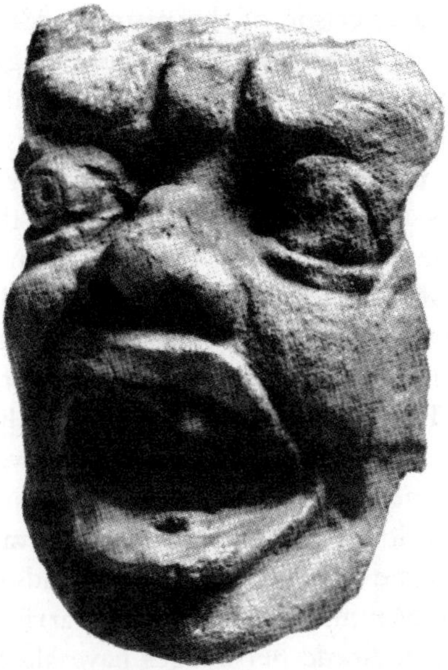

Fig. 195: Painted clay head of Mara's warrior. Kuva. 7th century AD. H = 22 cm. (Museum of History of the Peoples of Uzbekistan, Tashkent).

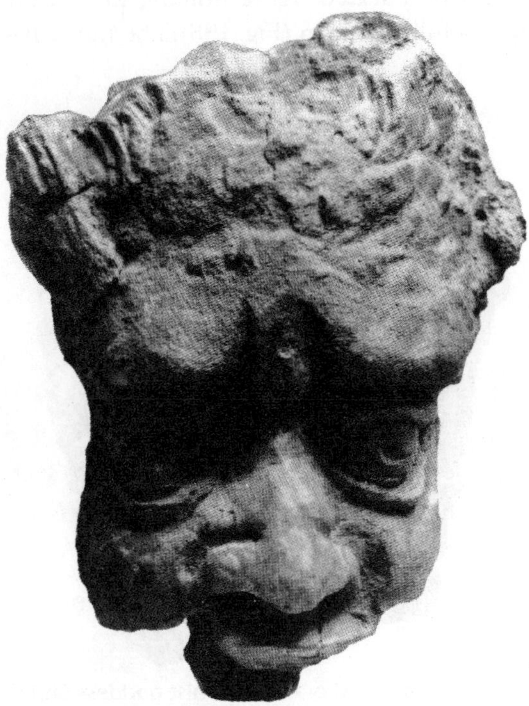

Fig. 196: Painted clay head of Manjushri. Kuva. 7th century AD. 25 × 18.5 cm. (Museum of History of the Peoples of Uzbekistan, Tashkent).

tranquil expression characteristic of the main Buddhist figures. This head has been associated with Shri-Devi.[514] She has elongated eyes with heavy eyelids and arch-shaped eyebrows and the typical subtle smile on the lips (Fig. 197). One of the most interesting aspects of this representation is the hairstyle, namely the manner of modelling the hair above the forehead, where two large locks are placed symmetrically in the centre. This detail remotely resembles the musician with the harp from Airtam in Bactria. A similar hairstyle can also be found on certain Gandharan sculptures. For example, the stone female bust from Taxila (Archaeological Museum, Taxila, Inv. no. DH'12-2347) dated from the second to third century AD shows the same hairstyle.[515] This manner of depicting hair also occurs on a Hariti representation from the British Museum (London, Inv. no. 1886-6-11-1).[516] Despite the chronological gap, there is a resemblance between certain figures in Bactrian plastic art and the works of Kuva. The similarities are noticeable first of all in the so-called 'grotesque' heads of the Kuva complex that have been called 'Manjushri' and 'Mara's Warriors'.[517] Similar figures with traits resembling demonic personages have already been mentioned above in connection with the Khalchayan reliefs. One of the heads from Kuevkurgan has a similar expression.

The find of a bronze seal at Kuva was unique.[518] It is a disk with the negative impression of a seated figure holding in its right hand a rhyton and in its left hand a full wineskin (Fig. 198). The figure has been associated

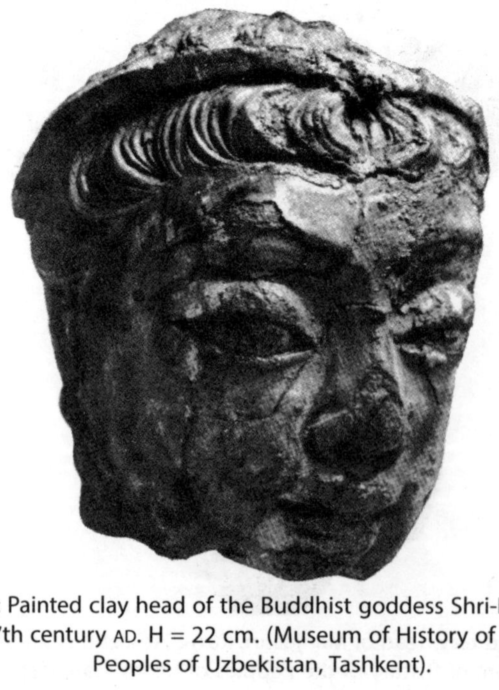

Fig. 197: Painted clay head of the Buddhist goddess Shri-Devi. Kuva. 7th century AD. H = 22 cm. (Museum of History of the Peoples of Uzbekistan, Tashkent).

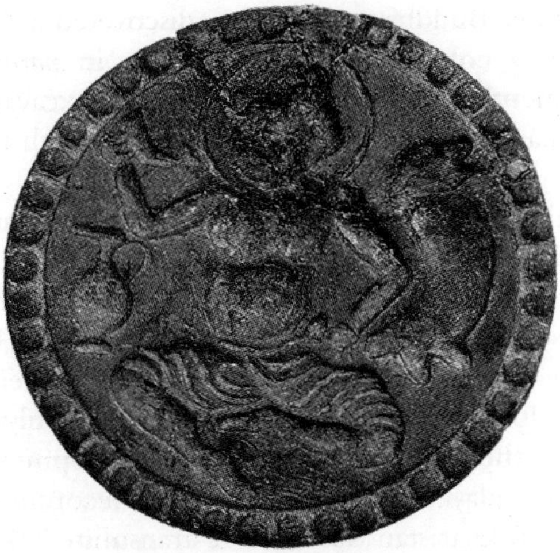

Fig. 198: Bronze seal with representation (in negative) of Kubera. Kuva. 7th century AD. Diameter = 5.7 cm. (Institute of Archaeology, Samarkand).

with Yaksha Kubera, a deity of the Hindu pantheon who also played a minor role in Buddhist religious art as one of the four *lokapalas* (local guardians). The seal was not found in a temple area, but in a dwelling quarter of the city. As correctly observed by V.A. Bulatova, the excavator of Kuva, the plastic works from this site reflect a faint influence from Bactrian art.[519] This influence can be detected in the general treatment of the face and hair, which resembles more the ethnic Bactrian and Sogdian population than Mongoloid types. The latter are seemingly rendered in the figurative complexes of Ak Beshim and the Krasnorechenskoe sites.

The Buddhist Complexes of Ak Beshim and Krasnorechenskoe

In the Early Medieval and Medieval periods, the number of Buddhist architectural constructions increased in the Semyrech'e and in southern Kazakhstan.[520] Although in antiquity it was mainly nomadic tribes (Turcs, Turgesh and Karluk) who lived in this territory, by the sixth century AD the process of settlement began and urban cultures developed. In the Chu Valley, many Buddhist monuments have been studied including temples and monasteries.[521] Numerous objects of art with representations of Buddha, *bodhisattvas* and other personages of the Buddhist pantheon were found there.[522]

In the early 1940s, a monastery and chapel were discovered by A.N. Bernshtam at Ak Beshim and Tortkul.[523] In the 1950's, L.R. Kyzlasov excavated a temple at Ak Beshim dated to the seventh to eighth centuries AD.[524] Then, a second Buddhist temple was discovered at the same site.[525]

In 1961, yet another Buddhist temple was discovered at Krasnaya Rechka, which contained a colossal figure of Buddha in *parinirvana* (reclining position). Subsequently, this temple was completely excavated. The Krasnaya Rechka temple has been, likewise, dated to the seventh to eighth century AD.[526]

Chronologically, all these complexes belong to the Early Medieval and Medieval periods and have a very distinct appearance. The iconographic peculiarities of the plastic works of these monuments are more similar to those of Chinese Turkestan than to those of Bactria-Tokharistan. This suggests that the influences came from the artistic centres of Chinese Turkestan, where local schools of wall painting and sculpture had formed. However, during the early phase of their development the Bactrian-Tokharistan school played an important role. Accordingly, the Buddhist culture of Bactria-Tokharistan was not a 're-transmitted' Buddhist figurative tradition in the direction of China,[527] but in reality Bactria-Tokharistan was one of the great centres of irradiation of Buddhist culture, embodying its high artistic achievements.

NOTES

1. Abdullaev et al. 1991, p. 68 no. 22.
2. Antonova et al. 1979.
3. Askarov and Shirinov 1993, fig. 50, nos. 9-10.
4. Pugachenkova 1973, fig. 1, no. 2.
5. Shaydullaev et al. 2003, pp. 202-5.
6. Bernard 1996, pp. 331-65.
7. Guillaume 1983; Francfort 1984; Bernard 1985; Veuve 1987; Rapin 1992.
8. Will 1979.
9. Will 1979, pp. 267-72.
10. Bernard 1968, pp. 111-51.
11. E.V. Zeymal' 1978; idem. 1983, pp. 65-110; Rtveladze and Musakaeva 1986, pp. 35-8.
12. Droysen 1952; idem. 1980.
13. Val'dgauer 1938, p. 216.
14. Shmidt 1929, pp. 23-4.
15. Abdullaev 1996, p. 54.
16. Val'dgauer 1924, p. 34.
17. Abdullaev 1996, p. 56.
18. Val'dgauer 1938, p. 35.
19. Bikerman 1985.
20. Ibid., p. 228.
21. Ibid., p. 227.
22. Ibid., p. 230, n. 64.
23. Bieber 1961, figs. 141, 142.
24. Bernard, on the basis of archaeological data from Ai Khanum, explains the formation

of Parthian Hellenistic art by the strong influence of Bactrian art. See Bernard 1973b, 1974, 1985. However, according to Koshelenko and Munchaev 1976, pp. 118-24, Hellenistic art in Parthia developed simultaneously.
25. Abdullaev 1995a, nn.1-3, p. 38.
26. Collignon 1907.
27. Amelung 1895.
28. Johnson 1927; Ujfalvy 1902; Anatolian Civilisations 1983, fig. 173, p. 75.
29. Edwards 1996, pp. 130-50.
30. Visconti 1824-6. This plastic style penetrated even small forms of art such as terracotta. In Bactrian art one can trace this style in certain figurines from Ai Khanum. See for example Guillaume and Rougeulle 1987, pl. XVII, figs. 7, 9, 12, 14; Abdullaev 1996, pp. 55-67, n. 1.
31. Maviglia 1914.
32. For the bibliography on Ai Khanum see Rapin 1992.
33. Salis 1912. See also Belov 1959.
34. Koshelenko and Munchaev 1976, pp. 122-3.
35. Ibid., p. 123.
36. Bernard 1982, pp. 148-59.
37. Spemann, 1885-1912, vols. I-IX, vol. III, part 1; Schrammen 1906; Winnefeld 1910; Winter 1908; Frankel 1890-5; Bruns 1949; Kahler 1948.
38. Bernard 1974, n. 5, pp. 99-114.
39. Bernard 1973a, pp. 623-25, fig. 13.
40. Bernard 1973a, fig. 15.
41. Bernard 1973b, p. 628.
42. Bernard 1974, n. 5, p. 110.
43. Facenna 1962; Facenna 1974, pp. 126-76; Schlumberger 1985.
44. Guillaume and Rougeulle 1987.
45. Ibid., Pl. XVII, 7, 9, 10, 12, 14.
46. Litvinskiy and Pichikian 2000, p. 14.
47. See for example the figurative complex of the Oxus Treasure in Dalton 1964.
48. Ibid., 1991, p. 159.
49. Ibid., pp. 189-94.
50. Ibid., p. 190.
51. Litvinskiy 2004, pp. 37-62, figs. 3-9. For other interpretations see Litvinskiy 2004, pp. 45, 46.
52. Bernard et al. 2004.
53. Ibid., p. 333.
54. Abdullaev 2006a, p. 108.
55. Litvinskiy, quoting N. Smirnova, mentions a similar hairstyle portrayed on some Euthydemus' coins, and a clay head from Takht-i Sangin. However, he writes: '... we could ascribe the Takht-i Sangin heads to Greco-Bactrian rulers. But a general comparison with Greco-Bactrian coins shows that their affinity resides rather in the style of execution, whereas specific correspondences are almost absent'. Litvinskiy 2004, p. 51.
56. Pichikian 1991, pp. 172-9, fig. 29.
57. Pichikian 1986, pp. 266-7, fig. 2.
58. Abdullaev 1988, fig.1.

59. The site comprised several hills (*tepa*) concentrated in a small area. Today all of these hills have been levelled for cotton fields. Only the name Khalchayan survives in that of the modern village.
60. Pugachenkova 1966 and 1971.
61. Ibid., pp. 189-90.
62. The coins clearly demonstrate the succession of Heliocles imitations and coins of the unknown king Soter Megas in northern Bactria. See, for example, Rtveladze and Pidaev 1981.
63. Paul Bernard 1987, p. 761 proposed this interpretation and the idea was further developed in Bernard and Abdullaev 1997; Abdullaev 1995c.
64. The tradition of depicting enemies in a grotesque manner is characteristic of Chinese art also. See, for example, Grum-Grjimaylo 1899.
65. Abdullaev 2007, pp. 93-4.
66. Abdullaev 1995c, p. 158, figs 7, 8.
67. Koshelenko, pl. CXLIII; Musakaeva 2004, pp. 76-87.
68. Abdullaev 1995b, pp. 174-5, fig. 6, 9.
69. Abdullaev 1995c, fig. 3.
70. In Abdullaev 1995c, p. 155, there is an error. The visit of Chang Ch'ien took place not in 123 BC but most likely in 129-128 BC.
71. Pugachenkova et al. 1978.
72. Belyaeva 1978, pp. 33-7.
73. Abdullaev 1995c, pp. 154-5.
74. Mitchiner 1976, p. 407, type 607.
75. Bernard 1987, p. 762.
76. The director of the excavation interpreted this figurine as female. See Pidaev 1978, p. 89. The figurine measures 5 cm in height. It was impressed in a mould in high relief with a flat back. The figurine was painted yellow.
77. Sulaymanov 2000, fig. 143, 1.
78. It is interesting to note that on the early Sogdian imitation with an archer one can see a similar type of armour with a high collar. See, for example, Mitchiner 1976, types nos. 652, 432.
79. Pugachenkova 1966, pls. XIV, XV.
80. Ibid., p. 183.
81. Ibid.
82. Bernard 1974, n. 5, p. 112.
83. Guillaume and Rougeulle 1987; Abdullaev 1996.
84. L'Or des Amazones 2001, n. 81.
85. Except for the imitations on Seleucid and Greco-Bactrian coins, which preserved the original form of hairstyle. See, for example, the imitation on the coinage of Heliocles in Masson 1956, pp. 63-75.
86. Pugachenkova 1966, pl. XXX.
87. Ibid., pl. XXIV.
88. Bernoulli 1905; Bieber 1961, fig. 455.
89. Bernard 1973a, p. 625, fig. 13.
90. Trever 1961, pp. 98-109.
91. Pugachenkova 1966, pl. XXI.
92. Abdullaev 2006b, p. 84, fig. 1.
93. Abdullaev et al., n. 125.

94. Stepnaya Polosa Aziatskoy Chasti SSSR 1992, pls. 65, 10.
95. Abdullaev and Badanova 1998, p. 191.
96. Pugachenkova 1966, p. 214, fig. XXXI .
97. Abdullaev 1987, pp. 76-80.
98. Rosenfield 1967.
99. Schlumberger et al. 1983.
100. Schlumberger 1985, pp. 63-4.
101. Vogel 1930, pp. 20-33.
102. Schlumberger 1961, pp. 77-95; Schlumberger et al. 1983; Fussman and Guillaume 1990.
103. Schlumberger 1985, pp. 63-5.
104. Schlumberger 1952; Schlumberger 1970; Schlumberger et al. 1983; Fussman and Guillaume 1990.
105. Schlumberger 1985, figs. 55, 56.
106. The inscription from Rabatak (Afghanistan) leaves no doubt that Kanishka himself ordered the setting up of the royal statues. See Sims-Williams and Cribb 1992 .
107. Sims-Williams and Cribb 1992.
108. For the translation and interpretation of the text see Mitterwallner 1986, pls. 1-2, pp. 52-62.
109. The technique of low relief was characteristic also of the early medieval period in Central Asian art, from which we have remarkable examples in the Pendjikent and Varakhsha complexes.
110. Schlumberger 1985, fig. 31.
111. Pugachenkova 1973, p. 117, fig. 33.
112. For ancient sources see Strabo, XI, VII, 3, Diodorus Siculus XVII; for medieval sources see Istakhri 1939, 300-4, Muqaddisi 2000, 325. See also V.V. Bartol'd 1965, vol. III, pp. 504-5.
113. Staviskiy 1972a.
114. Nevertheless, not from Termez, but from Jumalaktepa (in the Surkhandarya region) comes a carved wooden head wearing a royal crown, see Abdullaev et al. 1991 n. 372.
115. Pidaev and Leriche 2003.
116. Pugachenkova 1973.
117. Pugachenkova 1945.
118. Bernard 1968, pp. 111. It would be interesting to compare the mineral composition of the stones employed at the sites of Ai Khanum and Old Termez. We do not exclude the fact that they could have come from the same quarry. As noted above, there was the possibility of transportation down the Oxus River. If we take into consideration that both quarries (Imam Said and Orlinaya Sopka) were located near the banks of the river, it would have been easy to ship the stone blocks downstream to the port of ancient Termez.
119. Bernard 1968, p. 118-20, figs. 5, 6.
120. Bernard 1968, p. 125.
121. Bernard 1973b, figs. 24, 25. Here should also be noted the Ionic capital of Asia Minor type from Takht-i Sangin. See Pichikian 1991, pp. 148-50, fig. 3.
122. Pugachenkova 1973, p. 85. A more detailed description of 'Orlinnaya sopka' is given by Staviskiy 2001, pp. 52-4.
123. Staviskiy 1979, p. 154.

124. Pugachenkova 1966, p. 132; Staviskiy 1979, fig. 135.
125. Schlumberger et al. 1983.
126. The Buddhist character of this object is not evident. Probably it belongs to the same type of dynastic architecture.
127. I.e. to AD 127. See Falk 2001.
128. Staviskiy 1972a, pp. 41-50.
129. Tyulyaev 1988, figs. 68, 69.
130. Staviskiy 1979, figs. 124, 127, 128.
131. Staviskiy 1977, fig. 42: a, e, j.
132. Pugachenkova 1982a, fig. 26.
133. It is in the repository of the Archaeological Museum in Termez.
134. Unfortunately they were destroyed in the bombing of the Museum building during the civil war.
135. This column base is unpublished.
136. Pugachenkova and Rempel 1960, fig. 2; Staviskiy 1974, fig. 73; Staviskiy 1979, fig. 89; Abdullaev et al. 1991, vol. 1, no. 92.
137. Al'baum 1975, p. 90, fig. 32.
138. Indian Museum, Calcutta – no. N.S. 4143; Government Museum, Mathura - no. A65. Mitterwallner 1986, pls. 22, 23.
139. Tissot 1985, p. 166, pl. VII.
140. Regarding the Zurmala stupa see Strelkov 1927, pp. 27-30; Strelkov 1928, pp. 41-7; Pugachenkova 1967a, pp. 250-9. The relief was published in Abdullaev, Rtveladze and Shishkina 1991, vol. I, n. 94; Abdullaev 2000c, fig. 2.
141. Abdullaev 2000b, p. 136.
142. British Museum, London, no. 1917-10-9-8. Tissot 1985, pl. XII, 1.
143. Tissot 1985, pl. XII, 3, 6.
144. Originally it was excavated by V. Kozlovskij and E. Nekrasova (see Kozlovskij and Nekrasova 1974, pp. 30-9). The archaeological investigation of this object was continued by the Uzbek-French Mission (MAFOUz) under K. Abdullaev. See Stride 2001, pp. 123-9.
145. Abdullaev et al. 1991, vol. 1, n. 96.
146. Ibid., pl. XVI, 10.
147. Abdullaev and Zav'yalov 1985, pp. 202-11.
148. Pugachenkova and Rempel 1960, pp. 48-9; Meshkeris 1969, p. 136; Iskhakova and Iskhakov 1978, p. 161.
149. On this subject see Abdullaev 1997/8.
150. The excavations were conducted by Sh. Pidaev.
151. Pidaev 1978, p. 90.
152. Pidaev 1999a, p. 135. The author writes that the ceramic complex of Mirzakultepa, dated by the coins of 'Heliokles' (1st century BC), is not equivalent to the ceramics of Old Termez (dated by the same coins of 'Heliokles'). This discrepancy is interpreted by the presence of 'bowls with hemispheric bases' in the ceramic complex of Old Termez that allows dating of the latter to the second century AD.
153. Mkrtychev 2002, pp. 174-5. The author categorically insists on the dating of the Buddha image to the first to second century AD, disregarding other opinions supporting an earlier dating to the first century BC.
154. See for example Bussagli 1996, where all of Chapter VI is devoted to this problem – pp. 323-79; in Russian see Pugachenkova 1982a, pp. 38-60.

155. For this question see Tissot 1987, pp. 77-84.
156. Cribb 1984; Tanabe 1994, V, X.
157. Falk 2001.
158. Facenna 1974.
159. See in detail Abdullaev 1997/8, pp. 161-77, pls. I-II.
160. Abdullaev 1997/8, p. 169.
161. Meshkeris 1969, fig. 23, b.
162. Il'yasov 2000, pp. 175-6, fig. 2.
163. Published here for the first time.
164. Pidaev 1978, pp. 73-4, fig. 23.
165. The first is dated to the year AD 40 and the second to the year AD 51. See Mittelwallner 1986, pls. 22, 23.
166. Tissot 1985, figs. 124-6.
167. Pugachenkova 1973, pp. 119-20, fig. 36. Regarding Barattepa, see Rtveladze 1974 p. 79.
168. Tissot 1985, pl. III, 2.
169. Pugachenkova 1973, p. 120.
170. Abdullaev 2000c.
171. Abdullaev et al. 1991, vol. 1, p. 150, n. 197.
172. Gupta 1985, p. 61, n. 61.
173. A similar figurine was found in the Kushan levels at Khaitabad with a ceramic complex dated to the third -fourth century AD. See Zav'yalov and Pidaev 2001, pp. 59-63, fig. 1.
174. A terracotta figurine from Old Termez. See Abdullaev 1997/8, pl. II, 4, probably represents the same iconographic type.
175. Tyulyaev 1988, fig. 197.
176. Nagarajunakonda Archaeological Museum. Tyulyaev 1988, fig. 211.
177. Peshawar Museum (no. 1844). Cited in L. Nehru 1989, fig. 14.
178. R.S. Gupta 1980, p. 3.
179. Abdullaev et al. 1991, vol. 1, no. 197.
180. Regarding Ismailtepa see Rtveladze and Hakimov 1973, p. 24.
181. Tissot 1985 pls. XXXIX, 3a; XXXI, 1.5.
182. Ismailtepa is located on the left bank of the Surkhandarya River, some 700-800 m from the bridge to the south-east of the centre of the Djarkurgan district. It is dated to the Kushan period. See Rtveladze and Hakimov 1973 pp. 24-5.
183. Huff (1995, pp. 269-74) characterizes this figurine as 'unusual'. In other publications it was identified simply as a 'Bactrian deity'. See, for example, Mkrtychev 2002, p. 178.
184. Tissot 1985, pl. XXIX, 1a, 2a.
185. Ibid., pl. XXXII, 10.
186. Gupta 1980, pp. 4, 9.
187. Sarnath Archaeological Museum (inv. no 5512). Egami 1988, n. 17, p. 164.
188. Abdullaev et al. 1991, vol. 1, n. 81.
189. Abdullaev 1995a.
190. Al'baum 1960, pp. 31-2, fig. 17.
191. Abdullaev 1997/8, pp. 166-7, pl. I, fig. 6; Abdullaev 1990, fig. 1.
192. Pugachenkova 1973, pp. 106-7, fig. 21.
193. Litvinskiy and Sedov, 1983, p. 146, tab. XXXII, 3.

194. Abdullaev and Sheyko, 1985 n. 7.
195. Abdullaev 1990, pp. 63-4, fig. 1, 6.
196. The figurine is published here for the first time. It is housed in the Termez Archaeological Museum.
197. Harle 1986, pp. 28-32, figs. 12, 15, 17, 18.
198. Khodjaev and Abdullaev 1990.
199. Gupta 1980.
200. Masson 1940a, fig. 55, p. 3.
201. Zhukov 1961, pp. 190-1, fig. 8.
202. Ibid., pp. 179, 190.
203. Joshi 1966.
204. Staviskiy 1969a, fig. 35, a,b.
205. Abdullaev et al. 1991, vol. 1, p. 151, n. 199.
206. Pidaev 1978, pp. 75-6, fig. 24, no. 2.
207. Meunie 1942, pl. XXIX, 90.
208. Rosenfield 1967, pp. 3, 8, 12-13, 22-8.
209. Turgunov et al. 1983.
210. Pugachenkova 1973, pp. 120-1.
211. Zav'yalov 1981, p. 67, fig. 1, 2.
212. Tyulyaev 1988, figs. 206, 207, 209.
213. Pugachenkova 1973, pp. 120-1, fig. 37.
214. Hackin et al. 1954, pl. 141, 17, 23, 163, 668.
215. Zav'yalov 1981 p. 67, fig. 1, 6.
216. A terracotta tile representing an amorous scene from Kampyrtepa has also been identified as *mithuna* (see Mkrtychev 2002, p. 179, p. 184, fig. 4), although the pose and the clothing are reminiscent of 'Eros and Psyche', albeit very transformed.
217. Kramrisch 1981, pl. XII, 42, 43, 44; Tyulyaev 1988, figs. 81, 86, 87.
218. Facenna 1974, figs. 39, 40.
219. Kala 1980, pp. 81, 86, 87.
220. Turgunov et al. 1983, n. 3.
221. Abdullaev and Zav'yalov 1985, p. 211.
222. The name Fayaztepa is derived from the name of R.F. Fayazov, the former director of the Termez Municipal Museum. See Al'baum 1990, p. 19, n. 2.
223. Excavations were conducted by L.I. Al'baum, member of the Institute of Archaeology. See Al'baum 1974.
224. Al'baum 1990, pp. 18-27.
225. Al'baum 1974, p. 56.
226. Tissot 1987, fig. 79. It should be noted that the modelling of the tree in the art of Mathura and especially in that of Gandhara is different. Sometimes the tree covers the figure of the deity like a kind of parasol, similar to that on the large stele with five figures from Shahr-i Bahlol or on a schist sculpture from Shahr-i Bahlol with the representation of Bodhisattva Siddhartha under the *sala*. See Tissot 1987, fig. 78.
227. Here we cite some of them: sculpture in gray schist from Tahti Bakhi, representing the seated figure of Buddha (Berlin Museum). See Tyulyaev 1988, fig. 168; Joshi and Sharma 1969, fig. 39, 40. A similar type of hair-do is portrayed on a plaque cited by Tissot 1985 p. 204, pl. XXVI, nos. 5, 7.

228. Tissot 1985, fig. 70, pls. XI-XII.
229. In my opinion, some iconographical features in the treatment of monks' images (for example the anthropological type, see Khojaev and Abdullaev 1990, pp. 24-7) testify to their local origins.
230. Al'baum 1974, p. 56; Al'baum 1975, p. 90, fig. 31.
231. Staviskiy 1979, fig. 105.
232. Tissot 1985, pl. I, no. 1.
233. See Pugachenkova 1982a, fig. 121.
234. Abdullaev 1990.
235. Ibid.
236. On later paintings of Balalyktepa from the sixth-seventh century AD this kind of dress looks like a long *khalat*. Does this mean a long period of use for this mode of dress? Or is there another explanation for this detail, for example as an element of nomadic dress worn over centuries by different ethnic groups? See the illustrations in Al'baum 1960.
237. Abdullaev 2003.
238. Al'baum 1990; Staviskiy 1998, fig. 28.
239. Mitterwallner 1986, pl. 6.
240. Schlumberger et al. 1983.
241. Al'baum 1975, n. 119.
242. Staviskiy 1979, figs. 38-48.
243. In this case there is an interesting comparison with the inscriptions from Karatepa. According to V. Livshits, the title and name would rather point to: 'an Aramaean clerk or soldier of Sassanian detachments, than Buddhist pilgrims' (Al'baum 1990, p. 26). In spite of the rigid policy of Zoroastrian priests in the eastern parts of Iran, in the late Kushan period the veneration of Buddha continued. See Lukonin 1969b, p. 43, n. 16.
244. Staviskiy 1995, pp. 191-202.
245. Bussagli 1978, p. 80.
246. Kruglikova 1979, pp. 122-5, fig. 2, 3, 4.
247. See, for example, Marshak 2005, pp. 47-55, figs. 33-44; An Hayao 2005, pp. 57-65
248. Al'baum 1974, p. 57.
249. Ibid.
250. Recent excavations at Fayaztepe showed that Buddhist constructions associated with so called Soter Megas coins can be dated to the first half of the first century AD. For new data on Fayaztepa, see Annaev and Annaev 2010, pp. 53-66.
251. Al'baum 1974, pp. 57-8.
252. Vertogradova 2000, pp. 43-6.
253. Denike 1927; Denike 1928; Masson 1940a, pp. 5-122.
254. Staviskiy 1969b, pp. 7-31.
255. See for example, Staviskiy 1969a, pp. 139-69; Staviskiy 1972b, pp. 67-100; Staviskiy 1987, pp. 282-9.
256. Staviskiy 1972b, p.74, fig. 21.
257. Ibid., p. 74, fig. 21b.
258. Abdullaev 2000c, fig. 2.
259. Abdullaev et al. 1991, vol. I, p. 104, n. 108.
260. Pidaev and Kato 2003, pp. 128-34.

261. Pidaev and Kato 2001, pp. 114-22; Pidaev and Kato 1999, n. 9-10, pp. 82-5; Pidaev and Kato 2000b, pp. 39-45.
262. Pidaev and Kato 2003, pp. 128-34.
263. Ibid., p. 133.
264. Pidaev 2002, no. 21.
265. A similar depiction of cobras is found on one of the worshippers on a relief composition dated to the first or second centuries AD showing the bathing of the new-born Buddha from Ghantasala (Sidorova 1971, fig. 84).
266. Mify Narodov Mira 1982, vol. 2, p. 195.
267. Pidaev 2002, no. 17.
268. Pidaev 2002, no. 23.
269. Pidaev and Kato 2006, figs. 3, 4.
270. Tissot 1985, pl. XII, no. 1.
271. Pidaev and Kato 2001, p. 119.
272. It should be noted that the trees have a long pyramidal crown resembling the indigenous poplar. On the dark green background there are long light green leaves with red fruits. The latter have such a fresh appearance that one suspects a later origin. These leaves and fruits are similar to the tree *sala* (*Shorea robusta*) popular in Buddhist art of the Indian subcontinent.
273. Staviskiy 1987, p. 287.
274. Pidaev 2002, no 28.
275. Staviskiy 1972b, p. 77.
276. Kruglikova 1979, pp. 123-43, figs. 2, 3, 4.
277. Kruglikova 1979, p. 144.
278. Staviskiy 1972a, pl.V.
279. Pidaev et al. 2001, pp. 112-13.
280. Pidaev and Leriche 2003, pp. 136-8, fig. 1.
281. Ibid., pp. 138-9.
282. Ibid., p. 138.
283. Ibid., p. 139.
284. Staviskiy 1977
285. Ibid., fig. 42, g.
286. Facenna 1974, vol. I., pp. 126-76.
287. I should like to express my deepest gratitude to Dr. T. Annaev for this communication.
288. Vyazmitina 1945a, p. 32; Vyazmitina 1945b, fig. 12.
289. Pugachenkova and Rempel' 1960, fig. 3-6; Pugachenkova 1979, figs. 153-4; 159-62; Staviskiy 1974, figs. 67-71; Staviskiy 1979.
290. Turgunov 1973, pp. 52-77.
291. Today it has been completely levelled.
292. Turgunov 1973, p. 55.
293. Facenna 1974, fig. 35.
294. Staviskiy 1974, fig. 81.
295. The figurine has been identified as 'a great Bactrian goddess'. See Turgunov 1973, p. 76.
296. Pugachenkova 1978b, figs. 68-9.
297. Pugachenkova et al. 1978.
298. Turgunov 1989, pp. 81-95.

299. Pugachenkova and Turgunov 1978, pp. 90-7.
300. Ibid., pp. 90-1.
301. Ibid., p. 92.
302. Ibid.
303. The materials are in the depository of the Institute of Art Research (Tashkent). See Pugachenkova and Turgunov 1978, p. 92.
304. Turgunov 1989, p. 93.
305. Pugachenkova and Turgunov 1978, p. 91.
306. Ibid., pp. 92-3.
307. Ibid., p. 93.
308. Bernard 1969, p. 344, fig. 20.
309. Pugachenkova and Turgunov 1978, p. 93.
310. Pugachenkova 1978b, fig. 19.
311. Ibid., p. 138, fig. 26.
312. The same ornamentation can be seen on the conical headdress of a prince from the same complex at Dal'verzintepa. See Pugachenkova 1978b, fig. 24, 25.
313. Pidaev and Kato 2003, p. 133.
314. Barthoux 1930.
315. Turgunov 1989, pp. 81-95.
316. Turgunov 2000, pp. 83-4.
317. Turgunov 1989, p. 93.
318. Turgunov 1989, p. 95.
319. Turgunov 2000, pp. 83-6.
320. Kavasaki 1997, pp. 49-50, fig. 25.
321. Pugachenkova 1989b, p. 15.
322. Turgunov 1989, pp. 94-5.
323. Antonini 1995, p. 267.
324. Abdullaev, 1997/8, pp. 161-77. For a map of the distribution of Buddhist terracottas see Abdullaev 1997/8 pl. I.
325. The terracotta figurine has not been published yet. I thank Mr. D. Rusanov for this information.
326. Several articles are devoted to this subject. For the latest bibliography see Abdullaev 2000b.
327. Rtveladze 1978, pp. 75-90.
328. Pugachenkova 1978b, pp. 115-43; regarding the temple, see pp. 130-43.
329. Ibid., pp. 142-3.
330. Ibid., pp. 132-3.
331. Ibid., p. 133.
332. Ibid.
333. Ibid.
334. Ibid.
335. Ibid., p. 140.
336. Ibid., p. 117.
337. Rudenko 1960, fig. 152, j; Chuvin 1999, fig. 18.
338. Abdullaev 1995c, fig. 6.
339. Cited in Nehru 1989, p. 331.
340. It is difficult to agree with Mkrtychev's interpretation of a terracotta plaque from Kanka (Tashkent region) representing a horseman (Mkrtychev 2002, p. 187, figs.

1-2). He proposes to see in this composition the 'Great Departure', while we can find only one comparable feature in it, namely the frontal pose of the figure. The image of the bearded rider wearing a tripartite crown and holding a spear has not the slightest similarity to young Prince Siddhartha. G. Bogomolov's interpretation of the plaque seems more acceptable. See Bogomolov 1986. Actually, in the art of Early Medieval Central Asia, especially in the nomad environment, images of riders were very popular and associated with a specific cult. To Kanka's terracotta plaque with a horseman one can add another plaque of the same type from Khodjent, dated fifth-sixth century AD. Drevnosti Tadjikistana 1985, no. 836.

341. Pugachenkova 1978b, figs. 65-7.
342. For example, from the same Dal'verzintepa ceramic complex, see Nekrasova and Pugachenkova 1978, pp. 143-61, figs. 75, 76.
343. Hackin et al. 1954.
344. Pugachenkova 1978a, p. 218.
345. Masson M. 1940a, fig. 50; Pugachenkova and Rempel 1960, fig. 63.
346. Meshkeris 1986, tab. II, I. This opinion was supported by T. Mkrtychev 2000, p. 165.
347. Abdullaev 1997/8, p. 166.
348. Pugachenkova 1982b, p. 254.
349. Gupta 1980.
350. Mkrtychev 2002, pp. 184-5.
351. In this context the term 'Central Asia' refers to the territory of the former Soviet Republics of Kirghizia, Tajikistan, Turkmenistan, and Uzbekistan.
352. (inv. no. 5043) Pugachenkova and Rempel 1960, fig. 63.
353. Rosenfield 1967, p. 33.
354. Cited from Rosenfield 1967, p. 33.
355. Rosenfield 1967, pp. 29-30.
356. It should be pointed out that representations of Jaina are clearly missing on the Kanishka coins.
357. Dandamaev 1974, n. 2, p. 30.
358. Koshelenko (ed.) 1985, pl. XXXVIII; Abdullaev et al. 1991. vol. II, no. 468; Suleymanov 2000, p. 194, fig. 153, 4.
359. Pugachenkova 1978b, fig. 75; Tissot 1985, pls. XXIV, XXXIII.
360. Cited in Pugachenkova 1982a, fig. 95.
361. Sulaymanov 2000, p. 199.
362. Ibid., fig. 173, no.1
363. Tissot 1985, pl. XXX, 5a, 5c.
364. Ibid., pl. XXVII, 7.
365. Lunina 1990, pp. 48-50, fig. 5.
366. Mkrtychev 2002, p. 195. N. Dvurechenskaya considers this detail a misunderstanding by the master. See Dvurechenskaya 2000, n. 2, pp. 128-9.
367. Dvurechenskaya 2000, pp. 125-33.
368. Vyatkin 1927, p. 24, fig. 21.
369. Marshak et al. 1996, pp. 47-56.
370. Ibid. p. 43. See also Marshak and Raspopova 1997/8, figs. 1a, b, 2, 3a, 3b. Evidence of ornamentation (such as the bracelet on the left hand and a flower in the left field) and other details suggest the identification of this image as a *bodhisattva* rather than as Buddha. It is possible that the inscription on the mouth of a jar

(from the same site) with the word *sutra* can indirectly be related to Buddhism. See Belenitski et al. 1986, pp. 320-1.

371. Karev 1998, fig. 1, 2.
372. Ibid., p. 108.
373. Abdullaev 2000d, pp. 173–5, fig. 1.
374. The pendant, from a private collection, is published here for the first time.
375. Staviskiy and Urmanova 1958; Staviskiy 1960.
376. Baybakov 2000 p. 200, fig. 1.
377. Litvinskiy 1975, pp. 191-8; de la Vaissière 2002.
378. Staviskiy 1997, p. 67.
379. Ibid., p. 88.
380. Ibid., pp. 87-90.
381. Al'baum 1953, pp. 57-60.
382. Abdullaev et al. 1991, vol. 2, n. 486.
383. Koshelenko (ed.) 1985, tab. CVI, 2, p. 394.
384. Pilipko and Masimov 1969.
385. Pugachenkova and Usmanova 1994, pp. 142-4; Usmanova 2000, pp. 1714.
386. Pugachenkova 1958, pp. 61-6.
387. Masson M. 1963, pp. 51-6; Pugachenkova 1967a, fig. 17.
388. Yagodin 2000, fig. 2.
389. For example, Afrasiab with the image of Avalokiteshvara mentioned above (Karev 1998).
390. Masson 1976, pp. 3-17.
391. Abdullaev and Annaev 1990, pp. 12-25.
392. Al'baum 1960.
393. Pugachenkova 1966, fig. 58; p. 102, figs. 68-9
394. Annaev 1984, p. 189.
395. Ibid.
396. Al'baum 1960, pp. 61-114; Annaev 1984, p. 189.
397. Annaev 1984, p. 191, fig. 3.
398. Ibid. fig. 4, nos. 1, 8, 14, 18, 25, 29, 31; fig.5, nos. 6, 7, 23-8, 33, 34, 36-9.
399. Ibid., pp. 192, 193.
400. Ibid., p.193.
401. Annaev et al. 1988, fig. 1.
402. Ibid., p. 82.
403. See, for example, Steblin-Kamenskiy 1997, pp. 173-244.
404. Annaev 1984, n. 2, p. 188.
405. Abdullaev 2001a, pp. 115-18.
406. The translation of the Surkh Kotal inscription is based on the reading of V. A. Livshits. See Lunin 1984: 41-2. See also Livshits 1969, pp. 55-60. For the bibliography of Western scholars see Livshits 1969. The other version (Version M) of the translation is based on the reading of Steblin-Kamenskiy (1981, pp. 333-4).
407. Turgunov et al. 1983, pp. 38-48; Abdullaev et al. 1991, vol. 1, no. 193.
408. Litvinskiy and Pichikian 2000, vol. 1; Litvinskiy 2001a.
409. Litvinskiy et al. 1985, pp. 84-110.
410. Sarianidi 1989, p. 72, fig. 27.
411. Bernard 1986, p. 256.
412. We can only suppose the existence of such cults, but there is no direct evidence for them.

413. Steblin-Kamenskiy 1997.
414. Tissot 1985, pls. XXV, XXIX.
415. Pugachenkova 1978a, p. 214.
416. Litvinskiy and Zeymal' 1971, pp. 76-8.
417. Kruglikova and Pugachenkova 1977.
418. Verardi 1988, n. 43. pp. 479-504.
419. Ingholt and Lyons (1957, fig. 272) associate this hair style with the late (AD 300-400) period of Gandharan plastic art. See also Tissot 1985, p. 204, pl. XXIV, no. 9.
420. Tissot 1985, pls. XXIX-XXXI.
421. Barthoux 1930.
422. Al'baum 1975, fig. 22, pl. XLI.
423. Belenitskij 1973, n. 14.
424. Al'baum 1975, fig. 23, 24. Another parallel can be found in a recently discovered relief on a ceramic fragment from Afrasiab. See Grenet, Gritsina and Ivanitskij 2003, fig. 2
425. Location of the ceramic finds after Annaev 1984, fig. 138. Room 1: 17, 27-8 – on the floor; 1-2, 19, 21, 23, 30 – found with sculpture. Room 2: 12, 20, 22 – found under the first floor. Room 3: 9, 10 – found over the first floor. Room 4: 13, 16 – found on the floor. Room 5: 8, 14, 18, 25, 29 – found on the floor. Room 6: 4, 6, 7, 11, 13, 26 – found on the floor.
426. Marshak 1961.
427. After Annaev 1984, fig. 139: 1.2
428. Location of the ceramic finds after Annaev 1984, fig. 139. Room 1: 1, 8, 10, 12, 15, 17, 19, 21, 29, 40, 42 – found on the floor; 2 – found together with sculpture. Room 2: 1 – found under the first floor; 4, 9 – found over the first floor. Room 4: 5, 15, 18, 24, 32 – found on the floor. Room 5: 6, 7, 23-28, 33, 34, 36-39 – found on the floor. Room 6: 3, 11, 14, 20, 41 – found on the floor. 30-32 – found in the pit in western part of the monument.
429. Lyonnet 1997, figs. 45, 7, 8, 9.
430. Abdullaev 2000a, pp. 116-17, fig. 1.2.
431. Masson 1976, p. 9. Masson 1977, pp. 138-43; Zav'yalov 1979.
432. Sycheva 1975; Annaev 1984, p. 196.
433. Litvinskiy 1973, pp. 97-102, pl. 43.
434. Pidaev 1974, pp. 32-41, figs. 6, 27.
435. Nekrasova 1976, p. 82, fig. 3.
436. Turgunov 1978, pp. 57-9, fig. 34.
437. The upper layers are dated more widely from the fifth to the seventh century AD See Al'baum 1960, p. 122; see also Annaev 1984, p.196.
438. Isamiddinov 1978, pp. 237-8, fig. 7.
439. Marshak 1970, pp. 34-5.
440. Here we mean the 'life of the sculpture according to the life of the site itself and its inhabitants'. This notion, but concerning the works of the classic period, was presented in the lecture by Professor V.D. Blavatski 'Life of the sculpture after its creation' in the winter of 1979 at the Institute of Archaeology. The paper has not been published.
441. Pugachenkova 1966, pp. 190, 214.
442. Sarianidi 1985, pl. 52.

443. Pugachenkova 1978c, n. 26.
444. Ibid., pp. 78, 79.
445. Sidorova 1971, fig. 79.
446. Kruglikova 1979, figs. 9, 10.
447. Grenet 1987, pp. 41-5, pls. XXIV-XXV.
448. Rosenfield 1967, fig. 13.
449. Ibid., fig. 96.
450. Ghirshman 1962, fig. 92.
451. Ibid., fig. 158.
452. Ibid., fig. 171.
453. Ibid., figs. 207, 209.
454. Ibid., figs. 216, 217.
455. Ibid., fig. 233.
456. Ibid., figs. 248, 250, 252.
457. Ibid., fig. 294.
458. Staviskiy 1974, fig. 116.
459. Ghirshman 1962, figs. 305 f., 309, 311 f., 316-19.
460. Ibid., fig. 259.
461. Pugachenkova 1966, pls.VII, XXXII.
462. Pugachenkova 1982a, figs. 129, 130, 131.
463. Bulatova 1972, p. 90, fig. 24.
464. Waldschmidt 1976.
465. For example, see Pugachenkova 1966, pls. XXX, XXXI.
466. Schlumberger et al. 1983.
467. Sims-Williams and Cribb 1992.
468. E.V. Zeymal 1967.
469. Staviskiy 1979, figs. 38, 40, 44, 48.
470. Schlumberger 1970, fig. 51.
471. Koshelenko and Serdityh 1986, pp. 300-6.
472. Abdullaev and Annaev 1990.
473. Ibid., p. 14, fig. 1a.
474. Zav'yalov 2008.
475. Masson 1977, pp. 138, 141.
476. Zav'yalov 2008, pp. 233-4.
477. Masson 1976, pp. 4-7.
478. Pilipko 1976, pp. 59-68, fig. 4.
479. Pichikian 1991, p. 159.
480. Pugachenkova et al. 1991, n.179.
481. Staviskiy 1969a, fig. 35.
482. Litvinskiy and Zeymal 1971.
483. T.I. Zeymal 1979; T.I. Zeymal 1988; Zeymal 1990, fig. 1.
484. T.I. Zeymal 1990, p. 256
485. Ibid., p. 260.
486. T.I. Zeymal 1962, pp. 35-47; Litvinskiy and Zeymal 1964, pp. 76-86.
487. Litvinskiy and Zeymal 1971, p. 15.
488. Ibid., p. 59
489. Ibid., p. 62.
490. Ibid., figs. 4-6.

491. Ibid., fig. 27.
492. Litvinskiy 1981.
493. Ibid., pp. 116-38, fig. 2.
494. Mullokandov 1990.
495. Ibid., p. 15.
496. Ibid., p. 17.
497. Vertogradova 1990.
498. Mullokandov 1990, p. 19.
499. Masson 1963, pp. 51-6.
500. The *stupa* discovered here was studied from 1960 to 1966, and the *sangharama* from 1971 to 1978. The results of the excavation of the Buddhist complex were published by Z.I. Usmanova (1977). The final publication of the archaeological research of this monument appeared in two articles: in Russian (Pugachenkova and Usmanova 1994) an English version of same article (Pugachenkova and Usmanova 1995).
501. Pugachenkova and Usmanova 1995, p. 56, fig. 7.
502. Ibid., p. 60.
503. Ibid.
504. Rtveladze 1974a.
505. Pugachenkova and Usmanova 1994, p. 152.
506. Pugachenkova and Usmanova 1995, p. 65.
507. Pugachenkova and Usmanova 1994, p. 159.
508. Koshelenko 2001, p. 207.
509. Rtveladze 1974a, pp. 231-5.
510. Pugachenkova 1958.
511. Bulatova 1972.
512. Bulatova 1961, fig. 24.
513. Ibid., fig. 23.
514. Abdullaev et al. 1991, vol. 2, p. 85, n 504.
515. Marshall 1951, p. 714, no 100.
516. Tissot 1985, pl. XXI, no. 2.
517. Bulatova 1972, fig. 23, 24.
518. Bulatova 1963, pp. 109-15.
519. Bulatova 1972, pp. 66, 76.
520. Goryacheva and Peregudova 1996; Goryacheva 2000; Baybakov 2000.
521. Baybakov 2000, p. 199.
522. Goryacheva 2000, pp. 205-12, figs. 6-12.
523. Bernshtam 1952; Bernshtam 1950.
524. Kyzlasov 1959, pp. 160-227.
525. Zyablin 1961.
526. Kozhemyako 1989.
527. This idea is supported by Staviskiy 1998; Staviskiy 2000, pp. 181-3.

3

Conclusion

The monuments of Buddhist art of northern Bactria-Tokharistan followed figurative traditions that reached back to antiquity. The Hellenistic and Kushan periods yielded the most representative complexes in the history of northern Bactrian art. Buddhist art of the Early Medieval period drew on the sophisticated artistic concepts of those earlier periods. Hellenistic art is demonstrated primarily by the two well-studied sites of Ai Khanum and Takht-i Sangin. Each in its own way laid the artistic foundation from which the Khalchayan complex evolved. The Khalchayan reliefs incorporated many elements of Late Hellenistic art and at the same time created a new style that was the forerunner of Kushan art. The subjects of the Khalchayan circle, clearly of secular character, were subordinated to a single cult, the cult of ancestors, which gained victory over other beliefs in the fight for the new territory. This cult of ancestors is similar to the dynastic cult personified in the statues of Surkh Kotal. The sculptural representations of Surkh Kotal can be compared on the one hand with the portraits of Vima Kadphises and Kanishka on the coins of these rulers, and on the other hand with statues from Mathura. The dynastic cult is also reflected by the sculpture of Kuevkurgan. However, if in the images of Khalchayan features and likenesses were very realistic, clearly distinguishing one individual from another, in the Kuevkurgan sculpture the portrait becomes lost under the influence of Buddhist iconography. The methods used for representing facial features now include eyes with exaggerated eyelids, lips with drilled orifices at the corners, and stamped details of the hair. All these are characteristic of the Buddhist plastic art used for modelling secular personages.

This phenomenon of individual portraiture in the sculpture of northern Tokharistan confirms the dominant role of Buddhist plastic art and its influence on the figurative art not only of Bactria-Tokharistan, but also on the artistic centres of neighbouring regions. The Buddhist figurative tradition continued to exist for a long time. At Ajinatepa and Kalai Kafirnigan, not only the sacred edifices, but also the rich sculptural decorations and wall paintings bear out the continuity of these traditions.

The Buddhist art of northern Bactria grew out of the figurative traditions of the preceding periods and, having succumbed to the influence of such plastic styles as that of Gandhara to a greater degree, and Mathura to a lesser degree, became one of the leading schools and movements in the artistic culture. It gave strong impulses to the development of art in Chinese Turkestan, where Buddhist centres proliferated in the Early Medieval and Medieval periods.

Bibliography

Abdullaev, K. 1987. 'Terracotta Antefix from Termez Museum'. *IAHCCA* 12: 76-80.

——— 1988. 'O kul'te Gerakla v Baktrii (Nekotorye voprosy ikonografii)'. *IMKU* 22: 26-34.

——— 1990. 'Ob Odnom Buddijskom Obraze v Koroplastike Baktrii-Toharistana'. *IMKU* 24: 60-70.

——— 1995a. 'Tikhe-Ärdokhsho-Khariti (k Voprosu o Kushanskom Panteone)'. *ONU* 1-2-3: 38-42.

——— 1995b. 'Armour of Ancient Bactria', in *In the Land of the Gryphons. Papers on Central Asian Archaeology in Antiquity*, ed. A. Invernizzi, pp. 163-80. Florence: Casa Editrice Le Lettere.

——— 1995c. 'Nomadism of Central Asia: The Archaeological Evidence (2nd-1st centuries BC)', in *In the Land of the Gryphons. Papers on Central Asian Archaeology in Antiquity*, ed. A. Invernizzi, pp. 151-61. Florence: Casa Editrice Le Lettere.

——— 1996. 'Ellinisticheskaya Traditsiya v Iskusstve Sogda i Baktrii'. *IMKU* 27: 52-67.

——— 1997a. 'Terrakotovaya Plastika Ai Khanuma'. *RA* 1: 55-67.

——— 1997b. 'K Voprosu o Severnyh Rubezhah Bactrii v Ellinisticheskuyu Epohu'. *RA* 4: 54-60.

——— 1997/8. 'Buddhist Terracotta Plastic Art in Northern Bactria'. *SRAA* 5: 161-77.

——— 2000a. 'K Voprosu ob Semantike Ornamentalnyh Motivov Kushanskoy Keramiki', in: *Materialy Mezhdunarodnoy Konferentsii, Posvyashcennoy 50-letiyu Nauchnoy Deyatel'nosti G. V. Shishkinoy*, ed. T.G. Alpatkina, S.B. Bolelov, O.N. Inevatkina, T.K. Mkrtychev, pp. 116-17. Moscow: Peresvet.

——— 2000b. 'Novye Dannye o Kushanskoy Terracote'. *VDI* 2: 125-36.

——— 2000c. 'The Buddhist Traditions in the Plastic Art of North Bactria', in *India and Central Asia (Pre-Islamic period)*, ed. E.V. Rtveladze, pp. 79-82. Tashkent: Fan.

——— 2000d. 'Une Image Boudhique Découverte à Samarkand'. *Arts Asiatiques* 55: 173-5.

——— 2001a. 'Svyaschennye Kolodtsy i Kul't Vody v Aveste', in *Avesto va Uning Insoniyat Taraqqietidagi Urni*, pp. 115-18. Tashkent-Urgench: Fan.

——— 2001b. 'La Localisation de la Capitale des Yueh-chih', in *La Bactriane au Carrefour des Routes et des Civilisations de l'Asie Centrale,* ed. P. Leriche, C. Pidaev, M. Gelin, K. Abdoullaev, pp. 197-214. Paris: Maisonneuve et Larose.

——— 2003. 'Nana in Bactrian Art. New Data on Kushan Religious Iconography Based on the Material of Payokurgan'. *SRAA* 9: 15-38.

——— 2006a. 'Nakhodki Ellinisticheskih Monet k Severu ot Amudar'i-Oksa'. *RA* 3: 106-15.

——— 2006b. 'Ob Odnom Makedonskom Obychae v Kostyume Sredney Azii'. *IMKU* 35: 83-91.

——— 2007. 'Nomad Migration in Central Asia', in *After Alexander Central Asia before Islam*, ed. J. Cribb and G. Herrmann, pp. 73-98. Proceedings of the British Academy 133. Oxford: Oxford University Press.

Abdullaev, K. and T. Annaev, 1990. 'Raskopki na Tsitadeli Zar-tepa v 1979-81 gg'. *IMKU* 23: 12-25.

Abdullaev, K. and E. Badanova, 1998. 'Bactrian Dress in the Achaemenian Period'. *Mesopotamia* 33: 189-218.

Abdullaev, K., E.V. Rtveladze, and G.V. Shishkina, 1991. *Culture and Art of Ancient Uzbekistan*. 2 vols. Moscow: Vneshtorgizdat.

Abdullaev, K. and K. Sheyko, 1985. 'Novye Postupleniya Terrakotovyh Statuetok v Termezskij Kraevedcheskij Muzey'. *ONU* 7: 51-3.

Abdullaev, K. and V. Zav'yalov, 1985. 'Buddiyskie Motivy v Gorodskoy Kulture Baktrii v Pozdnekushanskiy Period'. *VDI* 4: 202-11.

Al'baum, L.I. 1953. 'Buddijskij Khram v Doline Sanzara'. *Doklady Akademii Nauk Uzbekskoy SSR* 86: 57-60.

——— 1960. *Balalyk-tepe. K Istorii Material'noy Kul'tury i Iskusstva Severnogo Tokharistana*. Tashkent: Fan.

——— 1974. 'Raskopki Buddijskogo Kompleksa Fayaz-tepe (po Materialam 1968-72 gg)', in *Drevnyaya Baktria*, ed. V.M. Masson, pp. 53-8. Leningrad: Nauka.

——— 1975. *Zhivopis' Afrasiaba*. Tashkent: Fan.

——— 1976. 'Issledovanie Fayaz-tepe v 1973 g', in *Baktrijskie Drevnosti*, ed. V.M. Masson, pp. 43-5. Leningrad: Nauka.

——— 1982. 'O Tolkovanii Karatepinskih Kompleksov (v Svete Raskopok Fayaz-tepe),' in *Buddiyskie Pamyatniki Kara-tepe v Starom Termeze*, ed. B.Ya. Staviskiy, pp. 54-63. Moscow: Nauka.

——— 1990. 'Zhivopis' Svyatilischa Fayaztepa', in *Izobrazitel'noe i Prikladnoe Iskusstvo. Kul'tura Srednego Vostoka. Razvitie, Svyazi i Vzaimodeystviya*, ed. G.A. Pugachenkova, pp. 18-27. Tashkent: Fan.

Altertümer von Pergamon 1885. *Altertümer von Pergamon*. Königlichen Museen zu Berlin. Vol. 11. Berlin: W. de Gruyter.

Altheim, F. 1959-62. *Geschichte der Hunnen*. Bd I-IV. Berlin: W. de Gruyter.

Amelung, W. 1895. *Die Basis des Praxiteles aus Mantinea. Archaologische Studien*. Munich: Bruckmann.

Anatolian Civilisations 1983. *Anatolian Civilisations. Catalogue of Exhibition May 22-October 30, 1983*. Vol. II. Greek, Roman, Byzantine. Istanbul: Turkish Ministry of Culture and Tourism.

An Hayao 2005. 'The Art of Glass Along the Silk Road', in *China: Dawn of a Golden Age, 200-750*, ed. James C.Y. Watt, pp. 57-65. New Haven and London: Yale University Press.

Annaev, T. 1984. 'Raskopki Rannesrednevekovoy Usad'by Kuevkurgan v Severnom Tokharistane'. *SA* 2: 188-200.

Annaev, T., Sh. Rahmanov, and A. Bobohodjaev, 1988. 'Zamok Kuchuktepa'. *IMKU* 22: 75-86.

Annaev, D. and T. Annaev, 2010. 'Arhitekturno-planirovochnaya Struktura i Datirovka Buddiyskogo Monastyrya Fayaztepa', in *Traditsii Vostoka i Zapada v Antichnoy Kul'ture Sredney Azii. Sbornik Statey v Chest Polya Bernara,* ed. Kazim Abdullaev, pp. 53-66. Tashkent: Noshirlik Yogdusi.

Antonini, S.C. 1995. 'The Dalverzintepa Temple', in *In the Land of the Gryphons. Papers on Central Asian Archaeology in Antiquity,* ed. A. Invernizzi, pp. 259-68. Florence: Casa Editrice le Lettere.

Antonova, E.V., N.M. Vinogradova and L.T. Pyankova 1979. 'O Letnikh i Osennikh Razvedkakh v Regarskom Raione v 1974 g'. *ART* XIV: 93-109.

Askarov, A. A. and T. Sh. Shirinov, 1993. *Rannyaya Gorodskaya Kul'tura Epochi Bronzy Yuga Sredney Azii.* Samarkand: Fan.

Avesta v Russkih Perevodah (1861-1996) 1997. Edition and Commentary by I.V. Rak. St. Petersburg: Izdatel'stvo Russkogo Hristianskogo Gumanitarnogo Instituta.

Bartol'd, V.V. 1963a. *Sochinenia*, vol. 1. Moscow: Nauka.

——— 1963b. *Sochinenia*, vol. 2, ch. I. Obschie Raboty po Istorii Sredney Azii, pp. 23-43. Moscow: Nauka.

——— 1963c. 'Turkestan v Epohu Mongol'skogo Nashestviya', in *Sochinenia*, vol. 1, pp. 4-75. Moscow: Nauka.

——— 1964. *Sochinenia*, vol. 2, ch. 2. Raboty po Otdel'nym problemam Istorii Sredney Azii, pp. 263-71. Moskva: Nauka.

——— 1965. *Sochinenia*, vol. 3. Raboty po Istoricheskoy Geografii. Moscow: Nauka.

Barthoux, J. 1930. *Les Fouilles de Hadda. Figures et Figurines, Album Photographiques.* Memoires de la Délégation Archéologique Française en Afghanistan VI. Paris: Librairie Diffusion De Boccard.

Baybakov, K.M. 2000. 'Novye Dannye o Buddizme v Semirech'e i Yuznom Kazahstane', in *India and Central Asia (Pre-Islamic Period)*, ed. E.V. Rtveladze, pp. 199-204. Tashkent: Fan.

Belenitski, A.M. 1973. *Monumental'noe Iskusstvo Pendjikenta.* Moscow: Iskusstvo.

Belenitski A.M., B.I. Marshak and V.I. Raspopova, 1986 'Raskopki Gorodischa Drevnego Penjikenta', *ART* XIX: 320-21.

Belov, G.A. 1958. *Altar' Zevsa v Pergame.* Leningrad: Aurora.

——— 1959. *Altar' Zevsa v Pergame. Al'bom Illustratsij.* Leningrad: Aurora.

Belyaeva, T. 1978. 'Zhiloj Dom Bogatogo Gorozhanina', in *Dal'verzintepe – Kushanskij Gorod na Yuge Uzbekistana*, pp. 33-7, ed. G.V. Pugachenkova, E.V. Rtveladze and B.A. Turgunov. Tashkent: Fan.

Bernard, P. 1968. 'Chapiteaux Corinthiens Hellénistiques d'Asie Central Découverts a Ai Khanum', *Syria* 45: 111-51.

——— 1969. 'Campagne de fouilles 1968 à Ai Khanum'. *CRAI* 1968: 313-55.

——— 1973a. 'Campagne de Fouilles a Ai Khanoum (Afghanistan) 1972'. *CRAI* 1972: 623-5.

——— 1973b. *Fouilles d'Ai Khanoum I (Campagne 1965, 1966, 1967, 1968).* Memoire de la Délégation Archéologique Française en Afghanistan, XXI. 2 vols. Paris: Librairie Klincksieck.

——— 1974. 'Ai Khanoum – Ville Coloniale Grecque'. *Archeologia* 5: 99-114.

——— 1982. 'An Ancient Greek City in Central Asia'. *Scientific American* 246. 2: 148-59.

——— 1985. *Les Monnaies Hors Trésors. Questions d'Histoire Greco-Bactrienne. Fouilles d'Ai Khanoum IV.* Memoire de la Délégation Archéologique Française en Afghanistan, XXVIII. Paris: Librairie Diffusion De Boccard.

——— 1986. 'Problemy Grecheskoy Kolonial'noy Istorii i Urbanisma Ellinisticheskogo Goroda Tsentral'noy Azii', in *Problemy Antichnoy Kultury*, ed. G.A. Koshelenko, pp. 249-57. Moscow: Nauka.

——— 1987. 'Les Nomades Conquérants de l'Empire Gréco-Bactrien. Réflexion sur leur Identité Ethnique et Culturelle', *CRAI* 1987: 758-68.

——— 1996. 'Marakanda-Afrasiab colonie grecque', in *La Persia e L'Asia Centrale da Allesandro al X Secolo. Atti dei Convegni Lincei* 127: 331-65. Roma: Accademia Nazionale dei Lincei.

Bernard, P. and Abdullaev, K. 1997. 'Nomady na Granitse Bactrii. K Voprosu ob Etnicheskoy Identificatsii'. *RA* 1: 68-86.

Bernard, P., Pinault, G.-J. and Rougemont G. 2004.'Deux Nouvelles Inscriptions Greques de l'Asie Centrale'. *Journal des Savants*, Juillet-Decembre 2004: 229-356.

Bernshtam, A.N. 1950. *Trudy Semirechenskoy Arheologicheskoy Ekspeditsii. MIA* 14. Moscow-Leningrad: Nauka.

——— 1952. *Istoriko-Arheologicheskie Ocherki Tsentral'nogo Tyan'-Shanya i Pamiro-Alaya. MIA* 26. Moscow-Leningrad: Nauka.

Bernoulli, J.J. 1905. *Die erhaltenen darstellungen Alexanders des Grossen.* Munich: Bruckmann.

Bichurin, N.J. (Iakinf). 1950. *Sobranie Svedenij o Narodah Obitavshih v Sredney Azii v Drevnie Vremena*, vols. I-II. Moscow-Leningrad: Izd tel'stvo Akademii Nauk SSSR.

——— 1954. *Sobranie svedenij o Narodah Obitavshih v Sredney Azii v Drevnie Vremena*, vol. III. Moskva-Leningrad: Izd tel'stvo Akademii Nauk SSSR.

Bieber, M. 1961. *Sculpture of the Hellenistic Age.* New York: Columbia University Press.

Bikerman, E. 1985. *Gosudarstvo Selevkidov.* Moscow: Nauka.

Bivar, A.D.H. 1956. *The Kushano-Sasanian Coin Series.* Varanasi: Journal of the Numismatic Society of India XVIII.

Bogomolov, G.I. 1986.'Izobrajenia Vsadnikov s Gorodischa Kanka'. *IMKU* 20: 69-79.

Bruns, G. 1949. *Der Grosse Altar von Pergamon.* Berlin: Gebr. Mann.

Bulatova, V.A. 1961.'Buddijski Khram v Kuve'. *SA* 3: 241-50.

——— 1963.'Bronzovy Shtamp iz Zhilogo Kompleksa VII-VIII vv. (Gorodischa Kuva v Ferganskoy Oblasti)'. *IMKU* 4: 109-15.

——— 1972. *Drevnyaya Kuva.* Tashkent: Fan.

Bussagli, M. 1978. *Central Asian Painting.* London: SKIRA.

——— 1996 .*L'Art du Gandhara.* Paris: La Pochoteque – Le Livre de Poche.

Chavannes, E. 1905 .'Les pays d'Occident d'après le Wei-lio'. *T'oung Pao* 5: 519-71.

——— 1907.'Les pays d'Occident d'après le Heou-Han chou'. *T'oung Pao* 8: 149-234.

Christensen, A. 1944. *L'Iran Sous les Sassanides.* Copenhagen: Levin and Munsgaard.

Chuvin, P. 1999. *Les Arts de l'Asie Centrale.* Paris: Citadelles et Mazenod.

Collignon, M. 1907. *Scopas et Praxitele, la sculpture grecque au IV siècle jusqu'au temps d'Alexandre.* Paris: Plon-Nourrit.

Cribb, J. 1984.'The Origin of the Buddha Image - The Numismatic Evidence', in *South Asian Archaeology, 1981*, ed. B. Allchin, pp. 231-44. Cambridge: Cambridge University Press.

Dalton, O.M. 1964. *The Treasure of the Oxus* (3rd edn.). London: The Trustees of the British Museum.

Dandamaev, M.A. 1974.'Novye Dannye o Religii v Persii na Rubeje VI-V vv. do n.e'. *VDI* 2: 18-33.

Denike, B. 1927.'Ekspeditsiya Muzeya Vostochnyh Kul'tur v Termez', in *Kul'tura Vostoka* I, pp. 9-18. Moskva: Izdatel'stvo Muzeya Vostochnyh Kul'tur.

Denike, B. 1928.'Ekspeditsiya Muzeya Vostochnyh Kul'tur v Srednyuyu Aziyu v 1927 goda', in *Kul'tura Vostoka* II, pp. 10-21. Moscow: Izdatel'stvo Muzeya Vostochnyh Kul'tur.

Diyakonov, M.M. 1953.'Raboty Kafirniganskogo Otryada', *MIA* 15: 147-86.

Drevnosti Tadjikistana. 1985. *Catalogue Vystavki*, ed. E.V. Zeymal'. Dushanbe: Donish.

Droysen, J.G. 1952. *Geschichte des Hellenismus*, vols. I-III Neue Ausg. Hrsg. Von E. Bayer.

——— 1980. *Istoria Ellinizma*, vol. I. Moscow: Nauka.

Dvurechenskaya, N.D. 2000. 'Terrakotovaya Plitka s Isobrazheniem Bodhisattvy iz Vostochnoy Kashkadar'i'. *RA* 2: 125-33.

Edwards, C.M. 1996. 'Lysippos', in: *Personal Styles in Greek Sculpture*, ed. Olga Palagia and J.J. Pollit, pp. 130-50. Cambridge: Cambridge University Press.

Egami, N. 1988. *The Grand Exhibition of Silk Road Civilisations: The Route of Buddhist Art*. Nara: Association for Silk Road Exposition.

Enoki, K. 1955. 'The Origin of the White Huns or Hephtalites'. *East and West* 3: 23-54.

——— 1958. 'On the Date of Kidarites'. *Memoirs of the Research Department of the Toyo Bunko* 17: 1-26.

——— 1959. 'On the Nationality of the Ephthalites'. *Memoirs of the Research Department of the Toyo Bunko* 18: 1-58.

Facenna, D. 1962. *Sculptures from the Sacred Area of Butkara I*. IsMEO, Reports and Memoirs, vol. II, Roma.

——— 1974. 'Excavations of the Italian Archaeological Mission (IsMEO) in Pakistan: Some Problems of Gandharan Art and Architecture', in *Central Asia in the Kushan Period*, vol. I, pp. 126-76. Moscow: Nauka.

Falk, H. 2001. 'The Yuga of Sphujiddhavaja and the Era of the Kusana'. *SRAA* 7: 121-36.

Francfort, A.-P. 1984. *Le Sanctuaire du Temple à Redans. Les Trouvailles. Fouilles d'Ai Khanoum III*. Mémoires de la Délégation Archéologique Française en Afghanistan, XXVII, Paris: Librairie Diffusion De Boccard.

Frankel, M. 1890-5. *Die Inschriften von Pergamon*, 2 vols. Berlin: W. Spemann.

Fussman, G. and O. Guillaume, 1990 *Surkh Kotal en Bactrane. Les Monnaies, par G. Fussman. Les Petits objets, par O. Guillaume*. Mémoires de la Délégation Archéologique Française en Afghanistan, XXXII. Paris: Librairie Diffusion De Boccard.

Gafurov, B.G. 1989. *Tadjiki*, vol. I. Dushanbe: Donish.

Ghirshmann, R. 1948. *Les Chionites – Hephtalites*. Le Caire: Imprimerie de l'Institut Français d'Archéologie Orientale.

——— 1962. *Arte Persiana. Parti e Sassanidi*. Milano: Rizzoli.

Goryacheva, V. D. 2000. 'Novye Nahodki Indo-Buddiyskoy Kul'tury v Kyrgyzystane', in *India and Central Asia (Pre-Islamic period)*, ed. E.V. Rtveladze, pp. 205-12. Tashkent: Fan.

Goryacheva, V. D. and Peregudova, S.Ya. 1996. 'Buddiyskie Pamyatniki Kirgizii'. *VDI* 3: 167-89.

Grenet, F. 1987. 'L'Athena de Dil'berzin', in *Cultes et Monuments Religieux dans l'Asie Centrale Préislamique,* ed. F. Grenet, pp. 41-5. Paris: Edition du CNRS.

Grenet, F., A.A. Gritsina and I.D. Ivanitskij, 2003. 'Raskopki Dvortsa Nasra Bin Sayjara'. *Arheologicheskie Issledovaniya v Uzbekistane* 2002: 50-5.

Grum-Grjimaylo, G.E. 1899. *Pochemu Kitaytsy Risuyut Demonov Ryjevolosymi?* St. Petersburg: V.S. Balashev.

Guillaume, O. 1983. *Les propylées de la rue principale. Fouilles d'Ai Khanoum II*. Mémoires de la Délégation Archéologique Française en Afghanistan, XXVI. Paris: Librairie Diffusion De Boccard.

Guillaume O. and A. Rougeulle 1987. *Les Petits Objets. Fouilles d'Ai Khanoum VII*. Mémoires de la Délégation Archéologique Française en Afghanistan, XXXI. Paris: Librairie Diffusion De Boccard.

Gupta, R.S. 1980. *Iconography of the Hindus, Buddhists and Jains*. Bombay: D.B. Taraporevala and Sons.

Gupta, S.P. 1985. *Masterpieces from the National Museum Collection*. New Delhi: National Museum.

Hackin, J., J.-R. Hackin, J. Karl and P. Hamelin 1954. *Nouvelles Recherches Archéologiques à Begram* (1939-40). Mémoires de la Délégation Archéologique Française en Afghanistan, XI, parts 1-2. Paris: Librairie Diffusion De Boccard.

Harle, J.C. 1986. *The Art and Architecture of the Indian Subcontinent*. London: Penguin Books.

Huff, D. 1995. 'An Unusual Type of Terra-cotta Figurine from north Bactria', in *In the Land of the Gryphons. Papers on Central Asian Archaeology in Antiquity*, ed. A. Invernizzi, pp. 269-74. Florence: Casa Editrice le Lettere.

Hulsewe, A.P.F. 1987. *China in Central Asia*. Leiden: Brill.

Il'yasov, J. 2000. 'Terrakotty Kampyrtepa'. *Materialy Toharistanskoy Ekspeditsii* I: 97-106.

Ingholt, H. and I. Lyons, 1957. *Gandharan Art of Pakistan*. New York: Pantheon Books.

Isamiddinov, M. 1978. 'Stratigrafia Er-Kurgan v Juzhnom Uzbekistane'. *SA* 3: 216-39.

Istakhri, A. 1939. *Kitab Masalik Al-Mamalik*. Tr. S. Volin. Moscow: Nauka.

Iskhakova, E.A. and M.Kh. Iskhakov, 1978. 'Terrakoty Dal'verzintepe', in G.A. Pugachenkova, E.V. Rtveladze and B.A. Turgunov, *Dal'verzintepe*, pp. 161-5. Tashkent: Fan.

Johnson, F.P. 1927. *Lysippos*. Durham N.C.: Duke University Press.

Joshi, N.P. 1966. *Mathura Sculptures. A Handbook to Appreciate Sculpture in the Archaeological Museum of Mathura*. Mathura: State Museum of Mathura.

Joshi, N.P. and R.S. Sharma, 1969. *Catalogue of Gandhara Sculptures in the State Museum*. Lucknow: State Museum of Lucknow.

Justin, 1954. 'Epitoma sochinenia Pompeya Troga'. Tr. A.A. Dekonski and M.I. Rizhski, ed. M.E. Grabar-Passek. *Vestnik Drevney Istorii* 2: 203-52; 3; 193-25; 21.

Kahler, H. 1948. *Der Grosse Fries von Pergamon*. Berlin: Gebruder Mann.

Kala, S.C. 1980. *Terracottas in the Allahabad Museum*. New Delhi: Allahabad Municipal Museum.

Karev, Yu. 1998. 'Statuetka Boddhisatvy Avaloketishvary iz Samarkanda'. *VDI* 1: 108-16.

Kavasaki, K. 1997. 'Matritsa iz Dal'verzintepa', in *Materialy Polevyh Issledovanij Uzbekistanskoy Iskusstvovedcheskoy Expeditsii*, ed. E.V. Rtveladze, pp. 49-50. Tashkent: Yani.

Khodjaev, T.K. and Abdullaev K. 1990. *Vneshnij Oblik Drevnikh Lyudey Uzbekistana (Skulptura i Plasticheskaya Rekonstruktsiya)*. Tashkent: Fan.

Klein, W. 1898. *Praxiteles*. Leipzig: Veit and Comp.

Koshelenko, G.A. (ed.) 1985. *Drevneyshie gosudarstva Kavkaza i Sredney Azii*. Moscow: Nauka.

Koshelenko, G.A. 2001. 'O Noveyshey Rabote Otnositel'no Sudeb Buddizma v Sredney Azii'. *VDI* 4: 200-11.

Koshelenko, G.A., K. Enoki and Z. Haidary. 1994. 'The Yueh-chih and their Migration', in *History of Civilizations of Central Asia*, vol. II, *The Development of Sedentary and Nomadic Civilizations, 700 BC to AD 250*, ed. János Harmatta, pp. 171-90. Paris: UNESCO Publishing.

Koshelenko, G.A. and R.M. Munchaev 1976. 'Raskopki na Gorodische Ai Khanum v 1965-68', in *Baktrijskie Drevnosti*, ed. V.M. Masson, pp. 118-24. Leningrad: Nauka.

Koshelenko, G. and Z. Serdityh 1986. 'Tsarskij Kul't v Greco-Baktrii', in *Problemy Ideologii i Kul'tury v Ranneklassovyh Formatsiyah*, ed. G.A. Koshelenko, pp. 300-6. Moscow: Nauka.

Kozhemyako, P.N. 1989. 'Otchet o Polevyh arheologicheskih Rabotah na Krasnorechenskom Gorodische. Raskop II', in *Krasnaya Rechka i Burana*, ed. P.N. Kozhemyako, pp 25-68. Frunze: Ylym.

Kozlovskij, V.A. and E.G. Nekrasova 1974. 'Stratigraficheskij Shurf na Tsitadeli Drevnego Termeza', in *Baktrijskie Drevnosti*, ed. V.M. Masson, pp. 30-9. Leningrad: Nauka.

Kramrisch, S. 1981. *Indian Sculpture*. Delhi, Varanasi, Patna: University Press.

Kruglikova, I.T. 1979. 'Nastennye Rospisi v Pomeschenii 16 Severo-Vostochnogo

Kul'tovogo Kompleksa Dil'berjina', in *Drevnyaya Baktria,* ed. I. T. Kruglikova, pp. 120-45. Moscow: Nauka.

Kruglikova, I.T. and G.A. Pugachenkova 1977. 'Buddijskoe Svyatilische (Raskop VI)', in *Dil'berjin,* ed. I. T. Kruglikova, pp. 61-90. Moscow: Nauka.

Kyzlasov, L.R. 1959. 'Arheologicheskie Issledovania na Gorodische Ak-Beshim v 1953-54 gg', in *Trudy Kirgizskoy Arheologo-Etnograficheskoy Ekspeditsii* II, ed. A.N. Bernshtam pp. 160-227. Moscow: Nauka.

Litvinskiy, B.A. 1973. *Keramika iz Mogil'nikov Zapadnoy Fergany.* Moscow: Nauka.

——— 1975. 'Rasprostranenie Buddizma v Sredney Azii', in *Central Asia in the Kushan Period.* Vol II. pp. 191-8. Moscow: Nauka.

——— 1981. 'Nastennaya Zhivopis' Kalai Kafirnigan', in *Kavkaz i Srednyaya Azia v Drevnosti i Srednevekov'e,* ed. B.A. Litvinskiy, pp. 116-38. Moscow: Nauka.

——— 2001a. 'Buddizm v Sredney Azii'. *VDI* 4: 188-99.

——— 2001b. *Khram Oksa.* Tome 2. Moscow: Vostochnaya literatura RAN.

——— 2004. 'Hellenistic Clay Portraits from the Temple of the Oxus'. *Parthica* 5: 37-62.

Litvinskiy, B.A. and I.R. Pichikian 2000. *Ellinisticheskij Khram Oksa.* Tome 1. Moscow: Vostochnaya literatura RAN.

Litvinskiy, B.A. and V.A. Sedov 1983. *Tepai-Shah. Kul'tura i Svyazi Kushanskoy Baktrii.* Moscow: Nauka.

Litvinskiy, B.A., Yu.G. Vinogradov and I.R. Pichikian 1985. 'Votiv Atrosoka iz Hrama Oksa v Severnoy Baktrii', *VDI* 4: 84-110.

Litvinskiy, B.A. and T.I. Zeymal 1964. 'Raskopki i Razvedki v Yuzhnom Tadjikistane v 1961 g'. *ART* IX: 76-86.

Litvinskiy, B.A. and T. I. Zeymal 1971. *Adjinatepe. Arkhitectura, Zivopis', Skulptura.* Moscow: Iskusstvo.

Livshits, V.A. 1965. 'Nadpisi na Freskah iz Afrasiaba', in *Tezisy Dokladov Sessii, Posvyaschennoy Istorii Zhivopoisi Stran Azii,* pp. 5-6. Leningrad: Nauka.

——— 1969. 'K Otkrytiyu Baktrijskih Nadpisey na Kara-tepe v Starom Termeze', in *Buddijskie Peschery Kara-tepe v Starom Termeze,* ed. B.Ya. Staviskiy, pp. 55-60. Moscow: Nauka.

L'Or des Amazones 2001. *L'Or des Amazones. Peuples nomades entre Asie et Europe, VIe siècle av. J.-C.-IVe siècle apr. J.-C.:* Musée Cernuschi, Musée des Arts de l'Asie de la ville de Paris, 16 mars-15 juillet 2001. Paris: Paris-Musées, Éditions Findakly.

Lukonin, V.G. 1967. 'Kushano-Sasanidskie Monety'. *Epigrafika Vostoka XVIII*: 16-33.

——— 1969a. *Kul'tura Sasanidskogo Irana v III-V vv. Ocherki po Istorii Iul'tury.* Moscow: Nauka.

——— 1969b. 'Srednepersidskie Nadpisi iz Kara-tepe', in *Buddijskie Peschery Kara-tepe v Starom Termeze,* ed. B.Ya. Staviskiy, pp. 40-6. Moscow: Nauka.

——— 1969c. 'Zavoevaniya Sasanidov na Vostoke i Problema Kushanskoy Absolyutnoy Khronologii'. *VDI* 2: 20-40.

Lunin, B.V. (compiled). 1984. *Istoria Uzbekistana v Istochnikah.* Tashkent: Fan.

Lunina, S.B. 1990. 'Izdelia Khudozhestvennogo Remesla Kesha', in *Kul'tuira Srednego Vostoka. Izobrazitel'noe i Prikladnoe Iskusstvo,* ed. G.A. Pugachenkova, pp. 48-50. Tashkent: Fan.

Lyonnet, B. 1997. *Céramiques et peuplement du Chalcolithique à la Conquête Arabe,* vol. 2, Prospections Archéologiques en Bactriane Orientale (1974-78). Paris: Éditions Recherche sur les Civilisations.

Maev, N.A. 1879. 'Ocherki Buharskogo Khanstva'. *Materialy dlya Statistiki Turkestanskogo Kraya* 5: 159-65.

——— 1906-8. *Istoria*. Tr. Yu. A. Kulakovski and A. Sonny. Issues 1-3. Kiev: S.V. Kul'zhenko.

——— 1871. *Rerum Gestarum Libri qui Supersunt*. Berlin: F. Eyssenhardt.

Marshak, B.I. 1961. 'Vliyanie Torevtiki na Sogdijskuyu Keramiku VII-VIII v'. *TGE* 5: 177-201.

——— 1970. 'Kod dlya Opisania keramiki Penjikenta V-VI vv'. *Statistiko-kombinatornye Metody v Arheologii*. Moscow: Nauka.

——— 2005. 'Central Asian Metalwork in China', in *China: Dawn of a Golden Age, 200-750*, ed. James C.Y. Watt, pp. 47-55. New Haven and London: Yale University Press.

Marshak, B.I., V.I. Raspopova and V.G. Shkoda 1996. 'Raskopki v Penjikente v 1995 g'. In *Novye Arheologicheskie Otkrytiya i Izuchenie Kul'turnoy Transformatsii*, ed. V.M. Masson, pp. 47-56. St. Petersburg: Izdatelstvo SPbGU.

Marshak, B.I. and V.I. Raspopova 1997/8. 'A Buddha Icon from Pandjikent'. *SRAA* 5: 297-301.

Marshall, J. 1951. *Taxila: An Illustrated Account of Archaeological Excavations Carried out at Taxila by the Government of India Between the Years 1913-14*. 3 vols. Cambridge: University Press.

Massal'skij, V.I. 1913. *Turkestanskij Kray*. St. Petersburg: A. Transhel'.

Masson, M.E. 1933. *Nahodka Fragmenta Skul'pturnogo Karniza Pervyh Vekov n.e.*, Materialy Uzkomstarisa 1. Tashkent: Uzkomstaris.

——— 1935. 'Skul'ptura Airtama'. *Iskusstvo* 2: 35-8.

——— 1940a. 'Gorodischa Starogo Termeza i ih Izuchenyie. Termezskaya arkheologicheskaya ekspeditsiya 1936 g'. *Trudy Uz Fan SSR. Seriya I, Istoriya, Arheologiya 2*. Tashkent: Fan.

——— 1940b. 'Termezskaya Arheologicheskaya Ekspeditsiya'. *KSIA* 8: 113-16.

——— 1953. 'Materialy Issledovanij po Arkheologii'. *MIA* 37 Moscow/Leningrad: Nauka.

——— 1963. 'Iz Rabot Juzhno-Turkmenistanskoy Arheologicheskoy Kompleksnoy Ekspeditsii Akademii Nauk Turkmenskoy SSR v1962 godu'. *Izvestiya Akademii Nauk Turkmenskoy SSR*, 3: 51-6.

——— 1968. 'K Voprosu o Severnyh Granitsah Gosudarstva "Velikih Kushan"'. *ONU* 8: 14-24.

——— 1975. 'K Voprosu o Severnyh Granitsah Gosudarstva "Velikih Kushan"'. *Tsentral'naya Azia v Kushanskuyu Epohu*, vol. 2, pp. 42-9. Moscow: Nauka.

Masson V.M. 1956. 'Drevnebaktriyskie Monety Chekanennye po Tipu Tetradrakhm Geliokla'. *Epigrafika Vostoka* XI: 63-75.

——— 1976. 'Kushanskie Poselenia i Kushanskaya Arheologia', in *Baktrijskie Drevnosti*, ed. V.M. Masson, pp 3-17. Leningrad: Nauka.

——— 1977. 'Zartepe – Kushanskiy Gorod v Severnoy Bactrii', in *Istoria i Kul'tura Antichnogo Mira*, 138-43. Moscow: Nauka.

——— 1985. 'Baktriysky Komplex v Kushansky Period', in *Drevneyshie Gosudarstva Kavkaza i Sredney Azii: Arkheologiya SSS*, pp. 250-72. Moscow: Nauka.

Maviglia, A. 1914. *L'Attività Artistica di Lisippo*. Roma: Loescher.

Meshkeris, V.A. 1969. 'Terrakoty iz Kara-tepe', in *Buddijskie Peschery Kara-tepe v Starom Termeze*, ed. B.Ya. Staviskiy, pp. 126-38. Moscow: Nauka.

——— 1986.'Indian Votive Syncretism as Reflected in the Coroplastics of Kushan Bactria'. *Information Bulletin* 11: 19-30.

Meunie, J. 1942. *Shotorak*. Mémoires de la Délégation Archéologique Française en Afghanistan X. Paris: Librairie F. de Nobele.

Mify Narodov Mira 1982. *Mify Narodov Mira. Entsiklopedia*, vols. 1-2. Moscow: Izdatel'stvo Sovetskaya Entsiklopedija.

Mitchiner, M. 1976. *Indo-Greek and Indo-Scythian Coinage*, vol. 5. London: Hawkins Publications.

Mitterwallner, G.V. 1986. *Kushana Coins and Sculptures from Mathura*. Mathura: The Government Museum of Mathura.

Mkrtychev, T. 2000. 'Buddijskaya Terrakota Baktrii-Toharistana: k Voprosu o eje Roli v Iskusstve i Kul'te', in *Materialy Mezhdunarodnoy Konferentsii, Posvyashcennoy 50-Letiyu Nauchnoy Deyatel'nosti G.V. Shishkinoy*, ed. T.G. Alpatkina, S.B. Bolelov, O.N. Inevatkina, T.K. Mkrtychev, pp. 162-167. Moscow: Peresvet.

Mkrtychev, T.K. 2002. *Buddijskoe Iskusstvo Sredney Azii*. I-X vv. Moscow: Iskusstvo.

Muller, F.W.K. 1918. 'Toxri and Kuisan (Kusan)'. *Sitzungsberichte der Kgl. Preussischen Akademie der Wissenschaften zu B.*, Philosphisch-Historische Klasse XXVIII. Berlin.

Mullokandov, M. 1990. 'Rannesrednevekovyj Buddijskij Monastyr Hishttepa v Hovalingskom Rayone Tadzhikistana'. *The Newsletter – International Association of the History and Culture of Central Asia* 17: 12-20.

Muqaddasi Al 2000. *Ahsan Al-Taqasim Fi Ma'rifat Al-Aqalim*. Tr. Basil Collins. London: Garnet UK.

Musakaeva, A. 2004. 'Monety Girkoda'. *IMKU* 34: 76-87.

Narain, A.K. 1962. *Indo-Greeks*. Oxford: Clarendon Press.

Nekrasova, E.G. 1976. 'Drevnyaya Keramika Sherabadskogo Oazisa', in *Baktrijskie Drevnosti*, ed. V.M. Masson, pp. 76-83. Leningrad: Nauka.

Nekrasova, E.G. and G.A. Pugachenkova 1978. 'Keramika Dal'verzintepe'. in G.A. Pugachenkova, E.V. Rtveladze and Turgunov *Dal'verzintepe* , pp. 143-61. Tashkent: Fan.

Nehru, L. 1989. *Origins of the Gandhāran Style: A Study of Contributory Influences*. Delhi, New York: Oxford University Press.

Nil'sen, V.A. 1966. *Stanovlenie Feodal'noy Arhitektury Sredney Azii (V-VIII vv.)*. Tashkent: Fan.

P'yankov, I.V. 1997. *Srednyaya Aziya v Antichnoy Geograficheskoy Traditsii*. Moscow: Nauka.

Pchelina, E.G. 1946. 'Drevnebuddijskij Monastyr' Kara-tepe'. *Doklady i Soobscheniya Istoricheskogo Fakul'tetfa MGU* 4: 12-18.

Pichikian, I.R. 1986. 'Paradnye Nozhny Greko-Baktrijskih Mechey', in *Problemy Antichnoy Kul'tury*, ed. G.A. Koshelenko, pp. 266-67. Moscow: Nauka.

Pichikian, I.R. 1991. *Kultura Baktrii. Ahemenidsckij i Ellinisticheskij Periody*. Moscow: Nauka.

Pidaev, Sh. 1974. 'Materialy k Izucheniu Drevnih Pamyatnikov Severnoy Bactrii', in *Drevnyaya Baktria* ed. V.M. Masson, pp. 32-41. Leningrad: Nauka.

——— 1978. *Poselenia Kushanskogo Vremeni Severnoy Baktrii*. Tashkent: Fan.

——— 1999a. 'K Voprosu o Poyavlenii Obraza Buddy v Koroplastike Baktrii'. *IMKU* 30: 133-7.

——— 1999b. 'Les chateaux du debut du Moyen Age dan la region du Surkhandarya'. *Dossiers d'Archéologie* 247: 64-7.

——— 2002. *New Finds of Uzbek Archaeology. Catalogue of Exhibition*, ed. Kyuzo Kato. Kyoto.

Pidaev, Sh. and K. Kato 1999. 'O Rabotah Uzbekistano-Yaponskoy Ekspeditsii na Karatepa v 1998 Godu'. *ONU* 9-10: 82-5.

——— 2000a. 'New Data from the Studies of Karatepa: The Buddhist Center of Old Termez', in *India and Central Asia (Pre-Islamic period)*, ed. E.V. Rtveladze, pp. 87-90. Tashkent: Fan.

——— 2000b. 'Predvaritel'nye itogi Issledovanij Uzbekistano-Yaponskoy Ekspeditsii na Karatepa v 1999 godu'. *ONU* 5: 39-45.

——— 2001. 'Arheologicheskie Issledovania na Buddijskom Tsentre Karatepa v Starom Termeze'. *AI* 2000: 114-22.

——— 2003. 'Arheologicheskie Issledovania Uzbeksko-Yaponskoy Ekspeditsii na Karatepa v Starom Termeze'. *AI* 2002: 128-34.

——— 2006. 'Arheologicheskie issledovaniya v Buddijskom Tsentre Karatepa'. *AI* 2004-05: 183-91.

Pidaev, Sh.R., P. Leriche, and O. Papahristu 2001. 'Novye Dannye o Raskopkah v Starom Termeze'. *AI* 2001: 112-13.

——— 2003. 'Arheologicheskie Raboty Uzbeksko-Frantsuzskoy Ekspeditsii na Gorodische Starogo Termeza'. *AI* 2002: 134-43.

Pilipko, V.N. 1976. 'Raskopki Svyatilischa Pozdnekushanskogo Vremeni na Gorodishce Zar-tepe', in *Baktrijskie Drevnosti*, ed. V.M. Masson, pp. 59-68. Leningrad: Nauka.

Pilipko, V. and I. Masimov 1969. 'Buddijskaya Statuetka iz Ak-kala (Srednyaya Amudarya)'. *SA* 3: 247-51.

Pugachenkova, G.A. 1945. 'Fragmenty Ellinisticheskoy Arhitektury Pravoberezhnogo Toharistana', in *Termezskaya Arheologicheskaya Kompleksnaya Ekspeditsiya* ed. M.E. Masson, vol. II, pp. 68-81. Tashkent: Izdatel'stvo Academii Nauk Uz SSR.

——— 1958. 'Gandharskaya Skul'ptura v Merve'. *Iskusstvo* 6: 61-6.

——— 1966. *Khalchayan. K Probleme Khudojestvennoy Kul'tury Antichnoy Baktrii.* Tashkent: Fan.

——— 1967a. 'Dva Stupa na Yuge Uzbekistana'. *SA* 3: 250-9.

——— 1967b. *Iskusstvo Turkmenistana.* Moscow: Iskusstvo.

——— 1971. *Skul'ptura Khalchayana.* Moscow: Iskusstvo.

——— 1973. 'Novye Dannye o Khudozestvennoy Kul'ture Baktrii', in *Iz Istorii Antichnoy Kul'tury Yuga Uzbekistana*, ed. G.A. Pugachenkova, pp. 78-128. Tashkent: Izdatel'stvo Imeni Gafura Gulyama.

——— 1978a. 'Dal'verzintepe i Nekotorye Obschie Voprosy Istorii i Kul'tury Severnoy Baktrii', in *Dal'verzintepe – Kushanskij Gorod na Yuge Uzbekistana*, ed. G.V. Pugachenkova, E.V. Rtveladze, B.A. Turgunov, pp. 176-221. Tashkent: Fan.

——— 1978b. 'Kvartal Keramistov (Dt-9)', in *Dal'verzintepe – Kushanskij Gorod na Yuge Uzbekistana*, ed. G.V. Pugachenkova, E.V. Rtveladze, B.A. Turgunov, pp. 115-43. Tashkent: Fan.

——— 1978c. *Les Trésors de Dalverzin-tépé.* Leningrad: Édition d'Art Aurora.

——— 1979. *Iskusstvo Baktrii Epokhi Kushan.* Moscow: Iskusstvo.

——— 1982a. *Iskusstvo Gandhary.* Moscow: Iskusstvo.

——— 1982b. 'Baktriysko-Indiyskie Sviazi v Pamiatnikakh Iskusstva', in *Drevniaya India*, ed. G.M. Bongard-Levin, pp. 244-65. Moscow: Nauka.

——— 1989a. *Shedevry Iskusstva Sredney Azii.* Moscow: Iskusstvo.

——— 1989b. 'V Poiske Kul'turnyh Tsennostey', in *Antichnye i Rannesrednevekovye Drevnosti Yuznogo Uzbekistana*, ed. G.A. Pugachenkova, pp. 13-32. Tashkent: Fan.

Pugachenkova, G.A. and L.I. Rempel 1960. *Vydayuschiesya Pamiatniki Izobrazitel'nogo*

Iskusstva Uzbekistana. Tashkent: Gosudarstvennoe Izdatel'stvo Khudozhestvennoy Literatury Uz SSR.

Pugachenkova, G.A., E.V. Riveladze and K. Kato (eds) 1991. *Antiquities of Southern Uzbekistan. Catalogue*. Tokyo: Soka University Press.

Pugachenkova, G.A., E.V. Rtveladze and B.A. Turgunov 1978. *Dal'verzintepe – Kushanskij Gorod na Yuge Uzbekistana*. Tashkent: Fan.

Pugachenkova, G.A. and B. A. Turgunov 1974. 'Issledovania Dal'verzin-tepe v 1972 g', in *Drevnyaya Baktria*, ed. V.M. Masson, pp. 58-73. Leningrad: Nauka.

Pugachenkova, G.A. and A. Turgunov 1978. 'Buddijskoe Svyatilische v Zagorodnoy Zone', in *Dal'verzintepe – Kushanskij Gorod na Yuge Uzbekistana*, ed. G.V. Pugachenkova, E.V. Rtveladze, B.A. Turgunov, pp. 90-7, Tashkent: Fan.

Pugachenkova, G.A. and Z.I. Usmanova, 1994. 'Buddiyskiy Kompleks v Gyuar-kale Starogo Merva'. *VDI* 2: 142-64.

——— 1995. 'Buddhist Monuments in Merv', in *In the Land of the Gryphons. Papers on Central Asian Archaeology in Antiquity*, ed. A. Invernizzi, pp. 51-81. Florence: Casa Editrice Le Lettere.

Rapin, C. 1992. La *Tresorerie du Palais Hellenistique d'Ai Khanoum. L'Apogee et la Chute du Royaume Grec de Bactriane. Fouilles d'Ai Khanoum VIII*. Mémoires de la Délégation Archéologique Française en Afghanistan XXXIII. Paris: Librairie Diffusion De Boccard.

Rosenfield, J. 1967. *The Dynastic Arts of the Kushans*. Berkeley, Los Angeles: University of California Press.

Rudenko, C.I. 1960. *Kul'tura Naselenia Tsentral'nogo Altaya v Skifskoe vremya*. Moscow-Leningrad: Izdatel'stvo Akademii Nauk SSSR.

Rtveladze, E.V. 1974a. 'Novy Buddiyskiy Pamyatnik v Starom Merve'. *Trudy Yuzhno-Turkmenskoy Arheologicheskoy Kompleksnoy Ekspeditsii* XV: 231-35.

——— 1974b. 'Razvedochnye Iizuchenia Baktriyskih Pamiatnikov na Yuge Uzbekistana', in *Drevnyaya Baktria* ed. V.M. Masson, pp. 74-84. Leningrad: Nauka.

——— 1978. 'Khram v Severnoy Chasti Dal'verzintepe', in *Dal'verzintepe – Kushanskij Gorod na Yuge Uzbekistana*, ed. G.V. Pugachenkova, E.V. Rtveladze, B.A. Turgunov, pp. 75-90. Tashkent: Fan.

Rtveladze, E.V. and Z.A. Hakimov 1973. 'Marshrutnye Issledovania Pamiatnikov Severnoy Baktrii', in *Iz Istorii Antichnoy Kul'tury Uzbekistana*, ed. G.A. Pugachenkova, pp. 10-34. Tashkent: Gafur Gulyam Edition.

Rtveladze, E. and A. Musakaeva 1986. 'K Istorii Denezhnego Obraschenia v Zapadnom Sogde. Klad Podrazanij Tetradrachmam Evtidema iz Bukhary'. *ONU* 6: 35-9.

Rtveladze, E.V. and Sh. Pidaev 1981. *Katalogue Monet iz Yujnogo Uzbekistana*. Tashkent: Fan.

Salis, A. 1912. *Der Altar von Pergamon; ein beitrag zur Erklarung des hellenistischen Barockstils in Kleinasie*. Berlin: G. Reimer.

Sarianidi, V. I. 1985. *Bactrian Gold*. Leningrad: Aurora Art Publishers.

——— 1989. *Khram i nekropol' Tillyatepe*. Moscow: Nauka.

Sastri, K.A.N. 1956. *A Comprehensive History of India*, vol. II. Calcutta: Orient Longmans.

Schlumberger, D. 1952. 'Le Temple de Surkh Kotal en Bactriane'. *JA* CCXL: 433-53.

——— 1961. 'The Excavations at Surkh Kotal and the Problem of Hellenism in Bactria and India'. *Proceedings of the British Academy* 47: 77-95.

——— 1970. *L'Orient Hellénisé. L'Art Grec et ses Héritiers dans l'Asie non Méditerranéenne*. Paris: A. Michel.

——— 1985. *Ellinizirovannyj Vostok*. Moscow: Nauka.

Schlumberger, D., M. Le Berre and G. Fussman 1983. *Surkh Kotal en Bactriane I: Les temples*. Mémoires de la Délégation Archéologique Française en Afghanistan, XXV. Paris: Librairie Diffusion De Boccard.

Schrammen, J. 1906. *Der Grosse Altar*, vol. III, part 2. Berlin: W. Spemann.

Shaydullaev, Sh., D. Huff and K. Rahimov 2003. 'Jarkuton – 2002'. *AI* 2002: 202-05.

Shmidt, F.I. 1929. 'O Neskol'kih Rannih Ellinisticheskih Portretah', in *Antichnyj Portret*, ed. K. Trver, pp. 23-4. Leningrad: Izdatel'stvo Academii Nauk SSSR.

Sidorova, V.S. 1971. *Skul'ptura Drevney Indii*. Moskva: Iskusstvo.

Sims-Williams, N. and J. Cribb 1992. 'A New Bactrian Inscription of Kanishka the Great'. *SRAA* 4: 75-142.

Spemann, W. 1885-1912. *Altertumer von Pergamon*, vols. I-IX. Kenigliche Museen zu Berlin, vol. III, part 1. Berlin: W. de Gruyter.

Staviskiy, B.Ya. 1957. 'Khuttal' v Soobscheniyah Kitaskih Putishestvennikov Suan-Tszyanya i Khoy Chao', *Izvestiya Odeleniya Obschestvennyh Nauk AN Tajikskoy SSR* 14: 87-90.

——— 1960. 'Raskopki Gorodischa Kuldor-Tepe'. *SA* 4:113-21.

——— 1961. 'O Severnyh Granitsah Kushanskogo Gosudarstva'. *VDI* 1: 108-14.

——— 1969a. 'Fragmenty Kamennyh Rel'efov i Detaley Arhitekturnogo Ubranstva iz Raskopok Kara-tepe 1961-64', in *Buddijskie Peschery Kara-tepe v Starom Termeze*, ed. B.Ya. Staviskiy, pp. 139-69. Moscow: Nauka.

——— 1969b. 'Osnovnye Itogi Raskopok Kara-tepe v 1963-64 gg', in *Buddiyskie Peschery Kara-tepe v Starom Termeze*, ed. B.Ya. Staviskiy, pp. 7-31. Moscow: Nauka.

——— (ed.) 1969. *Buddijskie Peshcery Kara-tepe v Starom Termeze*. Moscow: Nauka.

——— 1972a. 'Kapiteli Drevney Baktrii'. *SA* 2: 41-50

——— 1972b. 'Raboty na Kara-tepe v 1970-71 gg', in *Buddijskij Kul'tovyj Tsentr v Starom Termeze*, ed. B.Ya. Staviskiy, pp. 67-100. Moscow: Nauka.

——— (ed.) 1972. *Buddijskij Kul'tovyj Tsentr Kara-tepe v Starom Termeze*. Moscow: Nauka.

——— 1974. *Iskusstvo Sredney Azii (Drevnij period)*. Moscow: Iskusstvo.

——— (ed.) 1975. *Novye Nahodki na Kara-tepe v Starom Termez*. Moscow: Nauka.

——— 1977. *Kushanskaya Baktria. Problemy Istorii i Kul'tury*. Moscow: Nauka.

——— 1979. *Kunst der Kuschan*. Leipzig: Seemann Verlag.

——— (ed.) 1982. *Buddijskie Pamyatniki Kara-tepe v Starom Termez*. Moscow: Nauka.

——— 1987. 'Buddijskij Kul'tovyj Tsentr Kushanskogo Termeza kak Pamyatnik Drevnih Sredneaziatsko-Indijskih Svyazey', in *Tsentral'naya Azia. Novye Pamyatniki Pis'mennosti i Iskusstva*, ed. G.M. Bongard-Levin, pp. 282-9. Moscow: Nauka.

——— 1995. 'Central Asian Mesopotamia and the Roman world. Evidence of contacts', in *In the Land of the Gryphons. Papers on Central Asian Archaeology in Antiquity*, ed. A. Invernizzi, pp. 191-202. Florence: Casa Editrice Le Lettere.

——— 1997. 'O Rasprostranenii Buddizma na Severe Sredneaziatskogo Mezhdurech'ya (po Materialam Arheologii)', in *Problemy Sovremennoy Arheologii*, pp. 45-74. Moscow: Drevnosti.

——— 1998. *Sud'by Buddisma v Sredney Azii*. Moscow: Nauka.

——— 2000. 'The Destiny of Budhhism in Central Asia in the First Millenium BC from the Perspective of Archaeological Data', in *India and Central Asia*, ed. E.V. Rtveladze, pp. 181-3. Tashkent: Mir Ekonomiki i Prava.

——— 2001. 'Gora Orlinaya – Hoja Gul'suar', in *Drevnyaya i Srednevekovaya Kul'tura Surkhandar'i*, ed. E.V. Rtveladze and Sh.R. Pidaev, pp. 52-4. Tashkent: Uzbekiston Millij Entsiklopediyasi.

Staviskiy, B.Ya. and Urmanova M.H. 1958. 'Gorodische Kuldor-tepe'. *SA* 1: 231-5.

Steblin-Kamenskij, I.M., 1981. 'Baktrijskij yazyk', in *Sredneiranskie Yazyki. Osnovy Iranskogo Yazykoznaniya,* ed. V.I. Abaev, M.N. Bogolyubov and V.S. Rastorgueva, pp. 314-47. Moscow: Nauka.

——— 1997. 'Ardvisur ili Aban-yasht', in *Avesta v Russkih perevodah (1861-1996),* pp. 173-244, tr. I.M. Steblin-Kamenskij. St. Petersburg: Izdatel'stvo Russkogo Hristianskogo Gumenitarnogo Instituta.

Stepnaya Polosa Aziatskoy Chasti SSSR 1992. *Stepnaya Polosa Aziatskoy Chasti SSSR v Skifo-Sarmatskoe Vremya. Arheologia SSSR.* Moscow: Nauka.

Strabo Geografia. Tr. and comm. G.A. Stratanovskij 1964. Moscow: Nauka.

Strelkov, A.S. 1927. 'Zurmala ili Katta-tepe Okolo Termeza'. *Kul'tura Vostoka* 1: 27-30.

——— 1928. 'Doislamskie Pamyatniki Termeza'. *Kul'tura Vostoka* 2: 41-7.

Stride, S. 2001. 'Sondage Stratigraphique dans le Secteur Occidental de la Citadelle de Termez (Chantier D)', in *La Bactriane au Carrefour des Routes et des Civilizations de l'Asie Centrale,* ed. P. Leriche, C. Pidaev, M.Gelin, K. Abdoullaev, V. Fourniau, pp. 123-9. Paris: Maisonneuve et Larose – IFEAC.

Sulaymanov, R.Kh. 2000. *Drevnij Nahshab.* Tashkent: Fan.

Sycheva, N.S. 1975. 'Keramika Kara-tepe', in *Novye Nakhodki na Kara-tepe v Starom Termeze,* ed. B.Ya. Staviskiy, pp. 88-148. Moscow: Nauka.

Tabari, 1977. *Geschichte der Perser und Araber zur Zeit der Sassaniden.* Tr. Th. Noldeke. Cambridge: Cambridge University Press.

Tanabe, K. 1994. 'Kanishka I's Coins with the Buddha Image on the Reverse and Some References to the Art of Gandhara'. *Orient* X: 31-56.

Tarn, W.W. 1951. *The Greeks in Bactria and India.* Cambridge: Cambridge University Press.

The Route of Buddhist Art. 1988. *The Route of Buddhist Art. The Grand Exhibition of Silk Road Civilizations* Catalogue. Nara: Nara National Museum.

Tissot, F. 1985. *Gandhara.* Paris: Librairie d'Amerique et d'Orient. Jean Maisonneuve.

——— 1987. *Les Arts Anciens du Pakistan et de l'Afganistan.* Paris: Desclée de Brouwer.

Trever, K.V. 1961. 'Baktrijskij Bronzovyj Falar s Izobrajeniem Dionisa', *Trudy Gosudarstvennogo Ermitaja: Kultura i Iskusstvo Narodov Vostoka* V: 98-109.

Turgunov, B. 1973. 'K Izucheniyu Airtama', in *Iz Istorii Antichnoy Kul'tury Uzbekistana,* ed. G.A. Pugachenkova, pp. 52-78. Tashkent: Gafur Gulyam Edition.

——— 1978. 'Dom Bogatogo Domovladel'tsa', in *Dal'verzintepe – Kushanskij Gorod na Yuge Uzbekistana,* ed. G.V. Pugachenkova, E.V. Rtveladze and B.A. Turgunov, pp. 57-9. Tashkent: Fan.

——— 1989. 'Raskopki Vtorogo Buddijskogo Khrama na Dal'verzintepe (Predvaritel'noe Soobschenie)', in *Antichnye i Rannesrednevekovye Pamyatniki Yuznogo Uzbekistana,* ed. G.V. Pugachenkova, pp. 81-95. Tashkent: Fan.

——— 2000. 'Characteristics of the Buddhist Monuments of Dal'verzintepa', in *India and Central Asia (Pre-Islamic period),* ed. E.V. Rtveladze, pp. 83-6. Tashkent: Fan.

Turgunov, B., V. Livshits and T. Rtveladze, 1983. 'Otkrytie Monumental'noy Nadpisi v Airtame'. *ONU* 3: 38-48.

Tyulyaev, C.I. 1988. *Iskusstvo Indii. III tysyacheletie do n.e. – VII v. n.e.* Moscow: Iskusstvo.

Ujfalvy, C. de. 1902. *Le Type Phisique d'Alexandre le Grand.* Paris: E. Leroux.

Usmanova, Z.I. 1977. 'Buddiyskiy Kompleks v Gyaur-Kale Starogo Merva'. *Sbornik Nauchnyh Trudov Tashkentskogo Gosudarstvennogo Universiteta* 533: 12-22.

——— 2000. 'Istoriko-Kul'turnye Svyazi Yuznoy Turkmenii i Indii v Drevnosti', in

India and Central Asia (Pre-Islamic period), ed. E.V. Rtveladze, pp. 171-4. Tashkent: Fan.

Vaissière, de la, E. 2002. *Histoire des Marchands Sogdiens*. Paris: Edition de Boccard.

Val'dgauer, O.F. 1924. *Antichnaya Skul'ptura*. Leningrad: Brokgauz i Efron.

——— 1938. *Etudy po Istorii Antichnogo Portreta*. Leningrad: Iskusstvo.

Verardi, G. 1988. 'Osservazioni sulla coroplastica di epoca Kusana nel Nord Ovest e in Afghanistan in relazione al materiale di Tapa Sardar, seguite da una precisazione sulla natura e la data delle sculture di Ushkur'. *Annali dell'Istituto Universitario Orientali di Napoli* 1988: 479-504.

Vertogradova, V. 1990. 'Glinyanye Tabletki s Tekstami iz Hishttepa'. *The Newsletter – International Association of the History and Culture of Central Asia* 17: 21-5.

Vertogradova, V.V. 2000. 'Karatepa – South-Eastern India: On the Finding of a New Brahmi Inscription in Karatepa', in *India and Central Asia (Pre-Islamic period)*, ed. E.V. Rtveladze, pp. 43-6. Tashkent: Fan.

Veuve, S. 1987. *Fouilles d'Ai Khanoum VI. Le Gymnase. Architecture, Ceramique, Sculpture.* Mémoires de la Délégation Archéologique Française en Afghanistan, XXX. Paris: Librairie Diffusion De Boccard.

Visconti, E.Q. 1824-6. *Iconographie Grecque.* 2nd edn. 3 vols. Milan: Rizzoli.

Vogel, J. Ph. 1915 'Explorations at Mathura: Excavations at Mat'. *Archaeological Survey of India. Annual Report 1911-1912*, pp. 20-133. Calcutta: Superintendent Government Printing.

——— 1930. 'La Sculpture de Mathura' in *Ars Asiatique*, vol. XV. Paris et Bruxelles.

Vyatkin, V.L. 1927. *Afrasiab – Gorodische Bylogo Samarkanda.* Tashkent: Izdanie Glavnauki Narkomprosa Uz SSR.

Vyazmitina, M.I. 1945a. 'Raskopki na gorodische Airtam', in *Trudy Akademii Nauk UzSSR. Termazskaya Arheologicheskaya Ekspeditsiya*, tome II, pp. 23-34. Tashkent: Izdatel'stvo Akademii Nauk ZzSSR.

——— 1945b. 'Keramika Airtama Vremeni Kushanov', in *Trudy Akademii Nauk UzSSR. Termazskaya Arheologicheskaya Ekspeditsiya*, tome II, pp. 35-64. Tashkent: Izdatel'stvo Akademii Nauk ZzSSR.

Waldschmidt, E. 1976. *Gandhara Kutscha Turfan. Einführung in die Frühmittelalterliche Kunst Zentralasien*. San Francisco: Chinese Materials Center.

Will, E. 1979. *Histoire Politique du Monde Hellénistique.* T.I. Nancy: Press Universitaires de Nancy.

Winnefeld, H. 1910. *Die Friese des Grossen Altar*, vol. VII. Berlin: G. Reimer.

Winter, F. 1908. *Die Skulpturen*, vol. VIII. Berlin: G. Reimer.

Yagodin, V.N. 2000. 'New Findings Relating to the Historical and Cultural Relations between India and Khorezm', in *India and Central Asia (Pre-Islamic period)*, ed. E.V. Rtveladze, pp 59-64. Tashkent: Fan.

Zav'yalov, V.A. 1979. 'Raskopki Kvartala Pozdnekushanskogo Vremeni na Gorodische Zartepe'. *SA* 3:141-53.

——— 1981. 'Pozdnekushanskaya Antropomorfnaja Terracota Zar-tepe'. *Kratkie Soobschenia Instituta Arheologii* 167: 65-7.

——— 2008. *Kushanshahr pri Sasanidah (po Materialam Raskopok Gorodischa Zartepa)* St Petersburg: Izdatel'stvo SPbGU.

Zav'yalov, V.A. and Sh. R. Pidaev 2001. 'Izobrazheniya Bodhisatv v Terrakotah Severnoy Baktrii Kushanskogo Vremeni', in *Drevnyaya i Ssrednevekovaya Kul'tura Surkhandar'i*, ed. E.V. Rtveladze and Sh.R. Pidaev, pp. 59-63. Tashkent: Uzbekiston Millij Entsiklopediyasi.

Zeymal', E.V. 1967. 'Monety Velikih Kushan v Sobranii Gosudarstvennogo Ermitaja'. *TGE* IX: 5-86.

——— 1978. 'Politicheskaya Istoria Drevney Transoksiany po Numizmaticheskim Dannym', in *Kul'tura Vostoka. Drevnost' i Rannee Srednevekov'e,* pp. 192-215. Leningrad: Avrora.

——— 1983. *Drevnie Monety Tadjikistana*. Dushanbe: Donish.

Zeymal', T.I. 1962. 'Arheologicheskie Raboty v Vahshskoy Doline v 1960 g'. *ART* VIII, 1960: 35-47.

——— 1979. 'Buddijskij Komplex Ushtur-Mullo'. *ART* XIX: 186-202.

——— 1988. 'Raskopki Buddijskogo Kompleksa Ushtur-Mullo v 1981 g'. *ART* XXI: 325-36.

——— 1990. 'Buddijski Monastyr' Ushtur-Mullo (Raboty 1982 g)'. *ART* XXII: 255-61.

——— 2000. 'Buddhist Monuments of Northern Tokharistan (Chronology and Periods)', in *India and Central Asia (Pre-Islamic period)*, ed. E.V. Rtveladze, pp. 77-8. Tashkent: Fan.

Zhukov, V.D. 1961. 'Arheologicheskaya Razvedka na Shahristane Khayrabad-tepe'. *IMKU* 2: 177-91.

Zyablin, L.L. 1961. *Vtoroy Buddijskij Khram Ak-Beshimskogo Gorodischa*. Frunze: Ylym.

Index